CW01337892

Critical Theory and Animal Liberation

Nature's Meaning

Series Editor: Roger S. Gottlieb, Professor of Philosophy, Worcester Polytechnic Institute

Each title in Nature's Meaning is created to have the personal stamp of a passionate and articulate spokesperson for environmental sanity. Intended to be engagingly written by experienced thinkers in their field, these books express the comprehensive and personal vision of the topic by an author who has devoted years to studying, teaching, writing about, and often being actively involved with the environmental movement. The books will be intended primarily as college texts, and as beautifully produced volumes, they will also appeal to a wide audience of environmentally concerned readers.

Integrating Ecofeminism, Globalization, and World Religions, by Rosemary Radford Ruether

Environmental Ethics for a Postcolonial World, by Deane Curtin

The Ecological Life: Discovering Citizenship and a Sense of Humanity, by Jeremy Bendik-Keymer

Sacramental Commons: Christian Ecological Ethics, by John Hart

Capitalizing on Environmental Injustice: The Polluter-Industrial Complex in the Age of Globalization, by Daniel Faber

Critical Theory and Animal Liberation, edited by John Sanbonmatsu

Critical Theory and Animal Liberation

Edited by
John Sanbonmatsu

ROWMAN & LITTLEFIELD PUBLISHERS, INC.
Lanham • Boulder • New York • Toronto • Plymouth, UK

Excerpts from John Abromeit's dissertation manuscript, "The Dialectic of Bourgeois Society" (University of California, Berkeley, 2004), are used by permission of the author.

The chapter by Ted Benton originally appeared in *Radical Philosophy* 50 (1988): 4–18. Used by permission.

A version of Carl Boggs's chapter appeared in Fast Capitalism, http://fastcapitalism.com/. Used by permission.

Parts of Karen Davis's chapter appeared in the "Minding the Animal Psyche" issue of *Spring: A Journal of Archetype and Culture*, www.springjournalandbooks.com. Used by permission.

The chapter by Denis Soron originally appeared in *TOPIA: The Canadian Journal of Cultural Studies* no. 18 (Fall 2007). Used by permission.

A version of John Sorenson's chapter appeared in *Green Theory and Praxis* 2, no. 1 (2006). Used by permission.

The chapter by Vasile Stănescu first appeared in the *Journal of Critical Animal Studies* VII, issue 1/11 (2010): 8–32. Used by permission.

Published by Rowman & Littlefield Publishers, Inc.
A wholly owned subsidiary of The Rowman & Littlefield Publishing Group, Inc.
4501 Forbes Boulevard, Suite 200, Lanham, Maryland 20706
www.rowmanlittlefield.com

Estover Road, Plymouth PL6 7PY, United Kingdom

Copyright © 2011 by Rowman & Littlefield Publishers, Inc.

All rights reserved. No part of this book may be reproduced in any form or by any electronic or mechanical means, including information storage and retrieval systems, without written permission from the publisher, except by a reviewer who may quote passages in a review.

British Library Cataloguing in Publication Information Available

Library of Congress Cataloging-in-Publication Data

Critical theory and animal liberation / edited by John Sanbonmatsu.
p. cm. — (Nature's meaning)
Includes bibliographical references and index.
ISBN 978-1-4422-0580-2 (cloth : alk. paper) — ISBN 978-1-4422-0582-6 (electronic : alk. paper)
1. Animal rights. 2. Speciesism. 3. Critical theory. I. Sanbonmatsu, John.
HV4708.C75 2011
179'.3—dc22 2010032055

™ The paper used in this publication meets the minimum requirements of American National Standard for Information Sciences—Permanence of Paper for Printed Library Materials, ANSI/NISO Z39.48-1992. Printed in the United States of America

This book is dedicated to my son, Emmanuel Sullivan. Your gentle love of the world, and of the myriad animals in it, shows us the way.

Table of Contents

Part III: Speciesism and Ideologies of Domination

Part IV: Problems in Praxis

Acknowledgments

I could not have gotten to the end of this long project without the support of my family, whom I wish to thank (Kira, Lisa, Yoshiro, Marianne, and Donna), as well as the critical feedback of a number of friends and colleagues, especially Zipporah Weisberg (my doppelgänger on so many theoretical and political questions). I would also like to thank my comrade, Barbara Epstein, and acknowledge the support of my good friends Thomas Hartl, Chris Bobel, Nancy Zeigler, Laurie Prendergast, Matt Goodman, Tess Oliver, Eric Begleiter, Jenny Staples, Laurie Crane, Sam Diener, and Valerie Sperling. I would especially like to thank Roger Gottlieb (series editor for Rowman & Littlefield), without whose obstinate faith this book might never have seen light of day. Roger has been a mentor, comrade, and colleague in the best and truest sense of all three words. I would also like to thank the faculty and staff of the Department of Humanities and Arts at Worcester Polytechnic Institute—particularly department head Kris Boudreau—for their collegial and administrative support while I worked on this project.

Several of the articles here are reprints, and I want to extend my thanks to the various presses that accommodated my requests. I would especially like to thank Peter Hallward and the other members of the editorial collective at *Radical Philosophy* for generously allowing me to reprint Ted Benton's "Speciesism = Humanism?" for a nominal fee, as well as Jody Berland, editor of the excellent Canadian journal *Topia* for permission to reprint Dennis Soron's essay on commodification and road kill. I would also like to thank Josephine Donovan for allowing me to reprint her essay on interspecies care; the editors of *Green Theory and Praxis* for permission to reprint an edited version of John Sorenson's essay;

the editors of *The Spring Journal* for permission to reprint Karen Davis's essay; and the editors of *Fast Capitalism*, the online journal, for the rights to Carl Boggs's article here. Last but by no means least, I would like to thank Sarah Stanton, my editor at Rowman & Littlefield, and her assistant Jin Yu, for their help and patience, as well as Karen Ackermann, my production editor.

I would also like to express my gratitude to acclaimed artist Sue Coe, who very generously agreed to let my publisher use her extraordinary artwork on the front cover of this volume.

Finally, this project would not have gotten off the ground at all if Renzo Llorente, one of our contributors, had not approached me years ago and suggested that the two of us edit a volume together on Marxism and animal rights. Much to my regret, owing to a variety of circumstances beyond his control, Renzo had to bow out of this project midway through. However, his intellectual stamp on our volume can be felt in a variety of ways, both large and small. *Renzo—Ti abbraccio.*

Introduction

One of my secret pleasures as a boy was to sit for hours poring over my father's collection of photography books. There, in *The Family of Man*, *Days to Remember*, and others, I saw disclosed the strange and varied wonder of the human condition, at least as it appeared to professional photojournalists at mid-century: children in Bombay lifting their smiling faces to the rain; Jackie Robinson, "first Negro in major league baseball"; the first television. There were also many disturbing pictures of grief, tragedy, and violence, indelible images of mob slayings and suicides, terrible industrial accidents and "the war in Indo-China." But of them all, one particular image haunted me the most: a group of Midwesterners standing in a circle in the snow, cheering on a young boy of about seven years old as he beat a fox to death with a baseball bat.[1] The boy, with a bright smile, stands with his legs firmly planted, as though waiting for a pitch that never comes. The fox, crouched, tongue lolling, exhausted almost to the point of death, gazes vacantly, a look of hopelessness or resignation visible in his pinched face. Then, dark against the blood-spattered snow, one sees the small, broken bodies of two other foxes, already dead. But what stands out most in my mind are the rosy-cheeked men (and a few women) in their winter clothes, standing shoulder to shoulder or kneeling in the snow to form a tight cordon of death around boy and fox. All of them are grinning. And it is this last detail, of ordinary human beings taking delight in the torture of a powerless individual, an animal, that still troubles me the most.

Many of us have encountered similar images, read similar accounts, of public spectacles in which atrocity has mixed incongruously with joy. What is it about the human condition that induces otherwise ordinary people to murder the powerless, whether human or nonhuman, with such evident pleasure? For it is indeed pleasure we see in faces of whites celebrating beside the sexually mutilated corpse of a hanged and burned black man in the American South,[2] pleasure that onlookers saw in the animated faces of Hutu men and women as they swung machetes against their defenseless Tutsi neighbors, singing,[3] pleasure etched in the smiles of Gestapo officers laughing as they kicked naked Jewish women cowering in the dust at their feet. "In Kaunas, Lithuania, where Einsatzkommando 3 operated," reads one account from World War II, "the Jews were clubbed to death with crowbars, before cheering crowds, mothers holding up their children to see the fun, and German soldiers clustered round like spectators at a football match. At the end, while the streets ran with blood, the chief murderer stood on the pile of corpses as a triumphant hero and played the Lithuanian national anthem on an accordion."[4] A German army colonel who came upon this scene later remarked: "At first I thought this must be a victory celebration or some type of sporting event because of the cheering, clapping and laughter that kept breaking out." Only when he got closer and the scene came into focus did he realize his perceptual error.[5]

The question posed by the chapters in this volume is how much closer we ourselves need to get to the reality of our own society's violence against other animals before we are able to perceive that violence for what it is—atrocity. When will we begin to see something fundamentally amiss in the ubiquitous pictures and TV images we see of grinning hunters posed beside the corpses of elk or deer, or of fishermen giving the thumbs-up sign beside heaped-up mounds of squid or crabs or other marine creatures dredged up from the deep and tossed up onto ship decks to suffocate, or to be beaten insensible with claw hammers and crowbars? At what point do we begin to suspect that something serious is wrong with our world—that something fundamental may be at stake—when we learn that workers at a pig farm kill sick or injured baby pigs by swinging them by their tails and smashing their heads against the concrete? Or when we read in the newspaper, over our morning coffee, that in Puerto Rico, "unwanted dogs, cats and even farm animals [are] hurled from bridges, intentionally crushed by vehicles or butchered with machetes," apparently as a form of recreation?[6]

Such ruthless and extreme acts of violence against other animals are in fact the norm in every society in the world. In France, wealthy gourmands can still arrange a private meal of roasted ortolan—the endangered songbird who, by tradition, has its eyes put out before being force-fed for weeks and then drowned in a snifter of brandy. In Spain, over 11,000 bulls are ritually tortured and killed before thousands of cheering human beings each year. In the Middle East, Muslims celebrate Eid and Ramadan by slitting the throats of hundreds of thousands of live goats, cheering as they struggle in pain, bleeding to death. In 2006, officials in southwestern Yunnan Province in China "killed more than 50,000 pet dogs in five days," after a few isolated cases of rabies appeared in the province. "Dogs being walked were taken from their owners and beaten on the spot. . . . Other teams entered villages at night, creating noise to get dogs barking, and then beating them to death."[7] In some instances, owners were forced to hang their own dogs in front of their houses, while their children looked on. Two years later, Chinese officials ordered a similar pogrom of cats in Beijing in preparation for the Olympic games. Hundreds of thousands of cats were rounded up, packed tightly into wire cages, then transferred to what Chinese observers termed "death camps" set up on the capital's periphery. There, they were killed outright or simply left to starve or succumb slowly to disease. Thousands more were sent to Guangzhou, apparently to be killed for their flesh—Chinese restaurants serve cat.[8]

But even such organized pogroms pale in significance beside the smoothly functioning planetary system of routine extermination—the gigantic, technologically advanced, mechanized apparatus whose sole function is to produce, destroy, and process the bodies and minds of thousands of millions of living beings each year. So normalized and naturalized has this violence become that we only become aware of its existence when the apparatus unexpectedly goes awry, threatening either public health or an industry's bottom line. Only then does an otherwise obscure system of mass killing emerge briefly from the background of daily life to enter the public's consciousness, and then only as spectacle. In 2001, thus, it was only when farm animals in Britain became sickened with foot-and-mouth disease (a purely commercial illness—most infected animals recover on their own), and the English and Irish states ordered the mass killing of six million cows and sheep—the animals' bodies were dumped into huge open pits and set afire, the smoke darkening skies over the British Isles and drifting across the Channel—that the hidden system of routine mass violence suddenly spilled out into the open. Three years later, a similar rupture in the narrative of normal slaughter occurred when the Asian poultry industry grappled with an outbreak of the H5N1 virus. Within weeks, *220 million* ducks, geese, and chickens, healthy and sick alike, were burned alive, suffocated, strangled, shot, and beaten with pipes—killed with savage and remorseless violence as though they themselves were to blame for the excruciating illness which their own squalid confinement and brutal treatment had made them susceptible to.

"So long as living creatures with physiological makeups very close to our own are reduced to resource-objects for human appropriation," Carl Boggs observes in his chapter in this volume, "virtually anything is possible." To which, however, we must add: *and everything is permitted*. The inner essence of fascism and totalitarianism, of atrocity, lies not in ideology as such, but in willed actions whose purpose is to show that there are *no limits* to what can be done to the individual, or even to entire classes of individuals. What finally links images of Americans murdering foxes in the Midwest to reports of the Einsatzkommando 3 murdering Jews in Kaunas—or rather, what allows us to recognize atrocity *as* atrocity, whether perpetrated against human beings or against other animals—is neither the joy, ruthlessness, or simply boredom of the killers, nor the helpless terror, anguish, and suffering of the defenseless victims, but the way the two become conjoined in a mode of action whose symbolic function is to demonstrate absolute superiority of one group over another. As Jacques Semelin writes in his authoritative discussion of the origins, nature, and political uses of genocide and massacre, it is the perpetrator's "situation of impunity" that enables him to feel pleasure "not only at making others suffer but by enjoying the all-powerful state over the victim who is completely at his mercy."[9] To witness atrocity—to see those wielding total power annihilate those who have no power at all—is to see ontologized or made real a relation which, until that moment, could only be expressed ideologically—namely, the *idea* of the worthlessness of the other, the other's lack of a right to exist. It was this ideology that defined the relation of the fascist state to its enemies in the 1930s and 1940s, and it is this ideology, this relation, which today lies at the deepest core of our relations with the other beings-in-the-world, those "others" who we reduce by that singular and utterly fraudulent sign, "the animal." Exposing this ideology, revealing its material and psychic underpinnings and limits, is the main objective of this book.

ANIMAL LIBERATION AND TOTAL CRITIQUE

Critical Theory and Animal Liberation is intended to draw into sharper relief the relationship between the human oppression of other animals and the thematic concerns and political commitments characteristic of the critical or Left tradition in social and political thought. While critical theory today encompasses a wide range of methodological and thematic approaches, including Marxism, feminism, existential phenomenology, Habermasian discourse theory, critical race theory, and queer theory, the term was first used in reference to the work of a group of Marxist sociologists and philosophers based at the Institut für Sozialforschung, or Institute for Social Research, in Frankfurt am Main in Germany. Though only two of the chapters in the present volume focus directly on the scholarly work of the Frankfurt School, as it came to be known, all of them are informed by the school's critical sensibility and spirit.

Founded in 1923 by Felix Weil, the son of a wealthy businessman who made his fortune (ironically) in the meat business, the Frankfurt School was intended as a Left-intellectual answer to the more conservative academic institutes then being funded by the social democratic German state. The purpose of the institute was to explore the role of social institutions and ideologies in perpetuating systems of authority and social hierarchy. The institute's theorists drew on the work of Marx and Freud as well as critical sociology and philosophy in an effort to analyze the deepest structural and psychological elements of fascism and capitalism. Herbert Marcuse, one of the most influential early members of the Frankfurt School, defined the institute's critical or "dialectical" theoretical approach this way in his 1968 preface to *Reason and Revolution*, his study of the influence of Hegel and Marx on social philosophy:

> Dialectical thought starts with the experience that the world is unfree; that is to say, man and nature exist in conditions of alienation, exist "other than they are." Any mode of thought which excludes this contradiction from its logic is [therefore] a faulty logic. Thought "corresponds" to reality only as it transforms reality by comprehending its contradictory structure.[10]

Critical theory thus sets out from a single intuition about the world—that the predominant values, institutions, representational schemata, and so forth of the prevailing social order are a distortion of the real, unjustly constituted in such a way as to prevent the world from becoming something other than it "is"; that is, from becoming what it *ought to be*. Critical theory thus rejects from the outset the ontological distinction in the positivist social sciences between facts and values. Rather than feign a neutral or disinterested stance toward the world—the image of the theorist as innocent abroad, unburdened by ethical or social *values*—the *critical* theorist sets out instead from a prior standpoint of normative sociological critique and existential refusal. Here there is no question of whether theory or practice comes first. As Marcuse writes, "praxis does not only come at the end but is already present in the beginning of the theory."[11] Confronted with a totality rooted in *unfreedom*, the critical theorist seeks to generate forms of knowledge and practice that are themselves "real"—which is to say, adequate to the task of comprehending, and changing, the totality of existing social fact. The goal of critical praxis, therefore, is to liberate humanity and nature too from the brutalizing logics of power that prevent us from realizing our capacities and essence as free, creative beings.

At least two affinities suggest themselves between the early Frankfurt School critique of capitalist society and the critique by animal liberationists of speciesism. First, as a *critical* theory, the critique of speciesism too sets out from the prior assumption or experience of the world as unfree, that is, from the intuition that human and animal "exist in conditions of alienation," and hence are "other than they are." Like the Frankfurt School critics, then, animal liberationists implicate by their critique not merely one aspect of the existing order, but the entirety of human history and culture. To take the claims and concerns of the animal liberationist critique seriously means to question existing economic arrangements, social norms, science and technology, cultural expression, and the foundational terms of social and political thought.[12] Second, animal liberationism is a critical theory, even the most fundamental critical theory, insofar as it shares with other emancipatory traditions the desire to redeem the conscious living *subject*, or person, from thoughtlessness, violence, and domination. Every form of radical praxis arguably has two moments. The first moment is phenomenological, the *revealing* of a suppressed mode of existence (the experiences of the oppressed). The second moment is normative and active—the affirmation of the oppressed subject's experiences through political struggle and the negation of the existing unjust order. We might say that the entire emancipatory tradition—the revolutionary commitment to universal freedom in thought and deed—is therefore grounded in the defense of the *person*, of consciousness, from the indignities and humiliations that power would impose upon it. Hence Rolf Wiggershaus's apt description of Max Horkheimer, the Institute's first director, as having been motivated by "indignation at the injustices being perpetrated on those who [are] exploited and humiliated."[13] Both Horkheimer and his close friend and colleage at the institute, Theodor W. Adorno, saw nonhuman animals to be among the most exploited and humiliated of living subjects. As Christina Gerhardt observes in her chapter "Thinking With: Animals in Schopenhauer, Horkheimer and Adorno," in seeking a way beyond (or through) Kantian rationalism via Schopenhauer's ethics of sympathy, both thinkers hoped to recuperate the animal other as a major subject of moral concern. Through their "shared nexus of concerns," vis-à-vis the animal and the human, the two sought a *politicized* morality in which concern for the other would stand as a kind of barrier to absolute violence. Herbert Marcuse himself (Horkheimer and Adorno's junior colleague at the Institute) appears to have shared their views of other animals. In *One-Dimensional Man*, for example, when Marcuse affirms the socialist view that existing human culture is a hell on earth, he immediately adds that "[p]art of this Hell is the ill-treatment of animals—the work of a human society whose rationality is still the irrational."[14] In *Eros and Civilization*, similarly, Marcuse invoked the myth of Orpheus in his call for a new, post-capitalist civilizational order that might "sing" the natural world back to life, restoring subjectivity to other animals. "In being spoken to, loved, and cared for, flowers and springs and animals [would at last] appear as what they are—beautiful, not only for those who address and regard them, but for themselves, 'objectively.'"[15] The search for a new mode of address to the natural world, a form of *Mitsein* or inter-being in which humans might learn to live alongside the other conscious beings without imposing their own violent categories and systems upon them, was in fact central to the Frankfurt School's ethical vision.

A stake for these early critics was not only the moral problem of nonhuman suffering at human hands, but the self-estrangement of our own animality, as well. As Zipporah Weisberg writes in her psychoanalytic critique of speciesism in these pages, "Animal Repression: Speciesism as Pathology," even as we oppress the other animals we also repress our own animal natures and cut ourselves off from any meaningful connection with the other beings. The result is "an unconscious sense of loss, melancholia, ambivalence, [and] guilt," among other neuroses. The human being "transforms itself into a kind of object—an unthinking automaton, a one-dimensional shell." Weisberg quotes the following vivid passage from Horkheimer and Adorno's *Dialectic of Enlightenment* (first published in 1944), on the torment and controlled killing of live animals in the scientific laboratories of the behaviorists:

> [They] apply to human beings the same formulae and results which they wring without restraint from defenseless animals in their abominable physiological laboratories. . . . The conclusion they draw from the mutilated animal bodies applies, not to animals in freedom, but to human beings today. By mistreating animals they announce that they, and only they in the whole of creation, function voluntarily in the same mechanical, blind, automatic way as the twitching movements of the bound victims made use of by the expert.[16]

Here the alert reader will hear the echo of earlier Romantic critiques of the experimental sciences, whose erstwhile technological innovations were seen only to confirm the species' lack of *moral* progress. As Mephistopheles remarks to God in Goethe's *Faust*:

> The little god of earth remains the same queer sprite
> As on the first day, or in primal light.
> His life would be less difficult, poor thing,
> Without your gift of heavenly glimmering;
> He calls it Reason, using light celestial
> Just to outdo the beasts in being bestial.[17]

As Susan Benston relates in her moving poem here, *Neuroscience* (the only creative writing included in this volume), the language, methodological protocols, and instrumental practices of contemporary technoscientific research on animals are evocative of medieval barbarism—and reminders of the ways in which modern human subjectivity remains rooted in a colossal bad faith. The scientist's religious language of "sacrifice" ironically underscores the heedless sacrifice of his own vaunted humanity. In Benston's imagery, the monkey strapped to a restraint table emerges as a Christ-like figure whose inability of consent to the humiliations and torments to which she is subjected mirrors the scientist's own inability to comprehend or "consent" to the sadistic role he has chosen to play out in the lab.

In tormenting other animals, the human scientist performs what Aaron Bell in "The Dialectic of Anthropocentrism," his chapter here, terms an "auto-vivisection": "one must cut into one's own being in order to remove or place to one side those features of oneself that are incidental and held in common with the rest of the 'natural world,' the 'meat' of one's being, in order to find that tissue which is essential to the human." As Bell argues, this excision of the animal *within* the human leads to what Hegel termed "radical evil," an extreme solipsism in which the subject—in this case, *Homo sapiens*—seeks to destroy all that is other. It was precisely such solipsism that led Horkheimer and Adorno to indict modern civilization for having reduced the universe to a "unified" cosmic hunting ground "in which nothing exists but prey."[18] Unable to recognize or acknowledge the animal other *as* other—that is, as a being worthy of being addressed as a "Thou" (see Josephine Donovan, this volume)—humanity subsequently falls into the ugly role of a universal Procrustes. Procrustes, it is to be recalled, was the dread bandit in Greek myth who alternately stretched or cut his guests' legs to fit his bed. According to the *Penguin Dictionary of Symbols*, the Procrustes myth represents "the perversion of idealism into conventionality and a symbol of the tyranny exercised by those who only tolerate the activities and opinions of others when they satisfy their own standards." This makes Procrustes a potent "symbol of totalitarianism, whether exercised by individual, party or state."[19] Or by the *species*. For as Karen Davis shows in her chapter here, "Procrustean Solutions to Animal Identity," the genetic, behavioral, and psychological manipulation of chickens and other exploited animal species produces the most excruciating and mutilated forms of animal being, as commercial animal industries wholly suppress their life-needs in the quest for profit.

Weisberg, Bell, Davis, and indeed all the contributors to our volume show that the compulsory forgetting, or repression, of our own animal essence—that is, of the knowledge that we human beings are always already caught up with the drama of *being animal* (desiring, feeling, experiencing, suffering, laboring, loving, and so on)—prepares the way for the unending catastrophes of modernity. This is to say that speciesism is both symptomatic of and constitutive of a total mode of domination. Negation of the animal other is not a side concern to the "real issues" facing human social life but the pivot around which our civilization itself has formed, the phenomenological *ground* upon which the figure of the human being continues to stand. As Horkheimer and Adorno observed:

> Throughout European history, the idea of the human being has been expressed in contradistinction to the animal. The latter's lack of reason is the proof of human dignity. So insistently and unanimously has this antithesis been recited by all the earliest precursors of bourgeois thought, the ancient Jews, the Stoics, and the Early Fathers, and then through the Middle Ages to modern times, that few other ideas are so fundamental to Western anthropology.[20]

The animal other is thus not only the material stuff of civilization—the flesh and bone, labor and intelligence we exploit for our purposes—but the psycho-semiotic medium upon which we inscribe the entirety of our culture, our philosophy, our cosmology. Hence Adorno's continual return to the problem of the animal: as Eduardo Mendieta points out in his chapter in these pages, "Animal Is to Kantianism as Jew Is to Fascism: Adorno's Bestiary," Adorno's whole philosophy was centrally a "critique of metaphysics and [of] its implicit positive anthropology that delimits the human and reason by invidiously excluding the animal."

In arriving at these conclusions, it is worth noting, both Adorno and Horkheimer seem to have been influenced by the work of the psychologist and social theorist Wilhelm Reich. Though not a member of the Frankfurt School, "Willi" Reich (as Adorno refers to him in his letters) was nevertheless a fellow traveler in the circles of critical philosophy of the 1930s, a maverick German intellectual who, like the sociologists and philosophers of the Frankfurt School, felt that the rise of fascism had thrown the most fundamental assumptions concerning European civilization into doubt. That Nazism could develop in such a culturally "advanced" society, one at the very height of its creative and technological powers, required a rethinking of the bases of Western civilization. It was in this spirit of a grand *epochē* or bracketing of Europe's own common-sense notions of modernity that Reich thought he had traced fascism and the authoritarian personality to a foundational hatred of the animal, a hatred which, he argued, had come to structure virtually the entirety of human consciousness and culture. Whether in man's "science, his religion, his art, or his other expressions of life," Reich wrote in *The Mass Psychology of Fascism*, first published in 1933, the "highest task of human existence" is held to be the 'slaying of his animal side' and the cultivation of 'values.'"

> Man is fundamentally an animal. . . . [Yet] man developed the peculiar idea that he was not an animal; *he* was a "man," and he had long since divested himself of the "vicious" and "brutal." Man takes great pains to disassociate himself from the vicious animal and to prove that he "is better" by pointing to his culture and his civilization, which distinguish him from the animal. His entire attitude, his "theories of value," moral philosophies, his "monkey trials," all bear witness to the fact that he does not want to be reminded that he is fundamentally an animal,

> that he has incomparably more in common with "the animal" than he has with that which he thinks and dreams himself to be. . . . His viciousness, his inability to live peacefully with his own kind, his wars, bear witness to the fact that man is distinguished from the other animals only by a boundless sadism and the mechanical trinity of an authoritarian view of life, mechanistic science, and the machine. If one looks back over long stretches of the results of human civilization, one finds that man's claims are not only false, but are peculiarly contrived to make him forget that he is an animal.[21]

This *episteme*, to borrow Foucault's term, has subtended and conditioned the whole of civilization from its beginning, providing the very basis of positive human culture. For centuries, our sciences and systems of knowledge have conspired to divide sentient life, conscious being-in-the-world, into two neat, mutually exclusive, and utterly fraudulent halves—"the human" versus "the rest."[22] Paradoxically, though, in distancing ourselves from the animal other, we end up disavowing our own humanity (itself, after all, a form of *animality*) embracing a "machine civilization" based in death-fetishism. "How is it possible," Reich wondered, "that [man] does not see the damages (psychic illnesses, biopathies, sadism, and wars) to his health, culture, and mind that are caused by this biologic renunciation?"[23]

It is striking that Reich, Adorno, and Horkheimer, all of whom were personally forced to flee Germany by Hitler, had no qualms about comparing the human treatment of animals to the treatment of Jews and other enemies of the Third Reich under fascism.[24] After the war, Adorno famously wrote that "Auschwitz begins wherever someone looks at a slaughterhouse and thinks: they're only animals," a once-obscure quote that recently has been given new life by animal rights activists and sympathetic scholars. In fact, pointed comparisons of our treatment of other animals to the Nazis' treatment of the Jews and others in the Holocaust are peppered throughout Adorno's work, sometimes showing up in the most unexpected places (including a study of Beethoven's music). As Mendieta observes here, Adorno drew an explicit link between Kant's denial of any meaningful subjectivity or moral worth to animals and the catastrophes of the twentieth century, including the rise of National Socialism. "Nothing is more abhorrent to the Kantian," he wrote, "than a reminder of man's resemblance to animals. This taboo is always at work when the idealist berates the materialist. *Animals play for the idealist system virtually the same role as the Jews for fascism*."[25]

Indeed, is speciesism itself not a form of fascism, perhaps even its paradigmatic or primordial form? The very word "massacre," Semelin observes, originally meant "putting an animal to death": human massacres of other humans have always been realized through the semiotic transposition of the one abject subject onto the other. "Killing supposedly human 'animals' then becomes entirely possible."[26] Adorno made a similar point in *Minima Moralia*, sixty years earlier: "The constantly encountered assertion that savages, blacks, Japanese are like animals, monkeys for example, is the key to the pogrom. The possibility of pogroms is decided in the moment when the gaze of a fatally-wounded animal falls on a human being."[27] What is crucial to bear in mind, however, as Victoria Johnson points out in her chapter here ("Everyday Rituals of the Master Race: Fascism, Stratification, and the Fluidity of 'Animal' Domination") the very "power of such animal metaphors depends on a prior cultural understanding of other animals themselves, as beings who are by nature abject, degraded, and hence worthy of extermination." The animal, thus, rests at the intersection of race and caste systems. And nowhere is the link between the human and nonhuman caste systems clearer than "in fascist ideology," for "no other discourse so completely authorizes absolute violence against the weak." In our own contemporary society too, Johnson emphasizes, we find daily life and meaning based on elaborate rituals intended to keep us from acknowledging the violence we do to subordinate classes of beings, above all the animals.

So numerous in fact are the parallels—semiotic, ideological, psychological, historical, cultural, technical, and so forth—between the Nazis' extermination of the Jews and Roma and the routinized mass murder of nonhuman beings, that Charles Patterson's recent book on the subject, *Eternal Treblinka: Our Treatment of Animals and the Holocaust*, despite its strengths, only manages to scratch the surface of a topic whose true dimensions have yet to be fathomed.[28] In the ideological mechanisms used to legitimate killing, in the bad faith of the human beings who collude with the killing through indifference or "ignorance of the facts," above all in the technologies of organized murder—practices of confinement and control, modes of legitimation and deception, methods of elimination (gassing, shooting, clubbing, burning, vivisecting, and so on)—the mass killing of animals today cannot but recall the Nazi liquidation of European Jewry and Roma. The late Jacques Derrida observed that "there are also animal genocides."[29] With uncharacteristic moral sobriety he wrote:

> [T]he annihilation of certain species is indeed in progress, but it is occurring through the organization and exploitation of an artificial, infernal, virtually interminable *survival*, in conditions that previous generations would have judged monstrous, outside of every supposed norm of a life proper to animals that are thus exterminated by means of their continued existence or even overpopulation. As if, for example, instead of throwing people into ovens or gas chambers (let's say Nazis) doctors and geneticists had decided to organize the overproduction and overgeneration of Jews, gypsies, and homosexuals by means of artificial insemination, so that, being more numerous and better fed, they could be destined

in always increasing numbers for the same hell, that of the imposition of genetic experimentation or extermination by gas or fire.[30]

What would it mean for us to come to terms with the knowledge that civilization, our whole mode of development and culture, has been premised and built upon extermination—on a history experienced as "terror without end" (to borrow a phrase from Adorno)?[31]

To dwell with such a thought would be to throw into almost unbearable relief the distance between our narratives of inherent human dignity and grace and moral superiority, on one side, and the most elemental facts of our actual social existence, on the other. We congratulate ourselves for our social progress—for democratic governance and state-protected civil and human rights (however notional or incompletely defended)—yet continue to enslave and kill millions of sensitive creatures who in many biological, hence emotional and cognitive, particulars resemble us. To truly meditate on such a contradiction is to comprehend our self-understanding to be not merely flawed, but to be almost comically delusional. Immanuel Kant dreamed of a moral order in which we would all participate as equals in a "kingdom of ends." But it is time to ask whether morality as such is even possible under conditions of universal bad faith and hidden slaughter, in the same way that we might ask whether acts of private morality under National Socialism were not compromised or diminished by the larger context in which they occurred.[32] When atrocity becomes the very basis of society, does society not forfeit its right to call itself moral? In the nineteenth century, the animal welfare advocate Edward Maitland warned that our destruction of the other animals lead only to our own "debasement and degradation of character" as a species. "For the principles of Humanity cannot be renounced with impunity; but their renunciation, if persisted in, involves inevitably the forfeiture of Humanity itself. And to cease through such forfeiture to be man is to become demon."[33] What else indeed can we call a being but *demon* who enslaves and routinely kills thousands of millions of other gentle beings, imprisons them in laboratories, electrocutes or poisons or radiates or drowns them? A being who tests the capacity of empathy in other beings by forcing them to choose between life-sustaining food and subjecting a stranger of their own species in an adjacent tank or cage to painful electrical shocks? And what does it tell us about the vaunted moral superiority of humankind that while the rat, the octopus, the monkey will forgo food to avoid harming another, the human researcher will persist in tormenting his captive, until he or she collapses in convulsions and dies? Do such tests, designed to detect the presence of empathy in other species, only demonstrate the paucity of empathy in our own? Above all, it is the existential question that haunts: Who, or rather what, are we?

ANIMAL RIGHTS AND THE COMPLICATED LEGACY OF THE LEFT

If the authors in this volume have a single shared objective, it is to provide a historical rather than metaphysical answer to this last question—that is, to illuminate the structural, economic, and psycho-social forces that give rise to speciesism as a total mode of domination. To pose the problem this way is to identify our project with the Left tradition. However, notwithstanding the recurring interest of early members of the Frankfurt School in the problem of speciesism, the Left with few exceptions has historically viewed human violence toward other beings with indifference. In fact, as John Sorenson shows in his chapter here, "Constructing Extremists, Rejecting Compassion: Ideological Attacks on Animal Advocacy from Right and Left," it is one of the ironies of social thought that the views of leftists and rightists converge on the question of animal rights. Both sides affirm the sovereign right of members of *Homo sapiens* to exploit and kill other living beings as they wish; both view animal liberation as a danger to established human society. To critics of the political right, the very idea of animal rights is a threat to free enterprise and a symptom of a "relativist," godless, and effeminate secular society in decline. (Pundits draw on masculine paranoia and nationalism to defend meat, circulating articles suggesting that vegetarianism is "making kids 'gay'" and "feminizing" America.[34]) In the United States, animal rights activists themselves have been portrayed as "enemies of the human race" who seem bent on outright "human extermination"[35]; far-right movements in other countries have similarly incorporated *species right* into their defense of ultranationalist sentiments.[36] Where the Right sees animal rights as a national apocalypse and a threat to free enterprise, however, the Left warns of the end of secular enlightenment and social progress. Peter Staudenmaier, for example, a student of the anarchist theorist Murray Bookchin, warns that animal rights is "'a moral mistake and a symptom of political confusion . . . anti-humanist and anti-ecological . . . at odds with the project of creating a free world.'"[37] Along the same lines, the ecological Marxist Joel Kovel describes animal rights activists as "fundamentalists" who "forget that all creatures, however they may be recognized, are still differentiated and that we make use of other creatures within our human nature."[38] In a similar vein, one writer on a Marxist listserv responded this way to an earlier post by a critic asking whether Hegel's "master-slave" dialectic might not be applicable to the relation between humans and animals: "Unless you've done a Vulcan mind-meld and know something I don't, animals are incapable of self-consciousness, or of any deliberative ethical judgment, hence the master-slave dialectic is irrelevant in this regard. Since I'm in favor of anthropocentrism, as is any rational human being, I wouldn't waste my time worrying about this."[39]

It is just such widespread, unthinking prejudice on the Left that has led liberal animal rights theorists like Robert Garner to conclude that neither socialism nor feminism has much to offer much from "an animal protectionist perspective." As Garner notes, there is nothing in the historical record to suggest "that at the level of praxis the theoretical case for incorporation has been accepted by anything more than a small proportion of feminists and socialists."[40] Whence this hostility of radical intellectuals to animal liberation as such?

The origins of the Left's hostility to animal rights can be traced back to the unresolved ambivalences and tensions at the heart of the humanist and Enlightenment traditions from which it sprang. On the one hand, the early modern period saw the rise of a secular-scientific worldview that "disenchanted" the living natural world and reduced all living beings—including human ones—to the status of mere things to be controlled. The humanist faith in "the dignity of man"—the principle from which all modern progressive movements eventually evolved—was from the start drawn in contradistinction to the perpetually degraded and irrational animal. Already by the early seventeenth century, the fate of nonhuman beings in the modern era had been decided in Francis Bacon's *New Atlantis* (1627), a utopian scientific novel that anticipates, and indeed provides the conceptual blueprints for, the genetic engineering of the twenty-first century. The triumph of vivisectionists and their proponents, including René Descartes, Nicholas Malebranche, Antoine Arnould, and Robert Boyle, among others, confirmed that the nonhuman animal would now be made productive for the human sciences.[41] The advent of modernity, and with it the descent of an "iron cage of reason," produced new modes of control and manipulation—the bureaucratized nation state, rationalization, new technologies of control, the homogenizing and standardizing effects of commodity fetishism, and so on—that trapped human and nonhuman beings alike.

But this is not the whole story, and it is important to resist the poststructuralist vogue in animal studies for simplistic denunciations of the Enlightenment.[42] For it is one of the ironies of the Enlightenment and secularization that it was also in this period, specifically in the century that followed the first advances of the scientific revolution, that nonhuman animals themselves became *humanized*, and here not only in the bad sense. Secularism and the Enlightenment led not only to new modalities of domination (above all colonialism), but also to procedural democracy, liberalism, socialism, the "rights of man"—and animal rights. With the spread of universalist and egalitarian ideals, it did not take a great leap of logic for some far-sighted individuals to see how other animals too might have an interest in freedom, liberty, and fraternity, or in not feeling pain.[43] Less than a decade after the storming of the

Bastille, an English reformer named Thomas Young wrote *An Essay on Humanity to Animals* (1798), in which he placed concern for other animals alongside "exertions . . . to diminish the sufferings of the prisoners, and to better the condition of the poor." Young vividly compared animal rights to "the interest excited in the nation by the struggles for the abolition of the slave trade" and suggested that both were signs of humanity taking small but meaningful steps toward social progress.[44] Many early proponents of vegetarianism and animal welfare in fact drew parallels with or personally participated in other liberal and radical causes for social emancipation, including abolitionism, prison reform, pacifism, women's rights, and workers' rights. The Scottish John Oswald converted to radical vegetarianism in the same moment that he became an anti-imperialist militant opposed to British colonialism in India.[45] Henry Salt, the most prominent and philosophically astute nineteenth-century advocate for animal rights, highlighted the connection between animal rights and the struggle to reform a capitalist system that was degrading to all beings, human workers and nonhuman animals alike. Salt was merely articulating the view of many other animal advocates at the time when he wrote in *Animals' Rights: Considered in Relation to Social Progress* (1894) that social reformers and animal rights activists alike were "working towards the same ultimate goal."[46]

Sadly, though, despite the broadly socialist and social democratic sympathies of animal rights proponents during the nineteenth century, few socialists in that period or in the century that followed were to acknowledge a tug of political conscience from the other side. The exceptions for the most part appear to have been feminists with socialist sympathies—Charlotte Perkins Gilman, for example, who portrayed the Amazonian inhabitants of her utopian novel *Herland* as vegetarian, or the anarchist Voltairine DeCleyre, who felt as passionately about the suffering of cats and dogs as she did about the oppression of the working class. Another exception was Peter Kropotkin, the Russian anarchist, who between 1890 and 1896 published a series of articles in the British journal *The Nineteenth Century* on the Darwinian case for the primacy of social cooperation (rather than the Spencerian emphasis on ruthless competition) in the animal and human worlds. Kropotkin not only acknowledged the advanced intelligence and emotional complexity of numerous other species besides our own, he also emphasized other animals' "joy of life" and "love of society for society's sake."[47] Other prominent nineteenth-century anarchist and socialist thinkers, including Mikhail Bakunin and Pierre-Joseph Proudhon, held similarly generous opinions of the cognitive and social capacities of the other species, though none explicitly advocated animal rights as such (Charles Fourier, however, did advocate "gentleness" in animal husbandry, and he boasted that donkeys in his utopian village of Harmony would "be much better housed and better kept than the peasants of the beautiful land of France"[48]). If such sentiments were a far cry from an explicit socialist critique of human domination, they were at least not dismissive of the notion that other animals might have lives and experiences that mattered, and they were not overtly hostile to movements promoting animal welfare. It therefore seems plausible that, had the early pluralism of anarchist and socialist thought been allowed to ferment and mature, radical thought might have developed in a more ecological, feminist, and animal liberationist direction. In the event, however, the brilliance of one socialist theorist was to outshine all the others, and in the consolidation of his staunchly anthropocentric vision of a "scientific" socialism, all thought to the suffering and oppression of other species was to be swept to one side for the next hundred years.

I am speaking, of course, of Karl Marx. It is well known that Marx and Engels held the animal welfare movements of their own time in contempt, placing "members of societies for the prevention of cruelty to animals" alongside "organisers of charity, temperance fanatics, [and] hole-and-corner reformers of every imaginable kind."[49] Engels himself was an avid fox-hunter, and neither he nor Marx thought to question the anthropocentric prejudices of their time, which they broadly accepted.[50] Despite his avowed intention of turning Hegel on his head (that is, right-side up), Marx never quite shook off the anthropocentric assumptions of the German idealists. Both Hegel and Kant had viewed freedom as the exercise and realization of an absolute, *human* freedom, and both denied that other animals, lacking such freedom, could have any intrinsic value of their own. Hegel's crypto-theological view of *Homo sapiens* as the pinnacle of creation, the ultimate expression of the self-consciousness of the universe, later found its way into Marx's historical materialism, in the latter's theory of the coming to self-consciousness of humanity through the praxis of the working class. Marx laid out his humanist conception of nature and of the purposes of human life at length in his extraordinary *Economic and Philosophical Manuscripts* of 1844. We might say that with Marx's *Manuscripts*, the modern humanist tradition that begins with Pico's *Oration on the Dignity of Man* in the sixteenth century and ends some four centuries later with Foucault's *The Order of Things* reaches its highest philosophical development and greatest spiritual expression.[51] Taking up Feuerbach's Hegelian conception of humankind as a self-conscious "species being," that is, a being whose life essence lies in its ability to lay hold of *itself* universally, as the total object of its own labor, consciousness, and will, Marx showed how the emergence of capitalism, and with it abstract labor, estranges human beings from one another as well as from internal and external nature. Rather than labor and produce "universally," or in accordance with the welfare of humankind as such, the individual treats both the species and herself as a mere means to an end—as a source of crude pleasures and self-interested desires. Compulsory wage labor effectively reduces human beings therefore to the status of *animals*—that is, to beings incapable of exercising genuine autonomy. Animals too are capable of suffering and of producing their own means of existence. They too are *sensuous* beings. However, human sensuous life is qualitatively different from nonhuman sensuous life. Our senses only become truly human when they cease to be "merely" animal. Only under conditions of universal freedom do we achieve proper historical self-consciousness as a species being (and so come to define our collective life purpose). Like other scientific thinkers of his time, therefore, Marx did not try to come to terms with the consciousness of other beings. For him, nature—including other animals—was indistinguishable from "man's body"—hence a resource for humans to develop and control as the means to their own self-flourishing.

As all this suggests, and as Ted Benton shows in careful detail in his important chapter, "Speciesism = Humanism?: Marx on Humans and Animals" (originally published in 1988 and reprinted here for the first time), Marx's account of the nature and purposes of human existence revolves around an insupportable dualism that places human being on one side and animal being on the other. But while such a dualism was relatively uncontroversial a century and a half ago, it is no longer scientifically credible today. After nearly five centuries of portraying other animals as little more than automata (one or another variant of the mechanistic "stimulus and response" model), modern science is at last confirming what most ordinary human beings have known for millennia—namely, that other animals feel and think and experience the world.[52] Both evolutionary biology and the new science of cognitive ethology in particular have proved Charles Darwin right: that the difference between *Homo sapiens* and the other animals is a difference in degree rather than kind. Other animals have memories and feelings, fall in love, experience loss, mourn their dead, suffer, reason, have distinct cultures, use tools, communicate with one another, and on and on. Dolphins address each other using specific whistles, which function as individual names.[53] Whales transmit cultural innovations across and within the generations.[54] New Caledonian crows have been observed to fashion tools out of leaves—and to take them with them when they change nests. At least one parrot was taught over a hundred words and could answer questions in English concerning the qualities of presented objects (round, four-cornered, soft, and so forth).[55] Elephants have been observed in the wild coming to the assistance of injured or wounded strangers, working together to save infants from drowning, using medicinal plants, and engaging in rituals for (or related to) the dead. Species as varied as orcas, bonobo chimps, and European magpies, among others, have passed the so-called "mirror test," acting in ways that show that they understand their image in the mirror to be of *themselves*.[56] But these are only a few examples of literally thousands available that show beyond any reasonable doubt that other species exist in temporal, meaningful, feeling, thinking worlds of their own. There is indeed every reason to believe that their worlds are at least as vivid and emotionally intense as our own, since the very capacities we fetishize as most valuable and meaningful in our own species—reason and speech—have probably dimmed or blunted our other sensuous capacities.[57] It is bracing to learn how *cognitively* and sensorily impaired we humans in fact are compared to many of the other species—for instance, to learn that the eyesight of wild turkeys is three times as acute as our own, that sharks perceive electrical fields, that the average bonobo can jump 30 percent higher than the top human athlete, or that the humble bar-tailed godwit, a seagoing bird, can fly 7,000 miles across the Pacific Ocean—nonstop. While no other terrestrial species has yet revealed itself to have our capacity for abstract, language-based reasoning, other animals do think, and some plan for the future, anticipate events, reflect on past experiences, and so on. Some primate species, including macaques, have been shown capable of discerning the internal mental states of other beings, including human beings (that is, to know whether subject A knows some fact X or not). In reality, though, it is hard to see how any socially complex organism, whether a bird, cetacean, or mammal could survive long in the world without a keen comprehension of the mental states and intentions of those around it. Moreover, while we are prone to think of the other animals as our perpetual cognitive inferiors, it turns out that at least some other species have more acute memory and high-level reasoning abilities than we do. The Clark nutcracker, for example, can remember the location of its nearly 3,000 individual food caches, hidden across 100 square miles of terrain; chimpanzees have easily defeated elite Japanese college students at short-term memory tests[58]; pigeons have bested U.S. college students in spatial reasoning exercises; and both pigeons and baboons have demonstrated a more robust capacity for "higher-order relational learning" than humans in controlled laboratory experiments.[59]

Other animals are *conscious* beings, they *exist* in the world. Phenomenologists exploring the nature of nonhuman consciousness have shown beyond any doubt that the other beings' phenomenological worlds, like ours, are richly rooted in personal meaning and signification.[60] While their experiences are therefore quite different from our own, the mere fact of their radical "otherness" does not therefore deprive their experiences or their existence of intrinsic existential and moral import. We need not deny or denigrate those qualities that may make human existence unique in order to at the same time affirm the cognitive, historical, and cultural capacities of other species.[61] In this connection, Benton's point is not simply that Marx's humanist view of other animals is obsolete, but rather and more crucially "that he was wrong [about other animals] in ways which undermine his own view of the desirability of a changed relationship between humanity and nature in the future communist society." Marx was "wrong about animals in ways which cut him off from a powerful extension and deepening of his own ethical critique of prevailing (capitalist) modes of appropriation of nature." At stake, then, in Marx's mistaken understanding of other species is the question of the *adequacy* of our own theoretical frameworks for envisioning forms of historical praxis in the present. For if we persist in constructing a liberatory politics on the ground of a fraudulent ontology—an insupportable division between human and nonhuman consciousness and experience—we cannot identify our own true emancipatory interests, let alone those of the other conscious beings.

Regrettably, however, for reasons that are probably rooted in the psychology of speciesism itself, the Left's view of the other animals has remained stubbornly unchanged since the last century. The chasm opened up by Marx between socialism and animal liberationism grew wider after the "hard" masculine turn of the Bolshevik Revolution: the Leninist emphasis on the necessity of using ruthless violence to wage and preserve the gains of revolution further postponed any possibility of a rapprochement between the two movements. The consolidation of Stalinism proved especially catastrophic, preparing the way for state ecological catastrophes—and massive animal exploitation and killing—in the U.S.S.R. and China.[62] Hence today's "leftist cluelessness"—as Carl Boggs acidly describes the attitude of many contemporary radicals toward human domination and killing of other beings. Whether such blind indifference "derives from sheer ignorance," he asks, "or the simple prejudice of an addicted population, or simply reflects an intellectual myopia—or some combination of these," ultimately matters less than the fact that by ignoring the question of speciesism "the Left has abandoned any claim to critical thinking, much less oppositional politics."

Yet the fact that the Left has hitherto ignored the animal question in no wise reflects on the actual relevance or moral and *political* import of that question. As Renzo Llorente remarks in "Reflections on the Prospects for a Non-Speciesist Marxism," his chapter here, "nothing [in fact] commits Marxism to speciesism". The argument made by Garner and other liberal animal rights theorists, that because socialists have largely ignored animal rights neither they nor feminists therefore have anything substantive or useful to offer from "an animal protectionist perspective," only begs the question of whether and how speciesism as a social structure and ideology intersects with other modalities of oppression and domination. For while it is true that most feminists and socialists have not taken animal liberationism seriously, it is also the case that many early socialists did not take feminism seriously, that leading suffragists were dismissive of the anti-slavery movement, and that many animal rights activists today remain blind to the many discursive connections between the treatment of animals and a mysogynist culture of male sexual violence against women. Existing prejudice is therefore a reliable guide neither to determination of the moral good nor to a practical sociology of power and oppression. In reality, both animal rights and socialism have a great deal to learn from one another. Indeed, several of our contributors suggest, they should be grasped as dependent parts of the same total critique of domination, exploitation, and systemic violence.

CAPITALISM AND THE STATE: SPECIESISM AS A MODE OF PRODUCTION

Notwithstanding the problems with Marx's anthropocentric and dualist ontology of freedom, the transcendence of speciesism can itself be viewed as part of our *Bildung* as a self-conscious species, as the formation of what Engels, in another context, termed "a really human morality." Both movements share an underlying normative commitment to "radical egalitarianism," as Llorente calls it, suggesting the theoretical basis for a "rapprochement" between the two traditions. In fact, neither animal liberation nor socialism can be conceived without the other.

First and foremost, as Mills and Williams suggest, "no social formation has been so deeply implicated in the maintenance and proliferation of the mistreatment of animals as capitalism."[63] Capitalism is not just one manifestation of human domination—it is the *highest, most maturely developed historical form* of that domination. Human beings have enslaved and killed other species for many thousands of years, but only in the modern period, under a new form of commodity relations, have living beings been reduced to pure objects. Marx's fourfold phenomenology of alienation under capitalism applies as readily to exploited animals as to factory workers.[64] As Henry Salt observed more than a century ago, "[i]n the rush and hurry of a competitive society, where commercial profit is avowed to be the main object of work, and where the well-being of men and women is ruthlessly sacrificed to that object, what likelihood is there that the lower animals will not be used with a sole regard to the same predominant purpose?"[65] Commodity fetishism and privatization destroy human and human–nonhuman solidarity, estrange us from nature, and compromise and weaken democratic institutions, stripping all living beings of any intrinsic value other than one—surplus value (commercial profit). As Dennis Soron shows in his chapter here, "Road Kill: Commodity Fetishism and Structural Violence," speciesism is articulated in and through a system of institutional violence—capitalism—which in turn assumes shape and meaning only through speciesism and its rituals of domination. Drawing attention to one of the most egregious yet neglected features of our de facto state of war against other animals—the hundreds of millions of animals maimed and killed annually on our highways and roads—Soron shows how the manufacture and marketing of sadistic "road kill" products mocking the suffering of nonhuman beings—including plush toys for children with tire tracks imprinted on the animal's back and fake intestines hanging out—reflects the hidden violence and alienating logic of commodity fetishism as such.) Capitalism, in short, is inimical to freedom *qua* freedom, human and nonhuman alike.

Contra the liberal view of speciesism as a set of mistaken (and hence more or less easily corrected) *beliefs* about the world, speciesism is a *mode of production* in its own right, in Marx and Engels' specific usage of that term as "a definite form of expressing . . . life, a definite *mode of life*." That is, speciesism is not a fixed ideology or an unchanging essence, but rather a complex, dynamic, expansive system that is materially and ideologically imbricated with capitalism as such. Speciesism is a thoroughly historical way of relating to other beings, just as capitalism itself is a thoroughly historical way of relating to nature as such. Among other things, this suggests that the misplaced emphasis in the liberal animal rights literature on the history of ideas, often at the expense of social history and of a more probing inquiry into the nature and origin of human violence, is missing the big picture. Much has been made by contemporary philosophers of Descartes's views of the mind and body, for example, but little of the emergence of capitalism or the consolidation of a new form of patriarchy in early modern Europe, even though it was the capitalist instrumentalization of nature, in combination with a newly emphatic system of male control over women, that formed the profane ground upon which the speciesist thought of Descartes, Bacon, Malebranche, and so on stood forth.[66] As Marx observed, "Descartes with his definition of animals as mere machines saw with the eyes of the manufacturing period, while in the eyes of the Middle Ages, animals were man's assistants."[67] Today, we see animals through the eyes of biotechnology and global finance capital. In other words, the way we produce our lives is organized around the way we view and treat the other animals, and this is a historical process.

The importance of the *animal* as one of the most important loci for the ongoing, fundamental composition of capitalism can be seen in the shift from a Fordist to a post-Fordist regime of capital accumulation. According to the Regulation school of Marxist theory, capitalism stabilizes itself by forming new "regimes" of capital accumulation, overcoming contradictions in the existing arrangement of forces by consolidating new forms of economy, society, state, and cultural life. The only transition that theorists have examined in any detail is that between Fordist and post-Fordist forms of production. The former, so named because of the mass assembly line developed by Henry Ford, was based (inter alia) on mass production of standardized goods, mass consumer markets, vertical lines of control, capital-intensive technological innovation, and the formation of a welfare state to stabilize labor–capital relations. Post-Fordism, by contrast, mixes mass production and standardization with "batch" or niche production and consumption, globally dispersed or horizontal lines of control, technologies based on computerization, a post-welfare or neoliberal state, and new forms of culture, family life, and sexuality. In this context, Regulation theory takes on a whole new look when viewed through the lens of speciesism as a mode of production. While Fordism is typically associated with the rise of the mass-produced automobile, Nicole Shukin points out that Henry Ford in fact modeled his storied auto assembly line at Highland Park "on moving lines that had been operating at least since the 1850s in the vertical abattoirs of Cincinnati and Chicago, with deadly efficiency and to deadly effect"—the same rationalized killing process immortalized in Upton Sinclair's *The Jungle* (published seven years before Highland Park opened).[68] American monopoly capital eventually took these earlier, relatively crude efforts at mass slaughter to a new levels of efficiency, streamlining technologies to raise, transport, and slaughter hundreds of thousands of pigs in gigantic factories.[69] The mass killing of nonhuman beings was thus central to Fordism, not to mention to the model of routinized, administratively efficient, spatially extended mass killing adopted by the Nazis to liquidate European Jewry, Roma, and other "enemies" of the capitalist German state under the Third Reich. The effectiveness of Fordism as a coherent regime of capital accumulation in fact owed a great deal to a new language and culture around the industrialized production and consumption of animal bodies, one that reinforced narratives of national strength, gender roles, home life, and so on. The ready availability of meat in particular was a key ideological and cultural feature of the 1920s–1950s period, particularly in forming a new consuming subject.[70] The stockyards and slaughterhouses of Chicago not only enabled the expansion of the middle class, they even helped, at a semiotic level, to stabilize and legitimate the capitalist state. Hence the slogan of the Republican Party during the presidential campaign of 1928, promising "a chicken in every pot . . . [a]nd a car in every backyard," which linked American prosperity to automobility and mass slaughter of animals.[71]

Today, the animal is one of the most important sites for the reproduction and expansion of post-Fordist capital. As Shukin writes, "animal and capital are increasingly produced as a semiotic and material closed loop," a "nauseating recursivity" in which "capital becomes animal, animal becomes capital."[72] As before, the Taylorized mass killing of nonhuman beings remains central to the economies of the industrialized nations.[73] The globalization of production and financialization of capital since the 1980s has made possible the spatial expansion of mass animal confinement and slaughter technologies and procedures to all four corners of the earth. Faced with the possibility of declining demand at home (in part as a result of increased public awareness of factory farms), U.S. companies have exported American-style meat consumption patterns to Asia, the Pacific Rim, North Africa, and Latin America. To meet the demands of a rising middle class that has come to expect cheap, readily available pig flesh, Chinese companies are hastily constructing mass killing facilities. A similar dynamic holds sway in Eastern Europe, where hundreds of small-scale family pig farms are being eliminated overnight and replaced by huge, concentration camp–style facilities owned and operated by giant U.S. agricultural interests.

What is key is that the appropriation and control of other beings is being organized along post-Fordist, rather than Fordist, lines. In place of Fordism's vertical lines of production we find animal slavery and killing being integrated horizontally, across globally dispersed commodity chains, and driven by finance capital. Mass standardization of animal products persist; yet more and more we see product differentiation and niche marketing, like the "batch production" of animal commodities like Kobe and Angus beef, new markets in so-called "free range" eggs and "humanely killed" veal calves, and what we might call ontological hybridization (as fish oil in orange juice, now standard fare in Tropicana juices). If the Fordist regime of accumulation required the construction of a new mass consumer whose desires could be standardized to fit the needs of manufacturers, the post-Fordist regime is interested in creating a fragmented market of savvy, educated consumers. The world ecological crisis and the rise of a determined animal rights movement has made it necessary for the animal industry to develop new psychological and discursive frames in civil society to justify the continued exploitation of nonhuman beings for sport and killing. Animal capital has to this end conjured into being a large, well-funded hidden army of consultants, lobbyists, and marketing and behavioral experts charged with the twin objectives of shoring up the ideological base of speciesism as a mode of production and undermining the credibility of animal rights groups (such as by branding the latter as irrational terrorists.)[74] Just as Fordism interpellated a new form of mass consuming subject, post-Fordism is "hailing" a new, post–animal rights consumer to preserve the overall regime of animal capital.

Responding to social movements promoting socially responsible consumption, for example, the Whole Foods directorate has found a way to encourage renewed consumption of other animals through the rhetoric of "green" capitalism and "humane" farming—that is, through commercially driven campaigns whose function if not purpose is to do an end run around animal rights. Instead of challenging a global political economy based on killing, popular writers like Michael Pollan and Barbara Kingsolver (sadly, a leftist) have advocated "locavore" consumption as the solution to the world environmental crisis. Such critics advocate the exploitation and home-grown killing of captive chickens, goats, and other animals, portraying such practices as ethically and ecologically ideal. But as Vasile Stănescu shows in his contribution to our volume, "'Green' Eggs and Ham? The Myth of Sustainable Meat and the Danger of the Local," the new liberal defense of "personal" and local killing is rooted in unsupportable ecological arguments and resonates in disturbing ways with the "romanticized *autochthonous* relationship with both the soil and the local" once seen in National Socialism. Locavorism not only papers over the violence and exploitation that attends backyard animal butchery; it also seems to have an affinity for misogynistic and potentially racist discourses. Far from being a liberatory movement, then, locavorism is entirely consistent with a post-Fordist, neoliberal order that favors localism over internationalism, batch production, "resistance" through consumption, and nativist sentiments that can be mobilized by the political right.

Under Fordism, technological innovation played a pivotal role, enabling new scales of efficiency and engendering new cultural media as means for shaping mass consumer behavior and desire. Technology plays a similarly pivotal role in post-Fordist capitalist relations and structures, with animals again a core component of the new order. Thus, the information revolution has made possible whole new scales of efficiency in animal exploitation, enabling a single farmer, say, to control the biological rhythms and behavior of tens of thousands of egg-laying hens at once using wholly automated means. Computers are used not only to control the environments of factory-farmed animals, but also to track markets and investment strategies and to design ever more efficient means for rendering animals into capital. If the exploitation of other animals is the original or most primitive form of value accumulation in human culture, we must never forget that it is also the most protean and hypermodern, a source of endless technical adaptation and variation. In 2010, for example, Hewlett Packard, the world's largest computer manufacturer, released a report making the case for turning fecal waste from concentration camps for hogs into fuel to power high-technology companies like Google and Microsoft—an effort to make even the biological waste of this ghastly *perpetuum mobile* of mass suffering productive for capital.

But such Rube Goldberg schemes aside, animals are proving central to the new regime of accumulation in more profound ways. Specifically, if in the

Fordist era animals played an exemplary role as depersonalized, factory-produced mass commodities, in the post-Fordist era they *become* the factories, generative sites for the batch production of living human organs or designer drugs (secreted by the glands of genetically modified animals). Just as capital has penetrated to the deepest recesses of the human psyche, molding sexuality, identity, and consciousness itself, so too has capitalist technoscience penetrated to the very core of animal being, manipulating goats, sheep, chickens, dogs, cats, and others at the level of ontology. Different modes of existence, of being-in-the-world, can now be "Taylored" to the needs of Big Pharma and the biomedical industry. Today's factory-pharmed chicken, its genetic sequence plotted out virtually on a computer, is merely the ontologized form of finance capital. As Karen Davis observes in her chapter on the Procrustes myth, broiler hens bred for maximum efficiency experience their own "industrialized" bodies as "a wracking construction of pains and pathologies, including cardiovascular disease, crippled skeletons, and necroses of the skin, leg joints, and intestines." The doom of factory-farmed animals, she writes, is not to be faced with extinction but on the contrary "to be proliferated in virtually endless . . . re-formations of their bodies to fit the procrustean beds of global industrial agriculture and research."

What drives these and other colonizations and distortions of the nonhuman person is not an ancient *idea*—speciesism "as such"—but rather the most advanced forms of finance capital. Hedge funds now trade in global pork belly futures and the cattle business. A watershed was reached with the creation of the Goldman Sachs Commodity Index in 1991, which reduced the leading agricultural commodities, including cocoa, wheat, and live cattle to a single abstract mathematical formula (other banks quickly followed suit, creating new commodity indices of their own).[75] The consequence was in essence to liberate agricultural products—including living animals—from consumer supply and demand, transforming them into an aggregate financial instrument. What drives increased cattle production today in Latin America (as elsewhere) are international monetary and banking institutions, backed by the ruthless power of the neoliberal state.[76] As Carl Boggs writes in his analysis here of "Corporate Power, Ecological Crisis, and Animal Rights," the destruction and destabilization of the global ecosystem is the logical outcome of a total civilizational modality rooted in contempt for other beings and powerful commercial interests. Capitalism's "relentless assault on nonhuman nature" and in particular on other sentient beings in particular is spelling the destruction of our living world, or at least great portions of it. Already, the world capitalist system has so poisoned and destabilized the global ecosystem, through toxic waste, habitat destruction, killing sports, the slaughter industries, and climate change, that thousands of sentient species have been forced to the brink of extinction. One in every four mammalian species is at risk of disappearing forever in the next few decades; the outlook for reptiles, amphibians, and many species of fish is no better. Animal liberation and capitalism are in sum not merely in tension with one another, they are mutually incompatible modes of civilizational development.

Finally, we might take especial note of the changing nature of the nation-state under post-Fordism and the importance of animals to the transition. As Boggs shows, it is the coercive power of the U.S. state—an imperial power harnessed by elites in the interests of expanding corporate power on a global, not merely national or regional scale—that virtually ensures that perpetual war is waged against the other beings of the planet. The capitalist state as such directly supports recreational killing of animals through its fish and wildlife "management" agencies, sets fraudulent "ethical" standards for the treatment of lab animals, pours billions of dollars into animal-based research, and of course provides huge public subsidies for the dairy and meat industries. Meanwhile, because animal exploitation is both a leading source of value under capitalist relations and a source of national power (both symbolically and economically), the state has set out to defend animal capital by repressing the social movements that threaten it.[77] In 2006, thus, the U.S. government approved the draconian Animal Enterprise Terrorism Act, a bill intended not merely to discourage the more militant, direct action wing of the movement—some of whose members have in fact engaged in property destruction, firebombings, or the intimidation of medical researchers—but to put the animal rights movement as a whole on notice that the state is willing to use its vast coercive powers to protect animal industries, which elites view as a linchpin of the economic order. The "return" of an authoritarian, post-liberal state—one of the characteristic features of the post-Fordist order—is therefore directly bound up with the animal question.

BEYOND LIBERALISM—TOWARD A RADICAL CRITIQUE

Having unpacked the relationship between capital and speciesism in some detail, we can now double back to consider the liberal position of animal rights theorists, articulated by Garner and implicit to most other analytic philosophical treatments of the subject, that neither socialism nor feminism have much to offer from an animal liberationist perspective. And here, we might turn the liberal objection on its head by asking whether liberalism itself—that is, liberal theory and liberal institutions (including, by definition, capitalism and the capitalist state)—offers a sturdy enough theoretical platform from which to mount a sustained challenge to speciesism.

Since first publication of Peter Singer's *Animal Liberation* in 1975, animal rights discourse has in fact been dominated by liberal, analytic moral philosophers—particularly Singer, Tom Regan, and (with rather less fanfare and self-promotion) the British ethicist Mary Midgley. These and a handful of other first-rate philosophers, including legal scholars like Gary Francione, David DeGrazia, and Steve Wise, deserve the lion's share of credit for the relative intellectual respectability of animal rights today. Though it is true that the animal rights movement as such preceded such writers by more than a century—Singer's *Animal Liberation* owed many of its horrific empirical descriptions of animal labs and factory farms to the archives and research of well-established activist groups like Friends of Animals—there is no question that the analytic philosophers armed a generation of activists throughout the world with powerful, well-reasoned arguments against factory farming, vivisection, the fur industry, and other institutions of violence and exploitation. It is therefore unsurprising that the liberal critique of animal exploitation has become over the years *the* critique of animal rights. Still, there are important epistemological and political limits to the liberal, analytical, moral critique of speciesism that need to be foregrounded.[78]

First, we must ask whether liberal moral philosophy can fully illuminate a social and existential problem of the scale and complexity of human species domination. What do we lose when we try to contain the cataclysmic violence we human beings enact on the minds and bodies of the other species within the arid terms of Anglo-American analytic philosophy? It is striking that the keenest and most enduring insights into what the human condition looks like when glimpsed through the lens of absolute evil have historically come to us from novelists, theologians, and Continental philosophers—that is, from the minds and hearts of such broadly-trained intellectuals steeped in the history of ideas and culture as Theodor Adorno, Emmanuel Levinas, Hannah Arendt, Karl Jaspers, Primo Levi, and Zygmunt Bauman, to name a few. Writing in the shadow of the concentration camps and the mushroom clouds over Japan, such critics achieved a depth of historical and spiritual insight into evil that one searches for in vain among the writings of even the most acclaimed analytic philosophers and ethicists of the same period, including W. V. Quine, A. J. Ayers, Stephen Toulmin, Kurt Baier, or R. M. Hare. The former set of critics framed the problem of evil in the broadest possible socio-political, historical, and existential terms. They depicted European genocide and nuclear holocaust not simply as an analytical problem or a failure of *ideas*, but as a profound challenge to the human condition. By extension and analogy, it is fair to ask whether it is possible to make sense of today's animal holocaust without invoking a similarly wide range of historical, sociological, philosophical, and even theological approaches.

A second drawback to framing the problem of human domination, a special problem of moral philosophy, is the vulnerablity of liberal thought in general to the overdeterminations of power. Feminist animal liberation theorists were the first to point out the problem with the moral analytic school's continued reliance on conceptual categories and methods drawn from the same masculinist well of rationality, disinterestedness, and objectivity that constitute speciesism as an ideology and historical practice.[79] Pioneered by Carol Adams and Josephine Donovan in the 1990s, the radical feminist critique introduced a much-needed historical and socio-political dimension to our understanding of speciesism, revealing the crucial roles that power and ideology play in the "othering" of animals and women alike. Patriarchy and speciesism are perhaps the two oldest and most fundamental ideologies of *Herrschaft* (or domination by a master race): the oppression of women by men and the oppression of nonhumans by humans have reinforced one another for centuries,[80] and the oppression of animals and women is justified on the basis of the two groups' presumed similarities to one another. As Catharine MacKinnon observes in a recent essay, both speciesism and patriarchy are based on a "natural" hierarchy, and though "a hierarchy of people over animals is conceded and a social hierarchy of men over women is often denied, the fact that the inequality is imposed by the dominant group tends to be denied in both cases."[81]

It is therefore perplexing and troubling that the leading male animal rights philosophers have by and large ignored, trivialized, or misrepresented the feminist critique of human domination.[82] It is especially striking how few male animal rights philosophers will admit that they actually *care* what happens to other animals, preferring either to write dispassionately about objective animal "interests" or deontological principles (an aversion to sentiment that can be traced to the traditional Western terror of the female body and "feminine" emotions like compassion) or, alternately, to strike an aggressive tone of angry militancy, replete with macho references to activists as "warriors." As Carol Adams notes in her chapter here, "After MacKinnon: Sexual Inequality in the Animal Movement," the absence of a feminist critique within the animal movement has diminished its moral authority and sapped its organizational efficacy.[83] The fact that PETA, for example, the largest animal rights group in the world, features pornography on its website—its "State of the Union Undress" intercuts images of maimed and suffering animals with a very young, thin white woman awkwardly stripping to reveal her shaved vulva—is a testament not merely to the appalling lack of feminist scruples within the movement, but to the power of a misogynist culture to define the discursive terms of even erstwhile "oppositional" social movement culture.[84] But as Adams writes, "[so] long as the movement refuses to acknowledge that it is a part of a dominant culture in which women's inequality still prevails, so long as it resists addressing . . . this inequality, it will unconsciously undermine its own vision for a new kind of society, one based on genuinely universal equality, justice, and caring."

The continuing failure by liberal philosophers and political theorists to see the relevance of feminist concerns, whether in animal liberation studies or in other arenas of critical theory, is in fact symptomatic of a wider tendency in liberal thought as such to abstract social problems from their historical context and thereby to neglect the complex sociology of power and systemic violence. As indicated above, over and over in the philosophical literature one encounters an erudite but overdrawn emphasis on the history of ideas, often at the expense of social history and a more probing inquiry into the nature and origin of human violence. Political economy, social and class position, gender and sexuality, and so forth matter less in the critique than the metaphysical spread of "ideas"[85] and a naïve faith in the redemptive power of philosophical argument alone.[86] Such accounts tend both to minimize the irrationality of speciesism—its rootedness in our minds, bodies, practices, discourses, institutions, identities, and so forth—and to occlude the structural preconditions and institutional underpinnings of speciesism as a set of diverse, overlapping modalities of domination. Certainly one shouldn't understate the power of ideas; but one shouldn't understate the overdetermination of ideas by social power, either. The trouble with the idealist bias in analytic philosophy is that it tends to lead either to voluntarism—for example, putting one's faith in changes in individual "lifestyle"—or to forms of analysis that seem oblivious to the many connections that link speciesism with other systems of power and dominance.

This returns us again to the province of Marx and to the lack of a clear anti-capitalist commitment within the mainstream animal movement. On the one hand, it is true that important animal welfare advances have been made within the framework of liberal capitalism: more legislative progress has been made on the animal question in the last ten years than in the previous two hundred. In 2002, for example, Germany added an animal protection clause to its constitution, and in 2008 the Spanish Parliament passed an unprecedented law granting human rights to other primates. Yet such reforms have so far been largely symbolic, and they have had no discernible impact on the pace or scale of animalcide at a global level. On the contrary, after a period of gradual decline in the number of animals killed in scientific laboratories worldwide during the 1970s to 1990s the total number appears to be increasing. The prospect for abolishing the unspeakable conditions of animals in factory farms, meanwhile, remains abysmal, despite growing public awareness that animal "agriculture" is one of the biggest causes of global climate change. In 2006, the U.S. government projected an 11 percent growth rate for jobs in the animal slaughter and processing industry over the next decade, and between 2003 and 2009 (before the recession of 2008), American dairy exports quadrupled, from $1 billion to $4 billion.[87]

Legislative reforms and lifestyle changes alone are therefore not enough to slow, let alone end, the juggernaut—we must also deal somehow with the underlying social relations that give rise to a total system of domination. So long as those relations remain intact, the future misery of billions of animals is ensured. It is thus no minor theoretical limitation in the published works of the leading liberal moral philosophers that nowhere in their pages does the reader brush up against a full-blown critique of capitalism. As Dennis Soron observes in his chapter, while the animal movement criticizes the treatment of animals *as* commodities, "it has tended to regard commodification less as [an essential] . . . feature of capitalist production than as a matter of morally inappropriate attitudes and behaviors.") But such blindness to the role that class stratification and social power more generally play in the animal–human equation cannot but blunt our analysis and seriously hobble the movement as a whole—to say nothing of the fact that it condemns billions of *human* animals too, to the misery, deprivation, starvation, violence, and war that capitalism produces each and every day.

Left unanswered in the liberal account, in short, is how we are to envision effective challenges to the animal holocaust in the absence of a penetrating critique of, among other things, patriarchy and male violence, the links between racialization and animalization, or the capitalist state as such—that structural bulwark for, and juridical guarantor of, the animal exploitation industry. To develop animal rights campaigns without an eye out for the deeper contradictions and tendencies of capitalist world system puts the movement at risk of merely displacing, rather than eliminating, particular forms of animal slavery. Pharmaceutical and biotechnology companies, for example, are already outsourcing animal experimentation to countries where "scientists are cheap and plentiful and animal rights activists are muffled by an authoritarian state"—in much the same way that the U.S. state under President Bush outsourced torture, and U.S. and European companies now routinely outsource jobs to Third World countries with weak labor and environmental standards.[88] As the CEO of an American pharmaceutical company in San Francisco explained in 2006, China offers "big benefits and a 5-year tax holiday." But the main incentives for relocating the dirty work to China are political. "Animal testing," the CEO told a reporter, "does not have the political issues [in China that] it has in the US or Europe or event India, where there are religious issues as well." The combination of economic and political incentives explains why "big Pharma is looking to move to China in a big way." Already, "in terms of animal supply . . . China is a good place to be, as it is the world's largest supplier of lab monkeys and canines—mostly beagles."[89] (Four years later, in 2010, Charles River Labs of Massachusetts, the world's largest supplier of research animals to the scientific community, in fact acquired WuXi AppTec, a Chinese research lab, in a deal totaling over $1.5 billion.[90])

CONCLUSION

Animal liberationism therefore cannot do without socialism, nor without Marx's critical phenomenology of capital. By the same token, however, if animal rights needs socialism, socialism without animal liberationism is itself false and one-sided.[91] If socialism is a mode of life in which humans live in harmony both with their own authentic natures and with the natural world, then it is unclear how a socialist movement premised on the domination of other animals cannot but contradict itself. Because we are animals ourselves, what "we" do to "them" we also do to ourselves—in two senses. First, in oppressing our kin, we become estranged from ourselves, placing ourselves in perpetual flight from our own embodied, desiring, suffering, and (potentially) rational selves. Second, to affirm a socialism without animal liberation is to affirm a civilization based on continual antagonism with the rest of nature. It is to suggest that an ideal society, a society of *universal* freedom and justice, could be founded upon enslavement, exploitation, and organized mass killing of *other persons*. Such a repugnant notion cannot be maintained, either in practice or in theory, without contradicting itself at its roots. A speciesist socialism thus contradicts itself causally and materially, because speciesism itself serves as one of the crucial ideological props of the capitalist system, a system which, in its anti-ecological iniquities, more and more poses a threat to human civilization itself.[92]

Hence the need to overcome the animal rights movement's liberal *weltanshauung* by bringing these two movements, socialism and animal liberation, into closer alliance, and indeed into coalescence. The chapters in *Critical Theory and Animal Liberation* argue that such a convergence between the two traditions is not only possible, but urgently needed.[93] And not just "two" traditions: many of our authors rightly insist on the need to set the structures of speciesism in the context of a much wider epistemological and social system of patriarchal violence. It is *men* as a class who are the primary efficient cause of the unhappiness of the world, the purveyors of what Erich Fromm (another early member of the Frankfurt School) termed a "necrophilic" civilization.[94] Our writers for this reason collectively speak to the need for a comprehensive, holist conception of praxis, a common language of politics, community, and liberation able to bridge the divide between socialism and feminism, race and class, North and South, human and nonhuman, masculine and feminine. Hence, the especial importance in these pages of Josephine Donovan's chapter—revised and with a new introduction by the author—"Sympathy and Interspecies Care: Toward a Unified Theory of Eco- and Animal Liberation." Donovan identifies four theoretical currents that seem to be converging: ecofeminism, Marxism, phenomenology, and sympathy theory. The latter two traditions in particular point the way toward a new societal order based on compassion for the suffering other, including and especially the most vulnerable class of sufferers, the other animals. Together, all four intersecting traditions "point to a recognition of the subjective reality of animals," for the first time creating "the possibility of a new unified theory of animal (and indeed human, indeed earthly) liberation."

Like the other writers gathered here, Donovan attempts less to spell out a comprehensive new approach than to clear the ground for one, not merely by drawing attention to the ideological and material conditions of speciesism but by noting the aporias, absences, and contradictions in contemporary political and social thought. Like the works of the early Frankfurt School, whose members sought above all to offer an image of *negation* of an existing order whose "positive" features in fact represent the negation or forgetting of the true bases of creaturely happiness, the chapters in *Critical Theory and Animal Liberation* thus offer only a promissory note on the redemption of humankind—the solace of critique in the face of overwhelming violence.

In this connection, it seems appropriate to bring our introduction to a close by recalling an especially poignant passage in Adorno's *Minima Moralia*. Describing his experience during his years of exile from Germany, when "in a mood of helpless sadness" he discovers himself using the incorrect subjunctive of a verb native to the dialect of his German home town, Adorno writes: "Language sent back to me like an echo the humiliation which unhappiness had inflicted on me in forgetting what I am."[95] We might say that the purpose of this volume, in seeking to bring the critical tradition to bear on "the animal question," is to restore the memory of what we were—or, rather, what we might become—before power inflicted unhappiness upon us: free, creative, ethical beings able to live in solidarity and harmony with one another and with other animals within a wider ecological order. Only by affirming such a memory, of a past that never was, might we discover a way of living in the present that does not concede the future to an unending terror.

I

COMMODITY FETISHISM AND STRUCTURAL VIOLENCE

1

Procrustean Solutions to Animal Identity and Welfare Problems

By Karen Davis

There are many ways to describe and allegorize our brutal treatment of other animals. But the one that seems most apt to me is the figure of Procrustes, that symbol from literature of tyranny and cruelly enforced order. In Greek mythology, Procrustes ("the stretcher") is a bandit who keeps an iron bed to which he forces people to conform. Watching his victims approach from his stronghold, Procrustes stretches or shrinks the bed in advance to predetermine their failure to fit into it so that he may torturously reshape them to suit his will. If the victims are too tall, he amputates their excess length; if they are too short, he stretches them to size. Procrustes, I suggest, is a particularly fit symbol of the false anthropomorphism humans use to force nonhuman animals to conform to constructions that are fundamentally alien and inimical to their very being. Because the needs and desires of animals and the wishes and desires of the humans who would exploit them seldom coincide, a Procrustean solution is sought whereby the animal/argument is either cut down to size or stretched to fit the agenda. Animals are physically altered, rhetorically disfigured, and ontologically obliterated to mirror and model the goals of their exploiters. The Procrustean solution thus ultimately resolves in what can only be termed a genocidal assault on nonhuman identity itself.

In "Why Look at Animals?" John Berger presents the environment of the zoo as a paradigm of extinction by incarceration, a form of genocidal anthropomorphism, in which a wild animal, with all of that animal's defining traits and activities, is reduced to a mere object in a fabricated, deadening setting. The space that modern, institutionalized animals inhabit, Berger writes, is artificial: "In some cages the light is equally artificial. In all cases the environment is illusory. Nothing surrounds [the animals] except their own lethargy or hyperactivity. They have nothing to act upon—except, briefly, supplied food and—very occasionally—a supplied mate."[1]

Animals on display are the objects of blind, and blinding, encounters between a human audience and the animals' human-imposed personas. Zoo-goers do not really *see* the animals they are looking at, and the animals being looked at have been "immunized to encounter" since "nothing can any more occupy a *central* place in their attention," Berger writes. Animals who break out of their phony images are punished (further punished, that is, since the condition of spectacular captivity—captivity for the sake of spectacle—is, of itself, the fundamental punishment) by being beaten, starved, isolated, sold, killed, or all of the above.[2] Zoo animals, so-called, are imprisoned in a world that expresses elements in human nature that no normal animals would voluntarily consent to enter or live in. Animals on display are manikins of their true selves in varying conditions of atrophy, apathy, "hysteria," or extinction. Defenders call zoos the "Noah's Ark" of the modern world. Philosopher Dale Jamieson responds that if zoos are "arks" protecting animals from extinction, then these animals are like "passengers on a voyage of the damned, never to find a port that will let them dock or a land in which they can live in peace."[3]

Likewise, animals on factory farms are imprisoned in a world from which their psyches did not emanate and which they accordingly do not understand and do not psychologically resemble. The case of chickens is emblematic. Chickens were the first farmed animals to be permanently confined indoors in large numbers in automated systems based on drugs. This model, which was developed by the U.S. poultry industry in the mid-twentieth century, has been exported abroad to become the leading model for animal agriculture throughout the world. What is crucial to bear in mind is that this model has been achieved by reducing the living animal rhetorically and biologically to machine metaphors derived from industrial technology. As early as 1927, a chicken breeder noted in *National Geographic* magazine that chicken and egg production across the United States was "rapidly assuming factory proportions."[4] In the 1970s, *American Poultry History 1823–1973* discussed the egg industry's manipulation of hens to produce eggs for human consumption in terms of a "continued emphasis genetically on smaller, more efficient but lighter-weight egg machines."[5]

Factory-farmed chickens are not only *in* factories; they are regarded by the chicken industry *as* factories that allow for a continually manipulated adjustment of their bodies to fit the iron conditions of commerce. According to *Commercial Chicken Meat and Egg Production*, the "technology built into buildings and equipment" is "embodied genetically into the chicken itself." Physical characteristics and behavioral attributes deemed "necessary for commercial performance objectives" should enable a "continued adaptation of chickens to the housing systems and management used by commercial producers."[6] As Michael Watts writes in "The Age of the Chicken," "[w]hat is striking about the chicken is the extent to which the 'biological body' has been actually *constructed* physically to meet the needs of the industrial labor process."[7]

From the standpoint of the birds themselves, a more excruciating image emerges. In the case of "broiler" chickens—chickens raised specifically for meat rather than for egg production—the "industrialized" body is a wracking construction of pains and pathologies, including cardiovascular disease, crippled skeletons, and necroses of the skin, leg joints, and intestines. According to John Webster, a professor of animal husbandry at the University of Bristol School of Veterinary Science, most of the painful leg disorders in broiler chickens and turkeys can be attributed to birds being forced to grow "too heavy for their limbs." The birds become so "distorted in shape" as to impose unnatural stresses on their joints, which are full of pain receptors.[8] Up to 50,000 birds per unit sit on their crippled legs in dark, manure-soaked, football-field-long buildings thick with pathogens and poisonous ammonia fumes. Within a few weeks, according to a contract grower for Simmons Foods, the birds "can hardly stand because their legs are so weak, and with no natural light or exercise, their joints are too soft to carry the weight."[9]

In the most encompassing sense, factory-farmed chickens are alienated from surrounding nature, from an external world that answers intelligibly to their inner world. There is nothing for them to do or see or look forward to; they are permitted no voluntary actions and are deprived of any opportunity for joy or zest of living. They just have to *be*, in an excremental, existential void, until we kill them. The deterioration of mental and physical alertness that occurs under these circumstances has been suggested by some animal scientists as a sign of temporary but not permanent suffering. According to this view, as long as an animal survives physically, "its adaptive mechanisms prohibit the occurrence of long-term suffering."[10] F. Wemelsfelder of the Institute of Theoretical Biology in the Netherlands rejects this assumption, noting that the loss of behavioral flexibility on which an animal's adaptive well-being depends "leaves an animal in a helpless state of continuous suffering."[11] Veterinarian Michael W. Fox points out that even if chickens and other factory-farmed animals may sometimes appear to be adapted to the intensive conditions under which they are kept, "on the basis of their functional and structural 'breakdown,' which is expressed in the form of various production diseases, they are clearly not adapted."[12]

In industrialized agriculture, the suffering of animals is obscured by the fiction of exploitation which proposes that the state of virtual inanition and passive "acceptance" of chronic, uncontrollable abuse, which psychologists call learned helplessness, is an aspect of the animal's inherent nature, hence the animal's "choice" or "benefit," which the exploiter merely facilitates into expression. An example of this way of thinking can be seen in what the agribusiness philosopher Paul Thompson refers to ironically as the "blind chicken problem"—ironically, because what he really means to propose is the "blind chicken solution." Thompson, who is a professor of agricultural food and community ethics at Michigan State University, calls breeding blind chickens for egg production "emblematic" of the "ethical conundrum" involved in adjusting the animal to fit the production system, "rather than adjusting the production system" to fit the animal. Since (he claims) blind chickens "don't mind" being crowded together as much as normal chickens do, what most people would consider a horrible thing to do—breeding blind chickens specifically to fit them for captive egg production in battery-cage buildings—really isn't so bad. On the contrary, "[i]f you think that it's the welfare of the individual animal that really matters, how the animals are doing," he says, "then it would be more humane to have these blind chickens."[13]

Thompson argues that animals produced through breeding who lack a given capacity to suffer pain, stress, or a specific pathology have not been "actively deprived" of a capacity they once had. Therefore, he claims, they cannot suffer like the "founder" animals (the original breeding stock) who have not had the capacity bred out of them. Whereas founder animals in inimical circumstances have worse welfare than their debilitated counterparts, genetic strategies that produce animals with debilitations that are specifically (but not "actively") tailored to fit the production environment—birds bred to live blind in battery cages, for instance—should perhaps be used.[14]

This argument presumes, of course, that any behavior of an exploited animal that is deemed to indicate "less stress" in that animal is of interest and value in the agribusiness environment only insofar as it can be shown to contribute to more profitable levels of production—more meat, milk, or eggs being extractable from the animal so used. Thus, for example, researchers at the University of Guelph in Ontario have announced that a particular genetic strain of blind chickens they are experimenting on does in fact lay more eggs in experiments designed to give egg producers "more tools to alter light[ing] techniques for higher performance" in commercially housed hens.[15]

Such findings (or claims of findings) interest researchers not only from a strictly commercial standpoint but from the standpoint that the laying of eggs in normal chickens is dependent on light to stimulate the hormonal activity on which egg formation depends. That is why egg producers burn light bulbs anywhere from 14 to 16 hours a day to simulate the longest days of summer inside the hen houses. By eliminating the need for light to stimulate hens to lay eggs, researchers can claim the feat of overcoming nature as well as saving the egg industry money on electricity. The claim can even be stretched into a stewardship argument, as when animal biotechnologists assure the public that the industry "will work proactively to assure good stewardship to animal care."[16]

Geneticist Bill Muir of Purdue University, who breeds chickens and quails to live passively in battery cages, says that "adapting the bird to the system makes more sense" than the other way around and can even accrue benefits if by "selecting for chickens that could tolerate the social stress, we also get chickens that could tolerate environmental stress," such as increased levels of pollution and microbial activity inside the buildings the birds are housed in.[17] Still another "solution" is the breeding of featherless chickens, a project that is well underway in the United States and elsewhere. According to Professor Avigdor Cahaner of the Hebrew University of Jerusalem's Faculty of Agriculture, who has been breeding featherless chickens for more than a decade, naked chickens are more efficient than chickens with feathers: "No feathers, no waste, less processing costs and less water use during processing. Even more interesting is that these birds do not waste costly nutrients for developing useless feathers."[18] In particular, he says, there is "a clear economic advantage" in growing naked chickens in hot, humid climates. Not only is their so-called performance improved, but the "welfare" of the chickens is improved by the genetic elimination of their feathers, according to Cahaner. He adds that "genetic material from his stock of featherless broilers can be shipped to interested partners at any time."[19]

ANIMAL GENOCIDE

Forcing our psychic pattern on animals who fit the pattern only by being "stretched" or "amputated" to conform is the very essence of the genocidal assault on nonhuman animal identity that, in addition to the direct extermination of millions of animals every day by humans, and expropriation of their land and homes, forms one of the strongest links to the experience of humans similarly treated, as in, for example, the experience of the Jews under the Nazis. By "genocidal assault," I refer to the concept of genocide as it was originally formulated by the Polish jurist Raphael Lemkin in 1944, to refer not only to the deliberate physical annihilation of a group by direct killing, but also to the destruction of the *identity* of the targeted group or groups, as in their "extinction" by incarceration and/or genetic manipulation, an extinction reflected in and reinforced by rhetorical formulations misrepresenting the targeted groups.[20] Recalling the experience of the Jews under the Nazis to illuminate the plight of nonhuman animals subjugated by humans, Roberta Kalechofsky writes of both victimizations that, "[l]ike the Jew," the animal is trapped in the "symbolism of another group. The animal's life and destiny are under the control of the symbolic signs of others."[21]

A concept of genocide in which physical, cultural, and ideological forms of victim annihilation are comprised allows us to consider humanity's relentless, wholesale assault on the individuals, families, communities, and bodies of other animal species as a genocidal project both in its own right and in the context of organized genocidal assaults by human populations on one another. Just as it makes sense to speak of a "genocidal relationship implemented through racism"[22] in the case of America's aggression in Southeast Asia, for example, so it makes sense to speak of genocidal relationships implemented through speciesism in the myriad examples of humankind's conquest of nonhuman animals and their living space.

The destruction and/or relocation and exile of countless animal species and remnant populations of animals, under the assertion of the human "right" to possess and impose our pattern on them and the land they inhabit (or inhabited), corresponds to the European colonial assault on the native human inhabitants of the African and American continents. It parallels the Nazi territorial expansionism known as *Lebensraumpolitik*. The Nazi politics of "must have" living space was an extension of the territorial expansionism boasted by the United States in the nineteenth century as its "manifest destiny" of conquering the Southwest and the Northwest, and islands in the Pacific and Caribbean, following its previous and continuing depredations and exterminations in South and Central America.[23]

The Nazi concept of "living space," as Enzo Traverso writes in *The Origins of Nazi Violence*, "was simply the German version of a commonplace of European culture at the time of imperialism."[24] This commonplace, which "postulated a hierarchy in the right to existence," consisted in "the principle of the West's right to dominate the world, to colonize the planet, and to subjugate or even eliminate 'savage peoples.'" In 1850, the American anthropologist Robert Knox called the extermination of native populations "a law of Anglo-Saxon America."[25] Expanding this theme, French anthropologist Edmond Perrier wrote in 1888: "Just as animals disappear before the advance of man, this privileged being, so too the savage is wiped out before the European."[26]

Clearly, civilization (so-called) has spread by both of these means. As Raphael Lemkin indicated, genocide represents the imposition of the oppressor's pattern of life on the life pattern of an oppressed group. The group is subject to the oppressor's laws, a process that may, but does not invariably, entail the complete and direct annihilation of the subjected group, vestiges and deformations of which may remain for shorter or longer periods despite, or at the behest of, the oppressing agency. Philosopher Jean-Paul Sartre noted, for example, that dependence on the labor of the subject people and the preservation of the colonial economy places restraints on the physical genocide that otherwise tends to proceed where no material advantage is to be gained from restraint. The dependence of the colonizers on the subject people protects them, to a certain extent, from physical genocide, even as "cultural genocide, made necessary by colonialism as an economic system of unequal exchange," continues.[27]

This model of genocide has parallels to the humans-over-nonhuman-animals model of conquest. An example is the maintenance of theme parks and zoo populations of animals otherwise targeted for extinction—gorillas, tigers, trumpeter swans, and many more remnant populations of animals whose approaching mode of existence is in the form of genetic material in storage facilities to be manipulated into resurrection in laboratories. In the case of the billions of chickens, turkeys, ducks, cows, pigs, and other animals who, like their wild counterparts, evolved to lead complex social lives in their own natural habitats and have shown their ability to revert to living independently of humans, that is, to become feral, the genocidal fate is not to be rendered physically extinct, but to be proliferated in virtually endless procrustean re-formations of their bodies to fit the procrustean beds of global industrial agriculture and research.

In considering the fate of chickens, a hideous twist on the myth of the phoenix emerges. The phoenix, it may be recalled, is the mythical Egyptian bird who rises eternally young out of its own self-made funeral pyre and has thus traditionally been regarded as a symbol of the indomitable spirit of life and the inexorable ability to be reborn from the ashes of death. In the light of animal agriculture, the phoenix takes on a sinister aspect. Chickens are unable to die and become extinct under conditions equivalent to their eternal rebirth in a bottomless pit. A further cruel irony consists in the fact that the ancient Egyptians are considered the original inventors of the enormous incubation ovens that became the model for the mammoth incubators that are used for hatching tens of thousands of baby chicks artificially, all at the same time, without a mother hen sitting on the eggs. From a mechanical phoenix-like matrix in Hell, the Egyptians provided the blueprint for producing the very "tidal wave of baby chicks" that flows invisibly across the earth today.[28]

Factory-farmed chickens are imprisoned in total confinement buildings within global systems of confinement and international transport. Baby chicks, turkey poults, and hatching eggs intended for breeding are stowed as cargo on flights from one country to another, adding to the billions of birds being crated in delivery trucks from hatcheries and brought to growout facilities to slaughter plants and elsewhere, up and down main roads and back roads all day every day. As noted by the agribusiness watchdog group GRAIN, which tracks and reports on the global spread of avian influenza and its sources, "[r]are are photos of the booming transnational poultry industry. There are no shots of its factory farms hit by the [bird flu] virus, and no images of its overcrowded trucks transporting live chickens or its feed mills converting 'poultry byproducts' into chicken feed."[29] In the Ukraine alone, nearly 12 million live chickens were imported in 2004. The Hastavuk Company in Turkey, which operates Europe's second largest hatchery, has the capacity "to produce over 100 million hatching eggs per year," many of which are exported to Eastern Europe and the Middle East.[30] Adding to this picture, nearly 25 million pigs were traded internationally in 2005, more than two million pigs per month.[31]

These animals are thus totally separated from the natural world in which they evolved. They are imprisoned in alien, dysfunctional, and disease-prone bodies genetically manipulated for food traits alone, bodies that in many cases have been surgically altered, creating a disfigured appearance—they are debeaked, de-toed, dehorned, ear-cropped, tail-docked, castrated, and (in the case of piglets), dentally mutilated—and always without painkillers. In the procrustean universe of animal agriculture, these brutal amputations can be made to sound sensible and even benignant. A poultry researcher writes, for example: "The emotion-laden word 'mutilation' is sometimes used in describing husbandry practices such as removing a portion of a hen's beak. . . . [However] removal of certain bodily structures, although causing temporary pain to individuals, can be of much benefit to the welfare of the group."[32] To control the debate between animal agribusiness and its adversaries, a poultry industry veterinarian has suggested that the word "debeaking" should undergo a procrustean facelift and instead be called "beak conditioning."[33]

Factory-farmed animals are imprisoned in a belittling concept of who they are. Disfigured and lumped together in a sepia-colored, excremental universe, huddled together awaiting their slaughter in a foreseeable future of featherless bodies and mutilated faces already come to pass, they appear to fit the human-created conception of themselves as mere raw material fit only for processing into human food products and animal byproducts. Nor is their predicament new so much as a further turn of the screw that, with genetic engineering and other refinements of unrestrained scientific violence to animals firmly in place, continues to turn.[34]

ANTHROPOMORPHISM

Ever since Darwin's theory of evolution erupted in the nineteenth century (*The Origins of Species* appeared in 1859), animal exploiters have invoked the word *anthropomorphism*—a term previously reserved to describe the attribution of human characteristics to the deity—to suppress objections to the cruel and inhumane treatment of animals and to enforce the doctrine of an unbridgeable gap between humans and other animals. Exceptions to this doctrine are made when the concept of continuity between species is necessary to justify a particular enterprise, such as the chicken genome project, in which the chicken is said to be "well positioned from an evolutionary standpoint to provide an intermediate perspective between mammals, such as humans, and lower vertebrates, such as fish."[35] The unbridgeable-gap doctrine is set aside any time an exploiter requires the formula that a particular use of animals, as in the case of genetic engineering, "has the potential to remarkably improve, not only animal health and well being, but also human health."[36]

The term *anthropomorphism*, as it is now used, refers almost entirely to the attribution of consciousness, emotions, and other mental states, commonly regarded as exclusively or predominantly human, to nonhuman animals. While there is no longer any scientific doubt regarding the physiological and anatomical continuity between human and nonhuman animals, the notion that evolutionary continuity between humans and nonhumans also extends to the realm of consciousness remains controversial. Until recently, about the only emotional capacity that scientists have been willing to grant unstintingly to animals is fear. Scientists have set up countless "agonistic" experiments to elicit fear and fighting in captive animals, perhaps because there is unacknowledged pleasure in inducing the emotion of fear in others and watching them fight to the death in controlled experiments. In contrast to fear and other stressful emotions, the emotional capacity for pleasure, happiness, and joy in animals is a far more contentious issue. Yet as University of Colorado biologist Marc Bekoff points out, "according to Darwin, there is evolutionary continuity among animals not only in anatomical structures such as hearts, kidneys, and teeth, but also in brains and their associated cognitive and emotional capacities."[37] As Bekoff observes, evidence of joy in animals is already "so extensive that it should hardly need further discussion."[38] Not everyone is willing to agree. University of Oxford zoologist Marian Stamp Dawkins criticized ethologist Jonathan Balcombe's book *Pleasurable Kingdom: Animals and the Nature of Feeling Good* for arguing (with copious illustrations) that animals can experience pleasure and happiness.[39] This idea, she said, threatens to usher an abandonment of "all standards of scientific reasoning," resulting in a chaos in which there will no longer be any distinction "between the anthropomorphism of Bambi and the scientific study of animal behavior."[40]

The irony of experimenting on animals to learn more about humans and cure human ills while (and by) defending an unbridgeable ontological gap between humans and other animals has frequently been noted. Richard Ryder quotes an 1885 commentator on the irony of scientists who "instruct us to cast aside the old theology which makes men different from the beasts of the field, inasmuch as he was created in 'the image of God,' and yet would arbitrarily keep, for their own convenience, the line of division which such a belief marked out between man and animals."[41] But using animals as we wish is based on precisely such ploys. The rhetoric of exploitation cuts and pastes nonhuman animal identity, just as scientists cut and paste the bodies of animals to fit human desires. Sometimes the animal is ennobled if there is something wild and warlike about "him" (the "noble steed," the "majestic wild turkey" who deserves the best gunshot), but usually not. Humans, by virtue of a shared verbal language, can aggressively challenge the profanation of their identity. By contrast, nonhuman animals such as chickens are powerless, short of human intercession, to protect their identity from being defiled, as when a hen is represented by egg producers as an "egg-laying machine," or as a symbolic uterus for the deposition of a human being's spiritual impurities, as in the Hasidic custom of *kaparos* ("atonements") in which chickens are configured as receptacles for practitioners' sins.[42] Likewise, the practice of vivisection—the invasion of a living creature's body with a knife or other instrument of direct physical assault—is based on the anthropomorphic construction of the nonhuman animal as a model for the human condition into whose body human diseases are injected in what is, in essence, a form of interspecies rape by a human of a nonhuman animal victim. As in rape, so in vivisection, the victim is not only treated as a receptacle for the victimizer's defilement; in both cases, the victim is also involuntarily made to appear as an aspect of the victimizer's identity, as when scientists call animals used in vivisection experiments "partners" and "collaborators" in the quest for knowledge. A biotechnology representative told an audience at a symposium on the future of animal agriculture that animals who are being modified and "recombined" every which way, to fit every conceivable purpose and whim, are "serving mankind" as part of an enterprise which "recognizes that animal welfare is of paramount importance and therefore has been and will continue to ensure that animal welfare is unsurpassed."[43]

FALSIFYING THE FATE OF

Throughout history, nonhuman animals have been represented as collaborating at the level of their destiny, if under no other determinable aspect, in their own destruction. Similar to the myths circulated by U.S. slave owners about their human "property" during the nineteenth century, animal victimizers typically insist that their victims don't mind their plight, or that they don't experience it "as you or I would," or that the victims are complicit in their plight, even, on occasion, to the point of gratitude. The victims, in other words, are not really innocent. Thus, for example, at his trial Nazi leader Adolf

Eichmann pleaded, regarding his deportation of tens of thousands of Jews to their deaths, that the Jews desired to emigrate and that "he, Eichmann, was there to help them."[44] This is not exceptional psychology, as students of sexual assault are well aware. Indeed, victimizers are very often likely to represent themselves, and to be upheld by their sympathizers, as the innocent parties in their orchestrations of the suffering and death of others. In *Eichmann in Jerusalem*, Hannah Arendt cites an Egyptian deputy foreign minister who claimed, for instance, that Hitler was "innocent of the slaughter of the Jews; he was a victim of the Zionists, who had compelled him to perpetuate crimes that would eventually enable them to achieve their aim—the creation of the State of Israel."[45] If you want to hurt someone and maintain a clean conscience about it, chances are you will invoke arguments along one or more of these lines: the slave/animal doesn't feel, doesn't know, doesn't care, is complicit, or isn't even *there*. In the latter case the victim is configured as *an illusion*.

This is a commonplace of victimizer psychology: the transformation of the sacrificial victim into a manifestation of something else in disguise, a being or spirit imprisoned in the manifestation that wants to be "let out," a "vermin" or viral infection that requires a bloodletting ceremony of purgation to protect the community, "race," or nation. In such cases, not only is the victim reconfigured to fit the victimizer's agenda, but the victimizer too is different from what he or she appears to be—a murderer, say, as in the portrayal of Hitler as "in reality" the benignly motivated liberator of a spiritual wish within the Jewish people to be free. Think also of U.S. president George W. Bush as the alleged "liberator" of the Iraqi people.

In the case of animals, their fate, for each individual him and her, is to be absorbed into a human-centered hierarchy in which the animals don't count, or even exist, apart from how humans use or have used them. *Our use becomes their ontology*—"this is what they are"—and their teleology—"this is what they were made for." To this day, animals are ritually sacrificed by Hindus whose practice is based on the idea that "the sacrifice of an animal is *not really the killing of an animal*." The animal to be sacrificed is not considered an animal but is instead "a symbol of those powers for which the sacrificial ritual stands."[46] In Hindu mythology, according to Basant K. Lal, "if a soul migrates to an animal form from a human life, it moves from a superior to an inferior form of life, and it does so because of its misdeeds while in the human form."[47] As in traditional Judaism, the Hindu attitude toward animals is not based on considerations about the animal as such but on considerations of how the animal advances the purificatory process leading to human salvation.[48] In Christianity, lambs disappear into the body and symbolism of Jesus Christ whereby they are elevated and redeemed into something that matters. In Buddhism, according to Christopher Chapple, the animal world is one of the lesser destinies, "along with the hell beings and hungry ghosts." Birth as an animal in the Buddhist tradition, although a basis for compassion, including the promotion of vegetarianism and other forms of nonviolence towards animals, is also a punishment for "evil deeds" and "deludedness."[49]

Accordingly, there is a long tradition of thought in which nonhuman animals are represented as not only benefiting from their victimization but as gratefully assisting in their own destruction, which is formulated as their liberation. In Greek mythology, the ox runs from the fields to the city and stands at the altar to be sacrificed, and a bird flies to the altar and delivers itself "into the hands of the high priest."[50] In Hasidic lore, flocks of wild doves come of their own accord to lie down under the slaughterer's knife.[51] It has been argued that the doctrine of metempsychosis—the belief that human souls can become trapped in "lower" life forms as punishment for their misdeeds—rather than promoting vegetarianism, favors the consumption of flesh, since slaughtering an animal releases the human soul imprisoned within.[52] Meat in these accounts does not remind one, as it came to remind former chicken slaughterhouse worker Virgil Butler, of "the sad, tortured face that was attached to it some time in the past," but only of the human sinner or penitent, whose superior identity is defiled by being trapped in an animal's body.[53] In Isaac Bashevis Singer's story "The Slaughterer," the rabbi seeks to convince the main character, Yoineh Meir, who does not want to slaughter animals, but is coerced into doing so, that everyone benefits from the slaughter: "When you slaughter an animal with a pure knife and with piety, you liberate the soul that resides in it. For it is well known that the souls of saints often transmigrate into the bodies of cows, fowl, and fish to do penance for some offence."[54]

Little has changed since earlier times. In today's world, advertisers tell consumers that pigs and cows and even children want to be turned into Oscar Meyer wieners. Rabbits "collaborate" with vivisectors to test cosmetics so that women can look pretty. Chickens want to be made into buffalo wings and Subway sandwiches. Hunters' lore is replete with the idea that prey animals want to be hunted and slain by the superior huntsman. In the rhetoric of exploitation—as opposed to the language of liberation—only by being sacrificed to "higher" forms of life via science, religion, entertainment, or edibility can animals be redeemed from being "just animals." Hence, whatever was or is done to them is said to be profoundly, if obscurely, justified by the wishes of the animals themselves. Nonhuman animals want to be raped, mutilated, imprisoned, and even murdered, if it will make them "higher" and more humanlike, or if they can at least serve the human interest. This is the essence of false anthropomorphism and of the genocidal erasure of the animal's true identity in favor of the abuser's image.

EMPATHIC ANTHROPOMORPHISM

The opposite of this narcissistic enterprise is empathic anthropomorphism, in which a person's vicarious perceptions and emotions are rooted in the realities of evolutionary kinship with other animal species, in a spirit of goodwill toward them. In contrast to the false anthropomorphism fashioned by animal exploiters, anthropomorphism based on empathy and careful observation is a valid approach to understanding other species, and in any case, we can only see the world "through their eyes" by looking through our own. This said, humans are linked to other animals through evolution, and communication between many species is commonplace. Reasonable inferences can be drawn regarding such things as an animal's body language and vocal inflections in situations that produce comparable responses in humans. Chickens, for example, have a voice of unmistakable woe or enthusiasm in situations where these responses make sense. Their body language of "curved toward the earth" (drooping) versus "head up, tail up" is similarly interpretable. As in comparing atrocities conducted by victimizers and experienced by victim groups, behavioral resemblances of nonhuman animals to ours don't require an exact match. One may consider these resemblances in terms of the common wellspring from which all experience flows, or in the form of a musical analogy, as in the theme of sentience and its innumerable manifestations harking back to the matrix of all sentient forms.

Anthropomorphism conceived in these terms makes sense. One may legitimately formulate ideas about animals and their needs that the rhetoric of exploitation seeks to discredit. One may proffer a counter-rhetoric of animal liberation based upon empathy and careful observation. As Jonathan Balcombe writes in *Pleasurable Kingdom*, "We cannot feel the hummingbird's response to a trumpet-flower's nectar, the dog's anticipation of chasing a ball, or the turtle's experience of basking in the sun, but we can imagine those feelings based on our own experiences of similar situations."[55] Consider, for example, this picture of a wild turkey mother leading her brood, including an errant youngster:

> They hurry along as if on a march to some particular point, sometimes tripping along in single file, one behind the other, and at other times scattered through the woods for fifty yards or more. When on these scattered marches it is pleasant to note some straggling youngster as he wanders out of sight of the main flock in an attempt to catch a fickle-winged butterfly, or delays by the wayside scratching amid the remains of a decayed log in search of a rich morsel in the shape of a grubworm. . . . [W]hen he discovers that he is alone . . . [h]e raises himself up, looks with his keen eyes in every direction for the flock, and, failing to discover them, gives the well-known coarse cluck. Then he raises his head high in the air, and listens intently for

> his mother's call. As soon as it is discovered that one is missing the whole flock stops, and the young turkeys raise their heads and await the signal from their mother. When she hears the note of the lost youngster, she gives a few anxious "yelps," which he answers, and then, opening his wings, he gives them a joyous flap or two and with a few sharp, quick "yelps," he goes on a run to join his companions.[56]

Empathic anthropomorphism, as this picture shows, is the opposite of the false anthropomorphism of, for example, the fighting cock, the circus elephant, and the Thanksgiving turkey. In cockfighting, roosters are forced to die in stylized rituals of masculinity having nothing to do with natural bird behavior in an actual chicken flock. So-called circus elephants are taken from their natural habitats and forced to perform human-contrived antics for human entertainment. Thanksgiving turkeys are maledicted as "dirty birds" that become magically clean only by being slaughtered, cooked, and consumed by "superior" humans. These constructions exemplify the kind of anthropomorphism on which animal exploitation depends. It consists of insisting that animals are not suffering, that they are happy and grateful to be exploited, despite a congeries of evidence to the contrary. If animal advocates say, for instance, that a hen in a battery cage or a chicken buried alive in his own flesh is miserable, they're accused of anthropomorphism—of attributing human feelings to chickens. If producers say that the chicken is happy or (as one egg producer rewrote the company language in response to criticism) "content," the claim is accepted as "science." Consider the latitude accorded to agribusiness philosopher Paul Thompson, cited above, whose claim that blind hens "don't mind" being crowded together in cages as much as do chickens who can see is accepted as a "science-based" proposition with a view to improved animal welfare in light of the blind chickens' alleged "reduced susceptibility to stress."[57] If blind chickens, or featherless chickens, or whatever genetically modified animal forms can be shown "quietly" to increase cost efficiency in the industrial environment, the procrustean solution can be represented as a "holistic fit between a farm animal and its environment."[58] That sounds reasonable.

A point to bear in mind in confronting these claims is that, as avian ethologist Lesley Rogers has emphasized, a docile or placid temperament is not synonymous with or a necessary sign of reduced intelligence or sensitivity.[59] Moreover, many factors can be mistaken for diminished cognitive capacity in industrially raised chickens and other factory-farmed animals, from the masking effects of their impoverished environments to the complex infirmities imposed upon them that often include unrelieved pain. As I wrote in my book *More Than a Meal: The Turkey in History, Myth, Ritual, and Reality*, rather than showing that chickens and turkeys are stupid, the fact that they become lethargic in continuously unstimulating commercial environments shows how sensitive these birds are to their surroundings, deprivations, and prospects.[60] Learned helplessness, which may as well be referred to as "learned hopelessness," is a pathologic reaction of living beings to pathogenic living conditions from which they cannot escape. Children warehoused from their infancy in institutions—like those discovered wasting away in Romanian orphanages in the 1990s—and wild animals forced to spend years behind bars, show similar apathy and atrophy of body and spirit.[61]

On the positive side, the ability of domesticated animals to respond alertly and appropriately to sensory and social stimuli, and to negotiate the physical, social, and emotional milieus in which they find themselves, say, at a sanctuary or in an adoptive home, indicates considerable intelligence, awareness, and learning potentials. If Sarah, a former battery-caged hen, climbed the stairs in the morning to get me downstairs to fix her breakfast after yelling from the bottom of the steps failed to produce results, was she not displaying purposeful adaptive intelligence? And what about Katie the "broiler" hen, who pecked at my pant legs to get me to bend down and hug her? Or consider Mila, a quiet-natured turkey rescued from a slaughterhouse who repeatedly calmed down her belligerent companion, Priscilla, and prevented her from attacking people by inserting herself between Pricilla and the intended target?

All of these birds arrived at our sanctuary in a state of pathological apathy and lethargy quite different from the expressive personalities that emerged under the influence of fresh air, soft grass, and attention to their needs, as well as the opportunity afforded them to make some decisions on their own. As Michael W. Fox has observed, freedom and well-being are more than intellectual concepts. They are "a subjective aspect of being, not exclusive to humanity, but inclusive of all life. This is not an anthropomorphic claim. It is logically probable and empirically verifiable."[62]

PROCRUSTEAN SOLUTIONS TO ANIMAL WELFARE PROBLEMS

Thus far we've considered the plight of sentient animals caught in the toils of agribusiness and other institutionalized predicaments in which they and their identities are forcibly reconstructed against their will to fit human purposes. The ethical conundrum posed by this arrangement has been represented in public debates mainly in terms of the fact that these animals can suffer. Animals are feeling beings. They are "subjects of a life," in philosopher Tom Regan's phrase, who are capable of experiencing what is being done to them.[63] The eighteenth-century utilitarian thinker Jeremy Bentham said that the question of how we treat animals is not "can they reason or can they talk, but can they *suffer*?" Adopting this principle, philosopher Peter Singer wrote in his book *Animal Liberation*, published in 1975, that the vital characteristic that gives a being the right to equal consideration of interests, including the right not to be tortured and treated like a thing, is "the capacity for suffering," including the ability for "enjoyment or happiness."[64]

But what if an animal's capacity to suffer and enjoy could be significantly reduced or even eliminated? What if scientists could create animals whose adjustment to abusive environments consisted in their being unable to experience their own existence, animals who were in essence the oblivious entities they are treated as being? This prospect may seem farfetched, but how distant is it? More than a decade ago an engineer predicted, fancifully but seriously, that the future of chicken and egg production would resemble "industrial-scale versions of the heart-lung machines that brain-dead human beings need a court order to get unplugged from."[65]

The creation of insentient, brain-dead animals to fit the procrustean systems of industrialized agriculture is most likely in the works already. Consider the forecast presented by avian ethologist Lesley Rogers in her book *Minds of Their Own: Thinking and Awareness in Animals*. In the industrialized farming of today, Rogers writes, "the identities of individual animals are completely lost." Chickens and other animals are seen only as bodies "to be fattened or to lay eggs." Their higher cognitive abilities are "ignored and definitely unwanted," and thus an ultimate aim of breeding programs is to obtain animals with minds "so blunted" that they will passively accept the worst treatment and living conditions.[66] Meanwhile, Rogers notes, the view of domesticated chickens as already stupid and brainless has more to do with how humans prefer to think about chickens than with the abilities of chickens themselves. There is no evidence, she says, that domestic chickens, or any other farmed animals now in commercial use, have been so cognitively impaired that they need no more stimulation than they receive in industrialized farming. Indeed, she writes that with increased knowledge of the behavior and cognitive abilities of the chicken has come the realization that "the chicken is not an inferior species to be treated merely as a food source."[67] However, the overt signs of sensitivity in chickens will continue to be, as they are now, suppressed by industrial conditions. A writer for the *The Guardian* described his impression of thousands of young chickens being raised for slaughter in a huge facility in the United Kingdom as "a sea of stationary grey objects."[68] The fate of chickens and other farmed animals is not to be treated as fellow creatures with feelings, but as pieces of meat and whatever else the market desires. They may have minds and consciousness, "but they will not be treated as such."[69]

For some critics of factory farming, the genetic engineering of animals to fit them to conditions from which they cannot escape is a welfare solution of sorts. The utilitarian philosopher Peter Singer exemplifies this view. Asked if he would consider it ethical to engineer wingless chickens to give them more space in battery cages, he replied that a wingless chicken would be an improvement "assuming it doesn't have any residual instincts" such as phantom limb pain (which debeaked chickens have been shown to experience). He added that "if you could eliminate various other chicken instincts, like its preference for laying eggs in a nest, that would be an improvement too." Asked if he would consider it ethical to engineer a "brainless bird, grown strictly for its meat," Singer said it would be "an ethical improvement on the present system, because it would eliminate the suffering that these birds are feeling. That's the huge plus to me."[70]

One may contest this viewpoint. For one thing, most people who hope for a genetic solution to the suffering of animals on factory farms (which agribusiness calls concentrated animal feeding operations, or CAFOS) have no idea of what actually goes on in genetic engineering laboratories where countless live animals are routinely being modified and trashed. For example, in 1994 I attended the First International Symposium on the Artificial Insemination of Poultry at the University of Maryland, College Park. In a talk entitled "Beyond Freezing Semen" (available in the published proceedings, which includes photographs of some of the procedures), Robert Etches, a researcher at the University of Guelph in the Department of Animal and Poultry Science, joked that his presentation might just as well be called "The Night of the Living Dead." He was discussing the experimental freezing and thawing of semen obtained from laboratory roosters (extracted by masturbating them) to create chicken chimeras—chickens with genes from other species inserted into their embryos. Of birds hatching with no outward sign of the desired change, he said, "We simply throw them away."[71]

From an ethical standpoint, genetic engineering is not a solution to the suffering of animals on factory farms; rather, it is an extension of the system and mentality that produced and produces such suffering in the first place. Suffering involves more than the sensation of an injury; it includes more than pain. Suffering refers to the sustaining of a harm, wound, or disease, painful or otherwise. Millions of birds and other animals are being tortured in laboratories, forced into mutilated forms of existence, then discarded with no more concern for them or their feelings than if they were paper clips. What, then, is the difference from the standpoint of a purely nominal "concern" for animals between surgical amputation of their body parts and genetic amputation of their body parts? Does anyone wonder how a wingless bird might feel? Are wings just mechanical appendages to the bodies of birds that can be excised or "deleted" at will to enhance the "welfare" of their progeny in the terrible places to which we consign them to satisfy our appetites? Could other aspects of their existence be adversely affected by having their wings removed that would offset any welfare advantage obtained in the tradeoff?

Dr. Eldon Kienholz, a professor of poultry nutrition at Colorado State University, described the experiments that he did on newborn chickens and turkeys in which he literally cut off their wings and tails to see if by doing so he could demonstrate a savings in feed costs, since feed would not be needed to grow wings and tails in birds raised for meat. Later, he wrote that some of these de-winged birds, as he called them, "couldn't get up onto their feet when they fell over." It wasn't pleasant, he wrote, "seeing them spin around on their side trying to get back onto their feet, without their wings."[72] This raises many questions, including whether a bird's wings are mere physical, expendable appendages, or whether they are an integral part not only of the body but of the very *being* of a bird. The neurologist Oliver Sacks discusses the persistence of what he calls "emotional memory" in people suffering from amnesia who have lost the ability to connect and recall the daily events of their lives, but who nevertheless appear to have "deep emotional memories or associations . . . in the limbic system and other regions of the brain where emotional memories are represented."[73] He suggests that these emotional memories, perhaps more than any other kinds of memories we possess, are what make us who we truly are in the most profound, though elusive, sense. The available evidence suggests that the consciousness of other animals, including birds (who more and more are found to resemble mammals cognitively), is also rooted in and shaped by emotional memory. Birds, too, possess limbic systems and other regions of the brain in which instincts and emotions are formed and coordinated, and they have been shown to share with humans a complexly evolved brain that processes information and gives rise to experience in much the same way as the human cerebral cortex.[74] Thus, scientists cite neurological evidence that the amputated stump of a debeaked bird continues to discharge abnormal afferent nerves in fibers running from the stump for many weeks after beak trimming, "similar to what happens in human amputees who suffer from phantom limb pain."[75] A "memory" of the amputated beak part persists in the brain, beak, and facial sensations of the mutilated bird even after healing has occurred. Scientists also cite the persistence of "ancestral memories" in intensively bred, factory-farmed chickens who, though they have never personally experienced so much as the ground under their feet, have "the same drive to scratch away to get their food," given the opportunity, as do their jungle-fowl relatives who spend long hours scratching away at the leaves of the forest floor to reach the tiny seeds of bamboo which they love.[76] Perhaps these deeply structured memory formations, retentions, and ineffable networks of knowledge in the body and brain of the factory-farmed bird give rise to "phantom limbic memories" in the individual—to subjective, embodied experiences in which even dismembered or mutilated body parts nonetheless awaken in the individual a distant memory of who and what he or she really *is*, ontologically.

We must assume, in other words, that other animals too have dimensions of interiority and proprioceptive awareness all their own, and that as a consequence of the surgical and genetic mutilation they experience, the grievous wounds they suffer are as much existential and psychic as they are physical. Wingless, featherless, blind, and brain-damaged, entrapped in the hell of humanity, do they recall their wholeness in the phantom limbic soul of themselves? And if they do, are such memories of their essential identity, eluding the procrustean blades of annihilation, experienced as a compensation or a curse? When hens in a battery cage fall asleep, perchance to dream, how do they feel when they wake up? We have become accustomed, through the environmental movement, to think of species extinction as the worst fate that can befall a sentient organism. But the chicken's doom is not to become extinct.

2

Road Kill

Commodity Fetishism and Structural Violence

By Dennis Soron

In early 2005, the New Jersey Society for the Prevention of Cruelty to Animals began a campaign to pressure Kraft Foods to remove its Trolli Road Kill Gummi Candy from the market. Activists argued that the candy, designed in the shape of cartoonishly mortified chickens, squirrels, and snakes imprinted with tire-treads on their backs, sent a disturbing message to children, encouraging them to be cruel towards animals. Responding to a public relations crisis, yet denying any intention to be callous about actual animal suffering, Kraft announced in late February that it would immediately cease production of the candy. Circulating as a quirky filler story through the Internet and the mainstream media in North America, this news was welcomed as a small victory among animal rights advocates and bemoaned among many others as further proof of the tyrannical power of political correctness. As minor as this case may have been, it reveals how opportunities for critically re-examining our collective relationship to animals are often bypassed, resolving into a simple contest between localized expressions of ethical concern and braying accusations of pleasure-killing moralism. Indeed, this incident provides an entry point into a more suggestive discussion than whether a specific product predisposes children to be unkind to animals, or simply represents a harmless form of gross-out humor.

Road kill candy and other similar products certainly demonstrate commercial culture's ability to wring opportunities for profit from the most abject circumstances. They also underline the extent to which, in the advanced capitalist world, the commodity form has come to overwrite habitual ways of seeing and relating to animals, draining their embodied experiences of moral or emotional significance. Although the controversy it generated was unique, Kraft's product is merely part of a broader market trend now transmuting the spectacle of dead animals on the road into saleable commodities. The California company Stuffe & Nonsense, for instance, produces Rikki-Tikki Roadkill, a tire-flattened version of Kipling's fabled mongoose, and also takes special orders for other species of road kill toys. Alongside its cloyingly cute stuffed bears, another American company, HankieBears, sells RoadKill Kitties, featuring bendable wire tails, missing eyes, and carefully stitched-in "road damage," and has recently expanded this line to include puppies. In a strange expression of global compassion, Cuddly Collectibles donates part of the profits from online sale of Meany Splat the Road Kill Kat to disaster relief efforts of the Red Cross and Habitat for Humanity. Other plush products of this kind abound on the market, including splayed animals that can be fastened to car or truck grilles, hats and slippers in the shape of squashed skunks and alligators, and even battery-operated dog toys that activate when squeezed, triggering the sound of tires squealing followed by a loud, comical splat. Although animal exploitation is a precondition of many consumer items today, road kill novelties like these represent a second-order form of exploitation in which the animal's expired body is offered up for consumption not simply as food or clothing, but as an image of its own ritualized abasement.

By transforming the animal's desecrated body into a spectacle and offering it up as a consumable thing abstracted from the violent encounter that caused its death, such commodities both bear witness to and dissolve responsibility for one of the most apparent consequences of our collective attachment to another commodity: the automobile. For most people in automobile-dependent regions of the world, the sight of animals laying dead on roadways—sometimes calm and intact, as if sleeping, sometimes gruesomely stretched out and pulverized into an unrecognizable mass by ongoing traffic—has become so routine as to seem like an inescapable fact of life. Notwithstanding the alluring imagery of advertisements portraying the car as a magical means of escaping from workaday drudgery and communing with wild animals in natural settings, automobile-oriented land use has become a primary threat to the integrity of ecosystems and animal habitat, with the car itself emerging as an apex predator in the landscapes reconfigured for its purposes. Although vast in its scale and implications, road kill is still a largely overlooked problem that has not been seriously taken up by major animal rights, environmental, or anti-car organizations. In the absence of any coherent moral or political discourse addressing the problem, commodity culture itself has effectively been delegated the task of reckoning with the meaning of the carnage on the streets, unmourned collateral damage of the automobile and the type of economic and technological progress it powerfully symbolizes.

Addressing this gap in the argument that follows, I will employ a flexible version of the notion of commodity fetishism to examine road kill both as the flashpoint for cultural anxieties lurking under the shiny surfaces of consumer capitalism, and as a structural problem arising from the spread of automobile-oriented transportation systems over the past century. While this concept has undergone many complex reformulations since Marx outlined it in the third volume of *Capital*,[1] my use of it will remain quite ecumenical, focusing on its ability to illuminate how road kill becomes visible in commodity culture and is constructed as an accident delinked from the system that produces it. In the broadest sense, commodity fetishism pertains to the processes through which capitalist commodity exchange detaches the value and meaning of objects from their social and material origins. Far from reflecting an a priori distinction between appearance and essence, Rosemary Hennessy argues, the concept underscores the commodity form's unique ability to effect a distinction "between what is visible and what is seeable"[2] at the level of everyday social life. As self-encapsulated objects imbued with economic and cultural values that seem to spring from their own being, commodities are the visible markers of historically organized social relations and productive processes that are ultimately seeable but not immediately apparent. In the classic Marxist formulation, a commodity is fetishized when it appears to us as an autonomous entity divorced from its origins in exploitative relations of production between capital and labor. In an expanded sense, fetishism also encompasses the colonial domination, environmental destruction, gender oppression, animal suffering, and other forms of exploitation that commodified social reality simultaneously incorporates and disavows.

The effects of commodity fetishism do not simply bear on the production of material goods, but on the production and reproduction of collective life more generally. As the expansionary logic of capitalism saturates social life with commodities, things—cars being a prime example—increasingly mediate our relationship to other people, the nonhuman world, and even our own bodies, identities, and capacities. Rationalized and abstracted from the complex network of relationships that make them possible, social structures and processes acquire a thing-like objectivity. Thus, Terry Eagleton writes, "the fact that social life is dominated by inanimate entities lends it a spurious air of naturalness and inevitability: society is no longer perceptible as a human construct, and therefore as humanly alterable."[3] This form of fetishism, however, is not simply a mystified understanding of the power of commodities, but an expression of the coercive power of capitalist market regulation. In a competitive, profit-driven economic system in which production and consumption are coordinated through the mechanisms of commodity exchange, the impersonal push and pull of market forces can have real and often tragic effects—either in the form of sudden crises or of cumulative social and ecological problems that the market's commodity logic cannot resolve. In the latter case, automobile transportation offers an excellent example of how the accelerated production and consumption of a single commodity, and the creation of a huge social and material infrastructure to support its use, gives rise to a "second nature" that acts back on humans and other animals alike with increasing hostility and violence.

VISIBLE, BUT NOT SEEN: MAKING SENSE OF "ROAD FAUNA"

As Hennessy suggests, the idea of commodity fetishism draws our attention to the socially constructed boundary between the visible and the seeable, calling upon us to theoretically and historically excavate the network of relationships and processes that has produced a particular object, but that is not immediately perceptible in its self-contained thinghood. Attempting to enhance the seeability of animal suffering amidst an ocean of decontextualized consumer goods, activists have often circulated disturbing images of abattoirs, vivisection facilities, fur farms, and so on, in order to conscientize people about ugly realities that are often obscured or denied in today's society. Contradicting the assumptions underlying this strategy, the stark visibility of broken animal bodies on roadways has generated mostly fatalism and disengagement, becoming as naturalized a part of contemporary landscapes as roads and automobile traffic themselves.

Since James R. Simmons published his pioneering book *Feathers and Fur on the Turnpike* (1938), the extent of the problem of "road fauna" has gradually become clearer, thanks largely to the independent efforts of various scientists, educators, and wildlife and humane societies.[4] As road ecologists Richard T. T. Forman and Lauren E. Alexander argue, the proliferation of roads and vehicles in North America over the past several decades has made this problem so acute that, setting aside the meat industry, automobile collisions now surpass hunting as the leading human cause of vertebrate mortality, accounting for over a million deaths per day in the United States alone.[5] Roger M. Knutson, founder of the International Simmons Society, estimates that the average density of "flattened fauna" on American highways now ranges between .429 and 4.10 bodies per mile, meaning that, depending on local conditions, a single trip of 1,000 miles could be the occasion for seeing 400 to 4,000 dead animals.[6] As shocking as these numbers are, they probably significantly undershoot the mark, since they do not account for the many wounded animals that stumble off the road to die out of sight.

This problem is significant not only for its physical impact upon the animals involved in accidents and its role in driving vulnerable species to the brink of extinction, but also for its growing influence over how people in automobile-oriented environments apprehend animals in their everyday lives. As cars and other forms of technology have increasingly come to shape contemporary experiences of the nonhuman world, road kill has become, alongside media images and branded consumer products, one of the dominant ways people encounter many species of animals. For every live creature a motorist in the United States today views along the roadside, as Knutson estimates in *Flattened Fauna: A Field Guide to Common Animals of the Roads, Streets, and Highways*, he or she is "likely to see anywhere from five to twenty-five animals plastered to the pavement."[7] Recognizing that many people today are likely to come across wildlife only after it has been rendered unrecognizable on the highway, Knutson's "field guide" provides a taxonomic scheme for identifying pulverized animals, even offering ironic tips for differentiating between mufflers and armadillos, and between hubcaps and turtles. In a literal sense, road collisions transform living creatures into inert objects of public display. The very banality of this everyday violence reinforces the tendency in commodity culture to regard animal bodies as things whose routine destruction inspires morbid curiosity, but never empathy or concern.

In spite of the palpable visibility of road kill, mainstream animal advocacy groups have failed to accord it any significant degree of critical attention. This failure is illustrated clearly in the case of People for the Ethical Treatment of Animals (PETA). Although PETA activists were involved in the Trolli Road Kill Gummi Candy protest, the organization itself has in recent years led a campaign that demonstrates no more sensitivity to the issue than that shown by Kraft. "Roadkill: Meat without the Murder" pitches PETA's message in an ingratiating manner to "die-hard meat lovers" who are tired of "guilt trips" from moralistic activists, urging them "to help save animals by scouring the streets and turning vehicular victims into vittles." Millions of animals are killed on highways every year, the campaign website argues, and this "natural, organic, and pesticide free" meat goes to waste while many other animals are raised for human consumption on brutal factory farms. To this extent, eating animals killed in accidents is a way to indulge in one's taste for flesh without supporting the atrocities of contemporary animal agriculture. Although laden with irony and calculated to tease meat eaters in some ways, this campaign falls in line with arguments made elsewhere by PETA president Ingrid Newkirk and with her embrace of other "victimless meats" such as laboratory-grown flesh.[8]

Leaving aside for now the environmental and utilitarian arguments for eating road kill, one of the interesting features of this campaign is the way it excludes certain forms of human-caused animal suffering from the ambit of compassion and ethical consideration:

> At PETA, we realize that squirrels are squished by Subarus and 'possums get plowed over by Pathfinders. We don't like it, but it happens. At least, with these animals, there's a good chance that Thumper was scampering about, happy and free, until that final moment when the Rabbit came around the corner. Odds are, he never knew what hit him.
>
> Such is not the case for all the cows, pigs, chickens, fish, and other commonly farmed animals who are unlucky enough to be born wearing the label "USDA meat." They have personalities and are quite capable of forming communities and relationships if given the chance. Instead, factory farms deny animals everything that is natural or enjoyable to them, condemning them to frustrating lives in filthy, cramped cages, stalls, and sheds, where only a steady diet of pharmaceuticals keeps them alive through the miserable and unnatural conditions.[9]

PETA's concern for factory-farmed animals contrasts sharply with its breezy dismissal of the fate of hundreds of millions of other creatures maimed and killed in collisions. The tone here is one of snickering bemusement, echoed in the playful alliteration, the reference to cartoon figures, and the jocular pairing and conflation of animals and automobile brand names. This calculated sense of ironic detachment is reinforced by the website's graphics, which feature an artfully blood-spattered car hood, photos of wounded animals over provocative captions ("It looks just like hamburger!"), and a masthead photo of a disfigured creature painted over by a yellow roadway line. PETA's critique of factory farms in this case hinges upon turning road kill itself into a fetishized object—one that can be pleasurably consumed, both physically and symbolically, without regard for animal suffering or the social processes that produced it.

Although extreme, PETA's campaign highlights the inability of contemporary animal advocacy groups to develop a coherent response to the problem of road kill. As Barbara Noske has argued, the largely urban-based animal movement's failure to address automobile hegemony is symptomatic of its tendency to frame animal oppression as a discrete moral issue disconnected from the wider social and ecological context in which it occurs.[10] With its outlook and practice heavily influenced historically by the moral philosophy of figures such as Peter Singer, David Nibert asserts, this movement has tended to eschew structural and institutional critique, typically regarding "individual attitudes and moral deficiencies as underlying the problem of animal oppression."[11] However institutionally embedded they may be, acts such as debeaking caged chickens or torturing lab animals are easily regarded as deliberate behaviors amenable to moral judgment. In contrast, animal deaths related to car use are more readily seen as random, unintentional, and hence beyond moral scrutiny. Indeed, apart from the occasional sadist, the majority of drivers seek to avoid animal collisions—whether to avoid harming another creature, or to simply protect themselves and their vehicles. Locating responsibility for road kill requires us to look beyond the plane of individual values and intentions, to consider how it, like automobility itself, is enmeshed with broader imperatives driving production, consumption, and government policy under late capitalism.

Ironically, the issue of road kill is most likely to be marginalized in critiques of animal oppression that explicitly target capitalist institutions and practices. As PETA's campaign shows, free-roaming animals killed in accidents are often seen as mercifully outside the capitalist commodity economy, in contrast to animals directly confined and exploited for profit by various industries. The animal movement has advanced powerful arguments against the treatment of other creatures as commodities, but it has tended to regard commodification less as a basic drive of capitalist production than as a matter of morally inappropriate attitudes and behaviors. Acceptance of the commodity status of animals, Gary Francione argues, underpins our "moral schizophrenia" toward them, leading us to hypocritically "love some animals, treat them as members of our family, and never once doubt their sentience, emotional capacity, self-awareness, or personhood, while at the same time we stick dinner forks into other animals."[12] Along similar lines, Craig Brestrup, in *Disposable Animals*, analyses how companion animals are treated as commodities by feckless "owners" who abandon them to premature death in shelters, often for the most trivial reasons. As he believes, the commodification of animals is a "moral failure" based on nonrelational, egocentric values that individuals can choose to either "affirm or reject."[13] While Brestrup offers a cogent psychological analysis of the devaluation of animals in commodity culture, he fails to consider that, as Noske notes, a large proportion of animals in shelters have not been willfully abandoned, but are displaced victims of automobile collisions.[14] The fate of these animals, and countless others killed on roads far from shelters, is not the consequence of individual moral failure, but the impersonal outcome of social and material structures that shape our collective patterns of habitation and mobility, as well as our relationships to the nonhuman world.

The concept of commodity fetishism enables us to retain a sense of moral opposition to the commodification of animals, while considering how this process is impersonally mediated through market exchange and tied in directly with capitalism's amoral imperatives of profit, accumulation, and expansion. Alongside the automobile industry, industries involved in the exploitation of animals are a central component of advanced capitalist economies today. Emergent segments of these economies, such as those associated with genetic engineering, involve an unprecedented manipulation and even patenting of animal life. As strict vegans well know, the bodies of animals are directly and indirectly incorporated into a vast array of consumer products, ranging from foodstuffs to clothing, cosmetics, pharmaceuticals, housewares, and even car products such as antifreeze, brake fluid, and tires. As Carol J. Adams asserts, the animal's living body is an "absent referent" in consumer society, continually fragmented and consumed as an object without history.[15] The meat at the supermarket, for instance, has been both physically transformed into a commodity dissociated from the living animal, and conceptually transformed into de-animalized categories such as "beef" or "pork." By this means, Bettina Heinz and Ronald Lee argue, "commodity fetishism in marketplace exchange removes the production process from the meaning of meat and, thereby, silences the slaughter of animals."[16] This severing of production and consumption, they suggest, has been amplified by global trade and the influence of marketing, enabling industry to continually intensify animal exploitation with little public opposition. In this regard, fetishism both constricts the meaning of meat by bracketing off the context of its production, and dramatically expands it by enabling marketing and other cultural practices to infuse the commodity with new values and connotations.

In one sense, the very visibility of road kill is a transgression of the fetishism that effaces animal suffering from commodity culture, signaling a return of the absent referent to the surface of public life. Unlike the unspeakable things that happen to animals behind laboratory doors and in factory farms, which leave little trace on the commodities on store shelves, road kill offers a highly conspicuous display of death and dismemberment. As I've suggested, the banality of road kill seems to undermine the hopes that some have placed upon the act of making animal victimization publicly visible. Jonathan Burt, for instance, drawing a strong link between visibility and the growth of moral awareness, has established a connection between the expansion of animal representation in photography, film, and other media, from the late nineteenth century onward, and the concomitant rise of animal welfare movements.[17] One reason road kill breaks this link is that it comes into view as the impersonal outcome of uncoordinated flows of traffic, rather than as an injustice perpetrated willfully by an identifiable agent. That said, Burt and others have perhaps underestimated the extent to which commodity culture and advanced technology have demoralized the visible, presenting us with an endless flow of depthless images that often produce sated detachment or disorientation rather than empathy and commitment to social change.

As Rosemary Hennessy has argued in relation to contemporary queer politics, "visibility" within commodity culture is by no means uniformly empowering, often leading to the commercial and symbolic exploitation of the subjects on display and to a denial of the materiality of their oppression.[18] In this context, coming to terms with the visibility of road kill requires us to consider how our prior understanding of animals as commodifiable, as subjects who are always latent or potential objects, enables us to emotionally and ethically dissociate from the fragmented form their bodies take through the mediation of human activity. As a human creation, "road kill" is just as de-animalized as "beef" and just as open to cultural meanings that are bracketed off from the embodied experience of the suffering animal. This is one reason that road kill imagery has been so readily adopted as a grittily authentic visual logo for everything from guitar pedals to lottery tickets, sports teams, and record labels. This process of dissociation is exacerbated in a social environment where animals are largely visible *as* commodified images and spectacles detached from their material bodies. As John Berger has argued, the physical marginalization of animals within urban-industrial life has been accompanied by a countervailing explosion of commodified images of them.[19] These stuffed toys, mascots, cartoons, picture books, nature shows, blockbusters, and so on provide us with consoling images of anthropomorphized creatures that express our yearning for connection with animals while turning them into projection screens for our own hopes and fears. Such images are themselves fetishes, abstract and simulated animal bodies invested with socially produced meanings and divorced from the material context of human domination.

Much like popular films such as *Babe*, *Chicken Run*, and *Charlotte's Web*, products like Trolli Road Kill Gummi Candy and Rikki-Tikki Roadkill explicitly acknowledge the fact of animal victimization while offering symbolic strategies for recontaining the anxieties that arise from this acknowledgement. Unlike the films, which show us exemplary creatures whose spirit and ingenuity enable them to escape being commodified like the rest of their kind, such goods simply collapse the boundary between animals and their commodified representations, rendering their plight as magically inconsequential as Wile E. Coyote's falls from cliffs. In the tradition of *Bambi Meets Godzilla*, their transgressive quality doesn't come from a realistic rendering of violent death, but from a gleeful trampling of conventional animal representations. The looming presence of physical violence is indirectly acknowledged in the disparity between road kill animals and their guileless cartoon counterparts, but only by rendering these animals so abject that they seem to invite and enjoy their own victimization. As Mike Michael argues, representations of road-killed animals today are often "cartoonified"—featuring comically protruding tongues, crossed and bulging eyes, buck teeth, expressions of dazed shock, and other stereotypical signs of imbecility. "By virtue of being cartoonified," he writes, "the corporeally traumatized animal can be portrayed as continuing to express surprise and display stupidity. That is to say, cartoonification at once warrants these deaths and serves in their partial denial."[20]

Other less representational road kill commodities also offer ways of expressing, enjoying, and symbolically recontaining anxieties arising from experiences of roadway carnage. Distilling death into a small bottle of clear fluid, for instance, *Liquid Road Kill* is—as its label announces—designed to smell "like the rotting carcass of a small animal that you might pass on the highway. You know the smell . . . it's so bad that you can't get your windows rolled up fast enough and it lingers inside your car for what seems like hours." Referencing a form of death that is abstract rather than particular, this product enables its owner to cap and selectively experience the smell of decaying flesh in an aestheticized manner, and to use it socially in pranks that confuse people with repulsive odors lacking any clear origin. Goods like these recuperate the unassimilated remains of road-killed animals within the commodity form, offering them up for consumption in ways that reaffirm human mastery. Clothing, jewelry, and other road kill accessories made directly from animal bodies illustrate this fusion of utility and symbolic mastery. Down Under Enterprises, for instance, is an Australian company that sells customized leather hats made from the skins of several road-killed animals and trimmed up with rattlesnake rib bones, mink jawbones, and "coon penis bone." This hat is utilitarian yet contemptuous, emphasizing absolute dominance over the dead animals—much like the wine goblets Viking warriors were fabled to have made out of the skulls of their vanquished foes.

This tension between the animal body's pure utility and symbolic value is particularly evident with respect to the status of road kill as food—or "road pizza" as it is colloquially termed. PETA notwithstanding, actual consumption of road flesh has remained marginal in contemporary culture, confined to circles of survivalists, utterly impoverished country dwellers, cryptic celebrities like Viggo Mortensen, and periodic "road kill cook-offs" in the rural United States. In purely symbolic terms, road kill cuisine is a diversified market sector—comprising an array of road kill cookbooks, spices and sauces, gag products such as Roadkill Helper and Campbell's Cream of Roadkill soup labels, and firms such as the Road Kill Cafe, a 1990s New England restaurant that served mock dishes such as "Smear of Deer," "Center Line Bovine," and "Outta Luck Duck." Following the lead of other steak-iron businesses, one California company sells The Original Road Kill Griddle, an embossed griddle that burns the words *road kill* into ordinary burgers and steaks, packaged along with road pylons that transform the cooking area into an accident scene. In this case, road kill literally becomes an abstract "brand" that makes conventional acts of consumption seem subversive. Eating simulated road kill is a source of perverse pleasure not simply because of the lingering threat of physical contamination, but because the public nature of the animal's death has symbolically polluted the meat. By breaking with taboo and enjoying the familiar taste of this "branded" meat, the consumer dissolves any lingering anxieties about messy roadway violence and, indeed, the whole status of animals as food.

"THE COMMODITY THAT IS EATING THE WORLD": AUTOMOBILES, CAPITALISM, AND STRUCTURAL VIOLENCE

The notion of commodity fetishism nicely captures the ambivalent and contradictory nature of capitalist "progress," whose blind drive for accumulation and expansion becomes an end in itself, unhinged from any non-economic measure of value, need, or rationality. The apogee of commodification, as Fredric Jameson has compellingly argued, is quantitative abundance alongside qualitative loss: the unique and distinct "ends and values" of various forms of life and activity are extinguished under the rein of abstract exchange value, which reduces everything "to a means for its own consumption."[21] Thus, in today's world, animal commodities and road kill novelties of every conceivable variety proliferate as biodiversity declines and species extinction rates reach record levels. At the same time, paved-over, placeless landscapes become populated with enchanted, animalized objects—Thunderbirds, Impalas, Vipers, Mustangs, Rams, Eagles, Rabbits—that mimic and memorialize the vital, organic life they destroy.

A recent Canadian television advertisement for the 2008 Ford Escape Hybrid[22] captures the unique combination of nostalgia and denial that the contradictions of automobility often inspire. In it, a family with a young daughter is driving slowly along an unpaved road through a pristine forest echoing with the sounds of birds and crickets, when they come upon a parallel "family" of deer. Because of the quiet hybrid engine, the otherwise skittish deer remain unperturbed as the humans roll to a stop, lowering their automatic windows to gaze in awe at the magnificent animals. After a poignant moment of eye contact between the human daughter and a young deer calf, the light green SUV pulls away, fading slowly into the verdant hues of the surrounding forest. Suddenly, a pine cone dislodges from a branch and falls to the forest floor, causing the deer to scatter in fright. At one level, this commercial is a clear plug for the eco-friendliness of hybrid technology, highlighting not only the quietness of the vehicles, but their ability to exist peacefully within primeval nature. At another level, it simply recapitulates one long-familiar motif in auto ads, whereby vehicles become a native part of the environment, affording us controlled experiences of natural wonderment, and allowing us to commune with wild animals that reflect suppressed parts of ourselves. Effaced from this idyllic picture are all identifiable features of the spaces in which cars most frequently move—the gridlocked traffic, expressways, intersections, overpasses, strip malls, parking lots, ex-urban business parks, fast-food signs, tract housing, roadside garbage, and—more to the point—dead animals. Ironically enough for Ford drivers, not only are deer the large mammal most often killed by auto collisions, but all animals vulnerable to road traffic are likely to be put in greater danger by quiet vehicles that are harder to hear in advance.

In spite of its cultural associations with freedom, progress, and technological mastery, Peter Freund and George Martin assert, the automobile has today become "the commodity that is eating the world"[23]: swelling rapidly in number, continually annexing more social and biophysical space for its purposes, demanding huge supplies of material and economic resources, generating levels of pollution and waste beyond the earth's sink capacity, and leaving a trail of other seemingly intractable social and ecological problems in its wake. The dramatic growth in the global automobile fleet over the past century is one powerful confirmation of Marx's famous dictum that capitalist economic growth presents itself in the first instance as "an immense accumulation of commodities." In the past sixty years, the number of motorized vehicles in the world has expanded almost twelve-fold, growing from roughly 70 million in 1950 to over 826 million in 2006—more than two-thirds of which are in North America, Western Europe, and Japan.[24] One researcher, drawing upon U.S. government statistics, predicts that the number of passenger cars in the world will surpass one billion by the year 2014, and will rise to an astounding four billion if motor vehicle density across the globe were to ever converge with that of the industrial world today.[25]

Although the environmental and health implications of such scenarios are dire, even current rates of automobile use are dangerously unsustainable. Aside from its insatiable demand for fossil fuels—which bespeaks its disproportionate responsibility for problems like smog, global warming, and geopolitical conflict in the Middle East—automobile transportation in the industrial world is also a key cause of toxic air and water pollution; health problems such as cancer, asthma, and lung disease; and the wanton destruction of wetlands, agricultural land, wilderness areas, animal habitat, and urban green space. Most notably, as I've discussed above, the automobile has been a leading agent of violence against diverse forms of animal life—including human life. In the century since Marinetti's famous *Foundation and Manifesto of Futurism* (1909),[26] whose tribute to the cleansing, technologically enhanced violence of modernity begins with a car crash narrative, automobile accidents have claimed over 30 million human deaths globally, escalating to approximately 1.2 million per year in 2005, and are poised to become one of the top three causes of human death in the near future.[27] Beyond fatal collisions, humans—and, presumably, the nonhuman animals who share the earth's air and water with us—are sickened and killed in even greater numbers by automobile-related pollution and toxic releases.[28] While the structural violence of automobile-oriented transportation systems has become increasingly pronounced, Freund and Martin argue, public discussion of its manifestations continues to address the exceptional rather than the normal, focusing largely on accidents, technological shortcomings, faulty regulations, and the irresponsibility of individual drivers.[29]

The overall lack of critical public discourse around the structural effects of automobile transportation suggests that this system has become so deeply integrated into the life of advanced capitalism as to seem like an innate fact of life. Although ubiquitous and ordinary, the car is—to borrow Marx's well-known term—a "social hieroglyph" that quietly encodes within itself key features of an entire mode of production and consumption. Indeed, Mark Dery provocatively asserts, the automobile is a symbolically potent "totem" of postwar capitalism, an "ever-present reminder of the assembly line that made industrial modernity possible, Ur-commodity at the heart of postwar consumer culture, essential ingredient in the rise of suburbia and the dereliction of . . . inner cities."[30] As John Urry argues, the automobile is not simply a material good, but the key node in a system of linkages between dominant economic, political, and cultural process in contemporary capitalism.[31] The production and consumption of automobiles has become an important economic indicator in its own right, and is directly correlated with aggregate consumption of fossil fuels, metals, plastics, rubber, and other materials and with ongoing growth in other sectors, including land development, construction, road maintenance, retailing, fast food, mining, and many other industries. Although the car offers drivers a sense of self-motivated freedom, this freedom is collectively enabled, heavily dependent upon political decisions that shape land-use and transportation options, and upon the vast collective resources devoted to the automobile's social and material infrastructure. Indeed, John Bellamy Foster argues, the coordinated efforts of economic and political elites have made the "auto-industrial complex" the key axis around which accumulation has turned for much of the past century.[32]

To this extent, sustaining high levels of economic growth and profitability has historically hinged largely upon fostering individualized forms of consumption and making the car culturally and physically indispensable for the majority of people in the over-developed world. In the first instance, the multi–billion dollar automobile marketing industry has become a significant agent of commodity fetishism, investing the car with complex connotations of freedom, power, status, and unrepressed animality, and helping to make it "the one commodity of the industrial age that holds out the greatest promise of liberation through the possession of things."[33] That said, intensive automobile use in the contemporary world is not simply a culturally induced habit, but a structurally induced need deriving from the pragmatic pressures of coordinating one's work, domestic, and leisure routines within a social and material environment where alternatives to the car are often impractical or nonexistent. By spurring a progressive fragmentation and dispersal of human settlements and unbundling key sites of everyday activity, Freund and Martin argue, "the very social organization of space that auto-centered transport fosters helps to further auto dependence and to mask any sense of realistic alternatives to automobility."[34] Routinely immersed in the "second nature" of car-dependent environments, the diffuse and incremental effects of automobile transportation, such as road kill, are difficult to immediately grasp as a structured whole, and seem far beyond the power of any individual to personally influence.

One of the most dramatic of the cumulative effects of automobilization has been upon animal habitat. Over the past few generations, automobile-oriented land use within and beyond urban areas has radically transformed the natural landscape, exposing many species of animals to new types of risk and danger to which it has been very difficult to adapt. As Richard T. T. Forman has argued, the modern road system is the "largest human object on earth" and one of the leading weapons in human society's large-scale assault upon biodiversity.[35] According to some conservation biologists, road building and sprawl, along with off-road driving, is now the single biggest threat to habitat loss in the industrial world.[36]

This process has led to an ongoing degradation and fragmentation of animal habitat, confining wild populations into enclosures too small for their needs and forcing animals to attempt road crossings for access to food, water, cover, migration routes, nesting sites, and potential mates. Of course, roads are not simply dead zones that animals are forced to reluctantly cross, but places that often carry a positive attraction for animals seeking to bask in the radiant heat of the pavement, dig into roadside food scraps, or simply to avail themselves of the most efficient and unobstructed route through fragmented terrain. Unsurprisingly, habitat fragmentation and road kill are currently among the main drivers of extinction for threatened species such as woodland caribou of the Pacific Northwest, Florida panthers, cougars, grizzly bears, and various types of lizards, tortoises, and birds. Overriding the mobility needs of other species, automobile-oriented transportation has extended human incursions into previously wild and unsettled areas, intensifying forms of residential and commercial "splatter sprawl" that create aggressively rationalized landscapes in which animals become, at best, nuisances or intruders.

In this light, as Mike Michael has emphasized, road kill is largely a structural byproduct of the continual mapping of automobility onto "animobility."[37] Michael's theoretical outlook, unfortunately, leads him first to unduly idealize and reify these discrete systems of mobility, and then to celebrate their interpenetration—in the form of road kill—as if this were a welcome, subversive example of postmodern hybridity and boundary-crossing. A better formulation is put forth by Barbara Noske, who argues that road kill and other structural effects of automobile transportation are the consequence of human mobility "becoming more and more unanimal-like"[38]—that is, more mechanized, disembodied, sensually attenuated, and abstracted from the complexity of places through which we travel. Encased within a "metal cocoon" that becomes their technologically enhanced prosthetic body,[39] drivers—like television viewers—gain access to a wider range of experiences, but such experiences are transformed by their "screens" into a rapid succession of visual impressions without context or independent value. The inability to respond morally and politically to the problem of road kill is, in this regard, partly related to the phenomenological experience of driving, in which speed and mastery go along with a flattening of experience to its visual dimension and a loss of affective involvement with the sensuous life around us.

In this cultural context, the radical "othering" of road kill—as a commodified spectacle of debased and dominated bodily difference—not only is morally problematic, but prevents us from seeing the fate of animals as a reflection of our own enduring vulnerability and mortality, as a reminder of how the social world we have collectively constructed also violates, objectifies, constrains, and oppresses members of our own species. Breaking through this type of fetishism will require more than isolated wildlife corridors and overpasses and other small gestures toward the development of a more animal-friendly auto infrastructure. Indeed, it will require a wholesale political challenge to automobile dependency, the auto-industrial complex, and—more broadly—the socially, psychically, and environmentally corrosive logic of commodification itself. Asserting this form of collective human agency is, ironically, one important step in developing a more ethical relationship to other animals and a richer appreciation of the pleasures and possibilities our own animal being.

3

Corporate Power, Ecological Crisis, and Animal Rights

By Carl Boggs

The global ecological crisis, deepening with each passing year, threatens the world as never before, an outgrowth of unrestrained corporate power that today colonizes every realm of human life. The crisis intersects with virtually every social problem, from declining public health to chaotic weather patterns, growing poverty, resource depletion, agricultural collapse, even military conflict. It goes to the core of industrialism and modernity, to relentless efforts by privileged interests to commodify and exploit all parts of the natural world, including most natural habitats and species within them. This increasingly devastating attack on nonhuman nature stems from the same corporate order that has brought to the world mounting environmental problems, militarism, resource wars, and global poverty. The power of a neoliberal international system based in the United States and a few other advanced capitalist nations is so great, moreover, that a crisis that earlier might have been contained now veers out of control, with few political mechanisms or counter-forces to resist it. Living habitats are being ravaged at such an alarming rate that the carrying capacity of the earth is now being exceeded, a process of destruction justified by resort to such high-sounding virtues as social progress, material prosperity, and national security. Since transnational corporations, bolstered by immense government and military power, recognize few limits to their quest for wealth and domination, anti-system movements will be forced to adopt increasingly radical politics—progressive socialization of the state and economy, alternative modes of production and consumption, a new paradigm of natural relations. This means nothing short of a qualitative break with longstanding patterns of development if the planet is to be saved from imminent disaster.

If a political shift of this magnitude seems utterly remote and utopian, that is to be expected: genuine alternatives to the global corporate–military tyranny are presently weak and fragmented, and what exists lacks strategic coherence. Some progressive forces retain the capacity to disrupt business-as-usual, others have the power to achieve limited reforms, but none pose any real threat to the power structure. There are no truly anti-system movements of any scope or permanence, including among the multitude of environmental organizations and groups, despite the urgency of the crisis. In the case of animal rights, three decades of popular struggles have shown that even modest gains have been won slowly, with great difficulty, and against imposing obstacles. Of course this problem is scarcely unique to the challenge of transforming natural relations: time-honored goals of disarmament, ending poverty, and conquering disease, for example, are today no closer to realization than they were many decades ago. Still, where struggles to dramatically uplift the world raise such compelling political and moral issues, pessimism or resignation is simply no option insofar as history shows that even limited victories can set in motion more far-reaching dynamics of change. In the existing state of affairs, moreover, an attitude of retreat makes less and less sense insofar as fissures and cracks in a seemingly efficient monolithic system have begun to widen and global capitalism reaps more and more of its own bitter harvest.

In such a universe we can anticipate that the fate of *nonhuman* animals will be many times worse, that other creatures too will be victimized without end by war and ecological assault—not counting those imprisoned and slaughtered each year by the tens of billions for food, sports, biomedical research, and entertainment. The struggle for animal rights—for fundamentally altered relations between humans and nature—intersects in many ways with the modern crisis, and thus also with the imperatives of future social change—a concern that can no longer be so easily dismissed as the rantings of a few isolated misanthropes. Three decades ago Peter Singer called for a new kind of liberation movement, one demanding a radical expansion of human moral horizons—above all, rejection of the horrors people have for centuries visited on other sentient beings, a condition historically viewed as natural and unchangeable.[1] For Tom Regan, the problem revolves around humans choosing to instrumentalize nonhuman beings as simple resources within an exploitative system that must be overturned *in toto*, a system that fails to recognize a crucial moral principle—that all sentient beings have inherent value, each the experiencing subject of life, each a conscious being with defensible interests, including the avoidance of human-inflicted pain, suffering, and death. Regan insists that we go beyond the ethic of "humane treatment" to embrace the goal of *abolitionism*, implicit in a strong rights position taken from the progressive side of liberal theory.[2] Once animal interests are situated within a larger social and ecological context, as they sooner or later must be, the struggle for human and animal equity becomes part of an integrated whole. Accumulated evidence shows that animal exploitation is tightly linked to the ecological crisis in many ways, a connection that unfortunately seems to have escaped most environmentalists and leftists. The findings are clear: the same animal nightmares produced routinely by agribusiness, the meat industry, and fast-food companies also brutalize humans, as employees facing harsh working and living conditions as well as consumers suffering the toxic health effects of a meat-centered diet. The animal-food economy also devours massive resources in the form of water, land, and energy while consuming nearly *half* of all grains and vegetables produced in a world facing imminent and drastic food shortages and generating more pollution and dangerous waste products than any other economic sector. This enormous meat complex is also the locus of increasing disease transmission worldwide, yet another blessing of free-market corporate capitalism.

Today the global corporate system constitutes an ominous threat to both human and nonhuman life, an exploitative, repressive, and unsustainable juggernaut that treats all living beings as resources within a swollen production and marketing regime, as disposable commodities far removed from any moral status. If within this system the oppression of humans and animals is deeply intertwined—a guiding premise of this chapter—it follows that pursuit of global justice entails new efforts to include groups (in this instance animals) previously excluded from the political calculus. At this point the ethical, political, and ecological case for advancing the interests of nonhuman sentient beings, for ending the regimen of institutionalized barbarism, is so overwhelming as to force debate from the realm of scientific evidence (do animals feel pain, etc.) to that of radical strategy. The main challenge ahead, therefore, is to reconstruct social and political theory to take fully into account the epochal struggle to transform natural relations within a broader, anti-system agenda of challenging the modern crisis. Aside from its marginal leverage within the radical-ecology movement, however, animal rights discourse has scarcely entered into or altered the work of Left/progressive groups in the United States. Paradoxically, theoretical contributions to our understanding of natural relations have appeared mostly *outside* the ambience of Left politics, from writers and activists with at best peripheral involvement in labor, socialist, anarchist, and left-liberal groups. Sadly, the result is that the project of animal rights remains alien to the major social-change enterprises of the current period.

INSTITUTIONALIZED BARBARISM

Efforts to overturn the system of animal exploitation will have to begin the difficult process of ideological delegitimation, that is, subversion of those hegemonic beliefs and attitudes that maintain speciesism in its multiple forms. Unfortunately, despite new theoretical inroads, the brutal treatment of other species remains outside what is considered respectable public debate, understandable given the corporate largesse involved, the huge propaganda apparatus employed by the food, gun, and biomedical interests, and the undiminished power of ingrained cultural traditions. The meat phenomenon alone amounts to something of a national secular religion, helping to shape perceptions of gender and class, national identity, and even race relations.[3] Influential philosophical, religious, and political traditions serve to justify and even celebrate the use of animals for every imaginable purpose, endowing human preferences with a veneer of moral righteousness and social progress: the major God-based theologies, exalted philosophers (Aristotle, Aquinas, Descartes, and Kant), Enlightenment rationality with its fetishism of technological and industrial growth. These traditions carry forward and help solidify the very imperatives of domination and speciesism that block any political solution to the modern crisis.

Radical voices of dissent, fortunately, can nowadays be heard with increasing frequency, many offering at least passing glimpses into an alternative, ecologically viable future, with natural relations in particular developing into a crucial zone of ethical contestation. Regan, the pioneering rights theorist, probably best articulates the thesis that no sentient being ought to be "viewed or treated as a mere receptacle or as one who has value merely relative to the interest of others."[4] Robbins, author of the seminal *Diet for a New America* and *The Food Revolution*, has done more than any other writer to ask humans to reflect on the torture that food animals are forced to endure. In a typical passage he states: "As I've learned what is done to farm animals in modern meat production, there have been times that I've not known how to live with the pain I felt. It can be overwhelming to think of each of these billions of creatures as individual beings with personalities and feelings, yet forced to endure such deprivation."[5] Gary Francione, in his comprehensive *Introduction to Animal Rights*, critically interrogates the ideology that says "animals are commodities that we own and . . . have no value other than that which we as property owners choose to give them."[6] Writing in *Beyond Beef*, a book deserving far more attention than it has received, Jeremy Rifkin argues: "The modern cattle complex represents a new kind of malevolent force in the world. In a civilization that still measures evil in very personal terms, institutional evil born of rational detachment and pursued with cold calculating methods of technological expropriation has yet to be assigned an appropriate rung on the moral ladder."[7] Jeffrey Masson, widely known for his excellent work on the varied and intricate subjective capacities that animals possess, writes in *When Elephants Weep* about "innocent sufferers in a hell of our own making" whose "freedom from exploitation and abuse by humankind should be the inalienable right of every living being."[8]

Such far-reaching critiques demand a fundamental break with speciesism, that is, the ethos of human supremacy in which the rest of nature is viewed as a font of resources for human appropriation—an ethos rationalizing cruelty and killing as necessary to civilized entitlements and conveniences. Humans are exalted as basically different from other species, an "undeniable" contention and scarcely a topic of rational debate when it comes to assessing the sorts of mental capabilities that people valorize. Historically it was thought that only humans possessed an immortal soul, or were the only beings capable of using tools, or were the only species that could build orderly societies. Following the great religions and the great philosophers, Enlightenment thinking has come to attach to humans a range of qualities identified as unique to the species—thought, reflection, morality, planning, and empathy. It turns out that most of these traits are possessed to varying degrees by members of other species, as modern research shows, although public views have not caught up with such findings. (As for tools, it is true that only humans have massively created and deployed them for the purpose of killing.) A greater problem for speciesism is that human behavior more often than not has little in common with this idealized self-conception; the dark side of humanity, extensively recorded across history, is either ignored or downplayed and contextualized. As Jane Goodall observes in *Through a Window*, the familiar hallmarks of humanity are violated millions of times daily within the mammoth torture complexes known as packinghouses, to say nothing of the never-ending chain of wars and other forms of mass murder that human beings have visited upon themselves over the centuries. "Cruelty is surely the very worst of sins," she writes. "To fight cruelty, in any shape or form—whether it be towards other human beings or non-human beings—brings us into direct conflict with that unfortunate streak of *inhumanity* that lurks in all of us."[9] Responding to self-serving human proclamations of a unique moral compassion, Singer points out "that we rarely stop to consider that the animal that kills with the least reason to do so is the human animal."[10] Routine killing under human auspices is practiced not only for food but for the even more questionable ends of sport, entertainment, and biomedical testing.

Animal rights agendas face stiff challenges from agribusiness, the meat industry, the media, biomedical interests, and the resistance bred of established lifestyles. Animal food production in the United States alone has increased no less than four times since the 1950s, despite the more recent spread of popular knowledge concerning the harmful effects of meat consumption. At present there are an estimated 20 billion livestock on earth. In the United States more than 100,000 cows and calves are slaughtered every day, along with 25 to 35 million chickens. The Tyson plant at Noel, Missouri, kills some 300,000 chickens daily, while the IBP slaughterhouse at Garden City, Kansas and the ConAgra complex at Greeley, Colorado both disassemble more than 6,400 steers a day.[11] All told 23 million animals are killed worldwide to satisfy human and food demands daily. In a McDonaldized society Americans now eat on average thirty pounds of beef yearly, with seemingly little concern for well-known health risks. Conditions of factory farming, said to be improved owing to reforms, are in fact worse by most standards—more crowded, more painful, more disease-ridden, more drug-saturated even than at the time of Upton Sinclair's classic *The Jungle* (written in 1906).[12] The great misery of animals subjected to such conditions and cut off from normal social life has brought few changes from within the political system. More than half of all animals (pigs, chickens, ducks, etc.) are afflicted with diseases like cancer and leucosis at the time of slaughter. The Federal Humane Slaughter Act supposedly ensured that animals would be rendered unconscious before being ripped to pieces, but Robbins and other critics estimate that as many as 90 percent are conscious as they are processed through the assembly-line terror.[13] The meat industry has virtual carte blanche to do whatever it wants with its commodities insofar as government monitoring ranges from sporadic to nonexistent—a situation that, as Robbins argues, amounts to a crime not only against helpless animals but against nature and indeed against humanity itself.[14] That such practices are so routine, so concealed from public sight, so ideologically sanitized hardly subtracts from the horrors. So long as living creatures with physiological make-ups very close to our own are reduced to resource-objects for human appropriation, virtually anything is possible.

The relentless assault on nonhuman nature is rooted in the same corporate–imperial order responsible for ecological crisis, militarism, resource wars, global poverty, and political repression. The old religious and philosophical belief systems notwithstanding, no rational defense of such barbarism has been brought forward—nothing beyond blind obedience and crude prejudice. As in comparable instances of ideological convention, prejudice takes many forms. Thus Masson writes: "It has always been comforting to the dominant group to assume that those in subservient positions do not suffer or feel pain as keenly, or at all, so that they can be abused or exploited without guilt or impunity."[15] According to such mindless bias, perfectly healthy, intelligent beings with normal survival impulses are deemed unworthy of life, their fear and misery met with (usually silent) contempt. Immersed in the meat complex materially, institutionally, and psychologically, most people cannot allow themselves to see anything unusual, much less unethical, in the pain and suffering of other creatures. Sinclair argued in *The Jungle* that anyone visiting a slaughterhouse would be quickly converted into vegetarianism, but alas, these zones of torture remain invisible to the ordinary person, far removed from the sanitized and convenient supermarkets, restaurants, and fast-food outlets.

Those profiting from the food, gun, and biomedical industries see absolutely no moral problem with the killing machine, which is fully protected by Constitutional freedoms. On the contrary, their work is understood to be for the benefit of all humankind—after all, meat is needed for good health, hunting gives individuals much-needed diversion, lab testing helps cure diseases, and circuses provide entertainment for children. Little in the way of explicit moral justification or even factual evidence seems required in support of such notions, since the blessings of human supremacy (God-given or otherwise) appear sufficient. As with other modes of domination, cruel and lethal practices are simply taken for granted by otherwise educated and progressive individuals. In reality *Homo sapiens* does exercise dominion over nature due to its obviously superior material and psychological advantages, an element of anthropocentrism that is hardly debatable. Of course humans seize every opportunity to claim special moral qualities, placing themselves above brutal nature and the "beasts" that populate it. Yet while it is no great intellectual triumph for humans to establish their primacy over nature—they have done so for millennia—the real question turns on the exact character that primacy assumes as it is historically played out. In the present context "dominion" (as spelled out in Genesis and other texts) has meant exploitation and abuse, that is, domination largely bereft of positive ethical content—although some recent works (for example Matthew Scully's *Dominion*) have sought to ground a defense of animal rights in religion.[16] A different kind of human obligation would point in the direction of *stewardship*, calling attention to equity, balance, ecological sustainability, and coexistence between humans and the natural world.[17] So far, however, human beings have done little to distance themselves from a brutal or Hobbesian state of nature, having repeatedly proven themselves the most destructive and murderous of all creatures.

The view of natural relations adopted here derives from Regan's philosophical work—namely, that all sentient beings have inalienable rights to be free of pain and suffering at the hands of humans.[18] For Regan, this line of thinking holds to several interrelated premises: (1) no moral justification exists for overriding animal interests in order to serve "higher interests"; (2) what matters is not specific intellectual or communication skills but rather the capacity to experience pain, suffering, and loss; (3) while much of nature is inescapably used by humans as resources to satisfy material and other needs, this logic should not extend to other sentient beings; (4) humans ought to be stewards of nature and other species within it to the extent possible; and (5) human and animal interests are closely bound together within the same social and historical processes. Moving from these assumptions, a guiding aim of social change should be the ultimate elimination of animal exploitation in all its forms. This rises to the level of a moral imperative: if barbarism cannot be justified by necessity or by ethical precepts, then all that remains is the force of habit, prejudice, and material gain.

While humans have always dominated nature, their capacity for harm and destruction—greater today than ever—can be progressively reduced through the introduction of an animal rights politics leading, eventually, to the end of speciesism or at least the diminution of its harshest manifestations. If the rights agenda is constrained by the very inequities of capitalism, as Ted Benton argues, that is surely no reason to reject rights-based reforms completely any more than we would consider jettisoning any of the multiplicity of long-established human rights.[19] In a state–corporate system where domination pervades the entire social landscape, the promise of full equal rights will always run up against limits in the form of wealth, power, and ideology. It follows that rights, given adequate legal codification, will have to be *deepened* as part of long-term social transformation. Conversely, any theory of animal interests will be inadequate unless integrated into a more comprehensive schema engaging issues of corporate power and ecological crisis, a challenge taken up in the following pages.

NEOLIBERAL ILLUSIONS

As with other areas of personal life now viewed as having larger public relevance, meat has traditionally been regarded as a private issue, in this case one's dietary choice—a matter of individual preference. The past few decades have witnessed some changes in popular attitudes toward meat, yet most people see no connections between meat and general social problems. And these connections are indeed plentiful: resource depletion, pollution, food shortages, deforestation, global warming, disease. *Worldwatch* magazine has observed: "as environmental science has advanced, it has become apparent that the human appetite for flesh is a driving force behind virtually every category of environmental damage, including the growing scarcity of fresh water, loss of biodiversity, spread of toxic wastes and disease, even the destabilization of countries."[20] This predicament is aggravated by the massive increase in global demand for meat in just the past four decades: with more than 6.2 billion humans on the planet, at least 90 percent consumers of meat, it takes no genius to see that the Earth's capacity for renewal is rapidly being outstripped. The source of astronomical profits for agribusiness, meatpackers, grocers, and the fast-food industry—in fact a bulwark of the entire corporate system—meat is today a decisive factor in altering planetary life.[21]

In a word, meat is highly unsustainable and is destined to become more so over time unless existing consumption patterns are reversed. It demands great reservoirs of energy in the form of fossil fuels—pesticides, fertilizers, transport, processing, and so forth—and this, along with enormous waste and toxins from animal farming, is the largest source of water and soil pollution. In the United States, moreover, cattle, sheep, and other livestock graze roughly 525 million acres of land, nearly two acres for every person in the country. Seventy percent of the land area in the West is used in grazing livestock.[22] In all, the percentage of grain in the United States that goes to feed livestock is a staggering 72 percent (including 80 percent of corn).[23] Great expanses of land worldwide have long been overgrazed, leading to soil erosion, while vast regions are being deforested to make room for animal grazing and farming. Half of all water is utilized in meat production, which, owing to toxins and runoff, also contaminates shrinking water tables. Overall, meat drains a staggering amount of resources and energy at a time when their availability is peaking or declining. In the case of global warming, livestock account for more than 20 percent of world methane emissions, not including fossil fuels used in agriculture and transport. Though the staggering material wastefulness and ecological dysfunctions of the meat industry are no secret, the sad reality is that as societies develop economically and their middle strata grow, meat consumption tends to increase sharply as it is widely considered a symbol of affluence and good living. The public demand for meat escalates at precisely the historical moment when arable land is shrinking, oil resources are peaking, soil is becoming depleted, and water supplies are more problematic than ever.

Meanwhile, agricultural surpluses dwindle and more than one billion people around the world are chronically hungry—a figure that is sure to increase dramatically. Although world grain output has tripled since 1950, with the introduction of fertilizers and high-yield seeds, such growth has reached an end as farmers globally are now, in Lester Brown's words, "faced with shrinking supplies of irrigation water, rising temperatures, the loss of cropland to nonfarm uses, rising fuel costs, and a dwindling backlog of yield-raising technologies."[24] At the same time, world meat consumption rose from 47 million tons in 1950 to 260 million tons in 2005, a fivefold increase, while out of 220 tons of soybeans produced globally (in 2005) just 15 million tons were consumed by humans. Since world population is expected to reach over 9 billion by 2050, life-support systems will obviously never be able to satisfy food demands of even close to that many people given present trends. The result is that we now have a degree of unsustainability that is taking the planet toward catastrophe.

Spurred by unfettered corporate expansion, neoliberal globalization thus subverts ecological balance by its very logic, and an often neglected component of this downward cycle is animal-based agriculture. Neoliberalism legitimates its unsustainable practices on a foundation of technocratic arrogance, mythological belief in free-market economics, an instrumental view of nature, and contempt for other species. If U.S. elites stand at the forefront of such thinking, they are hardly alone: the global ecosystem has little value to corporate ideology in *any* setting, for that would intrude on profit making. Insofar as sustainability requires developmental balance, respect for nature, limits to growth, and renewal of resources, a transformed relationship between humans and animals logically follows, as does a worldwide move toward population reduction.

This last point deserves further elaboration. World population is expected to double over the next 50 years, at which time a sustainable economy—assuming present trends—will be a long-forgotten possibility. Rapid population growth brings a steady decline in per capita resources, increase in toxic wastes and pollution, extreme crowding in major cities, intolerable demands on public infrastructure, drastic loss of biodiversity, diminution of remaining species, and intensified global warming well beyond anything currently imagined. Food and water resources will be consumed far past crisis levels. Both agriculture and industry will be stymied, spreading poverty, joblessness, social chaos, ecological breakdown, and general calamity.[25] Since a sustainable human population has been estimated to be roughly two and a half billion people, we can assume that a population of 12 billion will tax planetary capacity to the point of catastrophe.[26] And if meat production continues anywhere close to present levels—and it is projected to rise sharply—the crisis will be simultaneously hastened and exacerbated. Unfortunately, at present no serious political counter-forces exist, and the United States has taken the lead in stonewalling even modest attempts to curtail global warming and related environmental threats. And very few observers (Left, center, or Right) have even posed the question of how meat production and consumption heavily weighs on sustainability.

For corporate managers across the globe, unlimited accumulation has always trumped social and ecological imperatives. Having for years pretended that global warming is a liberal myth, the George W. Bush administration was forced to backtrack, but still insisted that any challenges could be met by benevolent functioning of the free market, itself a conservative myth. In December 2005 more than 10,000 delegates from 189 countries met in Montreal to discuss how to reverse climate change, but the United States (source of no less than 30 percent of all greenhouse emissions) sought to obstruct reform efforts as its chief negotiator, Harlan Watson, walked out of the proceedings, continuing a rejectionist pattern established at the Earth Summit in Rio de Janeiro in 1992. (The Copenhagen talks in 2009 yielded no better result.) If a sustainable economy requires emphasis on the process of natural renewal, then neoliberal globalization—by far more exploitative, coercive, and destructive than in the past—can no longer be tolerated by either humans or other species. Under existing conditions, nature cannot begin to renew itself, meaning that conscious human intervention, relying on those special ethical and political qualities people claim to possess, is an urgent imperative. (Anthropocentrism *in this sense* cannot be denied, and in fact ought to be welcomed.) Ecological balance depends on a shift away from corporate agendas, toward a regimen of public goods, long-term social planning, renewable energy resources, reduced population levels, and a vegetarian-based agriculture—now less a matter of individual preference than of collective survival. How theorists and activists of the Left have managed to avoid this constellation of issues remains one of the great puzzles of the current period.

ADDICTED TO MEAT

If it can be said that the United States is addicted to militarism and war, as the volume *Addicted to War* graphically puts forth, then it might equally be argued that the nation is addicted to meat and all that comes with it, including the fast-food mania. A major difference is that meat permeates the entire society to a degree even beyond the culture of militarism and war. Psychological habituation occurs and is reinforced on several levels—political, economic, cultural, personal, even religious—and is reproduced by agricultural, industrial, and service networks that have grown dramatically over the past few decades. Fast food alone has exploded since the 1970s, helping reshape the entire American landscape: home, school, media, sports, and workplace.[27] According to Eric Schlosser, Americans spent $134 billion on fast food alone in the year 2000, more than was spent on college education, personal computers, or new cars.[28] Animal products now fuel the modern industrial system everywhere, a (false) symbol of human prosperity but also a source of mounting social, workplace, health, and environmental ills. Poor people and youth are most heavily targeted by fast-food advertising campaigns indifferent to the great harm their products bring to the workers who manufacture them, human health, the environment, and the animals they disassemble.

Rifkin shows how the beef complex, long ago seen as a vehicle of modernity, developed historically alongside an Enlightenment project fixated from the outset on the total commodification of nature.[29] Scientific discovery, technological innovation, and industrial growth were all harnessed to the sprawling meat enterprises that in the United States became especially valued as part of the frontier expansion. At the time of the westward push meat was a dominant economic and cultural force, reinvigorating the capitalist ethic of material acquisition and the masculine ethic of rugged individualism.[30] Since then the cattle system celebrated in hundreds of Western books and movies has become a pervasive element of the social order, a staple of the American diet, site of bountiful profit making, and a nightmare for animals that Sinclair was just the first to bring to (U.S.) public attention. By the 1950s meat could be linked to the rise of suburbia, the automobile culture, and an expanding electronic media that helped drive McDonaldization, a food regimen integral to fast-paced urban and suburban lifestyles while the apparatus itself (both production and consumption) came under Fordist operating principles: uniformity, speed, efficiency, standardization, and affordability. All the historical components of animal farming and meat processing were thoroughly rationalized, generating and satisfying public demand for hamburgers, hot dogs, steak, luncheon meats, and related fare. Workers at factory farms, slaughterhouses, canning plants, and fast-food outlets were mostly recruited from low-wage minority labor and subjected to alienating, routinized, toxic, and dangerous jobs involved in the disassembling of animals. Used in literally hundreds of industrial and food products, beef alone generates huge profits for corporations like ConAgra, Cargill, Tyson, IBP, and McDonalds. Cattle were (and are) dehorned, castrated, injected with hormones and antibiotics, sprayed with insecticides, and transported to automated slaughterhouses before being killed, then broken down into countless marketable parts, ultimately to wind up at butcher shops, stores, and restaurants. The same ritual is repeated for chickens, ducks, pigs, sheep, turkeys, and other creatures, by the millions each day, all subject to similar assembly-line horrors.

As McDonalidization appears to symbolize modernity in food production and consumption, meat has evolved into one of the most saleable commodities for corporations that benefit from mobile lifestyles dependent on relatively cheap energy sources. Champions of advertising and marketing, the meat companies fiercely resist government regulation precisely in that sector (food) most desperately in need of it to monitor health threats, toxic emissions, harsh working conditions, and extreme cruelty to animals. The industry has emerged as a bastion of right-wing politics infatuated with neo-Darwinian economics, including union busting and the fight against the minimum wage.[31] If those who run the meat empires have nothing but reckless contempt for their own workers and only slightly better regard for consumers, what can be expected of their treatment of those millions of hapless creatures processed through the extermination chambers? As Ken Midkiff observes, "[i]n the concentrated feeding operations, animals are treated as nonsentient beings, as if incapable of feeling pain."[32] Schlosser's vivid account of life at ConAgra's giant plant near Greeley, Colorado reverberates with horrific narratives right out of *The Jungle*. There, hundreds of thousands of cattle are squeezed together in huge feedlots, so close they can barely move, handled as nothing but units of production. Animal wastes, toxic runoff, and chemical emissions fill the slaughterhouse, spreading disease to cattle and humans alike. Workers are powerless cogs in a rationalized machine operation that similarly reduces them to manipulable objects. At Greeley, Schlosser reports three overpowering odors—burning hair and blood, grease, and a rotten-egg smell from hydrogen sulfide—with people, animals, and meat all contaminated by the same toxins and pathogens.[33] This uniquely American contribution to food production is now being exported to every corner of the globe.

Aside from the military, no sector of American society matches the frightening consequences of the meat complex: ecological devastation, food deterioration, routinized violence, injury, disease, and death to both humans and animals, and unaccountable corporate power. The health of consumers addicted to fast foods loaded with fats, salt, sugar, and calories worsens with each passing year, marked by a growing obesity epidemic connected to health problems like cancer, heart disease, diabetes, and chronic infections. The American junk-food diet, now more often than not a source of habituation at an early age, must be considered one of the great contemporary tragedies. As mentioned, public awareness of health problems stemming from meat consumption has recently increased, thanks to a new generation of critics and such documentaries as *Diet for a New America*, *McLibel*, *Supersize Me!*, and *The Corporation*. No doubt too the alarming scope of health problems, afflicting even the very young, has given rise to something of a backlash. In response, the meat industry has stepped up its propaganda crusades, hoping to short-circuit any thoughts people might have of turning to vegetarianism. Consumers are told, falsely, that meat is essential to good health, that it is an indispensable source of protein and other nutrients, that vegetarianism is a silly and harmful fad, that "barnyard" animals are treated with great care, and that critics of meat addiction are behaving like "food dictators" and "lifestyle Nazis." People are warned against the sinister and intrusive schemes of a "culinary police," Big Brother taking over the kitchen. Lobbies like the National Cattlemen's Association and the American Meat Institute, reinforced by friendly diet crazes like those of Robert Atkins, have waged multi–billion dollar media counteroffensives to persuade Americans that meat is the (only) path to true health and a sign of prosperity.[34] Meanwhile, despite abundant scientific, medical, and environmental evidence to the contrary, the familiar habits live on with daily reinforcement from the corporate media.

The terror that animals routinely experience at the hands of humans has for several decades been a taken-for-granted part of everyday existence, far removed from any possible set of ethical concerns. Of course such a collective sense of denial owes much to simple habit rooted in traditions, customs, and lifestyles, readily justified (and fiercely protected) as culinary preference. Yet where addiction of this sort causes extreme harm to the environment, to animals, and of course to the addicts themselves, much deeper explanations seem in order. Beyond the role of an indefensible speciesism, there is the power of transnational business interests that help define media culture, but that is not all. The break with old habits, however destructive, is more difficult where such habits are legitimated by hallowed belief systems, long inscribed in religion and philosophy, that celebrate the supremacy of *Homo sapiens* over an objectified nature. When people are questioned about what they eat, for example, they instinctively fall back on time-honored myths inherited from Christianity, Judaism, Cartesian and Kantian notions of human superiority, Enlightenment (scientific, technological) views of progress, or simple liberal-capitalist norms of possessive individualism. From these traditions it is a logical (and all too quick) journey to the factory farms, packinghouses, fast-food enterprises, hunting clubs, and biomedical labs. Criticism of such traditions strikes most people as nonsensical, an unwarranted intrusion into their personal lives and values. Barriers insulating people from the daily carnage are just as much ideological as physical (distance from source), permitting comfort in detachment in the same way that victims of technowar remain unseen by the perpetrators. What Western religion, philosophy, and political ideology instill is a conviction of human uniqueness and superiority: "man" possesses a level of intellect, communication skills, language, and emotional capacity that other species cannot match. While humans are capable of distinctly moral discourses and noble actions, "wild" animals are trapped in their biological immediacy—crude, primitive, violent, devoid of ethical impulses. The gulf is seen as unbridgeable. Such self-serving mythology conflicts with Darwinian evolutionary principles, but it does give humans a sense of entitlement over nature—easy justification for exploiting other species for food and other ends.[35]

Great distance and concealment allow people to isolate themselves from atrocities, so that moral discourses around animal interests readily fall on deaf ears; removed from sight, the pain and suffering does not register on the supposedly empathetic human psyche. Of course relatively few people are directly involved in the killing apparatus, while fast-food outlets and supermarkets (employing millions) package meat as just another customer item like bread, cereal, and soft drinks. The harm done to living creatures is relegated to the margins of social life, rarely broached as a topic of conversation, much less a source of moral outrage. Paradoxically, however, it is people's intimate daily connection to animal flesh as a food staple that renders meat addiction so difficult to break, or even to grasp as a problem. The end product of killing is viewed as vital to culinary and health benefits, reinforced through a constellation of daily habits, tastes, rituals, ceremonies, and special occasions, often linked to traditions and/or psychological identities. Habit further requires powerful defense mechanisms: denial, cynicism, insulation, or cultivated indifference. Any challenge to meat eating, moreover, can quickly be taken as an insult to personal rights often associated with sensitive religious, national, or ethnic traditions. Few meat eaters are prepared to hear that their food decisions are somehow unethical, harmful, and costly to human well-being, the environment, and animals possessing traits little different from those of domestic pets. Like other destructive behavior, the meat habit is embedded in complex social relations as well as ideological beliefs, thus working its way into systems of domination. An ostensibly premium, nutritious food, meat has long signified good health and strength while more mundane foods (grains, vegetables, and fruits) were associated with inferior, cheap diets of the poor and lower classes. Even today meat (above all beef) represents *power*, especially masculine power of the sort wielded by strong leaders and warriors, a kind of special nourishment needed to carry out tough work. Writes Carol Adams: "According to the mythology of patriarchal culture, meat promotes strength; the attributes of masculinity are achieved through eating these masculine foods."[36] A meat-centered diet is still regarded as a source of great virility. With the planet driven past its ecological limits, and with meat consumption more wasteful, destructive, and unhealthy than ever, humans remain locked in a closed universe of myths and addictions, immobilized by years of inbred practices.

Collective addiction can easily serve as a psychological bulwark of established interests, but in the end it provides no excuse for sidestepping important ethical choices. As Gary Francione points out, "[m]any humans like to eat meat, they enjoy eating meat so much that they find it hard to be detached when they consider moral questions about animals. But moral analysis requires at the very least that we leave our obvious biases at the door. Animal agriculture is the most significant source of animal suffering in the world today, and there is absolutely no need for it."[37] Radical change will insist upon moral and psychological as well as economic decisions that the vast majority of people anywhere will be reluctant to support, especially since habits are so deeply rooted in social institutions. Meat consumption is sustained at high levels by such vigorous corporate advertising and marketing that any significant break with existing patterns appears unlikely—that is, unless the modern crisis intensifies to the point where it *forces* basic alterations in daily life. For such alterations to occur, human–animal relations would finally have to be subjected to a full recasting. One might argue that, as in the case of the impact of fossil fuels on global warming, a sharpening crisis has already shown that it can provoke changes in both the social and ecological realms. If humans are indeed endowed with unique intellectual and moral potential, not to mention a capacity to plan for the future, then a new historical path ought to be within sight.

THEORETICAL MYOPIA

As I have indicated, how theorists and activists have managed to avoid this constellation of issues remains one of the great puzzles of the current period. As Francione observes, addictive human behavior can seem to justify an impulse to ignore the moral and political consequences of such behavior; some of the worst human crimes across history were rooted in longstanding habit and custom, later to become the targets of resistance and change. Critical reflection implies a willingness to reconsider *any* personal or institutional practice known to be harmful to others or to the common good. In the case of natural relations, as we have seen, barbarism rooted in human convenience and monetary profit not only thrives but is legitimated within the media and popular culture. However, if meat addiction is deeply implicated in the modern crisis across many fronts, then we are faced with a new set of *political* challenges. Such critics as Robbins, Rifkin, Masson, and Schlosser have written extensively about some of these connections, calling at least tacitly for decisive changes in the whole system of food production and consumption, but progressive/Left responses have given rise to one long deafening silence. It is probably no exaggeration to say that human–animal relations have been systematically ignored within the Marxist and labor traditions, and to a lesser extent within liberalism, major social movements, and community organizations. Important Left journals (*The Progressive, Monthly Review, Dissent, Z Magazine, The Nation*) have, with only rare exceptions over many decades, closed their pages to the discourse, as if the matter of animal interests were something of an ideological embarrassment.[38] For progressives, animal rights work has been dismissed as the misguided work of a motley assemblage of pet extremists, eco-misanthropes, and fringe New-Agers. Whether such leftist cluelessness derives from sheer ignorance or the simple prejudice of an addicted population, or simply reflects an intellectual myopia—or some combination of these—is difficult to tell. The problem is that, in the area of natural relations at least, the Left has abandoned any claim to critical thinking, much less oppositional politics, following instead the safe contours of mainstream ideology and its defense of powerful interests and conventional wisdom. Meanwhile, animal rights activism has generated one of the largest and most influential movements of the past two decades.

Such theoretical paralysis on the Left assuredly runs deep, as does a preferential weighting of issues that exhibits an irrational contempt for nonhuman nature. One might suspect that the growing impact of animal exploitation on the environmental predicament, its role in sustaining corporate power, and its connection to miserable working conditions, the spread of disease, and worsening of human health—problems historically championed by progressives—might in fact *compel* serious engagement. But nothing along these lines has happened. The Left has exhibited total disregard for the contributions of highly-accessible critical public intellectuals like Singer, Regan, Robbins, Rifkin, and Masson, among others. Despite its radical implications, this work has scarcely resonated among progressive writers, journals, groups, and movements otherwise dedicated to open and critical thought. The reasons for such deficiency of critical spirit surely fall along psychological as well as intellectual or political explanations. Lifestyle habits clearly matter, but the religious and philosophical traditions mentioned above still exercise hegemonic power.

On the other hand, animal rights discourse has its own distinct limits, in at least three ways. First, theorizing often follows rather narrow, exceedingly abstract lines of inquiry, with animal concerns isolated from wider social and ecological priorities. Second, the rights concept so prevalent in framing animal interests is tied overwhelmingly to questions of individual moral choice, a product of the liberal tradition in which motifs of social structure, institutional power, and ideology are de-emphasized. Benton writes that "[t]he problem for the rights perspective is not that it purports to offer protection too widely but, rather, that it is too restrictive in the purchase it gives to moral concerns."[39] These points logically intersect with a third: even the most far-reaching critiques of speciesism fall short of political articulation, with change posed largely in terms of personal ethics and detached from general strategic choices. Most attempts to reconceptualize human–animal relations fail to confront the weight of corporate power and supporting liberal-capitalist institutions. Beneath the façade of democratic practices we face a corporate system that, in the United States above all, pursues agendas guaranteed to bring ecological calamity. With its civilized flourishes and high-minded discourses, this system is integrated by a growing concentration of economic, governmental, and military power intent on world domination. It is a global order legitimated by Enlightenment ideology which, as William Leiss says, approaches "the kingdom of nature . . . like any other realm subject to conquest by those who command the requisite forces."[40]

The question at this juncture is not whether humans really dominate nature—the capacity to do so is undeniable—but what *form* their intervention will or should take. Liberal-capitalist development, merging technocratic and market principles, is fueled by conquest and exploitation, turning vital ecosystems into lifeless machines, reservoirs of accumulated wealth and power. Nor is the question one of people simply *using* nature to advance their own interests, since the only alternative would be total depopulation of the planet so that no water, foodstuffs, metals, wood, and paper could ever be extracted—an extreme approach to sustainability, to put it charitably. Again, the problem turns on precisely what forms human use of the natural habitat will take, including whether the developmental model will be sustainable, consistent with the Earth's biospheric potential. Any radical break with past ecological dysfunctions will require a new mode of natural relations including a qualitative leap forward in the human treatment of animals.

Marxism and the socialist politics it inspired throughout the twentieth century accentuated class struggle in some form, the anticipated prelude to large-scale social transformation—a negation of liberal capitalism, in theory if not always in practice. Yet, in its main strategic formulations (above all social democracy) Marxism followed liberalism in its attachment to Enlightenment values, rapid industrial growth, and maximum exploitation of nature. Classical Marxism held that human alienation could be abolished by eliminating the capitalist division of labor, a necessary stage in the full realization of species-being, or ultimate liberation. Nineteenth-century socialists—not only Karl Marx and Friedrich Engels but Karl Kautsky, George Plekhanov, and others—inherited a strong modernizing faith in science and technology, in the blessings of economic development. The egalitarian side of Marxism signaled a radical shift in what it meant to be human, but it never went so far as to redefine human–nature or human–animal relations, a hardly surprising void given the ideological constraints of the period. The positivist, scientistic side of Marxism, wedded to an implicit speciesism, militated against any such reformulation. Marxism was also *productivist* in its obsession with economic forces as the driving force of history as the determinant of a new society.[41] Again, such theoretical bias was inevitable given the *Zeitgeist* of the times: Marxism, after all, gained ascendancy during the early modern period, forged between 1840 and 1880, and then reached its peak in the decades preceding World War I, reflecting established intellectual currents of the time and place (Europe), including a strong optimism in the future of technology and the industrial order.

It has been argued that Marx (and later Marxists), despite the ideological confinements of time and place, arrived at a conceptual framework universally relevant not only to class struggle but to ecology. The socialization of production, a shift toward egalitarian class and power relations, a breakdown of the division between urban and rural life, an emphasis on collective consumption—all this is said to point toward a model of sustainable growth resting on a balanced relationship between humans and nature.[42] Whether this imputed vision effectively counters a productivist fixation on limitless industrial growth and triumph over scarcity is problematic, but even if we recognize an ecological Marx we are still left with his well-known silence regarding natural relations. There is little in Marx (or indeed later Marxists) to indicate serious theoretical reflection on this issue, nor indeed has anyone ever made such a claim. As Benton, generally sympathetic to Marx, observes, the overall thrust of the theory is to give humans a *freer* hand in utilizing the natural world for human purposes, with class struggle a vehicle of the "humanization of nature."[43] The much-celebrated "humanism" of the early Marx actually replicates the deep-seated speciesism of Western religious and philosophical thought. For Marx, following in the tracks of Descartes, Kant, and Hegel, humans are innately creative and self-reflexive, potentially free to remake history, while nonhuman creatures are trapped within a pre-designed biological realm. Instead of an organic connection between humans and animals, sharing the same ecological fate as Darwinian theory affirmed, Marx saw dualism and opposition between the two—a tendency that would become more pronounced in later, more crudely materialistic, variants of Marxism.

Twentieth-century Marxists were no more likely to address ecological issues than were the founders: Western Marxists like Rosa Luxemburg, Karl Korsch, Antonio Gramsci, Georg Lukacs, Jean-Paul Sartre, and Herbert Marcuse took up a range of distinctively non-productivist concerns—culture, aesthetics, bureaucracy, the family, media, and so forth—but, with the partial exception of Marcuse, seemed hardly more interested in ecology than were nineteenth-century thinkers, despite occasional abstract discussions of nature. The environment would become a challenge taken up by theorists *outside* the Marxist tradition, since for Marxism (and socialism) change was a project for and by *humans* struggling to conquer nature—"conquer" meaning here what we normally define as exploitation. Nowhere, of course, did issues related to ecological crisis, much less animal rights, get placed on the political agenda. By the time writers like Rachel Carson, Murray Bookchin, and Barry Commoner began calling public attention to ecological problems in the 1960s, Marxism was already in decline.[44] The crucial point is that the underlying productivism of Marxist/socialist thought imposed strict limits on its capacity to reconceptualize natural relations; it has had little more to offer than liberal capitalism.

By the early twenty-first century, strong attempts to merge ecology and Marxism were under way not only within and around Green parties and movements but in socialist circles, yet reconceptualization of natural relations in line with an ethic of animal rights had made little headway. Now as before, animal interests, where considered worthy of intellectual discourse, are explored in isolation from other problems, while those other problems are usually taken up separately from questions of animal rights. As for Marxism, John Sanbonmatsu has recently pointed out that the familiar theoretical impasse remains: although the global economy depends increasingly on the cultivation, killing, and disposal of billions of animals yearly, this horrific reality continues to be untheorized (in fact *untheorizable)* within the socialist tradition.[45] In this regard little has changed since the time of Marx and Engels: only human consciousness matters, only human suffering and pain enter the political calculus. Thus Joel Kovel, in an otherwise incisive work on the ecological crisis, maintains that animal rights concerns are "fundamentalist" and "forget that all creatures, however they may be recognized, are still differentiated and that we make use of other creatures within our human nature."[46] Left unexplained here is just what element of human nature (itself a problematic concept) justifies the practice of institutionalized barbarism. An article by Marxists Theresa Ebert and Mas'ud Zavarzadeh elevates blind prejudice to higher levels, arguing that human consumption of meat ("real food") is essential to the "proletarian diet" since it furnishes healthy, high-protein, strength-giving nutrition to workers who depend on it for every ounce of physical energy. As they put it in boosting the fraudulent Atkins diet, "[m]eat is the food of the working people; a food of necessity for the class that relies on the raw energy of its body for sustenance." In contrast to the sophisticated "bourgeois diet" containing a large proportion of grains, vegetables, and fruits, animal foods give workers exactly what they need while these upper-class foods are more appropriate for people with abundant leisure time to savor the "Zen moment." The authors conclude that such dietary opposites reflect a social order now in the process of splitting up into two great classes.[47] Leaving aside their total contempt for animal welfare and seeming ignorance of the way in which agribusiness, meatpacking, and fast-food corporations make obscene profits off both human and animal misery, Ebert and Zavarzadeh faithfully repeat every myth passed on by the meat interests—that animal foods are the most nutritious, are needed for physical strength, are the best thing for mundane lifestyles, and are easier and less time consuming to prepare. In fact these foods are just the opposite of what the authors pretend—their harmful effects well documented by thousands of hardly-secret studies conducted in the United States alone, as explored in such texts as Robbins' *The Food Revolution.* Reflecting on such an ill-informed diatribe, one is tempted to conclude that meat addiction is a much deeper problem for the progressive Left than for mainstream or even working-class culture. As the ecological crisis veers out of control, the limits of Marxism become more obvious by the day—and these limits are all the more glaring when it comes to animal rights. Yet its conceptual apparatus still offers crucial insights into the workings of economic power, corporate globalization, and class domination, vital to deciphering the nature of material forces in a transformed world.

Ecological politics, still relatively embryonic in its modern incarnation, grows out of an uneven legacy of theories and movements, the ideal of which has been to overcome the destructive consequences of industrialism and to restore balance between society and nature. Its radical, at times utopian, vision has followed a trajectory largely independent of Marxism, grounded in themes of local community, environmental renewal, mutual aid, limits to growth, and generalized opposition to hierarchy. What might be called "ecocommunalism" or "ecosocialism" passes through the seminal ideas of Jean-Jacques Rousseau, utopian socialism, anarchism, Peter Kropotkin, and the later contributions of modern anarchists and "left-Greens" like Bookchin. This rich tradition embraces a distinctly anti-authoritarian outlook—meaning hostility to the entire fabric of domination—and a fierce dedication to what might be called an ecological renaissance. Here we have something along the lines of a radical or "Green" democracy, defined through ongoing popular struggles for local self-management.

Bookchin's social ecology, an extension of classical anarchist thought and developed across prolific writings going back to the early 1960s, represents probably the most sophisticated ecological radicalism today. His theory is shaped by a "dialectical naturalism" in which efforts to transform history and nature, society and environment, unfold simultaneously, leading to organic community—a process defined by local struggles against multiple forms of domination: class, bureaucratic, racial, gender, cultural, and ecological. An ecological society would mean full realization of "free nature" through human self-activity, fully dependent on the revival of natural relations and the locus of an entirely new consciousness. In Bookchin's words, "[s]uch a change would mean a far-reaching transformation of our prevailing mentality of domination into one of complementarity, in which we would see our role in the natural world as creative, supportive, and deeply appreciative of the needs of nonhuman life."[48] Here the human and nonhuman worlds would be intimately connected, reunited after long centuries of harsh opposition and conflict. Bookchin inherits the political radicalism of Marx in his embellishment of dialectics and popular struggles to overthrow capitalism, but he goes beyond it in two important ways: a view toward overturning *all* modes of domination and a commitment to ecological reconstruction that is at best only implicit in Marxism.

But when it comes to animal rights Bookchin remains just as implacably attached to Enlightenment values and speciesism as Marxism. Indeed, animal interests are roundly dismissed as "misanthropic," a form of "primitive" ecocentrism he sees, incorrectly, as a logical manifestation of deep ecology (DE). For Bookchin, DE and animal rights share a mystical anti-humanism that inevitably undercuts radical politics. Humanity possesses a singular capacity to reappropriate "first nature" and create an elevated "second nature" grounded in reason, planning, and creativity, qualities that set humans apart from other species confined to the biological realm—a view that places Bookchin squarely within the mainstream of Western philosophy.[49] Other species remain tied to "genetic imperatives" and immediate needs of survival, so that "freedom . . . is not attainable by animals."[50] As we have seen, "special" attributes of human beings might be compatible with freedom (in human terms) but have absolutely no relevance to an abiding interest that other species might have in avoiding misery and death at the hands of their ("free") human masters—a moral issue Bookchin never confronts. Again, what matters here is the *specific* relationship humans are able to establish with nature—that is, whether dominion becomes conquest in the form of institutionalized barbarism, or something altogether different. In the final analysis, humans possess nothing special that can ethically justify the terror of slaugherhouses, lab testing, and hunting, although they obviously have the *power* to carry out such practices. In Bookchin's social ecology, we end up with an emancipatory theory of radical (human-centered) transformation that supports an arrogant speciesism where animals have no protection against whatever horrors people decide to visit upon them. As with neo-Marxism, social ecology has been impervious to the radical influence of animal rights theory and practice since the early 1980s.

Reacting against Marxism and social ecology, DE—its influence on Green currents has been strongly felt over the past two decades—looks to systemic change in human–nature relations, marked by an ecocentric break with modernity and industrialism. DE shares with social ecology a rejection of all forms of domination but, given the depth of the ecological crisis, identifies natural relations as the privileged site of human efforts to transform the world. It dismisses liberal environmentalism and its narrow project of limited reforms in favor of a deeper paradigm change in consciousness, lifestyles, and values that would define the new community. DE rejects the Enlightenment legacy *tout court*, urging limits to economic growth, bioregional living arrangements, population reduction, self-sustaining agriculture, and unyielding reverence for natural habitats. More fundamentalist DE theories call for a return to preindustrial society, consistent with basic Green principles of equality, democracy, peace, spiritualism, and ecological renewal. As George Sessions argues, human self-activity is attainable only through organic unity with the surrounding ecosystem.[51] Many DE currents adopt the view that virtually *any* human intervention in nature is destructive and must be avoided. The modern crisis, according to this extreme formulation, would be surmountable only at that point when humans finally exit the scene—a view bringing charges of misanthropic and even fascistic politics. Most variants of DE, it must be said, retreat from such dogmatism.

DE theory stresses moral obligation to nature and living systems within it, a biospheric equality that conflicts sharply with the requisites of industrial society. Departing from Marxism and social ecology, DE argues for full-scale transformation of social life and natural relations consistent with the abolition of speciesism or anthropocentrism. This is no contrived "second nature" but rather progressive adaptation to "first nature," transcending the age-old dualism between society and nature, humans and other species. Here the DE agenda seems compatible with animal rights given its reverence for nature and attraction to "wild nature" unspoiled by human contamination.[52] Yet the theory both exceeds and falls short of animal rights objectives as spelled out in this chapter. First, its moral stance covers the entire natural world, beyond individual sentient beings to include natural habitats as such (trees, water, insects, even rock formations as well as animal species) within an interconnected ecological system. It transcends and even trivializes "rights" to embellish all life forms, so that animal interests fall short of what needs to be considered as part of a deep ecological revolution. Beyond the formal (one might also say legalistic) goal of rights, radical change insists upon a qualitative shift in the economy, social structures, lifestyles, and popular consciousness—all indispensable for planetary survival.

At the same time, DE ecocentrism runs up against its own limits and contradictions. If animal rights discourse lacks a holistic, global outlook, DE offers no theoretical construct that would prohibit institutionalized barbarism as the system is currently maintained. Within DE thinking it has been easy for partisans to hedge on their rejection of anthropocentrism which, in any case, mistakenly poses the question of human domination itself as opposed to looking at how precisely that domination unfolds. The result is that deep ecologists lean toward an open, malleable attitude regarding how individual members of other species are expected to be treated in actuality. As Arne Naess writes, reflecting the tone of many DE passages: "[m]y intuition is that the right to live is one and the same for all individuals, whatever the species, but the vital interests of our nearest [i.e., humans], nevertheless, have priority."[53] He goes on to defend the use of animals as "resources" for human appropriation,[54] and one finds scattered references throughout DE literature to the acceptable use of animals as food sources. At another point Naess writes that humans should be allowed to intervene in nature "to satisfy vital needs," clearly a departure from the ethic of biocentric equality.[55] Lacking a theory of rights or its equivalent, biospheric egalitarianism shades into a vague general orientation, leaving moral and political space for humans to continue their meat addictions and related activities. Ecological radicalism is not so "deep" as to interfere with the brutal treatment of animals if that treatment can be viewed as contributing toward "satisfying vital needs." Conceivably "wild nature" would remain untrammeled, but in other locales sentient creatures would be eligible for merciless abuse at the hands of their human betters.

Another difficulty with DE is that its exit from modernity—indeed its very idea of organic bioregionalism—turns out to be rather abstract, a utopian fantasy. Modernity is so thoroughly a part of the existing world, so embedded in social institutions and practices for so many generations, that ambitious moves to escape its global reach would lead to immediate calamity—even conceding the possibility of such an escape. The idea of abolishing all or even most human intervention into the natural world, which no DE theorists has in fact ever concretized, winds up as just another hopeless romantic myth. Biocentric equality, itself a fanciful *human* construct, is so far beyond any realizable goal that down-to-earth political action is rendered moot. It is hardly surprising that in the sphere of animal rights DE lacks specificity: natural entities from elephants to shrubs, insects, and rocks appear to enjoy the same putative moral standing, however nebulous and subject to myriad qualifications. The grandiose notion of extending moral status across the entire ecological landscape seems on the surface laudatory enough but, as Tim Luke observes, such sacralization of nature fails to rise above a vague sense of "moral regeneration" devoid of political meaning.[56] Despite its deep, radical formulations, therefore, DE in itself offers little guide to an animal rights strategy, much less to a political way out of the modern crisis.

LIBERATING THEORY

We have yet to arrive at a theory of animal rights sufficient to engage all dimensions of the challenge. Both Marxism and social ecology, though vital departures for analysis and change, are much too attached to Enlightenment rationality, with its fetishism of technology and deeply-ingrained speciesism, to inspire any revolution in natural relations. Their view of animal rights is essentially one of contempt—where the issue is not ignored altogether. DE, on the other hand, breaks with Enlightenment ideology and affirms the moral standing of living habitats and the integrity of nonhuman species, but retreats so far into romanticism that it cannot by itself furnish any strategic way forward. The theory contains vague references to moral renewal and organic community that have no relevance to actual political outcomes, including animal liberation. Further, as we have seen, its stated position on animal rights is ambiguous at best. As for the animal rights movement itself, both in theory and in practice it has veered toward insularity, cut off from larger social and ecological concerns even as it generates militant and often highly effective popular struggles. The discourse has regularly been framed as a set of normative ideals to be achieved within the liberal-capitalist order, in the tradition of earlier rights movements. While this is eminently understandable, the problem is that no far-reaching animal liberation (or ecological) project can be sustained without challenging domestic and international corporate power, though partial reforms benefiting animal welfare (e.g., no-kill zones, hunting bans) do obviously matter and ought to be defended. As David Nibert argues, social changes leading to the liberation of both humans and animals are mutually reinforcing, fueled by a common material exploitation that goes back thousands of years.[57]

My argument here then is that a new theoretical synthesis is urgently needed, incorporating dynamic elements of Marxism, radical ecology, and animal rights, if the modern crisis is to be fought with any hope of success. Corporate capitalism has grown ever more authoritarian, exploitative, violent, and unsustainable over time, nowhere more so than in the United States, thus forcing political strategy along a more radical path. If the crisis is a product of multiple and overlapping factors, then countering it means proceeding along diverse fronts: class and power structures, the globalized economy, culture, ecology, natural relations. Even the most transformative change, however, can occur only within the parameters of an already existing urban, modernized order, part of a lengthy historical process, as opposed to any sudden "exit" from the present, or immersion in wild nature.

An expanded moral sensibility requires the normative obligation to other life forms, species, and individual sentient beings—a sensibility basic not only to animal rights but to historical ideals of social justice, democracy, peace, and sustainability. Such ideals demand no mythical biocentric community for their actualization, but they do assume prohibitions against exploitation, torture, and killing in any form, which clearly applies to institutionalized barbarism of the sort perpetrated against billions of sentient creatures today. As Herbert Marcuse, never known for his embrace of animal rights, observed in the 1960s, human beings in their great wisdom have managed to create a general "Hell on earth," and a significant "[p]art of this Hell is the ill-treatment of animals—the work of a human society whose rationality is still the irrational."[58] Today Marcuse would probably agree that the struggle to overcome the dualism of society and nature, humans and other species—barely theorized so far—ought to inform any future radical politics worthy of the name.

Whatever its lacunae in conceptualizing natural relations, Marxism remains indispensable to this project, its class analysis and anti-capitalist theory vital to forging anti-system movements against transnational corporate power. The most imposing problems of the current period, including worker exploitation, global poverty, militarism, and ecological decline, cannot be grasped, much less reversed, in the absence of class-based movements that break with the hardened rules of corporate globalization—a dialectic best theorized within the Marxist tradition. A deep flaw in Marxism is filled by social ecology, given its more systemic view of ecology and sharpened attention to the multiple forms of domination. Attuned to the complex ensemble of relations, social ecology resists the productivism and class reductionism that works against a full ecological Marxism. On the other hand, deep ecology (including ecofeminism) embraces a more distinctly subversive outlook toward natural relations, conferring moral status on *all* of nonhuman nature. Neither Marxism nor social ecology rival DE in the sense of gravity it attaches to habitat destruction and the global ecological crisis, in its potent critique of rampant industrial growth and obsessive pursuit of material abundance. Criticized (for the most part inaccurately) for its misanthropic ideas, DE calls for alternative modes of agriculture, production, and consumption in harmony with sustainable development—a viewpoint scarcely articulated within the Marxist tradition. Such a qualitative shift in social and ecological arrangements is necessary because, as the Pimentels observe, "[h]umanity is approaching a crisis point with respect to the interlocking issues of population, natural resources, and sustainability."[59]

The final and perhaps most contentious element of the synthesis, animal rights, calls attention to an institutionalized barbarism that has been routinely ignored but which does much to sustain corporate wealth and power, thereby helping further intensify the modern crisis. For the short term, like other protocols and standards, the rights of animals ought to find universal codification in the U.N. Charter, the U.S. Bill of Rights, and every other national constitution. Viewed over the long term, insofar as animal interests pose far-reaching challenges to the status quo regarding agricultural practices, the industrial system, diet and health, natural relations, and the ecological crisis, any movement that addresses the general interests of animals has undeniable anti-system potential. Taken to new historical levels, animal rights, in tandem with the great moral questions it raises, clashes with those megacorporate interests—agribusiness, fast food, biomedical, media, and Big Pharma among others—that will stop at nothing in their efforts to amass greater wealth, power, and profits. Nascent struggles to overturn institutionalized barbarism represent a blow, however limited, against escalating human assaults on nonhuman nature, perhaps opening a new phase in the development of a truly liberatory politics.

II

ANIMALS, MARXISM, AND THE FRANKFURT SCHOOL

4

Humanism = Speciesism?

Marx on Humans and Animals

By Ted Benton

> Nature is man's *inorganic body*—nature, that is in so far as it is not itself human body. Man *lives* on nature—means that nature is his *body*, with which he must remain in continuous interchange if he is not to die. That man's physical and spiritual life is linked to nature means simply that nature is linked to itself, for man is a part of nature.[1]

In the quotation above from the *1844 Economic and Philosophical Manuscripts*, Marx is by no means stating merely a shallow-ecological, enlightened self-interest of the species.[2] The view of communism which structures the whole of the *Manuscripts* gives a central place to a proper ethical, aesthetic, and cognitive relationship to nature as inseparable from true human fulfillment. This fundamental insight of Marx's in the *Manuscripts* is well worth holding onto. However, there are two elements in the argument of the *Manuscripts* which seem to me to sit very uncomfortably alongside the naturalism of the above-quoted passage and its possible deep ecological reading. These elements are, first, the use of the human/animal contrast as Marx's central device in the ethical critique of the estrangement of labor under regimes of private property, and, second, the specific content Marx gives to his vision of human emancipation as involving the "humanization of nature."

With regard to the human/animal opposition the argument is, very roughly, as follows. The estrangement of labor is supposed by Marx to have disastrous effects on human beings, their relations to one another, and their relationships to their external, material world. These disastrous effects can be summed up by saying that the estrangement of labor reduces human life to the condition appropriate to that of animals, and, within human life, inverts the relation between the human and the animal. The overcoming of estrangement means restoring to human beings their properly human status and relationships to one another and to the rest of nature. But what *is* the rest of nature? Does it include other animals? Marx's use of the metaphor "inorganic body" suggests not. On the other hand, nothing Marx says in connection with that metaphor can be sustained unless animals *are* included. A human life dependent upon the forces and mechanisms of inorganic nature, unmediated by other forces of life, is impossible. There is no reason to think Marx actually thought it possible. And, notwithstanding the arguments of some that the *possibility* now exists of a satisfactory human life which does not rely on the consumption or exploitation of other animals, the phrase "man lives on Nature," written in 1844, must have included within its reference a whole range of uses of animals as a source of energy in agricultural and industrial labor processes, as well as for food, entertainment, and companionship.

Now, if, for Marx, human emancipation involves a qualitative transformation of our relationship with the rest of nature, a "humanization" of nature, and if nature includes other species of animals, then human emancipation must involve a transformation in our relations to other animals. But what could this transformation be? A literal "humanization" of them in the sense of "rendering them human" by selective breeding (or, for us, genetic engineering)? Or, as with the rest of nature, a deliberate alteration of their character so that they better fulfill human purposes (i.e., a continuation of those breeding and "husbandry" practices whereby farm animals have been rendered more productive and docile, pets more "domesticated," companionable, child-like in appearance, and so on)? If either of these were intended by Marx, his critique of the estrangement of humanity from nature would lose all its force: the "humanization" of animals (as part of nature) in either of these senses would be a continuation and augmentation, not a transcendence, of the treatment of animals under capitalism, and indeed, in precapitalist societies too. Moreover, Marx draws on an absolute and universal, not a provisional and historically transcendable, opposition between the human and the animal in grounding his ethical critique of the capitalist mode of life. If what is wrong with these societies is that humans are reduced to the condition of animals, then the transcendence of capitalism, in restoring humanity to the human, simultaneously restores the differentiation between the human and the animal. If what is wrong with capitalism is, essentially, that it does not differentiate the human and the animal, then the antidote to capitalism must offer to restore the proper differential. But this is precisely what the notion of "humanization" seems to deny. The ontological basis of the ethical critique of capitalism (embedded in the notion of estrangement) appears to be inconsistent with the coherent formulation of its transcendence (in particular, the notion of "humanization" in relation to animals as part of nature). As I shall suggest later, this dilemma can be resolved by a revision of the ontology of the *Manuscripts* which nevertheless leaves intact a good deal of the ethical critique of capitalist society.

HUMANITY AS "SPECIES BEING"

Central to Marx's account of human nature is the claim that man is a "species being":

> Man is a species-being, not only because in practice and in theory he adopts the species (his own as well as those of other things) as his object, but—and this is only another way of expressing it—also because he treats himself as the actual, living species; because he treats himself as a *universal* and therefore a free being.[3]

This "universality" of human theoretical and practical activity distinguishes humans from (other) animals. The sensory, cognitive, and transformative powers of other animals are exercised "under the dominion of immediate physical need." They produce "in accordance with the standard and the need" of their species. Humans, by contrast, who know how to produce in accordance with the standard of *every* species, only *truly* produce in freedom from immediate physical need, and take the *whole* world of nature as the object of their practical, aesthetic, and cognitive powers.

Whereas animals produce to meet the needs of themselves or their young, the activity of individual human beings is, at least potentially, a part of the activity of the species as a whole. Not only, then, is human activity universal in the sense that it takes the whole world of nature as its object, but it is also universal in the sense that it is a species-wide activity. The activity of each individual is not a mere *instance* of its type, but, rather, a living *part* of an interconnected whole—the activity or "life" of the species.

In separating individual life from the life of the species and inverting their proper relationship to one another—as occurs under capitalism—the estrangement of labor imposes upon humanity a mode of existence in which its distinctive species attributes cannot be manifested. Human potential remains unactualized, development is stunted, and powers are exercised in a distorted or inverted way.

The character of "man" as a species-being, then, is not a manifest, empirically detectable feature in contemporary societies. It is, rather, an as-yet unachieved potential. The achievement of this potential is the work of the human historical process. So, implicit in the idea of humanity as a species being is also the idea of humanity as a *historical* being. And by this is meant not simply a being whose activities and forms of association change through time. In addition, these changes of manifest activity and forms of association have a cumulative and directional character, an overlying pattern in terms of which we can make sense of each successive phase or period. To say that the human species is historical in this sense is to say that the species as a whole undergoes, in the historical process, something analogous to the development undergone by both individual human beings and other animals in their transition from embryo through infancy to childhood. Only in the adult are the potentials of the infant fully actualized. The development of the individual is the process of its self-realization. So, in the case of the human species, communist society is the form under which what was merely potential in earlier historical phases becomes actual. The historical process is the developmental process of humankind, through which its species-powers are fully developed and its distinctive species-character is realized.

The analysis of the estrangement of labor shows that there is no necessary or universal connection between the developmental process of the species and the developmental process of the individual. Where labor is estranged, the development of the species occurs at the cost of individual development. On the other hand, the historical development of the species is a precondition for the development of the distinctively human powers of individuals. Humans are different from other animals, then, in that they undergo development at the level of the species (*historical* development) as well as at the level of the individual. In the human species, the development of the species may take place at the cost of stunting or distorting the development of individuals, but, in the long run, full development of the individual with respect to the most distinctively human characteristics is only possible on the basis of a high level of development of the species. None of these considerations apply to other animals, which, for Marx, have a fixed, species-characteristic relationship between need, instinct, and transformative powers, each producing "in accordance with the standard and need of the species to which it belongs."[4]

What makes possible this supra-individual development in the human case is the distinctive character of human activity as "free, conscious activity":

> Yet the productive life is the life of the species. . . . The whole character of a species—its species-character—is contained in the character of its life activity; and free, conscious activity is man's species-character.[5]

A being who freely and consciously engages in a practice is able to reflect critically upon that practice, to change it in line with its existing or newly formulated purposes. Free, self-conscious transformative practice, then, has within it a potential for change and development which the direct and instinctual need-meeting activity of (other) animals does not have. And since this "productive life" is the life of the species, to characterize its development—the development of human productive powers—is to characterize what is essential to the formative process of humanity itself:

> It is just in his work upon the objective world, therefore, that man really proves himself to be a *species-being*. This production is his active species-life. Through this production, nature appears as *his* work and his reality. The object of labor is, therefore, the *objectification of man's species life*: for he duplicates himself not only, as in consciousness, intellectually, but also actively, in reality, and therefore he sees himself in a world that he has created.[6]

And, again:

> But since for the socialist man the *entire so-called history of the world* is nothing but the creation of man through human labor, nothing but the emergence of nature for man, so he has the visible, irrefutable proof of his *birth* through himself, of his *genesis*.[7]

The historical developmental process, then, is to be understood as a multifaceted and progressive augmentation of human transformative powers vis-á-vis nature. This process can be understood as one of human *self*-creation, or *self*-realization, in that the *bearer* of these powers is transformed along with the object of their exercise (nature). In particular, human cognitive powers ("science") underlie the development of productive powers and are themselves developed through reflection upon the outcomes of productive activity. Human sensory powers are likewise developed along with the transformation of the *objects* of human perception: the power to create beautiful objects and the growth of aesthetic sensibility in the human subject are internally related to one another. And, finally, the *purpose* of transformative activity is itself historically transformed as humans acquire new needs in the course of their historical self-development. The historical self-creation of humanity, then, is a process in which human transformative, sensory, aesthetic and cognitive powers and liabilities are transformed and augmented, along with a transformation of the structure of human need itself. But this process is not one that takes place in vacuo, so to speak. It would make no sense to speak of these powers, liabilities and needs without some notion of their object: "nature."

The species-wide and communal project through which humanity creates itself is summed up by Marx as the "humanization of nature." Nature as an external, threatening, and constraining power is to be overcome in the course of a long-drawn-out historical process of collective transformation. The world thoroughly transformed by human activity will be a world upon which human identity itself has been impressed, and so no longer a world which is experienced as external or estranged:

> [I]t is only when the objective world becomes everywhere for man in society the world of man's essential powers—human reality and for that reason the reality of his *own* essential powers—that all *objects* become for him the *objectification* of himself, become objects which confirm and realize his individuality, become *his* objects.[8]

And this applies not merely to the objects of human practical, transformative powers, but also to the world as object of human sensory and cognitive powers ("man is affirmed in the objective world not only in the act of thinking, but with *all* his senses").[9] These quotations, and others like them, suggest a certain view of the transformation wrought by human history in the relationship between human beings and their natural environment. An external, limiting, conditioned relation between the two is transformed in favor of an internal, unlimited, unconditioned (i.e., universal) relation that amounts to a fusion of identities. The conflict between humans and nature is overcome in favor of an incorporation of the natural into the domain of the human without residue. Only when the *whole* world is appropriated cognitively, aesthetically, and practically can humanity itself be fully realized:

> This communism, as fully developed naturalism, equals humanism, and as fully developed humanism equals naturalism; it is the *genuine* resolution of the conflict between man and nature and between man and man—the true resolution of the strife between existence and essence, between objectification and self-confirmation, between freedom and necessity, between the individual and the species.[10]

This historical vision is clearly incompatible with the content of Marx's metaphor, elsewhere in the same text, of nature as "man's inorganic body," the insistence upon the *permanent* necessity of the "metabolism" between humans and their natural environment as a condition of survival. The reality of nature as a complex causal order, independent of human activity, forever sets the conditions and limits within which human beings, as natural beings, may shape and direct their activities. These materialist theses about the relationship of humanity to nature, which are elsewhere also assented to by Marx, are absent from this utopian and idealist vision of human emancipation.

Marx insists that the proper relation between the human species and its natural environment is not reducible to instrumental, need-meeting activity (important though this of course is). A properly human relationship with nature is a many-faceted relationship in which aesthetic, cognitive, practical, and identity-forming aspects are communally realized. This multi-faceted, properly human relationship to nature is one which not only meets need, but has itself *become* the prime human need.

These ideas are powerful, persuasive, and very much in line with modern environmentalism. But when we turn to Marx's specification of the *kind* of relationship to nature that would realize these values their critical potential is vitiated. If we can be at home in the world, be properly, humanly, connected with the world only on the basis of a thorough-going transformation of it in line with our intentions, then what space is left for a valuing of nature in virtue of its *intrinsic* qualities? If we can "see ourselves in," or identify only with a world which *we* have created, then what is left of our status as *part* of nature? Nature, it seems, is an acceptable partner for humanity only insofar as it has been divested of all that constitutes its otherness, insofar, in other words, as it has become, itself, human. This view of a properly human relationship to nature is certainly far removed from a utilitarian, instrumental one, but its value-content is no less anthropocentric. It is, indeed, a quite fantastic species-narcissism.

THE OPPOSITION BETWEEN THE HUMAN AND THE ANIMAL

We have seen that for Marx, (other) animals are characterized by a certain standardized fixity in their mode of life. Insofar as they are able to act transformatively upon external nature they do so in accordance with a definite "standard," characteristic of their species, and their activity is oriented to the meeting of their individual needs (also fixed and characteristic for each species) and those of their offspring. By contrast, human beings act upon the external world in a way which is free, self-conscious, and socially coordinated. Because of these distinctive features of human life activity, their forms of association and modes of practical engagement with the world are subject to directional historical transformations. What distinguishes humans from animals, in other words, is something which only becomes manifest in the course of human history itself.

The contrast between the human and the animal is, then, a contrast both between humans and other animals and between fully developed humanity and undeveloped humanity. History itself is a *real* part of *natural history*—of nature developing into man.[11] The process of historical development is a movement from animal-like origins to a fully human realization, and this is so with respect not only to our powers and liabilities, but also with respect to need. Even when human transformative powers are well developed but the estrangement of labor has not been overcome, truly human needs are not manifested. The worker experiences need and is constrained to meet need in a manner which belies his true human potential, resembling, rather, the animal mode of experiencing and satisfying need.

Underlying both Marx's concept of historical development and his critique of estrangement, then, is a contrast between what he variously calls "crude," "physical," or "animal" need, on the one hand, and "human" need, on the other:

> It (the animal) produces only under the dominion of immediate physical need, whilst man produces even when he is free from physical need and only truly produces in freedom therefrom.[12]

And again:

> The *sense* caught up in crude practical need has only a *restricted* sense. For the starving man, it is not the human form of food that exists, but only its abstract existence as food. It could just as well be there in its crudest form, and it would be impossible to say wherein this feeding activity differs from that of animals.[13]

Marx's attempt, in passages such as these, to provide an account of human nature in terms of a thorough-going opposition between the human and the animal is very much in line with the mainstream of modern Western philosophy and such more recent disciplines as cultural anthropology and sociology. The conceptual oppositions nature/culture, animal/human, and body/mind play a foundational, structuring role in the theoretical edifices that dominate these disciplines.

For each of these disciplinary matrices, an opposition between the animal and the human implies also an opposition *within* the human between what is animal(-like) and what is truly human. In the paradigm dualist philosophy of Descartes, for example, the contrast between persons and animals implies a contrast within the person between a spatially extended bodily mechanism and a self-conscious thinking substance. What is distinctive and valued in human nature is emphasized and its unsullied autonomy preserved, but at the cost of rendering unintelligible the *connections* between humans and the rest of nature and, within persons, between those aspects which are and those which are not distinctively human.

Now, Marx's utopian vision of an eventual reunification of humanity with itself and with nature seems, at first encounter, to promise a way out of the dilemmas posed by such dualist ways of thinking. However, the systematic use of human/animal contrasts in his early work tells against this. These contrasts are not presented as historically transcendable. On the contrary, the human potential for historical transcendence is precisely what *differentiates* us from animals. Whatever changes take place in our human relationship to nature, animals are, and will remain, mere animals.

The philosophical and ethical difficulties of the dualist aspects of Marx's early writings are in fact quite formidable, not only in their own right, but also in terms of other aspects of Marx's overall intellectual and practical project. Consider, first, Marx's "external" dualism of the animal and the human. I'll deal, in turn, with each of the characteristics through which Marx elaborates the opposition:

1. Animals are mere instances of their species, whereas humans relate also as part to whole to theirs. This is Marx's reference to the open-ended capacity of humans for social cooperation. For Marx this is potentially, though not yet actually, a species-wide cooperation in a common species-specific project. But the very cultural diversity that Marx's notion of "free creativity" also recognizes must render implausible his historical projection. What grounds are there for expecting a spontaneous merging of geographically discrete and culturally diverse lines of historical development and visions of the future? What reasons are there for supposing that humans have the potential to evolve non-coercive forms of social coordination on the gigantic scale required?

On the animal side of Marx's contrast, subsequent ethological study has revealed a wealth and complexity of social life in other species. In the case of such animals as dogs, cats, and herd animals such as sheep and cattle, their very sociability was a necessary initial requirement for their distinctive human uses. So also was a degree of malleability and openness in their forms of sociability. If we leave aside, then, what is merely speculative in Marx's contrast—his as-yet-unfulfilled historical projection—the picture is one of highly differentiated and species-specific capacities for and forms of sociability as between animal species. The extent and form of human sociability is, indeed, distinctive, but this is no less true of any other social species. The capacity for and disposition to social coordination of activity *as such* is therefore not a distinctive feature of our species.

2. Humans take the whole world as the object of their activity, whereas animals appropriate the world only partially and according to the fixed standard of their species. Again, the human side of this opposition is misleading. Certainly it is a plausible extrapolation from the past expansion of the geographical scope of human activity to suppose that one day the whole surface of the globe may bear the imprint of human intentional activity—the last of the rainforests and wildwoods destroyed or cultivated, the poles populated and industrialized, the oceans farmed or rendered sterile by accumulation of toxic wastes, and so on. But what is now supposed to be true of the large-scale, immensely complex and interacting mechanisms of chemical and physical cycling and energy transfer in the biosphere suggests that our species would

destroy itself (and many others) by the unintended consequences of its own activity long before such a "utopian" possibility were actualized. All transformative activity presupposes a distinction between those attributes of its objects which undergo alteration and other attributes of the objects, conditions, and agents of the activity whose persistence, unaltered throughout the process, is indispensable to it. Because of this, even if we suppose a limitless increase in human technical powers in any imaginable direction, the notion of a residueless subordination of the world intensively or extensively to human purposes is incoherent.

On the animal side of this contrast, again, ethological studies reveal great diversity among other animal species with respect to the extent, nature, and intra-species variability of their interaction with their environments. As Marx notes, birds build nests that are to a considerable extent species specific in the materials used, site chosen, and design. Nevertheless many species show considerable adaptability in all respects, especially if confronted with non-standard environmental conditions. Inventing, making, using, and inter-generational teaching of the use of tools are now well recognized as powers of nonhuman primates, notably chimpanzees. That there are profound differences in these capacities between humans and other species is clear, but it remains true that such profound differences also separate nonhuman animal species from one another. For his intellectual purposes, Marx exaggerates both the fixity and limitedness of scope in the activity of other animals, and the flexibility and universality of scope of human activity upon the environment. At the same time he abstracts from diversity among nonhuman animal species, and obscures human ecological diversity by way of a global historical extrapolation. Each of these intellectual tactics contributes to the formation of a dualistic categorical opposition instead of a recognition of complex patterns of species-specific diversity.

3. Humans possess historical potential, whereas animals exhibit fixed, standardized modes of activity from generation to generation. This contrast presupposes the first two, but goes beyond them in important respects. To get clarity about how the contrast works, and to see the difficulties in the way of sustaining it in this form, it is first necessary to unpack the notion of "historical potential" and that of "historical development" with which it is closely connected in Marx. First, it is important to distinguish between powers, or capacities, on the one hand, and potentials on the other. To attribute a power or a capacity to, say, an organism, is to say that it is *able* to do something (even though it may not be in *fact* doing it—it may never have done it). To attribute a *potential* is to say that it has the capacity to acquire some future capacity or power which it presently does not have.

Now, Marx's notion of a historical potential includes at least the idea of potentials as possessed by associated groups of individual organisms. Humans characteristically produce means of subsistence, for example, through some form of more-or-less stable pattern of combination of the activities of more-or-less numerous individuals. The productive powers of the group are certainly different in degree, and might indeed be argued to be different in kind from those possessed by individuals. This distinction between individual and group capacities can also be sustained for other social species of animals. Social bees and wasps, beavers, and predators such as lions, hyenas, and others are all species in which subpopulations form more-or-less stable groupings that possess capacities not possessed by individuals independently of their grouping.

But can we speak of group *potentials* as distinct from mere group *capacities*? Are there, for groups, analogues of the processes of development and learning at the level of individuals which might serve as the foundation for a cumulative acquisition of powers through time? Do groups augment their powers of coordination of their own activity, or of transforming their environments? To the extent to which they do we may speak of "collective potentials." In fact, collective potentials are probably possessed in any significant degree only in some mammalian social animals, and to a high degree only in the human case.

Clearly, a good deal needs to be said by way of elaborating and defending these distinctions. But enough has been said to enable me to at least state my case against Marx's use of the concept of historical potential in sustaining his opposition between humans and animals. On the human side of the opposition, it seems to me that the attribution of *species* historical potentials to humans is, to say the least, highly speculative. Certainly this is so if we try to follow Marx in saying which potentials these are (humanization of nature, and so on). Further, the normative connotation that the notion of potential generally carries in Marx does not seem obviously to carry over into historical potentials, whether individual or collective. The individual historical potential to deliver megadeaths at the press of a button is dependent upon the realization of the collective historical potential to construct high-tech weaponry. But how do we value this historical achievement? Do we recognize in it just one aspect of the historical unfolding of human nature, a dimension of human fulfillment, along with our increased capacities for curing the sick, making the deserts bloom, and so on? If we take this option, then it entails recognizing that humans have, as part of their nature, a potential for destructiveness, for evil. In this event, human well-being and the pursuit of happiness may require us to find ways of suppressing or blocking off some of our potentials. Well-being and the "good life" cannot be identified straightforwardly with the fulfillment of our human potential.

The alternative option would be to keep the positive normative connotations of the notion of potential, refusing to recognize *as* potentials those historical possibilities whose realization would be undesirable—evil, destructive, and, ultimately, self-destructive. This option strikes me as a particularly indefensible form of speciesist special pleading. The temptation toward utopian blindness to the causal importance of those individual and collective historical possibilities denied the status of potentials is both strong and dangerous. As Mary Midgley has eloquently shown, the human/animal opposition has served as a convenient symbolic device whereby we have attributed to animals the dispositions we have not been able to contemplate in ourselves.[14] The point of these considerations is to suggest that if Marx turns out to have been right in supposing that only humans have historical potentials, it does not follow directly from this that any great gulf stands between the animal and the human with respect to their *moral* status.

The significance of this point becomes clearer if we look at Marx's contrast from the animal side of the divide. As we have seen, many animal species display a complexity, diversity, and adaptability in their behavior that is denied in Marx's view of them as rigidly stereotypical in their species-characteristic modes of life. For many nonhuman animal species it is possible to speak defensibly of developmental and learning potentials, of simple collective powers, and even to a limited extent of collective potentials. Some evidence exists of cultural transmission of learned skills in the cases of some species of primates but not (as yet, at least) of any generation-by-generation cumulative direction in these collective skills.[15] This *does* seem to be a distinctive feature of humans by contrast with all other animal species currently inhabiting the earth. It is, however, worth noting that this is a purely contingent matter. There is no a priori reason for supposing that some other species might not evolve these potentials in the future, and there are good empirical grounds for thinking that our planet has previously been inhabited by other primate species that *did* have historical potentials.

Now, the *moral* contrast which Marx draws between the *historical potential* of humanity and its estranged, distorted, stunted, *merely animal* mode of existence under the dominion of estranged labor is only effective on two conditions. First, it is necessary to equate the fulfillment of human historical potential with the well-being, the flourishing, of humans in their forms of association with one another and their material environment. I have just suggested that this equation is not justified.[16] Second, it is necessary to attribute to human beings the capacity to exist in two contrasting states: as merely existing, or surviving, as beings whose "crude," "physical," or "merely animal" needs are met (as mere bearers of the capacity to work, and to physically reproduce that capacity), or, by contrast, as nourishing, as fulfilled, as "fully human."

But the place of the reference to "animal needs," here, and the associated use of the human/animal contrast to sustain the ethical critique of human estrangement, requires a *denial* of this capacity in the animal case. Animals, we must suppose, merely exist. As animals they have merely animal needs and the satisfaction of these needs is both necessary and sufficient for the existence and reproduction of the life of the individual and its species. But if, as we have seen, (some) animals, too, have developmental, learning, species, context, and collective capacities and potentials, then here also it must be possible to distinguish between mere existence on the one hand, and flourishing, well-being, and the fulfillment of diverse potentials on the other. The mere fact of distinctively human historical potentials does not obliterate *either* the ethical distinction between flourishing and merely existing for other animals or its ontological presupposition.

The point here is not just that Marx was simply wrong about animals.[17] It is rather that he was wrong in ways which undermine his own view of the desirability of a changed relationship between humanity and nature in the future communist society. Connectedly, he is also wrong about animals in ways that cut him off from a powerful extension and deepening of his own ethical critique of prevailing (capitalist) modes of appropriation of nature. Moreover, the pathological distortions from the properly human mode of life which Marx attempts to capture in his concept of "estrangement" or "alienation" are in important respects paralleled in the modes of life imposed upon animals by precisely the same structures of social action. The treatment of animals as mere means to external purposes, the forcible fragmentation of their life-activity, and the dissolution of their social bonds with one another are, for example, features of commercial agriculture which have become progressively intensified since Marx's day with each technical reorganization of agricultural production. The ethical critique of such practices should not be seen as an *alternative* to a Marxian critique of modern capitalist forms of labor-discipline, but, rather, an extension and a deepening of it. But Marx's contrast between the human and the animal cuts away the ontological basis for such a critical analysis of forms of suffering shared by both animals and humans who are caught up in a common causal network.

4. Marx's attribution to animals of a fixed and standardized mode of activity in relation to nature and his apparent failure to recognize in any significant way the social life of nonhuman animals are both at work in his use of the phrases "physical need" and "animal need" as if they were equivalent. This suggests a denial of the complexity and diversity of the emotional, psychological, and social lives of other animals. Such a denial renders merely rhetorical Marx's characterization of history as "nature developing into man," and cuts off two significant sources of insight into human nature and history. The first, which would require giving serious theoretical content to the idea of

"nature developing into man," would be an inquiry into the prehistorical origins of the human species and the processes of our differentiation from other primate lineages. The second, in part dependent for its rational justification on the first (i.e., a recognition of the kinship of humans and other animals), would be a comparative psychology and ethology in which what is genuinely distinctive about human beings could be viewed in the light of what is shared between human and nonhuman animals. That these lines of enquiry have a long post-Darwinian history of politically tendentious and methodologically suspect misuses[18] is not a sufficient reason for a wholesale abandonment of the enterprise. While there is certainly plenty of room for legitimate controversy within modern evolutionary theory, it is no longer reasonable to deny the main claims of the evolutionary perspectives in relation to human ancestry in some primate stock and our kinship with contemporary primates. Unless social scientists wish to stand with the flat earthers, the Inquisitors, and the bible-belt creationists, they have no choice but to engage with the questions posed by our animal origins and nature.

AGAINST MARX'S DUALIST VIEW OF HUMAN NATURE

Perhaps, however, the most telling arguments against the dualist aspects of Marx's early work relate to the dualism *within* human nature that follows from the external dualism of the animal and the human. It is characteristic of dualistic approaches, balking at the prospect of a comprehensively idealist view of our nature, to recognize an animal component, layer, or aspect within the human. The human *is* an animal, but an animal with a special something extra which makes all the difference—soul, mind, will, self, reason, and so on. Marx's early writings, as we have seen, still fall within this tradition.

Insofar as humans work only to meet their subsistence needs and do not experience their work as a need in itself, their activity is mere animal activity. Insofar as their leisure activities, their eating and drinking, their "dressing up," and so on are ends in themselves, segregated from the wider species-project, they are mere "animal functions." When the starving man is fed "it would be impossible to say wherein this feeding activity differs from that of animals."[19] This reproduction of the animal/human opposition within the domain of the human involves a sequestering of certain of our needs, powers, functions, and activities as animal, or animal-like, from others (generally more highly valued and assigned a more fundamental ontological status) that are designated "human."

The main objections to this broad strategy for understanding what humans are can be usefully placed into three groups.

1. Those powers, needs, activities, functions (etc.) that fall on the human side of the divide are represented as a self-sufficient, sui generis, autonomous complex, which is thus rendered unintelligible in relation to the rest (the animal side) of human life. But what sense could be made of, for example, human powers of reasoning in abstraction from the bodily needs and activities in which they are exercised? In Marx's own case, the ethical ideal for humanity is a mode of being which integrates the diverse activities of persons within a coherent communal project. Such a notion of integral self-realization remains incompatible with the residual dualism of the *Manuscripts*.

2. Those powers, activities, needs, functions (etc.) which fall on the "animal" side of the division are correspondingly profaned as, perhaps, rather shameful residual features. Their continued, uncomfortably insistent presence, eruptions, and interruptions are demeaning and rob us of the full sense of self-respect to which we feel entitled. A combined dread and contempt for bodily existence and function is barely disguised in much philosophical dualism. It provides grounding and sustenance for the valuation of mental over manual labor, of masculinity ("cultured") over femininity ("natural"), of reason over sentiment, of mind over matter, and of the "civilized" over the "savage." It makes for a culture that is guilt-ridden, fearful, and confused over such fundamental features of the shared human and animal condition as sexuality and death.

3. The dualist philosophical heritage is at work in many of our most problematic contemporary institutional forms and practices. The development of modern health care as a form of organized, high-tech "body mechanics" (at its best) detecting, diagnosing, and correcting defects in the bodily machine, has an unmistakable Cartesian legacy about it. The pertinence of the psychological, emotional, cultural, and socio-economic aspects and contexts of the person to both the causation of and recovery from disease has been widely understood only in recent years.[20] It has yet to gain the central place it deserves in policy disputes and health-care reform. In other areas of public policy, too, a segregation of "basic" (that is, physical) needs from "higher" (emotional, cultural, self-realizing) needs underlies priorities of welfare state provision in such areas as housing, the setting of nutritional standards, and even in education.[21] A great deal of overseas aid policy, too, neglects the cultural, socio-economic, and environmental contexts within which such "basic" needs as food and shelter are met. The sequestering of classes of need from one another, often well motivated, equally often is disastrous in its consequences. Needs that are inseparably interconnected both in the way they are experienced and in the interweaving of their causal conditions of satisfaction are all too often abstractly targeted in single-priority interventions which bring

extended chains of unintended consequences in their wake. The environmental and social cost of the export of "green revolution" technologies to large parts of Asia and Latin America is a case in point.[22]

NATURALISM WITHOUT REDUCTIONISM OR SPECIESISM?

In what remains, I shall offer a sketch for an alternative reading and reconstruction of Marx's early *Manuscripts*, centered on those elements that tell against both philosophical dualism and idealism and that favor, rather, a naturalistic but still not reductionist view of human nature. A view, that is, that gives due place to the specificity and distinctiveness of the human species, but does so without compromising what remains defensible in Marx's assertion that "man is part of nature."

Some of the most promising textual materials for his alternative approach are to be found, not surprisingly perhaps, in the manuscript entitled "Critique of the Hegelian Dialectic and Philosophy as a Whole."

> *Man* is directly a *natural being.* As a natural being and as a living natural being he is on the one hand endowed with *natural powers, vital powers*—he is an *active* natural being. These forces exist in him as tendencies and abilities—as *instincts.* On the other hand, as a natural, corporeal, sensuous, objective being he is a *suffering,* conditioned and limited creature, like animals and plants. That is to say, the *objects* of his instincts exist outside him, *objects* independent of him; yet these objects are *objects* that he *needs*—essential *objects,* indispensable to the manifestation and confirmation of his essential powers. . . . *Hunger* is a natural *need;* it therefore needs a *nature* outside itself, an *object* outside itself, in order to satisfy itself, to be stilled.[23]

In this passage, Marx is asserting the status of humans as natural beings, a status they share with (other) animals and with plants. As natural beings there are three interconnected features which humans share with other living beings. First, they have natural needs whose objects lie outside themselves, independent of them. All living things, for example, have nutritional needs. The objects of these needs—foodstuffs—exist independently of them. Second, all living beings have natural powers which enable them to satisfy these needs, and natural tendencies ("instincts") to exercise them. Third, this need-satisfying activity in relation to external objects is essential to the "confirmation" or "manifestation" of the essential powers of the species.

In other words, interaction with external nature is necessary for the survival of all natural beings. Each species of natural being has its own distinctive mode or pattern of interaction with nature—its own species-life. And finally, (a member of) each species only fully manifests its essential nature—only becomes what it has the potential to be—in virtue of its participation in this distinctive species-life.

"But," Marx goes on to say, "[m]an is not merely a natural being: he is a *human* natural being. That is to say, he is a being for himself."[24] Having begun to speak of human nature in a thoroughly naturalistic way, Marx appears, again, to pull back and re-establish a dualistic opposition, this time between the "human" and the "natural." However, there is no necessity for such a reading. The "human" here can be understood as a qualification, a specification, or subdivision *within* the natural, rather than its opposite. This remains a form of naturalism, in that what humans share with other natural beings is regarded as ontologically fundamental, and is accordingly given priority for purposes of understanding and explaining what humans are and how they act. But it is not a reductionist naturalism in the sense that it allows for a full recognition of the specificity and distinctiveness of humans, their forms of sociability, and their potentials within the order of nature. Whereas dualist and idealist accounts of human nature fix upon features that are held to distinguish us from (other) animals and elaborate their views of human nature upon that basis, a naturalistic approach begins with the common predicament of natural beings and moves from that basis to render intelligible their specific differences in constitution, structure, and modes of life.

Each species has its own characteristic species-life. Organisms can confirm or manifest their essential powers only within the context of their species-life, and so can be said to flourish only when the conditions for the living of the mode of life characteristic of their species are met. For each species, then, we can distinguish conditions for mere organic survival—the meeting of minimal nutritional requirements, protection from predators, and so on—from conditions for flourishing, for the living of the species-life. But *how* this distinction is made, the specific survival-conditions and nourishing-conditions that are identified, will vary from species to species. The empirical determination of such conditions is at least part of the content of the sciences of ethology and ecology.

So far, then, my alternative, non-dualistic reading of Marx's early *Manuscripts* has yielded a significant shift in the conceptual means for dealing with Marx's central theme in this text: the estrangement of labor. Under regimes of private property, conditions which enable the survival of workers are provided but the conditions for them to confirm their powers and potentials in the living of their characteristic species-life are denied to them. A distorted and pathological mode of life is the consequence. This theme can be further specified and elaborated with little if any loss of the ethical power of Marx's critique, but with the double gain that precisely the same framework of analysis can be applied in the critique of the mode of life imposed upon many of the other living species caught up in this distorted mode of human life, and that Marx's highly speculative notion of a distinctively human "species historical" potential is rendered redundant.

A naturalistic specification of human nature, I have suggested, would be a matter of differentiating out and then elaborating our specific features from an initial recognition of the common core of natural beinghood that we share with other living creatures. But this process of differentiation, of saying what is specifically human, can all too easily fall into a dualistic mode. If it becomes centered on a specification of those powers, potentials, requirements, and so forth possessed by humans "over and above" those they share with animals, the approach falls short of naturalism. This is not to deny that there *are* things (reading, writing, talking,[25] composing symphonies, inventing weapons of mass destruction, and so on) that humans and only humans can do. Rather, it is to say that those things that only humans can do are generally to be understood as rooted in the specifically human *ways* of doing things that other animals also do. It is this feature that I want to emphasize as the hallmark of a naturalistic approach.

What this approach might mean in practice can, perhaps, be illustrated by way of a study of Marx's treatment of the concept of need in the *Manuscripts*. As we have seen, Marx speaks variously of "crude," "physical," or "animal" needs, contrasting them with "human needs." In some passages it seems as though human needs constitute a separate, *sui generis* class of needs, set over and above our "animal" subsistence needs and peculiar to us as humans. We may distinguish two broad types of human need in this sense. First, what might be called self-realization needs:

> The *rich* human being is simultaneously the human being in need of a totality of human manifestations of life—a man in whom his own realization exists as an inner necessity, as *need.*[26]

Marx seems to suggest that such inner needs for self-realization, for the fulfilment of potential, are possible only for self-conscious beings, and even then are only fully acquired on the basis of an extended process of historical development.

The second class of distinctively human needs is similarly linked with our status as self-conscious beings, but not necessarily with our historicity. Marx speaks of the elements of our external environment ("plants, animals, stones, air, light. etc.")[27] as constituting "spiritual nourishment" insofar as they are objects of human science and art. Over and above the need (which they share with other animals) to physically appropriate nature, humans have spiritual needs to aesthetically and cognitively appropriate nature. This reading is strongly suggested by such passages as this:

> It (the animal) produces only under the dominion of immediate physical need, whilst man produces even when he is free from physical need and only truly produces in freedom therefrom.[28]

There are, it seems, two possible kinds of human practice in relation to nature: one, physical-need satisfaction, which we share with animals; the other, spiritual (aesthetic, cognitive) need-satisfaction, which is special to us and constitutes production in the "true" sense. This distinction reappears in the later works as a distinction between the realms of "necessity" and of "freedom."

However, an alternative, naturalistic reading of the passage is also possible. To qualify as properly human, it is necessary not that production have no relation to the satisfaction of physical need, but rather that it should not be performed under the *dominion* of *immediate* physical need. Leaving aside Marx's apparent equation of the animal with the "not-properly-human," Marx can plausibly be read as making a distinction not so much between practices that satisfy different needs, as between different modes of satisfaction of common needs. The satisfaction of aesthetic and cognitive needs does not *require* the performance of further practice, over and above the practices through which physical needs are met. In a fully human or "true" practice of production, physical needs would be met in a *way* that was aesthetically and cognitively satisfying. For at least this sub-class of "human" needs, then, we can say that they are not a sui generis complex of requirements, over and above the physical needs, but that they are, rather, requirements which bear on the manner of *experiencing, identifying, and satisfying* the physical needs. Let's take the physical need for nutrition as an example.[29] This need is common to both humans and other animals. Some non-human animals, but not all, have sufficient psychological and behavioral similarity to ourselves for us to speak non-metaphorically and unequivocally of them as experiencing hunger and searching for and consuming food. For all such animals the objects and substances which can count as food are a subset only of the total range of objects and substances that would satisfy their nutritional requirements. Moreover, only some modes of acquiring and consuming these objects and substances are characteristic of the mode of life of the species concerned, or are activities in which their specific powers and potentials are exercised or fulfilled. The feeding activities actually engaged in by such animals are the overdetermined outcome of inherited predispositions, learning, and environmental opportunity structures.

All this is true of humans and many other species of animals, especially mammals and birds. So, in the passage quoted above, Marx's parallel between the feeding activity of the "starving man" and that of animals is undermined. Neither for humans nor for other species can we simply equate the mere satisfaction of nutritional requirements with the feeding activity characteristic of the species. The distorted, or pathological, relation to food induced by starvation in humans is not an animal or animal-like relation to food, but a specific distortion or pathology of *human* feeding activity. But this mistaken equation of the pathologically human with the animal aside, Marx's comment is susceptible of an illuminating and naturalistic interpretation. What makes the relation of the starving man to food a pathological one is that the object of hunger exists *merely* as food; its sole significance is that its consumption will satisfy the hunger. Such feeding activity is performed under the domination of immediate need. This feeding activity is means/ends activity, not activity with its own intrinsic satisfaction. It is also activity in which the aesthetic, cognitive, and spiritual dimensions of human activity are missing.

On this naturalistic reading, then, what makes the difference between a fully or "properly" human way of satisfying hunger, and a less-than-human or pathological way of satisfying the same need, is the presence or absence of intrinsic cognitive and aesthetic satisfactions in the activity through which the need is satisfied. We can now get closer to answering the question, what are the enabling conditions for the satisfaction of hunger to take a properly human form? In addition to the availability of nutritional items in the environment and the technical powers on the part of persons to appropriate them, these enabling conditions must also include appropriate aesthetic and cognitive rules and resources.

To say that there is an aesthetic, cognitive, normative, spiritual—in other words cultural—dimension to the way in which humans meet their physical needs, and that this is indispensable to their meeting of these needs in a "properly" human way, might look like a covert return to dualism. But this is not so. The key point, here, is that the starting point for the analysis is the recognition of a need which is common to both humans and nonhuman animals. The specification of the distinctively human then proceeds not by identifying a further, supervenient class of needs possessed only by humans, but rather by identifying the species-specific *way in which* humans meet the needs they share with other species. This leaves open the door to making further illuminating contrasts and comparisons between humans and other species, and it avoids the effacement of the manifold differences among nonhuman animals in their ways of satisfying their physical needs.

But what of those needs—self-realization needs—which appear to be peculiar to self-conscious and historical beings? Again, it is not required by the form of naturalism I want to advocate that the reality of such needs should be denied. Rather, the commitment is to viewing them as *in some sense* consequential upon those needs that are common to natural beings, or upon the species-specific ways in which those common needs are met. Explanatory strategies in relation to such supervenient needs would be to make them intelligible in terms of the (ontologically) more fundamental common needs. Marx's attempt to explain the fragmentations and distortions of human personal and social life under capitalism as consequences of a pathological relationship to nature is clearly one such strategy that would be defended. What Freud does with the concept of sublimation is another clear case of an attempt to explain in a non-reductionist way the rootedness of some distinctively human activities (aesthetic and scientific, for example) in needs and propensities (sexuality and affectivity) that we share with other species.

To conclude, the suffering imposed on other species, the fragmentation and distortions of their lives associated with our current system of social and economic life, has much in common with the plight of many humans under these relations. If we recognize the continuities between humans and other species in our social and psychological as well as organic needs, then the ethical case for transformation of those relations is clear: liberation of nonhuman animals as well as full human emancipation require it.[30] Other animals may be sufficiently like human beings to be properly considered as moral subjects and as the bearers of biographies. Ethical considerations must therefore enter into our dealings with them. It is evil to continue to treat them merely as instruments or resources to be exploited for specifically human purposes.

5

Reflections on the Prospects for a Non-Speciesist Marxism

By Renzo Llorente

I.

"'Animal Liberation,'" Peter Singer once observed, "may sound more like a parody of other liberation movements than a serious objective."[1] If this is true of animal liberation per se, then the topic of Marxism and animal liberation will surely strike many as the very apotheosis of parody, as the seeming absurdity of such a juxtaposition is surpassed only by its utter predictability. Yet, however justified one's initial skepticism, there are in fact a number of affinities between the two traditions of Marxism and animal liberation,[2] as Ted Benton, for one, has argued in his book *Natural Relations*.[3] However, since the publication of Benton's book more than 15 years ago, scant progress has been made in the attempt to link these two emancipatory perspectives, despite a burgeoning literature on animal liberation and animal rights (not to mention the continuing efforts by writers of a Marxist persuasion to unite Marxism with other progressive movements). A glance at Angus Taylor's survey of the literature and debates concerning animal liberation, *Animals and Ethics*,[4] proves highly instructive in this regard. A comprehensive inventory of the issues and controversies surrounding the question of animal liberation, the book's very thoroughness attests to the dearth of serious study concerning the affinities between animal liberation and Marxism, or socialist thought generally. At the same time, Taylor's account ends up highlighting, albeit unwittingly, some of these very affinities, whether in discussing the radicalism of animal liberation's emancipatory pretensions (most notably on account of its attempted redefinition of the moral community), the sheer number and scope of activities and institutions vulnerable to its critique (i.e., implicated in the practices that it condemns), or the likely protractedness of its struggle (which recalls the assumption, endorsed by most radicals, that the achievement of an enduring socialism will require a long, multi-generational enterprise).[5] In addition, Taylor explicitly endorses the view that "the animal-liberation movement is unlikely to succeed in its goals unless it joins forces with other movements challenging the assumptions of industrial society."[6] In short, Taylor's study in effect provides the grounds or rationale for the project of uniting Marxism and animal liberation, while confirming the near nonexistence of attempts to do so heretofore.[7]

In the hope of reviving and advancing the project inaugurated by Benton and encouraged by Taylor's study, I should like to consider the grounds for a rapprochement, both theoretical and practical, between Marxism and the animal liberation movement. Needless to say, given the scope of this topic, in this chapter I can attempt little more than a preliminary exploration of a few fundamental issues. With this aim in mind, in the first section below I examine a number of factors and considerations, including some alleged antagonisms between these two traditions, that appear to explain the indifference of most Marxists, and leftists in general, toward animal liberation. I argue that all of the alleged incompatibilities are largely spurious, while leftists' other common misgivings concerning animal liberation all reduce to speciesism, which is, I suggest, indefensible. I also argue that nothing commits Marxists in particular, or leftists generally, to speciesism. In the following section, I review some of the fairly obvious, but nonetheless significant, parallels between Marxism and animal liberation. In the last of the paper's major sections, I defend the claim that we find a basic affinity between Marxism and animal liberation on a more fundamental level in the *radical egalitarian* orientation that defines both perspectives. The chapter concludes by suggesting that in addition to the other arguments advanced in the chapter, the commitment to moral progress present in Marxism provides good reason for Marxists to lend their support to animal liberation, and that this is in fact what they ought to do.

II.

There can be little doubt that Marxists, and leftists in general, have paid scant attention to the contemporary animal liberation movement since the advent of the latter in the mid-1970s. Such neglect appears especially conspicuous in light of Marxists' interest in (and efforts to engage with) many of the other "new social movements"—for instance, the environmental movement, the peace and disarmament movement, the women's movement, the anti-nuclear movement, and the lesbian and gay liberation movement—that began to coalesce at roughly the same time. Indeed, it would seem that most on the Left do not even view animal liberation *as* a new social movement,[8] even though many activists of a broadly socialist persuasion have assimilated some of the concerns central to animal liberation, such as the condemnation of factory farming and the corresponding ethical concern with food consumption habits. But whether or not this is the case, the animal liberation movement, and the philosophical literature devoted to its issues and concerns, has by and large been ignored by leftists, including Marxists,[9] or else been treated disparagingly: it is not insignificant that the pioneering animal liberation activist Henry Spira was first introduced to the movement through a dismissive treatment of it in a Marxist journal.[10] (The converse of Left indifference to animal liberation, on the other hand, is probably relatively unusual; that is, it seems to be the case that supporters of animal liberation also generally support more traditional social justice causes.[11]) How are we to explain this indifference to animal liberation among people who otherwise oppose and challenge exploitation, oppression, and domination, an indifference which suggests that many on the Left do indeed continue to regard animal liberation as "a parody of other liberation movements"?

Surely the most common reason among Marxists, and leftists generally, for neglecting the cause of animal liberation is the same reason that most people, whatever their political persuasion, continue to display indifference toward this movement: a more or less conscious adherence to *speciesism*, which in its most general sense can be defined as discrimination on the basis of species membership. That is to say, we practice speciesism whenever we treat the interests of other species with less consideration or respect—less, that is, than we would accord comparable *human* interests—merely because the bearers of those interests are not human beings. (When it is a matter of interests that human beings do not have, speciesism characteristically takes the form of ignoring those interests altogether, or granting them only the most minimal consideration.) Among those whose indifference to animal liberation is motivated mainly by speciesism, it is useful to distinguish, following a classification proposed by James Rachels, between those who adhere to "*unqualified speciesism*" and those who adhere to "qualified speciesism." According to Rachels, if one adheres to *unqualified speciesism*, "the bare fact that an individual is a member of a certain species, unsupplemented by any other consideration, is enough to make a difference in how that individual should be treated." For the adherent of *qualified speciesism*, on the other hand, "species alone is not regarded as morally significant," yet "species-membership is correlated with *other* differences that *are* significant" (e.g., "Humans, it might be said, are in a special moral category because they are rational, autonomous agents").[12]

Whereas unqualified speciesists believe that animals are entitled to little or no moral consideration by virtue of their non-membership in the class of *Homo sapiens*, those who profess a qualified speciesism maintain that it is animals' lack of certain crucial abilities or qualities which excludes them from moral consideration, abilities or qualities that are distinctive of human beings and possessed by nearly all of them.

Before addressing the question of speciesism in more detail, let us consider some of the other sources of Left or Marxist indifference to animal liberation, that is, reasons which seem not to be of an outright speciesist nature. One of the most important reasons no doubt derives from the conviction that there exists a fundamental incongruity or incompatibility between human emancipation and animal liberation, as though the interests of animals were without exception contrary to the interests of (socio-economically) oppressed humans, and in particular those of the working class. Notice that this view need not be motivated by speciesism. That is, one might hold that there are in fact many *genuine*, truly insurmountable conflicts of interest between animals and humans and that careful consideration of these cases establishes that, in every instance, human interests should take precedence because of the *actual* characteristics of the humans and animals involved. This reason for neglecting animal liberation proves largely groundless, however, for it rests on a dubious premise: as a matter of fact, there seem to be few genuine, major conflicts between the interests of oppressed humans and those of oppressed animals. As Singer has written, "We do not have to sacrifice anything essential, because in our normal life there is no serious clash of interests between human and nonhuman animals."[13] To be sure, Singer, and others who insist on the absence of any "serious clash of interests," may well exaggerate somewhat, especially if we bear in mind that genuine advances toward animal liberation, such as the total elimination of factory farming, would certainly adversely affect some human interests in the short run—indeed, interests of special concern to Marxists. After all, the abolition of this method of food production would undoubtedly create some economic upheaval, including pervasive unemployment for workers employed by the factory-farm industry as well as those employed by the numerous other industries and commercial operations dependent upon it (producers of farm supplies, food distributors, slaughterhouses, the meatpacking industry, and so on). Still, insofar as the adverse economic impact of eliminating the major causes of animal exploitation and human-induced harms—factory farming, most forms of animal experimentation, the use of animals for entertainment in circuses, bullfights, rodeos, and so on—would be mainly *short-term*, Singer's claim seems plausible enough.[14] Unless one is willing to claim that, say, the introduction of computerized automation in industry is, or a reduction in weapons production would be, a bad thing because these measures generate some temporary unemployment, it is difficult to maintain that animal liberation entails harm to *essential* human interests.

Another reason for Left indifference to animal liberation, and likewise one that need not necessarily be motivated by speciesism, is the limited time and energy of activists: since one cannot possibly devote one's efforts to every worthy cause, choices must be made and priorities set. The trouble with this sort of justification for a radical's indifference is that it rests on a false dilemma, given the very minor cost of adopting certain important measures, and in general the ease with which most of our duties in this regard can be discharged.[15] For, as Mark Rowlands points out, the measures that animal liberation requires are essentially *negative obligations*—"obligations *not* to eat meat, to *not* wear fur or leather, to *not* use products tested on animals, etc. . . . [While] fulfilling positive obligations takes time, fulfilling negative obligations generally does not."[16]

Yet another reason for Marxists' neglect of animal liberation may stem from the tactical political concern not to alienate workers by championing causes which may prove quite alien to their lifestyle or sensibility. It is a concern that recalls the attitude of certain traditionally minded leftists in the 1960s who condemned various practices, habits, attitudes, and so on of radical, countercultural youth on the grounds that a sympathetic tolerance of such things would alienate working-class Americans. Yet just as this belief proved to be short-sighted—most working-class Americans eventually came to accept much of the new socio-cultural sensibility, and it is probably safe to assume that those who did not (or have not) would never be receptive to radical economic measures, either—it seems rather doubtful that a defense of animal liberation will tend, in the long run, to alienate many workers.

Finally, it would be an error to ignore altogether another source of indifference, one of some importance insofar as the classic texts continue to shape the mindset—and not just the politics—of many Marxist militants: the views of Marx and Engels themselves.[17] While Marx and Engels never occupied themselves with questions bearing on the moral status of animals, their works do contain a few random remarks which convey an unambiguously dismissive attitude toward those who devoted themselves to the cause of animal welfare. Recall, for example, the passage from the *Communist Manifesto* in which Marx and Engels, in the course of delineating "Conservative, or Bourgeois, Socialism," lump "members of societies for the prevention of cruelty to animals" together with "organisers of charity, temperance fanatics, [and] hole-and-corner reformers of every imaginable kind."[18] We might also note Engels' derisive reference, in a very similar vein, to vegetarians and "anti-vivisectionists" in "On the History of Early Christianity."[19] At a deeper level, Benton has elucidated "the use of the human/animal contrast as Marx's central device in the ethical critique of the estrangement of labour under regimes of private property."[20] Which is to say, a concept as central to Marx's thought as the concept of "estrangement," or "alienation," turns out to be predicated on a division between human and nonhuman animals.

As I have tried to demonstrate, several of the common reasons for Marxists' (and leftists') typical indifference to animal liberation are either unsound or else reduce to speciesism. This conclusion prompts two questions: is speciesism morally defensible? Is there anything that commits Marxism to speciesism? I will not be addressing the first question here. Instead, I will simply state that I consider speciesism untenable, and note that a cogent defense of speciesism has yet to be offered.[21] Of course, if speciesism does ultimately prove indefensible, then Marxists ought to reject it, cleansing their views and positions of any speciesist presuppositions. Yet for our present purposes it will suffice to address the second question and establish that, regardless of whether or not some modified form of speciesism is ultimately shown to be sound, there are no elements essential to Marxism that commit this doctrine, or its adherents, to speciesism.

Whether we focus on more or less practical and/or political considerations or attend to more foundational issues, there is, I submit, nothing that commits Marxism to speciesism. As for the former, there are, as I have suggested, no essential clashes of interest between those who are the victims of class oppression and those who suffer from species oppression. Crudely put, a defense of animals' interests is by no means detrimental to the interests of the working class, for it does not adversely affect the economic interests of this class, nor does it frustrate the attainment of its political objectives, nor does it serve to reinforce the structural stability of capitalism.

On a more fundamental theoretical level, the grounds for assuming that Marxism need not entail speciesism are even clearer. The main reason is that a consistent materialism—particularly if it is informed by an evolutionary understanding of human beings—militates against the assumption of a radical opposition between human beings and all other species, an assumption that is normally one of speciesism's essential premises. To be sure, Benton's study documents how, in one sense, speciesism underpins and structures Marx's analysis of estrangement. After noting that "Marx's contrast between a fulfilled . . . human life, and a dehumanized, estranged existence can also be applied in an analysis of the conditions imposed by intensive rearing regimes in the case of non-human animals," Benton points out that "the 'humanist' philosophical framing of Marx's concept of estrangement renders extension of that analysis beyond the human case literally unthinkable."[22] At the same time, he shows that Marx's account also contains numerous passages acknowledging and emphasizing an awareness of the human–animal continuum, an outlook that is, needless to say, more consistent with his professed materialism, not to mention modern evolutionary thought. In short, to the extent that a certain speciesism is constitutive of Marx's (or any rate the early Marx's) own thinking, Marx's views are inconsistent with his own commitment to a thoroughgoing materialism, which must acknowledge the kinship, with all its implications, between human life and other forms of animal life.

III.

My remarks in the preceding section were intended to show that there are hardly any grounds for the view that Marxism is essentially incompatible with, let alone antithetical to, animal liberation. This is, of course, to make a *negative* case for fusing the two movements, since it amounts to insisting merely on the absence of impediments to such a fusion. Yet one can also make a case for fusing, or in any case linking, socialism and animal liberation in light of their natural affinities as social movements. Indeed, not only is it the case that Marxists and animal liberationists both denounce and oppose domination, exploitation, and oppression; in their analyses, they draw our attention to structures and patterns of domination, exploitation, and oppression that often prove remarkably similar, just as they tend to reveal similar methods for obscuring or masking these injustices. Moreover, it is clear that there also exist striking affinities between Marxism and animal liberation in terms of the sheer radicalism and scope of their respective emancipatory pretensions. While we cannot explore any of these similarities at great length (and I do not wish to imply that such a list by any means exhausts the noteworthy parallels), it is worthwhile to consider them briefly.

As just noted, we find one of the most striking parallels between animal liberation and Marxism in the fact that the structures and patterns of systemic exploitation, domination, and oppression that they confront prove remarkably similar. Consider, for example, animal liberationists' central concern with the form of raising and managing livestock commonly known as factory farming. What motivates those concerned with animal welfare to condemn the practice of factory farming are the countless harms endured by the animals raised in this manner, harms that include more or less extreme constraints on their normal development, functioning, and behavior, as well as experiences of acute—frequently unrelieved—physical pain. It is not often appreciated, however, that their strictures against factory farming, especially when spelled out in more concrete detail, bear a great resemblance to Marxists' objections to the organization of labor within a paradigmatic capitalist factory. As Benton rightly remarks, "a good deal of the content of Marx's contrast between a fulfilled or emancipated human life, and a dehumanized, estranged existence can also be applied in an analysis of the conditions imposed by intensive rearing regimes [i.e., 'factory farming'] in the case of non-human animals."[23] Moreover, the cause of these injustices proves to be the same in both cases. Indeed, *The Agricultural Dictionary* defines "factory farming" as "a type of farming which is usually operated on a large scale according to modern business efficiency standards, solely for monetary profit."[24] In this regard, the most noteworthy difference between the cases of exploited workers and exploited animals surely lies in the *degree* of exploitation. As Benton notes in an article coauthored with Simon Redfearn, "The Politics of Animal Rights—Where Is the Left?" "[f]arm animals have become objects of economic calculation and technical manipulation, like any other material input factor,"[25] a fact which those engaged in factory farming openly acknowledge. For example, a brochure issued by the New South Wales Department of Agriculture tells us that "a piggery must be imagined as being similar to a factory with raw goods (breeding stock and feed) going in one end and the finished article (pork and bacon) coming out the other."[26] Given such structural similarities, it is little wonder that the same concepts prove applicable in analyzing the oppression of both workers and animals.

Another significant parallel between Marxism and the animal liberation movement arises from the fact that similar methods and techniques conceal, and help to sustain, the oppression of "intensively reared" farm animals and exploited workers. In other words, there is a patent similarity with respect to the methods, or operations, that inhibit awareness of the injustices, that is, the morally unacceptable conditions underpinning our system of food production and the provision of many consumer goods and services. Marxists must of course often grapple with the complexity of the production and distribution process and marketing techniques which serve to obscure, or preclude altogether, an appreciation of the harms endured by workers—an unwholesome work environment, inadequate pay, the complete absence of worker autonomy, a crippling division of labor, strict regimentation of the work routine, and so forth—in the creation of many goods and services that we enjoy, and whose ready availability we take for granted. In this connection, Frederic Jameson has written of "the 'effacement of the traces of production' from the object itself, from the commodity thereby produced. . . . [I]t suggests the kind of guilt people are freed from if they are not able to remember the work that went into their toys and furnishings."[27] By the same token, it is clear that, as Benton and Redfearn observe, "the institutional forms and the marketing images of the meat industry conspire to ensure that the 'process disappears into the product' still more decisively than is the case with all other commodities. Increasingly the consumers of meat buy it in highly processed forms, packaged in such a way as to offer as few reminders as possible of its status as a part of the corpse of a dead animal."[28] Needless to say, in both cases these obstacles to understanding, these barriers to transparency, also constitute considerable impediments to liberation.

A third essential similarity between Marxism and animal liberation concerns their respective emancipatory pretensions and the radicalism of their challenges to existing society. As for the emancipatory pretensions of animal liberation, it is worth noting that, as in the case of Marxism, it is often claimed that animal liberation transcends the sectional interests of one oppressed group, that it would serve to eliminate other kinds of oppression as well—namely, various human oppressions. To use Singer's expression, "Animal Liberation Is Human Liberation Too."[29] Singer's point, at least in the context in which this particular phrase appears, is that the universal adoption of vegetarianism—an essential measure in the opinion of practically all animal liberationists—would redound to the benefit of human beings (and hence workers) as well as animals, given the massive waste involved in feeding grains to livestock in order to produce meat[30] (quite aside from any benefits of global vegetarianism for human health and the environment). Yet the claim that animal liberation would bring human liberation in its train can, and has, been construed and defended in at least two other senses as well. First, some liberationists insist that animal liberation promises a *gustatory* liberation, in that an end to the psychologico-cultural dependence on a carnocentric diet makes possible the emergence of—and frees us to experience and satisfy—new tastes and appetites. In this sense, a vegetarian lifestyle, so the argument goes, promises an enrichment of our lives, rather than a form of impoverishment or sacrifice.[31] It is, in effect, an argument that is analogous to one sometimes made with the aim of consolidating progressive men's support for feminism. The advance of feminism, on this view, benefits men, too—indeed, *liberates* them—insofar as it entails a negation of traditional gender roles, and thereby enables men to act and live in ways that were previously unavailable to them.

The other argument to the effect that animal liberation constitutes human liberation appeals to an intuitive notion of moral improvement: inclusion of (at least some) animals within the moral community and due recognition of our moral obligations toward them would, according to this argument, enhance our moral caliber, enable us to achieve greater ethical consistency, and perhaps even help us to reach a higher stage of humanity. Indeed, Henry Salt, one of the first people to explicitly link the embrace of animal liberation to a commitment to progressive social reform, placed considerable emphasis on this particular argument in his classic *Animals' Rights*, published more than a century ago. "Our true civilisation, our race-progress, our *humanity* (in the best sense of the term)," writes Salt, "are concerned in this development; it is ourselves, our own vital instincts, that we wrong, when we trample on the rights of the fellow-beings, human or animal, over whom we chance to hold jurisdiction."[32]

A final similarity worth mentioning is the fact that animal liberation, like Marxism, would plainly entail a profound transformation of society, owing to the redefinition of the moral community that it proposes. As Steven Sapontzis writes, "Animals are the most extensively and thoroughly exploited group on earth. Consequently, liberating animals would have the largest impact on our lives of any moral reform movement to date."[33] Sapontzis' claim is hardly an overstatement: a major change in the moral status that we accord to many types of animals, with the corresponding redefinition of our duties toward them, would obviously produce a radical transformation of countless habits, customs, laws, institutions and so forth. The widespread adoption of vegetarianism alone would require considerable changes in individuals' lifestyles, to say nothing of the broader socio-economic restructuring that would need to take place.[34]

This radicalism is surely one reason, and not the least important, that animal liberation is perceived by many as threatening, even subversive, in a manner that is reminiscent of the way that the prospect of socialist revolution produces unease even among many who would stand to benefit most from it. Indeed, it is probably the case that a commitment to animal liberation, with the adoption of moral vegetarianism that it usually involves, arouses greater animus and/or incomprehension among one's (non-liberationist) peers than, say, the defense of radical left-wing political views in front of those peers who happen to be conservative. This is unsurprising if we bear in mind various considerations, which are worth noting briefly.

To begin with, complicity with the practices condemned by animal liberationists is more difficult to ignore, deny, or conceal, given that so many mundane yet essential activities (e.g., meals) are based in obvious ways on the ruthless exploitation of animals. Moreover, it is far easier to radically diminish one's implication in animal exploitation through simple lifestyle choices (diet, purchasing habits, etc.) than to reduce one's implication in other systemic forms of group oppression (along class or gender lines, for example), where our role in maintaining and perpetuating the oppression is more indeterminate and ambiguous, and certainly appears less direct; consequently, a person is more likely to react in a defensive or resentful manner if we somehow highlight her role, however modest, in sustaining the oppression of animals. Also, the moral reform implied by a commitment to animal liberation involves a series of measures that most people identify with a retrograde development, even a de-modernization of sorts, at least insofar as they require that certain "privileges" or "gains" that are often construed as hallmarks of development and progress—abundant, high-quality meat in one's diet, for example, or the availability of a variety of leather goods—be voluntarily renounced. As if these factors were not already enough to generate apprehension and hostility among many who have not yet embraced animal liberation, let us not forget that a commitment to animal liberation requires us to rethink and substantially alter certain activities, such as meals, that are usually thought of as pre-political and morally neutral; accordingly, the demands of an animal liberation advocate are likely to be perceived as particularly alienating: she seems to be calling into question and politicizing activities and relationships that are the basis for some of our most basic bonds with one another.[35] Finally, we must not forget that most people still assume that animals, unlike oppressed human beings, do not even form a part of the moral community, and hence to demand a certain level of moral consideration for animals will no doubt sound bizarre, even vaguely threatening, to their ears.

IV.

In the preceding section I mentioned some of the most noteworthy affinities or, to use Benton's language, complementarities,[36] between Marxism and animal liberation at a somewhat superficial level. What I now wish to argue is that there also exists a much more fundamental, normative affinity between Marxism and animal liberation, one that explains the opposition to domination, exploitation, and oppression that characterizes both movements. This normative affinity consists, I submit, in a commitment, central to both Marxism and animal liberation, to *radical egalitarianism*. In saying that both movements or doctrines rest on radical egalitarian foundations I do not necessarily mean to claim that the underlying egalitarian principle is the same in both cases. However, I do indeed contend that the respective egalitarian principles are not only compatible, but also in some sense akin to one another.

While various theoretical currents coexist within the animal liberation movement, it is fair to say that most of those who espouse animal liberation either appeal directly and explicitly to the principle of *equal consideration of interests*, or else proceed from a framework which could readily incorporate this principle. (To be sure, it is also true that animal liberationists sometimes appeal to the far more basic precept of non-maleficence—"Do not cause harm"—along with, or even instead of, this principle[37]; but here I wish to focus on the more refined and specific grounds for their defense of animals' welfare.) It is a principle that, as David D. DeGrazia puts it, "require[s] giving equal moral weight to the relevantly similar interests of humans and animals."[38] Accordingly, for one who adheres to the principle of equal consideration of interests, similar interests, if affected in roughly the same way (adjusting for the differences between the bearers of those interests), will be accorded the same moral significance.[39] By the same token, dissimilar interests may furnish grounds for dissimilar treatment, although the interests themselves must nevertheless be given equal consideration. Thus, an interest in avoiding pain and suffering, for example, should, according to this principle, be given equal consideration with other such interests, whether or not the bearer of the interest happens to be a human being. Hence, if two beings are subjected to levels of pain that, given their respective physical constitutions, amount to comparable levels of distress, the moral evil attaching to the pain inflicted ought to be reckoned roughly the same in both cases. In any event, it is clearly appropriate to regard the "equal consideration of interests" principle as an expression of one type of radical egalitarianism, since this principle enjoins an enormous expansion of the moral community, requiring as it does that we consider the interests of all beings affected by an action or policy, regardless of their species membership. Thus, insofar as this principle underpins animal liberation, it is correct to say that animal liberation is based on a kind of radical egalitarianism.

As for Marxism, the commitment to a form of radical egalitarianism is also fundamental, albeit less explicit. Indeed, G. A. Cohen—who ranks equality with community and self-realization as core Marxist values—is surely correct in remarking that "all classical Marxists believed in some kind of equality, even if many would have refused to acknowledge that they believed in it and none, perhaps, could have stated precisely what principle of equality he believed in."[40] As the scope of this paper hardly allows for a proper treatment of Marxist egalitarianism or the controversies regarding Marx's own, apparently ambiguous, attitude toward equality,[41] I will confine myself to discussing two passages that illustrate Marx and Engels' commitment to equality, and one of which formulates a principle of equality comparable to the "equal consideration of interests" principle. (The radical character of Marxist egalitarianism will become evident below.)

The first avowal of egalitarianism that I have in mind is the well-known passage from *Anti-Dühring* in which Engels claims that "the real content of the proletarian demand for equality is the demand for the *abolition of classes*. Any demand for equality which goes beyond that, of necessity passes into absurdity."[42] A state of classlessness would, it seems to me, plainly constitute a form of radical egalitarianism, for, besides offering a far more profound equality than the standard alternative conceptions of political and social equality, such a social order would be most likely to yield the rough equality of condition conventionally associated with the term "radical egalitarianism." Indeed, it is these profoundly egalitarian ramifications of classlessness—along with the norm of fairness that classlessness presupposes and embodies—that prompted Kai Nielsen to remark, in response to doubts about Marx and

Engels' commitment to equality, that "unless we want to attribute a very extensive confusion to Marx and Engels, we cannot say that they valued classlessness and did not value equality as a goal."[43]

The second passage that I wish to cite as illustrating the Marxist commitment to egalitarianism is the famous slogan that appears in the *Critique of the Gotha Program*: "From each according to his ability, to each according to his needs!"[44] While Allen Wood, for one, doubts whether this proposition reflects any basic endorsement of equality per se,[45] it seems to me far more reasonable to interpret it as an essentially egalitarian slogan, for the reasons that Nielsen cites. The principle, notes Nielsen, enjoins that "[w]e are *all* to be treated equally in that way. The desideratum is that for each and every one of us our needs are to be satisfied. We cannot rightly or fairly ignore *anyone* here. This is to give expression (in a partial way) of what it is to have a society of equals."[46] Even if one concedes the basic egalitarianism underlying the *Critique*'s dictum, however, it is easy to overlook its similarity to "the equal consideration of interests" principle. Yet this similarity appears clear once we realize that "needs," in the sense relevant to Marx's slogan, are best understood as "general essential interests."[47] Therefore, to insist that the treatment of a given individual is to be determined in accordance with his needs is to say, in effect, that the treatment of a given individual is to be determined in accordance with certain interests that the individual has. If, in addition, Nielsen is correct in maintaining that Marx's principle means that "we are *all* to be treated equally in that way," then this principle in fact proves quite similar to the "equal consideration of interests" principle.

But to the extent that the latter part of the principle proclaimed in the *Critique of the Gotha Program* differs from the "equal consideration of interests principle," could it, too, be applied in a non-speciesist manner? Benton argues that there is in fact "no ontological obstacle to its extension beyond species boundaries,"[48] and he would seem to be right. Nonhuman animals plainly have needs—some of which are of course comparable to human needs—and it is relatively unproblematic to identify and satisfy many of these needs (which would generally entail merely negative duties on the part of humans). In short, as with the "equal consideration of interests" principle, there is no reason not to apply the precept "to each according to his needs" to nonhuman animals as well as to human beings; in both cases the restriction to human beings in the application of this principle turns out to be morally arbitrary, for the restriction is based on criteria which are themselves morally irrelevant. Consequently, if we consider the principle "From each according to his ability, to each according to his needs!" an essential element of Marxism, there are additional grounds for assuming that Marxism need not rest on any form of speciesism.

V.

At the end of the last section, and in section II, I claimed that there is nothing in the basic structure or outlook of Marxism that commits it to speciesism. This is a relatively weak claim, but there are in fact good grounds for making a much stronger claim, namely, that certain considerations actually incline Marxism to an anti-speciesist position. By way of conclusion, let us briefly examine some of these considerations.

In a familiar passage in *Anti-Dühring*, Engels remarks,

> The seizure of the means of production by society puts an end to commodity production. . . . Anarchy in social production is replaced by conscious organisation on a planned basis. The struggle for individual existence comes to an end. And at this point, in a certain sense, man finally cuts himself off from the animal world, leaves the conditions of animal existence behind him and enters conditions which are really human.[49]

Engels' main point, of course, is that with the advent of socialism, human beings will be able, for the first time, to take control of their own destiny and so truly free themselves—likewise for the first time—from the domination by unconscious forces and blind necessity, which have conditioned and constrained their existence up to now and prevented human history from amounting to anything more than, in Marx's words, "the prehistory of human society."[50] The passage might therefore be read, especially in light of the reference to the "animal kingdom," as furnishing grounds for the endorsement of speciesism in the post-capitalist era, since in at least one sense this would be the first time that there would exist a clear demarcation between humans and other animals, the first time that we truly transcend our, as it were, *contingent animality*. At the same time, if we bear in mind Engels' own claim elsewhere in *Anti-Dühring* to the effect that "a really human morality" "becomes possible only at a stage of society which has not only overcome class contradictions but has even forgotten them in practical life,"[51] we might just as plausibly construe the passage cited as pointing to a *transcendence* of speciesism. For the latter passage makes clear that one of the important ways in which every human being "leaves the conditions of animal existence behind him and enters conditions which are really human"—or, as another translation puts it, "emerges from mere animal conditions of existence into really human ones"[52]—has to do with her moral capacity. Let us assume that by a "really human morality" (*wirklich menschliche Moral*) Engels means a morality that not only reflects unfettered moral agency but also exemplifies morally praiseworthy traits and dispositions; that is, let us assume that in this context "human" is nearly synonymous with "humane"—"marked by compassion, sympathy, or consideration for humans or animals" (Merriam-Webster's Collegiate Dictionary), and thus means something like "worthy of human beings" in a moral sense. In short, let us assume that the emergence of "a really human morality" amounts to substantial *moral progress*.[53] If this is the case, one would expect that the successor to a class-skewed morality should be a moral outlook which radically enlarges the moral community and the scope of our moral obligations, just as moral progress over the ages is often depicted as an "expanding circle" of moral consideration,[54] and much in the way that successive advances in political emancipation (i.e., the extension of basic rights to previously disenfranchised groups—slaves, religious minorities, women, etc.) have produced corresponding enlargements of the political community, along with increased political obligations on the part of the state. In sum, if moral progress requires the elimination of speciesism and the establishment of a classless society will facilitate or engender substantial moral progress, then we should expect a classless society to develop a moral outlook devoid of the speciesism that has characterized nearly all moral codes and attitudes throughout history.

Let us hope that in the future Marxists will take their inspiration from the latter interpretation of Engels' remarks, and that they will come to appreciate that the animal liberation movement is, for reasons discussed in this paper, anything but a "bourgeois diversion." If Marxism as a whole evolves in this direction, incorporating a concern for oppressed and exploited animals into its theoretical and political outlook, Marxist socialism will finally offer the promise of a truly *universal* emancipation.

6

Thinking With

Animals in Schopenhauer, Horkheimer, and Adorno[1]

By Christina Gerhardt

> This world seems to be heading for a catastrophe, or more precisely, already to be in its throes. . . . Humans do not appear as subject of their destiny, but rather as objects of a blind process of nature, and the reaction of moral sentiment to this state of affairs is compassion.
>
> —Max Horkheimer[2]

> In his day Schopenhauer held it to be the particular merit of his own moral philosophy that it also included a view of our treatment of animals, compassion for animals, and this has often been regarded as the cranky idea of a private individual of independent means. My own view is that a tremendous amount can be learnt from such crankiness.
>
> —Theodor W. Adorno[3]

Animals, often neglected in studies of Adorno and Horkheimer, are of central importance for an understanding of their views on a wide variety of concerns, from a theory of the political to questions of ethics in a world after Auschwitz. Adorno and Horkheimer link their engagement with animals to larger questions of history and aesthetics, proposing that a revised reading of the status of animals and our relationship to them would open up alternative historical and aesthetic models. Animals, they argue, belongs to a complex set of concepts that are always already suppressed. The first task, then, is to lift and preserve the suppressed element, in this instance, animals. But Adorno and Horkheimer do not merely propose that we invert dominant paradigms, that is, that we give preference to animals over humans, for an inversion of paradigms would merely replace one underlying problematic structure, hierarchy, with another. Rather, they restore the focus on the dialectical tension between these constructions and on what generates these tensions in the first place. What follows is a consideration of how Adorno and Horkheimer's discussion of animals opens the door for a different model of ethics.

The entire corpus of Adorno's writings is traversed by rhetorical figures and dialectical images of animals and animality. Animals are a trope not only in Adorno's *Minima Moralia* (1951) and in his "Notes on Kafka" (1953) but also in the reflections on metaphysics and Auschwitz at the end of *Negative Dialectics* (1966), and in *Aesthetic Theory* (1970).[4] While the trope of animals assumes different shades of meaning depending on its specific context within Adorno's oeuvre, it consistently highlights the inhumanity of humans. Decisive here is the affinity of animals with "the non-identity of identity." Animals remind us that nature for Adorno is not only the condition of possibility for reading the self, humans, and culture but also for radically questioning the concept of otherness and our relation to it.

Animals figure prominently in Horkheimer's writings as well. They appear not only in "Materialism and Morality" (1933) and in *Dämmerung* (1934, written under the pseudonym of "Heinrich Regius") but also in "The End of Reason" (1941). And as John Abromeit points out, "Horkheimer was an active member of the Society for the Prevention of Cruelty to Animals in New York in the 1930s."[5] While the figure of animals takes on different meanings in Horkheimer's writings depending on the particular context in which it appears, it consistently reveals the shortcomings of philosophical and historical models that neglect a materialist base. Animals instantiate the attempt to return a materialist base both to historical and idealist models. For Horkheimer, animals underscore that humans are not superior and that precisely when they believe they are, their alleged superiority may well be based on a forgetting of the very real materialist conditions on which they depend and with which they interrelate. To remedy this, Horkheimer reminds us of the need to think with, to have compassion, *Mitleid*. In this way, when animals appear in Horkheimer's writings, they question how humans relate to concepts of otherness, of alterity.

Horkheimer and Adorno's obsession with animals has not escaped their attentive readers. For example, Robert Savage tells us that Adorno's obsession with animals ranged from his childhood to his adult life.[6] Adorno's fascination begins with frequent visits to the zoo during childhood, whereupon Adorno "took particular delight in . . . herbivores, such as hippopotamuses, rhinoceroses and even wombats."[7] He constructed a private mythology for his immediate family during his childhood and later for his closest friends. For example, Adorno addressed his mother as the "hippopotamus mare," his aunt Agathe as the "tigress," his father as a "wild boar," and later his wife Grete as "the giraffe." Adorno's interest in the herbivores and wombats remained with him into adulthood. Upon his return from exile in 1949, Adorno went so far as to write the director of the Frankfurt Zoo, Bernhard Grzimek, and request that wombats be reintroduced to the zoo's holdings, and he offered to write in support of the director's campaign to have safari hunting outlawed. As Adorno put it, although his support had nothing to do with the official duties of the Institute for Social Research, they were "much more aligned with the deeper impulse that such an Institute obeys, if it wants to be right in its humane responsibilities."[8]

Additionally, biographies of Adorno call attention to the significance of animals for Adorno.[9] For example, Detlev Claussen notes that for Adorno, "solidarity with animals, expanded to solidarity with all living things, recalls the suppression of internal and external nature, recalls domination."[10] Stefan Müller-Doohm, too, lingers on how important animals were to both Adorno and Horkheimer, discussing a song, "The Return Home of the Mammoth with a Trunk," that Adorno composed in February 1941 about Horkheimer's return to New York: "What's driving there in the car and sticking out its long trunk? / It's a mammoth, it's a mammoth and it's driving home."[11] And in "Bringing Nature Back In" (from his *Adorno: Disenchantment and Ethics*), Jay Bernstein argues that "Adorno's gamble, the gamble animating his late works, is that the immanent critique and correction of the dualisms of idealism's concept of the concept, as the philosophical apotheosis of identity thinking, will bring anthropomorphic, living nature into view."[12] I agree with Bernstein's observation that Adorno is trying to bring nature back in, but would argue the inverse: rather than correcting idealism in order to bring nature into view, Adorno brings anthropomorphic, living nature into view, in order to correct the dualisms of idealism and thereby avoid nefarious consequences.[13] As Savage concludes in the aforementioned article, Adorno believes the ethical treatment of animals and humans to be related.

While Horkheimer and Adorno's discussion of animals is inscribed into a whole network of historical, aesthetic, and philosophical concerns, it plays its most crucial role in their reading of the politics of ethics. Writing in *Negative Dialectics* about Kant's account of practical reason and ethics and about Auschwitz, Adorno indicates that at the end of a long humanistic tradition, the individual stands confronted with the figure of animality. Adorno suggests that the individual is "left with no more than the morality for which Kantian ethics—which accords affection, not respect to animals—can muster only disdain: to try to live so that one may believe himself to have been a good animal."[14] In other words, according to Adorno, precisely that animal Kantian ethics regards with such disdain should not be the source of derision, but instead the guide to morality. In what follows, I take up this thread and scrutinize Horkheimer and Adorno's rhetorical employment of animals, by considering how it offers a critique of the Kantian account of practical reason, how it draws on Schopenhauer's moral philosophy, and how Horkheimer and Adorno's discussion of animals offers a different model of ethics.

DIALECTIC OF ENLIGHTENMENT

The best foundation for this constellation of concerns can be found in Horkheimer and Adorno's well-known co-authored study *Dialectic of Enlightenment* (1944).[15] In this volume, written during their time in exile, Horkheimer and Adorno offer a dialectical criticism of the Enlightenment, seeking to expose its blind spots, in order to further its ideals. In particular, Horkheimer and Adorno explore a path from Kantian idealism and its moral aspirations to the totalitarianism of the Nazi regime and the horrors of the Holocaust.[16] To be sure, enlightenment, as it appears in the title of the work, does not refer exclusively to Kantian idealism. As even a cursory glance at the volume's contents will reveal, it begins roughly 2,500 years earlier with Homer's *Odysseus*, includes a discussion of De Sade's *Juliette*, and concludes with an analysis of the contemporary Western culture industry. In other words, enlightement does not refer strictly to the Enlightenment era. But even when it does, it has often been misread to be a rebuttal of Kantian idealism; it is instead the very opposite: references to the Enlightenment in this work mark an attempt to redeem the useful components of Kantian philosophy while remaining attentive to and critical of its shortcomings. What Horkheimer and Adorno sought to provide in *Dialectic of Enlightenment* was what Adorno came to call an "immanent critique"—in this instance, of Kantian philosophy and in particular of his moral philosophy.

As early as 1931, in his inaugural lecture in Frankfurt, "The Actuality of Philosophy" (1931), Adorno stated that if one wanted to avoid the political mistakes of the past, one would have to come to terms with problematic moments in the philosophical models that set the stage for those events. As Adorno put it, "[o]nly a fundamentally undialectical philosophy oriented toward ahistorical truth could fathom that the old problems could be disposed of in that one forgot them and started fresh from the beginning."[17] To presume that one could start with a clean slate would be preposterous.[18] Such a gesture would be constitutively unenlightened in its foreclosure of an understanding of the relationship of Enlightenment thinking to its own history.[19] Equally problematic, however, is the practice of heaping new philosophical ideas onto the pile without first examining their own internal contradictions. Adorno admonishes us to seek answers within the model itself. He writes, "I said that the riddle's answer was not the 'meaning' of the riddle in the sense that both could exist at the same time. . . . The answer was contained within the riddle, needs to be constructed out of the riddle's elements, and destroys the riddle."[20] In this way, Adorno undertakes what he calls immanent critiques, that is, critiques that pursue the inner logic of an argument, seeking to shore up its hidden fault lines or where its logic betrays its aspirations. By offering an immanent critique of Kant, Horkheimer and Adorno sought not to dismiss Kant but to preserve aspects of his thinking. Both Horkheimer and Adorno were, in fact, deeply Kantian.

Adorno was one of the most Kantian members of the Frankfurt School perhaps as a result of his early encounter with Kant: he was only 15 years old when he read Kant's first critique with Siegfried Kracauer, a family friend 14 years his senior. That Kant remained central to Adorno's thinking is evidenced by the fact that Adorno focused on Kant's philosophy in his major speculative works: *Negative Dialectics* (1966) and *Aesthetic Theory* (1970). Additionally, Adorno also frequently taught courses on Kant: in 1951, Adorno offered a seminar on "Kant's *Critique of Judgment*"; in 1954 and 1959, Adorno gave lecture courses on "Kant's *Critique of Pure Reason*," in which he laid bare the contradictions of Kant's philosophy; in 1955, he taught a course on Kant's *Critique of Practical Reason*; and in 1963, he offered a lecture course on "Problems of Moral Philosophy," which sought to provide an account of Kant's moral theory. Reading through Adorno's ouevre, it thus becomes clear how central Kant was to Adorno's thinking throughout his life. It is with, rather than against, Kant that Adorno critiques Kant's philosophy. Horkheimer, too, was strongly influenced by Kant's philosophy.[21] As Martin Jay puts it, "From Kant, however, he [Horkheimer] took certain convictions that he would never abandon."[22] The influence of Kant on Horkheimer throughout his life is evidenced by his 1922 unpublished dissertation on Kant entitled "Zur Antinomie der teleologischen Urteilskraft" and his 1925 Habilitation "Kants Kritik der Urteilskraft als Bindeglied zwischen theoretischer und praktischer Philosophie"[23] And it formed the locus of many of his later studies, for example, of *Eclipse of Reason* (1947), whose German title *Zur Kritik der instrumentellen Vernunft* (1967) reveals more clearly that it is playing off and working against Kant, and of "Zum Begriff der Vernunft" (1951) and of "Kants Philosophie und die Aufklärung" (1962).

One of the ways Horkheimer and Adorno sought to critique Kantian idealism in *Dialectic of Enlightenment* was by studying the relationship between humans and animals. In a section entitled "Man and Animal" Adorno and Horkheimer describe the structure of this relationship as posited by the Enlightenment: "The idea of man in European history is expressed in the way in which he is distinguished from the animal. Animal irrationality is adduced as proof of a human dignity."[24] That is, the animal functions as other to the human: the animality of animals is an index of what humans have overcome and no longer are. Yet this distinction between man and animal is not merely one of disambiguation or of contrast, it also sets up a hierarchical structure of domination.[25] Horkheimer had put this argument differently in "The End of Reason," an article he authored about the same time that he and Adorno were working on *Dialectic of Enlightenment*. Here he delineates the problematic relationship between man and nature as follows: "The age-old definition of reason in terms of self-preservation already implied the curtailment of reason itself. The propositions of idealistic philosophy that reason distinguishes man from the animal (propositions in which the animal is humiliated . . .) contain the truth that through reason man frees himself of the fetters of nature. This liberation, however, does not entitle man to dominate nature (as the philosophers held) but to comprehend it."[26] In *Dialectic of Enlightenment* Horkheimer and Adorno discuss how man's relationship to nature and to animals forms part of the larger ideology of domination as follows: "The essence of enlightenment is the alternative whose ineradicability is that of domination. Men have always had to choose between their subjection to nature and the subjection of nature to self."[27] The problematic relationship of humans to animals, whereby humans instrumentalize animals, establishes—Adorno and Horkheimer argue—a deeply vexed basis for moral conduct.

SCHOPENHAUER

Key to revising the pitfalls of Kantian idealism, in Horkheimer and Adorno's eyes, was the concept and practice of compassion for animals, something Adorno and Horkheimer borrowed from Schopenhauer, as Adorno's *Lectures on Moral Philosophy* indicate. In these lectures, Adorno takes up Kant's *Groundwork of the Metaphysics of Morals* and the *Critique of Practical Reason*, emphasizing the limits of Kantian moral philosophy. The lectures, which were written in preparation for the chapter on freedom in *Negative Dialectics*, were preparation for a planned book on moral philosophy. Adorno stated that this third volume—taken together with *Negative Dialectics* (1966) and *Aesthetic Theory* (1970)—was to "represent what I have to throw onto the scale" or what he had to say on the subject of moral philosophy.[28] (Unfortunately, with Adorno's passing in 1969, neither his *Aesthetic Theory* nor the planned third volume were seen through to completion.) Critiquing "the idea of reason as an ultimate end of mankind,"[29] Adorno cites Schopenhauer and specifically his discussion of animals: "In his day Schopenhauer held it to be the particular merit of his own moral philosophy that it also included a view of our treatment of animals, compassion for animals, and this has often been regarded as the cranky idea of a private individual of independent means. My own view is that a tremendous amount can be learnt from such crankiness."[30]

In Adorno's eyes what has often been dismissed as mere crankiness actually provides the grounds for a radically different relationship between humans and animals that does not think of animals as mere things but rather as beings worthy of compassion. [31]

Adorno's observations are based on Schopenhauer's *On the Basis of Morality* (1840).[32] Schopenhauer, too, like Horkheimer and Adorno, pursued an immanent critique of Kant to salvage aspects of Kantian idealism as a basis for morality. Thus, the first third of Schopenhauer's *On the Basis of Morality* forms a critique of Kant's moral philosophy as laid out in three works: *Groundwork of the Metaphysics of Morals* (1785), *Critique of Practical Reason* (1788), and *The Metaphysical Principles of Virtue* (1797).[33] Schopenhauer criticizes Kant's account of reason for how it deems animals not as equals worthy of our compassion but rather as creatures that allow us to exercise our compassion for other humans. As Schopenhauer points out, Kant, in paragraph 17 of his *The Metaphysical Principles of Virtue*, states that "cruelty to animals is contrary to man's duty to himself, because it deadens in him the feeling of sympathy for their sufferings, and thus a natural tendency that is very useful to morality in relation to other human beings is weakened."[34] Schopenhauer argues, "thus only for practice are we to have sympathy for animals. . . . I regard such propositions as revolting and abominable."[35] To Schopenhauer, they are indications not of the humanity of humans but of the inverse: their inhumanity and their incapacity to reason. Adorno agrees, stating:

> I believe that Schopenhauer probably suspected that the establishment of total rationality as the supreme objective principle of mankind might well spell the continuation of that blind domination of nature whose most obvious and tangible expression was to be found in the exploitation and maltreatment of animals. He thereby pointed to the weak point in the transition from subjective reason concerned with self-preservation to the supreme moral principle, which has no room for animals and our treatment of animals. If this is true, we can see Schopenhauer's eccentricity as a sign of great insight.[36]

What matters to Adorno is "changing the circumstances that give rise to the need for it [the idea of compassion]."[37] As he tells us further on in his lectures, "the pity you express for someone always contains an element of injustice toward that person; he experiences not just our pity but also the impotence and the specious character of the compassionate act."[38] In order for pity or compassion to work, one must, as Adorno puts it, change the hierarchical structure that sets rational humans over animals, and that allows only pity, to one that allows com-passion or em-pathy (feeling with). As Schopenhauer, who made compassion a central principle of his ethics, writes: "This compassion alone is the real basis of all free justice. . . . Only insofar as an action springs from it, does it have moral value, and those actions which follow from any other motive whatsoever have none."[39]

Horkheimer, too, discusses how Schopenhauer's critique of Kant's account of reason suggests a different model of ethics based on *Mitleid*. In his 1960 talk, "Schopenhauer Today," held on the hundredth anniversary of Schopenhauer's death, Horkheimer argues that for Schopenhauer, "the heroic even the holy life . . . is the consequence of suffering and rejoicing with others, of sharing in the lives of others; perceptive humans cannot stop fighting horror until they die. . . . Even the last utopian escape which his teacher Kant . . . wanted to offer . . . was to Schopenhauer, in the face of the horror of this earth, only rationalistic deception."[40] Here, his argument dovetails with Adorno's somewhat later 1963 lectures on moral philosophy on Kant and Schopenhauer (mentioned above). That is, he lingers on the concept of suffering with others (*Mitleid*), drawing on Schopenhauer as a corrective to shortcomings of Kant's moral philosophy. In his *On the Basis of Morality*, Schopenhauer had asked:

> But how is it possible that a suffering that is not *mine*, that does not affect me, nevertheless immediately becomes my own motive, and one capable of moving me to act? It is possible only insofar as I *feel with* [*mitempfinde*] the suffering, that I feel it as *mine*, yet still not *in me*, but in *someone else*. . . . This presupposes that I, so to speak, identify myself with the other so that consequently the boundary between the I and the non-I is for the moment dissolved: only then . . . I no longer grasp him as the empirical perception discloses him, that is, as someone alien to me, indifferent to me, completely different from me, rather, I suffer with him *in him* despite the fact that his flesh does not encompass my nerves.[41]

As Arne Johan Vetlesen puts it, in Schopenhauer "the capacity for suffering, not the (Kantian) capacity for reason, establishes the criterion for a full-fledged moral status, hence in Schopenhauer such status is ascribed to all living creatures."[42] Vetlesen argues that Schopenhauer builds his entire moral theory on the basis of compassion. Horkheimer gleaned a revised basis of moral conduct from Schopenhauer and he, too, used it in order to critique Kantian moral philosophy.

Horkheimer's interest in Schopenhauer came early in his career. As Martin Jay puts it, "Horkheimer, who set the tone for all of the Institute's work, had been interested in Schopenhauer and Kant before becoming fascinated with Hegel and Marx."[43] According to Jay, Horkheimer had been a keen reader of Schopenhauer since his time studying French together with Pollock in the 1930s: "[T]he first book in philosophy Horkheimer actually read was Schopenhauer's *Aphorisms on the Wisdom of Life*, which Pollock gave him when they were studying French together in Brussels before the war."[44] John Abromeit adds that "Horkheimer must have been taken immediately by Schopenhauer's *Aphorismen*, for when he discovered a copy of Schopenhauer's collected writings in a second hand bookstore a few weeks later, he bought it right away and proceeded to deepen his knowledge of the philosopher he would refer to a few years later as his 'exalted spiritual [*geistiger*] father.'"[45] Additionally, "both he and Lowenthal were members of the Schopenhauer Gesellschaft at Frankfurt in their student days."[46] Horkheimer's "expression of interest in Schopenhauer in the 1960s, contrary to what is often assumed, was thus a return to an early love, rather than an apostasy from a life long Hegelianized Marxism."[47]

To some extent, this becomes obvious when reading Horkheimer's early writings, such as *Anfänge der bürgerlichen Geschichtsphilosophie* and *Dämmerung*, the latter published under the pseudonym "Heinrich Regius." Although Schopenhauer is not explicitly mentioned in either piece, the concept of suffering with others or *Mitleid*, which was to play such an important role in Horkheimer's moral philosophy throughout his life, figures prominently. In the former, Horkheimer argues that a science that takes no account of the suffering, misery, and limitations of its period would be entirely lacking in practical interest. In the latter, Horkheimer argues that while those living in misery have a right to material egoism, it was base to think that "the improvement of material existence by a more useful structuring of human conditions was the most important thing in the world."[48] It was "not merely the principal, immediate goal, a better provision of the necessities for humanity" which depended on this improvement, "but also the realization of all so-called cultural or ideal values."[49] In all of this, as Rolf Wiggershaus points out, "there was an echo, which was not heard in his inaugural lecture in 1931, of the Schopenhauerian consciousness of the finiteness, physicality and *solidarity of creatures,* rather than the activist pathos of German idealism."[50] It is precisely this Schopenhauerian "solidarity of creatures" that Horkheimer underscores as an antidote to Kantian moral philosophy.

CONCLUSION

In sum, since both Horkheimer and Adorno were Kantian from early on, they shared an interest in addressing what they saw as the blind spots of his moral philosophy. Thus, Horkheimer and Adorno call their readers' attention to animals in order to suggest a radically different moral philosophy: one based on *Mitleid* or compassion as proposed by Schopenhauer. And yet, although their interests and argument in *Dialectic of Enlightenment* overlaps in these ways, discrete priorities also distinguish their primary concerns.

Adorno's interest in Schopenhauer's revision stemmed from three main interests: a commitment to Kantian moral philosophy; a concern with the relationship between humans and nature; and a commitment to a revision of the structural relationship between humans and animals, which antedated arguments that would appear in Adorno's *Negative Dialectics*. Horkheimer's interest revising Schopenhauer, meanwhile, stemmed from a somewhat different set of concerns: a commitment to revising Kantian philosophy from an idealist to a materialist form; an interest in calling attention to Schopenhauer's revisions to this end; and, finally, an interest in and commitment to the relationship between humans and nature in general and, in particular, between humans and animals.

What emerged then in their jointly composed opus, *Dialectic of Enlightenment*—a work which sowed the seeds for many of Horkheimer and Adorno's future endeavors, such as Horkheimer's writings on materialism and Adorno's work on moral philosophy—was in many ways a shared nexus of concerns based on both Horkheimer's and Adorno's prior intellectual interest in Kant and in animals. Importantly, Horkheimer and Adorno argued that the relation of compassion can be universalized, which has radical consequences for models of ethics. In this way, reading Horkheimer and Adorno through animals opens up a new side of their thought on the one hand, while on the other hand this reading provides a new perspective on animal ethics. At the heart of Horkheimer and Adorno's analysis of the animal is a revision of how we conceive of difference or the other, with obvious and real implications for our relations to animals.

7

Animal Is to Kantianism as Jew Is to Fascism

Adorno's Bestiary[1]

By Eduardo Mendieta

In 2001 Jacques Derrida was awarded the Theodor W. Adorno prize, which the city of Frankfurt am Main confers upon those who in the spirit of the Frankfurt-based Institute for Social Research pursue interdisciplinary work that cuts across the sciences, humanities, and arts.[2] Derrida's speech, entitled "Fichus," is surely one of the most important essays in the Derridian corpus, for in it he lays out in rather unequivocal terms the ways in which his work stands within the tradition of the Frankfurt School.[3] At the source of much of his thinking and preoccupations stands the towering figure of Walter Benjamin. Derrida in fact asks why there is no Benjamin prize, when so much of Adorno's work is dependent on Benjamin, and when so much of contemporary thinking is so enduringly nurtured by his mangled intellectual corpus. After fascinating discussions of Hegel, Freud, the question of language and national identity, and what it means to be a German Jew, Derrida offers the abstracts, "in the style of a TV guide," of seven chapters that would make up the contents of a book that would "interpret the history, the possibility, and the honor of this prize."[4] It is chapter seven of this hypothetical book that I want to briefly discuss as a way to introduce my concerns in this paper. Derrida notes that this last chapter would be the one that he would most enjoy writing, "because it would take the least trodden but in my view of the most crucial paths in the future reading of Adorno."[5] This chapter would deal with Adorno's animals, or what I have here called in the subtitle "Adorno's Bestiary." To give us a TV guide–style abstract of the question of the animal in Adorno, Derrida focuses on two texts in Adorno. The first is a fragment that is now in his posthumously published book on Beethoven. The passage reads, and I quote Adorno now:

> Ethical dignity in Kant is a demarcation of differences. It is directed against animals. Implicitly it excludes man from nature, so that its humanity threatens incessantly to revert to the inhuman. It leaves no room for pity. Nothing is more abhorrent to the Kantian than a reminder of man's resemblance to animals. This taboo is always at work when the idealist berates the materialist. *Animals play for the idealist system virtually the same role as the Jews for fascism*. To revile man as an animal—that is genuine idealism. To deny the possibility of salvation for animals absolutely and at any price is the inviolable boundary of its metaphysics.[6]

Derrida follows closely this passage, remarking on the German terms used and highlighting in particular the uses of "taboo," and "insult." But then Derrida glosses the text, introducing a turn of phrase that he finds extremely important: "Fascism begins when you insult an animal, including the animal in man. Authentic idealism (*echter Idealismus*) consists in *insulting* the animal in man or in treating a man like an animal" (181, italics in the original). Derrida immediately evokes the "but on the other hand," and turns our attention to another set of fragments in Adorno's work. The fragment in question is now part of *Dialectic of the Enlightenment*, and it is entitled "Man and Beast." Derrida is making reference in this fragment to a sentence in which Adorno and Horkheimer call in question the opposite attitudes to "insulting" and "reviling." Derrida paraphrases the following sentence: "The precondition of the fascist's pious love of animals, nature, and children is the lust of the hunter. The idle stroking of the children's hair and animal pelts signifies: this hand can destroy. It tenderly fondles one victim before felling the other, and its choice has nothing to do with the victim's guilt."[7] Derrida notes that these passages urge us to "fight against the ideology" that is concealed in the Nazis' "troubled interest" in animals and nature, to the point of vegetarianism.[8] Derrida is in fact drawing our attention to the dialectical tension between the insult against the animal in the human that is the foundation of fascist genocide, and the fascist's pseudo zoophilia, which is concealed in the Fuhrer's love of his dogs and his supposedly obsessive vegetarianism.

I want to remark on three aspects of Derrida's concluding chapter on animals in his hypothetical book, and in particular on his not-so-subterranean relationship to critical theory. First, there is the highly charged and potentially polemical character of Derrida's comments, in which he links Kant to fascism, and putatively to the ecological and animal questions of the twentieth and twenty-first century, by way of a Jew who survived the holocaust. What is also noteworthy is that Habermas was present at this speech, and that both were during the fall and winter of 2001 beginning a sort of collaboration and intellectual friendship. It was around this time that both Derrida and Habermas were being interviewed by Giovanna Borradori for what later became *Philosophy in a Time of Terror*.[9] Here one may suggest that Derrida is making a point about the Kantian turn of second-generation critical theory, one that both forgets and occludes the animal in man. The second remark concerns Derrida's proclaimed happiness were he to write this chapter. The fact is that he did write such a chapter, or in fact, he wrote several versions of this chapter. As is well known, Derrida was lecturing on the animal, the beast, sovereignty, and reason toward the end of his life. In fact, as Adorno developed a bestiary, Derrida also developed his own bestiary, but one that he wanted to call with the dual names of zoopoetics and zootheologies.[10] (Here I must make reference to Cary Wolfe and David Wood's indispensable works on the question of the animal in Derrida's work, in lieu of even a synoptic overview.[11]) This brings me to the third remark, and that is that Derrida, as the faithful and tireless reader that he was, had discovered a vast and unexplored dimension of Adorno's work when he noted that the question of the animal (which should not be written or thought in the singular according to Derrida) is, to repeat, the "least trodden" and the most significant in the future appropriation of Adorno's work. In the following, therefore, I want to focus on the trope of the animal in Adorno's work, one that acts as a hinge between Adorno's negative anthropology, on the one hand, and his critique of totalitarian reason, on the other. I will also discuss the way in which Adorno's notion that "nothing is more abhorrent to Kantianism" than to be reminded of the animal semblance of humans is related to a cognate though hardly explored notion in Adorno's work, namely his notion of "natural history." I will conclude by returning to Derrida in order to raise the question of the historicity of the animal–human question, and the role that a historical materialist philosophical anthropology can play in the context of an age of in which animal extermination and extinction converge.

ADORNO'S ANIMAL ETHICS: TO LIVE AS IF ONE HAD BEEN A GOOD ANIMAL

There is a picture of Adorno that has become iconic not just of Adorno's relationship to the world, but also of the ethereality and obscurity of his writing. The picture, which is now on the cover of the dusk jacket of the recently released massive biography of Adorno by Stefan Müller-Doohm, indeed portrays a man lost in thought, his gaze fixed in the distance, but aimed inwardly. His lips are slightly open, but downcast, as if about to say something or anticipating an expression of horror or regret. Martin Jay described well this picture, which also was on the cover of his book on Adorno: "the cumulative effect produced by the photo is powerful, showing us a man brooding in subdued sadness about the untold horrors of his life time."[12] Yet, there is another photograph that is as telling of Adorno. The photograph was taken around 1943, when Adorno lived in California. It portrays him at his desk, turned backwards looking at the photographer. His desk is cleared, though to the right there is a table with trays filled with papers. The desk, an ungainly contraption towering over him, is decorated with animal figurines. There are two giraffes, a gazelle, and a horse. To his left there is a large sculpture of what appears to be two peacocks rubbing heads, bowing to each other. Perched on one of the levels of the cabinet that rises over the desk is a little stuffed teddy bear. Adorno is wearing his glasses, and there is a smile on his lips.

Adorno in fact had a great fondness for animals. We now know that he used to visit quite frequently the Frankfurt Zoo with his mother and his aunt, whom he called a second mother. He had a great affection for large, slow, patient herbivores, such as hippopotamuses, rhinoceros, and wombats. This sentiment he avowed without subterfuge or shame. In a letter to Bernhard Grzimek, the director of the Frankfurt Zoo, dated April 23, 1965, Adorno wrote:

> Would it not be wonderful if Frankfurt Zoo could acquire a pair of wombats? I have fond memories of these friendly and cuddly animals from my childhood and would love to be able to see them again. . . . And may I also remind you of the existence of the babirusa, or the horned dog as I suppose it is called in English, which was also one of my favorite animals during my childhood; a delightful bizarre pachyderm. I hope it hasn't become extinct in the Malaysian archipelago? And lastly, what is the situation with the dwarf hippos they used to have in Berlin?[13]

Early in his life he imagined himself as Archibald the rhinoceros, and referred to Gretel, his wife, as the modern giraffe. Horkheimer was identified with the mammoth, and there is a drawing by him paying tribute to his animal soul, in which the mammoth is shown trying to shave and carries the note: "mammoth self[-]shaving must be difficult." There is a very telling, though playful, letter from the late 1930s from Adorno to Horkheimer, written while Adorno was in England:

> The rhinoceros king Archibald has a golden crown with a fat pear and golden layers of skin over his eyes, but stands aloof from active government. He is having an affair with the giraffe "Gazelle," occasionally wears a silk-grey pair of pajama trousers, and has published a pamphlet, the pan-humanist manifesto. It has appeared in the publishing house of the united jackals and hyenas. For years he has been working on his magnum opus. It is called "The Rhinoceros Whip," and is the theoretical groundwork of a society that includes the animals.[14]

As Detlev Claussen notes in his recent biography of Adorno, Adorno and Horkheimer refer to each other as pachyderms not only because of their thick skins, but also because of their placid temperaments and ability to digest mountains of literature as though it were grass.[15] It would be inappropriate and entirely contrary to the entwinement between the private and public in Adorno's work to dismiss these musings and playful assimilation into the animal. There is an unmistakable continuity between Adorno's lifelong fascination and identification with animals, and what he wrote and argued in his philosophical writings. We ought to take seriously what Adorno wrote in his letter to Horkheimer quoted above, namely that he aimed to develop a "theoretical groundwork of a society that includes the animals." This groundwork would entail developing a new anthropology and a new metaphysics in which the animality of humans would be acknowledged, and space would be made for a "natural history" that would point us in the direction of a future progress that is truly mindful of the incompleteness of our humanity. Here we cannot fail to remark on the similarities between Adorno's concern with the animal in the human, and Herbert Marcuse's rescue of the Orphic and narcissistic eros that counter the violence and brutality of the Promethean myth. These similarities are not only at the level of the content of images, allegories, and metaphors, but also at the level of methodology: that is to say, both Adorno and Marcuse seek to use myth against reified and ossified rationality.[16]

In a discussion from 1956 between Horkheimer and Adorno, the latter affirms: "philosophy is truly there to redeem what lies in the gaze of an animal. [Die Philosophie ist eigentlich dazu da, das einsulösen, was im Blick eines Tieres liegt]."[17] In a letter of congratulations to Horkheimer on his 70th birthday from 1965, Adorno wrote, "You [Du] once told me that I treat animals like humans, and you humans like men. There is something there."[18] What is "there" is a dialectical move to see in animals humans and in humans animals, precisely what the project of a natural history aims to keep in the foreground. A passage in *Minima Moralia* expresses explicitly this movement. In paragraph 68 Adorno considers the way in which the gaze of the animal and what looks like an animal are related:

> The possibility of pogroms is decided in the moment when the gaze of a fatally-wounded animal falls on a human being. The defiance with which he repels this gaze—"after all, it's only an animal"—reappears irresistibly in cruelties done to human beings, the perpetrators having again and again to reassure themselves that it is "only an animal" because they could never fully believe this even of animals.

Here, the license, and even perhaps the imperative to exterminate another human being appears when the animal gaze peers through the eyes of the human—the human that gazes back like a wounded animal. We need to read paragraph 68 in conjunction with paragraph 33, entitled "out of the firing line":

> Cinema newsreel: the invasion of the Marianas, including Guam. The impression is not of battles, but of civil engineering and blasting operations undertaken with immeasurably intensified vehemence, also of "fumigation", insect-extermination on a terrestrial scale. Works are put in hand, until no grass grows. The enemy acts as patient and corpse. Like the Jews under Fascism, he features now as merely the object of technical and administrative measures, and should he defend himself, his own action immediately takes on the same character . . . Consummate inhumanity is the realization of Edward Grey's human dream, war without hatred.

War without hatred means war that has become a cleansing operation, an operation to fumigate and exterminate a vermin, a plague. The enemy is no longer human, but a vermin. The pivot, though, is the formulation, "like Jews under Fascism," which recalls the other equivalence: "animal is to Kantianism as Jews are to Fascism." If we inure ourselves to the animal gaze, which is a gaze that addresses our unaccomplished humanity, we already have extinguished our subjectivity, and have eviscerated it of anything that would give worth to its preservation.

What kind of subjectivity is worth preserving, and how could it be preserved in such a way that it allows itself to be addressed by the gaze of the animal other? Part of the answer is to be found in the first excursus of the *Dialectic of the Enlightenment*, which deals with Odysseus. Here, Odysseus is read as a prototype of bourgeois subjectivity, but also as a cipher for the struggle against nature, on the one side, and myth, on the other. Odysseus's misfortunes and adventures are a travail against the irrational forces of nature, but also against the irrational force of rationality bent on self-preservation. Odysseus epitomizes the way in which "the history of civilization is the history of the introversion of sacrifice—in other words, the history of renunciation."[19] Homer's Odysseus captured the tragedy to which humans are condemned by civilization, namely to destroy in themselves that for which they surrender themselves to society. Odysseus, at the same time, personifies the promise of that for which we submit ourselves to so much privation and self-denial: a return home against the will of the gods, the overcoming of fate. Between this tragedy and promise is profiled a way out, namely not to reject in us what is nature, but also not to succumb to its mimetic violence. "At the moment when human beings cut themselves off from the consciousness of themselves as nature, all the purpose for which they keep themselves alive—social progress, the heightening of material and intellectual forces, indeed, consciousness itself—become void, and the enthronement of the means as ends, which in late capitalism is taking on the character of overt madness, is already detectable in the earliest history of subjectivity."[20] The birth of subjectivity in fact is inaugurated by the instrumentalization of what is nature in us and of external nature itself into means for our survival. The task, thus, is to dethrone the reversal of means into ends, and to establish properly the correctly lived life, a life or form of living that looks to the other, as other, and sees in it a challenge to our hitherto narrowly conceived humanity. If our humanity is not yet accomplished, it is because our proper relation to our animal others is not yet established. The task of humanization is not the rejection of nature in us, but its proper recognition in us. To paraphrase Marx's comments in his 1844 *Economic and Philosophic Manuscripts*, via Adorno, then, the humanization of nature is also the naturalization of humanity.[21]

The last sentence of paragraph 68 in *Minima Moralia* speaks to this task: "[t]he mechanism of 'pathic projection' determines that those in power perceive as human only their own reflected image, instead of reflecting back the human as precisely what is different. Murder is thus the repeated attempt, by yet greater madness, to distort the madness of such false perception into reason: what was not seen as human and yet is human, is made a thing, so that its stirrings can no longer refute the manic gaze."[22] This manic gaze is the gaze of that subjectivity born of the sacrifice of nature in us that refuses to be gazed back at by that which it claims it has vanquished and prevailed over. This nature must be insulted, because it was the source of our torment and reminds us of our own weakness and dependence on it.

Yet, there is something that is between nature and socialized society that forces us to look at, and be looked at by, nature in such a way that our being nature is ever present and recollected. This is the work of art. Philosophy redeems what lies in the gaze of the animal by rescuing what is preserved in the expression of works of arts. It is through art that humans are able to neutralize instrumental reason bent on dominating nature. Indeed, the work of art is dialectics at a standstill in that it exemplifies what it seeks to overcome by precisely highlighting what it is: always mimesis, always remembrance, always the self-confessing avowal that is an anti-commodity commodity that never renounces its announcement of the *promise de bonheur* by renouncing utopia in the now. In his last book, *Aesthetic Theory*, Adorno talks about the relationship between semblance and expression in artworks. It is through semblance that artworks communicate, but they communicate neither what they portray nor the subjectivity of the artist that imprints them with life. Artworks communicate the non-identical through their semblance of the object. But just as importantly, works of art communicate or express not a formed and fully autonomous subjectivity, but rather what Adorno called, "the protohistory of subjectivity." As he wrote in *Aesthetic Theory*, "Artworks bear expression not where they communicate the subject, but rather where they reverberate with the protohistory of subjectivity, of ensoulment, for which tremolo of any sort is a miserable surrogate. . . . The expression of artworks is the nonsubjective in the subject: not so much the subject's expression as its copy: there is nothing so expressive as the eyes of animals—especially apes—which seem objectively to mourn that they are not human."[23] Through artworks, nature peers back at humans, but also the yearning for a rightly lived humanity gazes mournfully at us, who see in artworks the stigmata of historical suffering, but also a primordial joy of living. Artworks are also above all about useless passions, the end without ends, the disinterested interest, and the pleasure for the sake of pleasure itself. The work of art is a playful charade. In this, it is also mimesis, and there we are harkened back to our species protohistory, as well as to our ontogenesis: once we were children, and as children we were innocent animals. Adorno writes: "In its clownishness, art consolingly recollects prehistory in the primordial world of animals. Apes in the zoo together perform what resembles clown routines. The collusion of children with clowns is a collusion with art, which adults drive out of them just as they drive out their collusion with animals. Human beings have not succeeded in so thoroughly repressing their likeness to animals that they are unable in an instant to capture it and be flooded with joy. . . . In the similarity of clowns to animals the likeness of humans to apes flashes up; the constellation animal/fool/clown is a fundamental layer of art."[24] This constellation is what makes of artworks the site for the expression of what is not human, albeit using human means.[25] Here art is indispensable to ethics; in fact, it is the groundwork for a moral philosophy.

If we read the statement Adorno made in 1956, that "philosophy is truly there to redeem what lies in the gaze of an animal," in tandem with the last section (153) in his *Minimal Moralia*—a book dedicated to Horkheimer—where he claims that "the only philosophy which can be responsibly practiced in face of despair is the attempt to contemplate all things as they would present themselves from the standpoint of redemption," then we can safely infer that Adorno would have been comfortable with the following statement: the only philosophy that we can practice responsibly today is one that would seek to redeem without prevarications the ethical appellation in the animal gaze. Such a philosophy would in fact combine two categorical imperatives, one imposed upon humanity by Hitler and the metonym of fascism, the other by Kantian derision and idealistic abhorrence of the animal in humanity. One categorical imperative would command: "to arrange their thought and actions so that Auschwitz will not repeat itself, so that nothing similar will happen."[26] The other would command: "to try to live so that one may believe oneself to have been a good animal [ein gutes Tier gewesen zu sein]."[27] One of the most astute analysts of Adorno's work, Gerhard Schweppenhäuser, notes with respect to this claim that if we are to take it seriously we have to ask not just, why should we be moral? but two further questions: why is morality immoral and immorality moral?[28] Schweppenhäuser holds that these two questions are implicit in all of Adorno's work on morality, especially in part three of the

Negative Dialetics, as well as in his lecture course from 1963 entitled "Problems of Moral Philosophy."[29] But as I have been suggesting, the imperative to "live so that one may believe oneself to have been a good animal," is related to Adorno's critique of metaphysics and its implicit positive anthropology that delimits the human and reason by invidiously excluding the animal and that which is not at the service of instrumental reason. Schweppenhäuser calls Adorno's ethics a negative moral philosophy, which rejects extant moral philosophy, as much Kant's as Hegel's, not only because of the way both are at the service of socialized society and the totalized totality, but also because bourgeois morality enshrines the autonomous free subject that is an empty shell, one immolated at the altar of subjectivity. There is no morality proper to human freedom, because humans as such have yet to realize their humanity in accord with their animal nature. Morality is negative, yet to be achieved, precisely because our humanity is yet to be achieved. Thus, Adorno's negative anthropology, an anthropology without anthropos,[30] is matched by a negative moral philosophy that denounces the immorality of what we take to be moral and discovers in the immoral the guide to what is moral. In *Negative Dialectics*, Adorno writes: "That man is 'open' is an empty thesis, advanced—rarely without an invidious side glance at the animal—by an anthropology that has "arrived. . . . That we cannot tell what man is does not establish a peculiarly majestic anthropology; it vetoes any anthropology."[31] If we cannot tell what the human is, precisely because it has yet to be achieved, we also cannot tell what the animal is. Just as Adorno develops a negative anthropology, he also traces the lineaments of a zoology without the animal—or rather and to be more precise, a philosophical animalistics without the animal. It would not be incorrect to refer here to Derrida's own project of a zoopoetics, a creation through and vis-à-vis the drawing of the lines within the continuum of the animal. Still, to speak of an anthropology without anthropos, a zoology without an animal, and a bestiary without the beast, is to speak of a historical materialism that thinks the natural as part of the historical and the historical as partly natural. In order to clarify Adorno's stand on his historical materialist philosophical anthropology and bestiary, we must take recourse to his views on what he called already in 1932 "the idea of natural history." As has been noted by Max Pensky, the concept of *Naturgeschichte* is "candidate for the most troubling and most resistant" concept in Adorno's thinking.[32] It is clear that it was originally formulated in terms of a critique of Heidegger's fundamental ontology and existential analytics, but later, it was retained and transformed into a critique of all attempts to assimilate nature into history and subjectivity into complete socialization. As the essay's translator has astutely noted, the closest conceptual analogue to *Naturgeschichte* is Horkheimer and Adorno's genealogy of primal subjectivity in the allegory of the Odyssey, as developed in the first excursus in the *Dialectic of Enlightenment*.[33] Natural history is neither *historia naturalis*, as was practiced by scholastic philosophers and theologians, who sought to read in nature the designs of some divine will and plan, nor is it nature as would be studied by the natural sciences, in which the changes in nature would be told in the form of a narrative. The key passage from the 1932 lecture is the following:

> If the question of the relation of nature and history is to be seriously posed, then it only offers any chance of solution if it is possible to comprehend historical being in its most extreme historical determinacy, where it is not historical, as natural being, or if it were possible to comprehend nature as an historical being where it seems to be most deeply itself as nature. . . . The retransformation of concrete history into dialectical nature is the task of the ontological reorientation of the philosophy of history: the idea of natural history.[34]

Natural history, contrary to the seeming oxymoronic ring of the expression, seeks to naturalize history and historicize nature in order to break through the reification of both: nature is not solely the repetition of the same, nor is history the ceaseless emergence of the new. The idea of natural history, in fact, turns out to be no more than a reconstruction of dialectical materialism. Nothing makes this more evident than Adorno's explicit claims in *Negative Dialectics*, where he inserts the above quoted passage from the 1932 lecture, and then proceeds to conclude the section entitled "Natural History" by quoting Marx from the *German Ideology*: "We can only know a single science, the science of history. History can be considered from two sides, divided into the history of nature and the history of mankind. Yet there is no separating the two sides; as long as man exists, natural and human history will qualify each other." This passage is then followed by Adorno's oblique gloss on it: "[t]he traditional antitheses of nature and history is both true and false—true insofar as it expresses what happened to the natural element; false insofar as, by means of conceptual reconstruction, it apologetically repeats the concealment of history's natural growth by history itself."[35] The category of natural history, therefore, can contribute to the dialectical cracking of a historical totality that sets up a sacrificial stage on which our humanity is immolated through its appearing as the supposed savage logic of nature.

"NATURAL HISTORY": WHAT FOLLOWS AFTER THE ANIMAL

In July of 1997 Derrida gave a 10-hour address at the Cerisy-la-Salle conference devoted to his work. The title of the conference was "The Autobiographical Animal."[36] Responding to a question afterward by Elisabeth Roudinesco concerning "animals rights," Derrida summarized how the key philosophers dealt with in his presentation—Descartes, Kant, Heidegger, Levinas, and Lacan—had broached the question of the animal:

> Now, when it comes to the relation to "the Animal," this Cartesian legacy determines all of modernity. The Cartesian theory assumes, for animal language, a system of signs without response: *reactions* but no *response*. Kant, Levinas, Lacan, Heidegger (much like the cognitivists [I would add to Derrida's list, Habermas and Honneth]) hold a position in this regard identical to Descartes'. They distinguish *reaction* from *response*, with everything that depends on this distinction, which is almost limitless. With regard to the essential and to what counts on a practical level, this legacy, whatever the differences may be, governs modern thought concerning the relation of humans to animals.[37]

Derrida proceeds to argue that the discourse of animal rights, which is predicated on human rights, replicates the logic and principles that have in the first place necessitated that we extend such protection to animals. The solution in fact turns out to be part of the problem, the medicine, the very source of the ailment:

> Consequently, to want absolutely to grant, not to animals but to a certain category of animals, rights equivalent to human rights would be a disastrous contradiction. It would reproduce the philosophical and juridical machine thanks to which the exploitation of animal material for food, work, experimentation, etc., has been practiced (and tyrannically so, that is, through an abuse of power).[38]

It is this contradiction that Adorno confronts squarely, but without flinching from it and deeming it a "disastrous" one. I want to conclude by arguing that Derrida is absolutely right to re-focus our attention in this hitherto little-explored aspect of Adorno's work, not just because it foregrounds a series of profound reflections that have immediate relevance for us today, as we face an unprecedented and irreversible ecological crisis, but also because it allows us to shed light on a methodological dimension of Adorno's work that seems to have lost some of its appeal and luster due to the linguistic turn of Frankfurt School critical theory.

Derrida's "The Animal that Therefore I Am (More to Follow)," which I cannot do justice to here, raises a series of extremely evocative questions, of which I will focus only on two.[39] The title, a play on French grammar that links the verb to be to "follow"—as David Will notes, "[a]n obvious play on Descartes's definition of consciousness (of the thinking animal as human)" which "also takes advantage of the shared first-person singular present form of *être* (to be) and *suivre* (to follow) in order to suggest a displacement of that priority, also reading as 'the animal that therefore I follow after.'"[40] Indeed, Derrida evokes the many valences of "to follow": to be after, to seek, to come after, to be next to, to be with, to be in a temporal chronology that is ambiguous as to whether the after is before or after, in the sense that the human is what comes after the animal, or that the human is in search of his or her animality. One of the things Derrida is alluding to, evidently, is the Darwinian notion that *Homo sapiens* comes after prior evolutionary extinctions or failures. We are thus in the grip of that realization that we are after all descendents of apes, and so we are also in the grip of the obsessive quest after our missing link. We are part of natural history, and humans cannot be explained without reference to that logic of evolution.

The temporal after, of the human that is after the animal in herself, is related to another important reflection in Derrida's lecture. Derrida in fact will formulate two hypotheses. The first hypothesis formulates that for over two centuries human beings have been "involved in an unprecedented transformation." And this "mutation" has affected what we call "imperturbably" the "animal or animals." Here Derrida notes the asymmetry between what has been happening to "the human" and what has not happened to the animal. On one side we have ceaseless change and transformation, on the other, immutability and stasis. Derrida wants to arrest and truncate the assumed historicality of the human and imputed ahistoricality of the animal. The transformation of humanity as is reflected in this putatively new consciousness about the animal is not and will not be described by Derrida as "historical turning point."[41] To describe it in such terms would be to reinscribe in the very attempt to think the human and the animal jointly the very line that has kept them separated from and alien to each other: that one has history, and the other does not; that one dwells properly in the historical, while the other dwells in timeless nature.

The second hypothesis is announced after Derrida has pronounced that "[t]he animal looks at us, and we are naked before it. Thinking perhaps begins there."[42] We must not overlook the striking similarity between Derrida's formulation and Adorno's formulation quoted above that "[d]ie Philosophie ist eigentlich dazu da, das einsulösen, was im Blick eines Tieres liegt (philosophy is truly there to redeem what lies in the gaze of an animal)."[43] The second hypothesis, nonetheless, is formulated in three paragraphs, which I will abbreviate for the sake of space in the following way: (1) that the abyss between the human and the animal does not have two edges; (2) that this rupture has a history; (3) that beyond this line that challenges its very tracing and legibility, is the multiplicity of the living.[44] Together, these three paragraph formulate the hypothesis that Derrida's work has been properly about limits, about their logics, their violences, and their transgressions. The subject of this second hypothesis is what Derrida calls *limitrophy*[45]: the turning of limits, the forms of limits, the turning of limits, among which, of course, is the limits of the human. In Adorno's language, then, Derrida's project has been "about transcending the concept by way of the concept"[46] by exploding and exposing the concept's historicity that is negated by being assumed to be a timeless category that is independent of both history and nature.

We have not ceased to be animals, and will never cease to be, for whatever is part of our evolution is still part of our natural evolution, just as numerous animals have not ceased to be animals even if they have co-evolved with humans. To refute and insult the animal in the human is to exile humans to an impossible pedestal, one from which it can fulminate and rain violence against that which it deems its inferior. Both Adorno and Derrida are resolute in their philosophical commitment to recognizing that we are inextricably woven into the natural history of all animals, and all that is living in general, even as we have sought to define ourselves by distinguishing ourselves from it. We are in the midst of crossing three important thresholds that will surely alter not just the meaning of what it means to be human, but also of what it may mean to be a nonhuman animal. The first has to do with the correlated processes of population explosion and mega-urbanization of humanity. Together, they mean as much the exacerbated stress on the planet as the inevitability of having to think of large sectors of humanity as surplus, redundant, even burdensome, humanity. We are at the point at which we are having to think of humanity as a plague on the planet and humanity itself. The population growth of humanity is exponentially and inversely related to the habitats of other animal species. The more humans and the more space they take up to live and to consume, the less space for other animals, the less other species can survive in macro- and micro-habitats. For this reason, we are facing what paleontologists have been calling the "sixth extinction." In 1993, biologist E. O. Wilson projected that about 30,000 animal and plant species were becoming extinct yearly. More recently scientists have began to argue that this estimate is actually higher.[47] In his 2002 book *The Future of Life*, Wilson offers a bleaker prospect when he affirmed that "at least a fifth of the species of plants and animals would be gone or committed to early extinction by 2030, and half by the end of the century."[48] What will become of the earth after such a massive extinction, on a scale larger than that occasioned by earlier earthly catastrophes? Humans may become extinct, and the earth will have become a "planet of weeds," as David Quammen put it.[49] The third threshold has to do with the genetic manipulation of genomes, both animal and plant alike. It is not only that we have been genetically modifying plants and animals, the so-called GMOs, some times even mixing animal and plant genomes. It is difficult not to expect that some scientist has not already engaged in some sort of genetic manipulation, whether therapeutic or enhancing, of the human genome. It is here where Adorno's concept and dialectical method of "natural history" becomes relevant. Neither a supererogatory ethics that grants to animals unique or elevated moral status, nor a mere utilitarian ethics of the preservation of animals, a kind of moral considerability of animals by proxy, will do. Adorno's historical materialism and negative philosophical anthropology remits us to an uneasy responsibility that is both simultaneously a responsibility for what is human and animal in us, and for the animal, without which we cannot be, both morally and materially. The animal in us gave rise to reason in us, but also to the affect that makes us vulnerable to the suffering in animal others and that guides our moral solicitude towards others. There is an aphorism by Leo Tolstoy that expresses beautifully what I take to be Derrida and Adorno's inchoate, if not explicitly avowed, positive response to the gaze of the animal: "[w]hen a man does not live as man, he is beneath the animal."[50] When man lives like a parasite and a plague, he is both less than human and less than animal. Let us learn to live like good animals, as Adorno put it when he reformulated the Kantian categorical imperative.

III

SPECIESISM AND IDEOLOGIES OF DOMINATION

8

The Dialectic of Anthropocentrism

By Aaron Bell

The ontological hierarchy of the human and animal established by the Western humanist tradition has largely been seen, even by its opponents, as part of an ideology that has benefited human beings. The instrumental reduction of "the animal" or "nature," a consequence of the anthropocentric subject's ability entirely to discount the significance of any considerations outside the purview of the human, is often seen as an enabling condition for the prolific development of Western (as well as Eastern) industrialized civilization. While in a sense this is true, I wish to call into question the supposed benefits of humanist anthropocentrism. My purpose here is to understand how the latent contradictions of humanist anthropocentrism have manifested themselves in a violent and self-destructive manner, fatal both to human and nonhuman life.

I will begin with a discussion of the genealogy of humanist anthropocentrism as a narrative of self-authorization and a means of self-definition. I will then discuss contemporary critiques of the ontological distinction between "man" and "animal" and the self-destructive violence that results from such a distinction. Finally, I will argue that humanist anthropocentrism, predicated on this ontological distinction, necessarily arrives at these moments of self-destruction because of its irrational formal structure—a structure that closely resembles what Hegel termed "radical evil."

In *Dialectic of Enlightenment*, Adorno and Horkheimer explain how the Enlightenment has become a source of catastrophe, subverting its express purpose of "liberating human beings from fear and installing them as masters."[1] By tracing the genealogical origins of instrumental reason to a primordial human past distorted by myth and violence, they reveal the currents of irrationality that have subtended the development of reason from its very beginning. The technologies of instrumental reason and the Enlightenment subject are Promethean developments, motivated by a fundamental lack and by a fear of and rage at a merciless external world. In the face of a dark world that terrorized a self that was "infinitely weak in comparison to the force of nature,"[2] human beings were driven to become stronger and more cunning in order to control nature before it could threaten to destroy them. The torch of reason was developed to enlighten the natural world so that human beings could make visible everything that might lurk or cower in the shadows of our ignorance. According to the logic of instrumental reason, everything must be called forth and laid bare, stripped of mystery and meaning, so that humans might make use of and disarm it.

As instrumental reason developed, the binary oppositions of man/animal and rational/irrational were produced as its underlying foundations. The production of a supposedly clean divide between the human and animal enabled the stabilized concepts of "Animal" and "Man." Adorno and Horkheimer draw attention to the co-constitutive feature of this relationship—"the [Enlightenment] idea of the human being has [always] been expressed in contradistinction to the animal. The latter's lack of reason is the proof of human dignity."[3] Thus, the identity of that which is human is established only in relation to non-identity with the animal. Furthermore, this distinction of human and animal facilitated Western civilization's establishment of a hierarchy of being. The Enlightenment subject is a being capable of possessing dignity, reason, and intrinsic meaning, while all others who fall outside of this identity occupy an inferior plane of being. Together, these two oppositions, the human/animal and rational/irrational, enable what Derrida calls "a veritable war of the species,"[4] where, as Adorno and Horkheimer put it, the "hunting ground [of the Enlightenment subject] then shrinks to the unified cosmos, in which nothing exists but prey."[5] Thus, we can see that both distinctions are crucial for the constitution of the human and the domination of nature. The distinctions enable and generate the technologies of the modern subject and instrumental reason, which are in turn necessary for the auto-authorizing constitution of the human narrative of exceptionality and supremacy.

As Adorno and Horkheimer explain, the development of reason has progressively filtered out any affinity or comparison between the human and the natural; mimetic activity, animism, and anthropomorphic conceptions of the natural world have all been eradicated as myth by enlightened reason. Any association between the human and the animal, be it through the shaman's mimetic impersonation of demons or animal spirits, or the "mystified" attribution of intrinsic meaning to nature, must be purged.[6] This is accomplished by placing the human animal entirely outside of nature. What was a distinction of degree gradually becomes a distinction of kind. The Judeo-Christian conception of man as made in the image of God represents a radical break from earlier metaphysical relationships which still retained features of animism and which acknowledged human vulnerability to forces external to itself. The Judeo-Christian narrative, with its grand origin story and mandate of human sovereignty over the undifferentiated mass of nature, becomes a catalytic moment in the development of anthropocentrism and the anthropocentric mythos of self-authorization. The supernatural origin of Adam, made in the image of God, signals the metaphysically sanctioned beginning of the reign of human beings and human history.

Conceptually, this creation myth enables the biological cycle of human procreation and death to be forcibly straightened into a time*line*, which by the eighteenth century allowed for the concepts of forward progress and the development and perfection of humanity. This stands in stark contrast to Enlightenment's characterization of nature as a grinding cycle of blind life and death which exists without progress or purpose. There is no organic purpose, no "end in itself" for nonhuman life: rather, "life" is paradoxically depicted as mechanical, a bloody machine which continually creates and destroys, recycling the organic matter that it produces without providing any meaning to its processes. Conceived this way, the cycle of nonhuman life can easily be transformed into a mere means to the end of humanity, an engine for the creation of raw resources to be utilized for human progress. The conceptualization of nature as machine is an important precondition for human development and ultimately the foundation for a collective human destiny. Human beings, generation after generation, must continue to improve their domination of nature, laboring on it to further improve the species itself. The singular personality of Man stands above this meaningless process, creating meaning through his labor, and in so doing forges for himself both a particular and collective destiny. By contrast, the conception of nature as a blind cycle without inherent value renders the lives of nonhuman individuals merely as particular instantiations of the universal, cogs in the machinery of *res extensa*. This self-authorized narrative becomes a primary means for the human animal to transition into the modern human being, which assures itself that it has a uniquely special destiny in contrast to all other life.

After giving us the key to the future, the God of Abraham, the father who granted us total dominion over the Earth, must be killed. And in the end it is imperative that we require no justification or license for our patricide. The dead patriarch must be discarded by enlightenment because our actions as children of God, despite being His favorites, are still mimetic—acting like a god is still acting like something other than what we are (human), which stands in the way of the total assertion of human transcendence. The death of God allows human beings to fully possess the world without mediation or constraint. Furthermore,

God, as divine creator, threatens to cast an aura upon all of His creations, even the natural world. Despite being given divinely sanctioned dominion over "every living thing that moveth upon the earth," the risk of even a limited or decayed aura surrounding nature is too great. After all, God also said that the creation of these living things was "good." God let us name all of the creatures of the earth, but this taxonomical privilege cannot offset the fact that we did not authorize the categorization of nature ourselves. Adam may have named all nonhuman life, but he did not name himself.

Once Enlightenment progressed to the point where human beings could be reconceived as the sole possessors of *logos*, the justificatory mechanisms of early history and the Judeo-Christian tradition came to seem antiquated and obsolete. While the authorization of the human right to dominate all other life, undersigned by God, was always already *self*-authorization, enlightened reason now presents itself as fully unsublimated and self-authorizing, freestanding and unabashed. The need to locate value and entitlement in some external, metaphysical source that led to the creation of religious myths is overcome: to paraphrase Kant, humanity has overcome its self-imposed modesty.

Humanist anthropocentrism now comes on the scene as a consciousness that recognizes only one meaningful distinction: that which is human and that which is not. Traditionally, this has been conceived of as a clean cut, a linear division that places the human on one side and the animal on the other. Contemporary post- or anti-humanist theorists have complicated this two-dimensional metaphor. The procedure of defining what is proper to the human entails not only Derridean "auto-biography," the construction of the self through the self-authorized narrative or "auto-definition" of what it means to be human in relation to the animal, but also what we might call *auto-vivisection*. Auto-vivisection because one must cut into one's own being in order to remove or place to one side those features of oneself that are incidental and held in common with the rest of the "natural world," the "meat" of one's being, in order to find that tissue which is essential to the human.

The recent work of Agamben is helpful in understanding the terms of this excision. For Agamben, the division between man and animal is accomplished through the use of an "anthropogenic machine" that constructs the zone of the human through "an exclusion (which is always already a capturing) and an inclusion (which is always already an exclusion)."[7] In other words, on the one hand, the machine empties that which is human of its animal content, and in so doing it constructs the human through the exclusion of the animal. On the other hand, it excludes what is human from the animal, thus designating what is excluded as human and the captured remainder as animal. Agamben concludes that the modern form of the anthropogenic machine constructs the human by excluding the "not yet human," by "isolating the nonhuman within the human."[8] Agamben defines as "bare life" what is left after the individual or group has been excluded from or fallen on the wrong side of the human/animal divide. Bare life is what exists after the anthropogenic machine has evacuated the human of those qualities and signifiers that make up the concept of the human proper, the "animal separated within the human body itself."[9] Personified in the neomort (human body after the death of the brain) and most horrifically in the Jew and Roma in the Holocaust, bare life can be understood as biological persistence without dignity, signaling the possibility of "a noncriminal putting to death."[10] Bare life, existing as the other to Enlightenment rationality, provokes the fear and violence that have always unconsciously animated Enlightenment's development "since the mere idea of the 'outside' is the real source of fear"[11] for the modern subject. The horrors that result from bare life are produced by the exclusionary logic of the unmediated distinctions of human and animal.

Although Agamben does not concern himself with speciesism as a system of domination per se, his analysis nonetheless sheds light on the discursive preconditions of that system. Derrida, by contrast, takes the issue of speciesism as a central problematic in his later work.[12] As Derrida observes, we are already mistaken as soon as we utter the words "Man with a capital *M* and Animal with a capital *A*,"[13] even before we attempt to place them on opposite sides of an insuperable divide. According to Derrida, to speak of the *Animal* (singular, generic), is to "utter an *asinanity*,"[14] that is, stupidly and violently to corral "a heterogeneous . . . multiplicity of organizations of relations between living and dead"[15] into the confines of a reductive concept. *Animal* is not just a word, it is a "name [men] have given themselves the right and authority to give to the living other."[16] *Animal* signifies one of the most egregiously reductive concepts in the history of Western civilization. But it is not simply a bad concept, it is an act of violence. "The Animal has no language, no tools, no history"—these are phrases that float through the halls of human history, unlocking door after door of cruelty. But what do they mean? What animal? Does one truly mean to implicate the millions of nonhuman species[17] in these statements, from the flea to Wittgenstein's lions and Koko the gorilla? What statement invoking the Animal could hold true for all nonhuman life? There is no *Animal* with a capital A: such statements are nonsense. Traditional, linear formulations of the human/animal distinction are therefore to be understood as what Derrida terms an "abyssal" limit, a rupture with "multiple and heterogeneous border[s]" that resists reification into a dichotomous border that would be "single and indivisible."[18] Understanding the distinction as a single boundary, even a permeable one, would reinstitute the conceptual leveling of nonhuman life into a homogenous territory that abuts the human. In opposition to this leveling, our task must be to understand this nonhuman territory as traversed by myriad intersections and boundaries, some of which do and some of which do not interact with the territory of the human, thus enabling us to discuss the issue in a non-anthropocentric manner.

Dogmatic and undialectical, the classic human/animal and rational/irrational distinctions are inevitably sources of violence, toward the human and nonhuman alike. One of the first human casualties of this violent enforcement of boundaries is Woman. According to Adorno and Horkheimer, "the woman is not a subject" for enlightenment.[19] Woman is conceptualized as "an embodiment of biological function, an image of nature,"[20] and thus exiled to an inferior plane of being, on the wrong side of the human/animal divide. This proto-feminist critique of the patriarchal violence of instrumental reason anticipates the insights of *The Sexual Politics of Meat* by Carol Adams as well as Derrida's concept of "carnophallogocentrism." Both positions trace the violence of anthropocentrism (carno), patriarchy (phallo), and reason (logo) to an interconnected network of concepts and discourses.[21] For Adams, the intersection between violence toward animals and women occurs as part of the same "logic of domination" and makes use of the "ready-made symbolic economy [produced by the violent exploitation of animals] that overdetermines the representation of women, by transcoding the *edible* bodies of animals and the *sexualized* bodies of women."[22] For Derrida, the intersection of these forms of violence is most clear in their shared use of a logic of exclusion. The "metaphysics of subjectivity . . . [is] constituted through a network of exclusionary relations"[23] which necessarily identifies certain groups as ineligible for the status of full subjectivity in order to define those who *are* candidates for full subjectivity.

According to Adorno and Horkheimer, Enlightenment becomes irrational and self-destructive because it relies on an exclusionary logic that attempts to "erase the dialectical tension"[24] between the categories of rational and irrational and human and animal. The unmediated relationship between these categories is a fiction, and the attempt to preserve the dichotomy results in contradiction and violence. Women are the first (human) victims of this contradiction, the social group contaminated by the animal par excellence. Patriarchy forces women to the margins of society, domesticating their existence through threats of male violence and denying them full subjectivity. Relegated to roles of care, support, and procreation, women end up resembling what Enlightenment characterizes as the cyclical and meaningless repetition of a nature without history or development. This stigma of the natural and the irrational is all that is necessary for continued persecution and exclusion.

To summarize: anthropocentrism's counterintuitive or dialectical reversals, which occur in moments of self-destructive violence toward human beings, are material manifestations of the otherwise latent contradictions of the ideology itself. The general irrationality of this mode of life is not an aberration or perversion of its internal logic. Rather, it is inextricably built into the formal structure of anthropocentric subjectivity. It remains for us only to describe the phenomenology of this structure, which in key ways resembles what Hegel termed "radical evil."

Hegel's account of radical evil is helpful here because of his insight into the self-deceptive and self-subverting nature of megalomaniacal subjectivity. For Hegel, radical evil is best understood not as a description of a type of action, but as a subjective comportment toward the world. What makes a subject evil *radically* (literally "to the root") is not the particular heinous acts he[25] is engaged in, but rather his relationship to those acts. Hegel characterizes this relationship as one "*empty* of all ethical *content*,"[26] where the individual sees himself as standing over and against the objective law and morality. Hegel agrees with Kant that ethical action must always be law-giving—if I will that this is right for myself, then I must will it universally, for everyone. Therefore, I cannot claim that something is good for others (universally), without also claiming that it is good for me (in particular), without being caught in a contradiction. To do otherwise, to act as though I am entitled to exclude my particular actions from the will of the true universal, is to commit an evil act. The subject who believes himself to stand completely outside of the moral order is evil in the most profound way.

According to Hegel, the radically evil subject is able to extricate himself from the objective moral order by embracing his own "*subjective emptiness*, in that he knows himself as this emptiness of all content and, in this knowledge, knows *himself* as the absolute."[27] In other words, by ironically turning to a lack, the individual is able to construct a grandiose narrative of entitlement. By recognizing the "subjective emptiness," or lack at the core of subjectivity, devoid of any content, the radically evil subject affirms himself as free to do whatever he will. In this moment of what Hegel calls "indeterminate freedom," the subject clearly recognizes the existence of the objective moral order yet holds himself over and above it. The subject not only recognizes that he is free to affirm or deny any value, but takes himself as the origin of value itself. Hegel imagines that the radically evil subject might say, "'You in fact honestly accept a law as existing in and for itself' [it says to others]; 'I do so, too, but I go further than you, for I am also beyond this law and can do *this or that* as I please. It is not the thing which is excellent, it is I who am excellent and master of both law and thing.'"[28] In recognizing himself as beyond and the master of the law, the subject's indeterminate freedom is characterized by a sense of whimsy or caprice—doing "*this or that* as I please"—and what Hegel identifies as *eitelkeit*, literally meaning "vanity" or "conceitedness." There is no experience of guilt for the radically evil subject because he—or she—"knows" himself or herself to be above it. As long as one feels guilt about one's immoral actions, or at least acknowledges that there is a higher authority or objective morality, there is hope for the subject's redemption or reform. But the subject who denies guilt or even the existence of an objective good must be feared above all others. As Pascal writes, "as for those open sinners, hardened sinners, undiluted, complete, and consummate sinners, *hell cannot hold them*."[29]

For Hegel, this ironic comportment toward the world is the ultimate evil, "an expression of an extravagant, self-indulgent (even self-deifying) subjectivism."[30] This form of subjectivity creates the total impossibility of transgression by the subject and the complete dissolution of moral subjectivity into evil. Everything becomes merely relative to the radically evil subject: the world itself can only become objective and real through *his* affirmation. Such an individual declares, "objective goodness is merely something constructed by my conviction, sustained by me alone."[31] The radically evil individual stands alone, conjuring up the chaos of the world into shapes of meaning and then smashing them to pieces according to his own arbitrary desire. This type of individual signals the death of good and evil because he denies their objective claim over him, and instead ordains himself as the sole arbiter of these values, along with all others. Evil can only be what he does not presently will, and good is nothing other than his will itself. The result is a transcendent moment of self-deification, in which the individual forgets his place as a metaphorical child of God, and sees himself as absolute, all-encompassing.

However, the radically evil individual is periodically reminded of the limits to his would-be omnipotence, as his volition collides with the structure of reality itself. For in fact, he is not the center of the universe, and his actions always occur in a context not of his making. The illusion of his supremacy is constantly challenged by his own reliance on others to simply survive, let alone to prosper. As a consequence, the radically evil subject must either acknowledge his own dependence on others to survive, and thus risk destabilizing the foundations of his grandiose self-narrative, or refuse to acknowledge the reality of his dependence and simply thrash and flail at the world like the inverted image of Oskar Matzerath, the main character of Günter Grass's *The Tin Drum* (who, at the age of three, chooses not to physically mature after witnessing the hypocrisy and irrationality of the adult world), until he is undone either by his own actions or by a reaction from the environment he rails against. It is probably because of this inherent instability that Hegel speculates on the possibility of a group of radically evil people forming a community in an attempt to compensate for the inherent instability of their way of being in the world. The radical evil subject, he writes, "may even form a *community* whose bond . . . above all [is] basking in the glory of this self-knowledge and self-expression."[32] Although Hegel is only speculating, it seems clear that this sort of self-narrative is inherently unsound and will inevitably be torn apart by its own momentum, whether it is instantiated in a community or a single individual. Radical evil militates against any authentic form of community or cooperation in a way that makes it structurally incompatible with any form of persistent social formation.

To return, now, to the anthropocentric gaze, we find that it too looks out upon the world and, like the radically evil individual, sees nothing but its own reflection. The rest of nature is reduced to "the chaotic stuff of mere classification,"[33] to be organized by the subject of logos in order to attain actuality and meaning. Like the radically evil subject, a sort of megalomania motivates the anthropocentric subject, which understands itself as the sole point of reference in an otherwise meaningless universe. Furthermore, as Derrida notes, the anthropocentric subject, like the radically evil individual and its indeterminate freedom, is defined by an emptiness or lack; and "from within the pit of that lack, an eminent lack, a quite different lack from that he assigns to the animal, man installs or claims in a single stroke *his property* . . . and his *superiority* over what is called animal life."[34] However, unlike the radical evil of the individual in Hegel's account, anthropocentrism is culturally sanctioned, hence persists through time as an institutionally stabilized phenomenon. The many practical limitations that finally render (individual) radical evil self-subverting have been either defused or omitted by the formal structure that anthropocentrism has evolved into over the history of Western civilization. Perhaps it is the historical scale of anthropocentrism that has allowed it to thrive while individual radical evil necessarily fails. A grandiose narrative scaled down to the life of an individual quickly becomes problematic; when inflated to the size of a society or civilization, however, it becomes a thing of truly awesome power, taking on the appearance of a "second nature." On the individual level, the deep irrationality and impractical nature of radical evil's egoism come to the fore almost immediately, whereas on a cultural level this sort of species-narrative has been able to persist and develop in a way that obscures and leaves latent these issues. As Goebbels remarked, the bigger the lie, the more it will be believed (a matter he knew something about).

By comparing Hegel's conception of radical evil to humanist anthropocentrism I have tried to show the way in which violent irrationality is implicit in the grandiose narrative and the logic of ontological exclusion of Western anthropocentrism. But I want to push this claim further still—to suggest that humanist anthropocentrism is not simply analogous to Hegel's conception of radical evil, it *is* evil.

The logic of exclusion deployed in the ontological distinction of human and animal and the radical evil of anthropocentrism have been the implements of unimaginable violence. The express, intentional purpose of anthropocentrism has been not only a "war of the species" but a war on empathy. As Derrida claims, the conflict, "accelerating, intensifying, no longer knowing where it is going, for about two centuries, at an incalculable rate and level,"[35] is "being waged . . . [by] those who violate not only animal life but . . . compassion" itself.[36] This radical evil is not content with the rationalized destruction of the lives of animals in infernal industrial farms—it works to eradicate pity for all that is other. Of all the things that Adorno meant when he said, "Auschwitz begins wherever someone looks at a slaughterhouse and thinks: they're only animals," perhaps this destruction of pity was what he meant to warn against most. The use of the same train cars designed to transport cows, the same crematorium ovens originally designed to burn animal bodies, the same electrified barbed wire enclosures used to intern animals before slaughter, makes the denial of the material similarities between the two events absurd, but the affinity between the two events is much more fundamental.[37] The denial of the significance of the other's suffering because she is "only an animal" is inextricably linked to indifference because she is "only" a woman, a black, a Jew, and so on. The "bare life" of the camps is the everyday existence of every factory farmed animal in the world. But the horror of the violence against animals is a kind of impossible genocide, a perpetual violence:

> [T]he annihilation of certain species is indeed in process, but it is occurring through the organization and exploitation of an artificial, infernal, virtually interminable survival. . . . As if, for example, instead of throwing people into ovens and gas chambers (let's say Nazi) doctors and geneticists had decided to organize the overproduction and overgeneration of Jews, gypsies, and homosexuals by means of artificial insemination, so that, being continually more numerous and better fed, they could be destined in always increasing numbers for the same hell, that of the imposition of genetic experimentation, or extermination by gas or by fire. In the same abattoirs.[38]

One could add to Derrida's horrific scenario the detail that the "undesirables" must now also be genetically altered in order to increase production, making their short lives even more hellish and grotesque. The process of domestication, taken to its logical conclusion, creates pathetic[39] and worse animals for us to butcher so that we can tell ourselves that we were right all along, that they were always already nothing but violent brutes to be disassembled and harvested. The violence and terror of industrialized violation that would drive any human being insane create terrified and bewildered animals that appear to verify the image of Descartes's beast-machines, as systems of blind behaviors and twitches.

By using the example of human suffering to illustrate his point about violence towards animals, Derrida is trading on the still-open avenues of compassion, those areas of suffering that still torture our conscience, in an attempt to short-circuit permissible pity into our consciousness of animal suffering. If we suffer for A, perhaps we can understand that we can and should suffer for B in a comparable situation. It is an admirable and generally effective strategy, but it also exposes the monstrosity of anthropocentrism's purpose—to render these comparisons themselves illegitimate (or, worse, incomprehensible), to close off even the possibility of pity, and to completely exclude animals from the moral circuit. Kant, along with Levinas to a lesser extent, accomplishes this exclusion in a particularly insidious way. Both thinkers acknowledge an imperfect ethical obligation to the animal, thus (implicitly) accounting for the phenomenological experience of compassion that healthy individuals feel in the face of nonhuman suffering, while precluding the animal from actually entering into the moral circuit. Kant claims that any obligation that we have to not cause needless suffering in animals comes from our duty to other human beings. Kant claims in his *Lectures on Ethics*, in a clear example of what Freud calls "the universal narcissism of men,"[40] that violence toward animals is only a problem because it can lead to violence and immorality *in humans*:

> if a man has his dog shot, because it can no longer earn a living for him, he is by no means in breach of any duty to the dog, since the latter is incapable of judgment, but he thereby damages the kindly and humane qualities of himself, which he ought to exercise in virtue of his duties to mankind . . . for a person who already displays such cruelty to animals is also no less hardened towards men.[41]

As Adorno has claimed elsewhere, there is a deep hatred of nature at the root of Kant's entire project, and it is on clear display in this passage. The master has no duty to the dog who has served him for its entire life once "it can no longer earn a living for him"—he is only prohibited from killing the dog because the act might harden his heart toward his fellow man. The rationality of the master who would wish to kill his no-longer-useful dog, an exemplar of the always already present bourgeois coldness typical of Kant's philosophy, is only a cause for alarm if this desire leads to the degradation of his "humane qualities" toward other human beings. Kant mercilessly ensnares the suffering of animals in exclusionary concern for human beings, effectively trapping and accounting for them in his system while discounting them. There are those who will immediately be put off by any comparison between factory farming and either slavery or genocide—we are comparing the meaningless existence of the animal to the lives of human beings, after all! This reaction is both tragic and perverse, simultaneously a product of and an enabling condition for the continual, irrational violence of anthropocentrism.

Freud noted in his well-known comments on what he termed "human megalomania" that "curiously enough . . . [anthropocentric violence] is still foreign to children."[42] Despite our wretchedness and failings, in a "wrong life" that can never be lived rightly, there is the hope that we can do better. The bad facticity of our distorted and distorting relationship to other animals and the rest of life is exposed as such by every generation of children who must be broken and indoctrinated, whose innocence must be sacrificed in order to continue in the logic of sacrifice. In the final aphorism of *Minima Moralia*, Adorno holds that "perspectives must be fashioned that displace and estrange the world, reveal it to be, with its rifts and crevices, as indigent and distorted as it will appear one day in the messianic light."[43] It seems that our one consolation is that this perspective, at least in relation to our treatment of other animals, obstinately returns and cannot be entirely snuffed out for as long as we continue to exist as a species.

If we are finally to abandon the self-aggrandizing narrative of anthropocentrism constructed in the West, we will have to begin by reconceptualizing the difference between humans and animals in a way that does not operate under a destructive exclusionary logic. Both for human beings and for animals, any cessation of violence under the current logic is only a momentary deferment, an armistice but never a peace. Even moments of apparent tenderness and compassion become grotesque symptoms of a corrupted order so long as this way of life is permitted to stand. As Horkheimer and Adorno observe in *Dialectic of Enlightenment*, "the fascists' pious love of animals, nature, and children is the lust of the hunter. The idle stroking of children's hair and animal pelts signifies: this hand can destroy. It tenderly fondles one victim before felling the other, and its choice has nothing to do with the victim's guilt. The caress intimates that all are the same before power."[44] The Nazi officer's arbitrary choice of who would survive (for another day) and who would be killed demonstrates the same terrible *eitelkeit* of Hegel's radical evil individual, who reduces every decision to a choice of "*this* or *that*."[45] The arbitrary nature of the decision is an exercise of power in its rawest form, and an uncanny reminder of our contemporary violence towards animals. For the same perverse arbitrariness at the core of the SS officer's decision holds sway in a society which dooms millions of animals to unimaginable suffering while pampering millions of others as "pets."[46]

Such interludes of apparent nonviolence are merely pauses between atrocities: as Levinas puts it, "the peace of empires issued from war *rests on war.* [Peace] does not restore to the alienated beings their lost identity."[47] War on the other, radicalized in the form of fascism, shows that "not only modern war but every war employs arms that turn against those who wield them. It establishes an order from which no one can keep his distance."[48] There is no safe ground for the "authentically" human individual—because there can be no authentic anthropocentrism, just as Adorno and Horkheimer claim that "there is no authentic anti-semitism." They write: "Just as . . . the victims are interchangeable: vagrants,

Jews, Protestants, Catholics . . . each of them can replace the murderer, in the same blind lust for killing, as soon as he feels the power of representing the norm."[49] The Jew in Auschwitz, the Palestinian in the West Bank, the Christian in Armenia, the enslaved African in the American South, women everywhere—they all have been reduced to the status of animal and they all could do the same to others. We all can be reduced to the "animal."

9

Animal Repression

Speciesism as Pathology

By Zipporah Weisberg

> *Be. And, at the same time, know what it is* not *to be.*
> That emptiness inside you allows you to vibrate
> in resonance with your world. Use it for once.
> To all that has run its course, and to the vast unsayable
> numbers of beings abounding in Nature
> add yourself gladly, and cancel the cost.
>
> —Rainer Maria Rilke[1]

Peter Singer defines speciesism as "a prejudice or attitude of bias in favor of the interests of members of one's own species and against those of members of other species."[2] This is certainly the fundamental *structure* of speciesism: the human species positions itself as superior to other species, and gives itself license to inflict egregious cruelties against them, simply by virtue of the fact that they are *not human*. Furthermore, it is well known that the justification for speciesism and the exclusion of other animals from ethical consideration remains the assertion of an insurmountable binary opposition between putatively rational humans and irrational animals. This dichotomy, which can be traced back to classical antiquity, began to have especial import in the early modern period with the arrival of Renaissance humanism; it has for the most part been consistently and uncritically reaffirmed in Western religious, philosophical, and scientific thought ever since. The rational human/irrational animal distinction has undoubtedly provided the justification for the instrumentalization and systemic torture and murder of other animals over the centuries. However, what is not wholly accounted for in the analysis of this binary opposition, or in the debates around the origins of speciesism as a whole, is the psychological dimension of animal hatred. Part and parcel of the system of apartheid which pits humans against other animals is humans' repression of their own animality. By "animality" I mean principally the *embodied consciousness* we have in common with other sentient beings and the intersubjective relationality this shared embodiment engenders.[3] Our fanatic denial of our own animality and our concomitant systemic brutalization of other animals throughout the millennia have had profoundly detrimental effects not only on our animal kin but also on our own psychic health. In short, a massive self-deception has been at play in the course of the development of Western civilization, which has proved not only immensely damaging to the welfare of other animals, but has also proven injurious to humans' psychological well being. Animal repression can result in or is even constitutive of an unconscious sense of loss, melancholia, ambivalence, guilt, and a host of other neuroses, on both an individual and a societal level. To properly understand and ultimately overcome speciesism, then, it is paramount that we examine the psychological mechanism of repression which results in undue torment for both the oppressed and the oppressors.

THE FRANKFURT SCHOOL'S THEORY OF REPRESSION

The early members of the Frankfurt School, especially Theodor Adorno, Max Horkheimer, and Herbert Marcuse, offer a starting point for our investigation of animal repression and oppression as they are arguably the first political theorists to acknowledge that this twin process of negation has resulted not just in misery for other beings, but in serious psychic and even cognitive injury to human beings. They extend Freud's theory of repression to suggest that civilization is built not only on the repression of drives but also on repression of "inner nature"—or human sensuousness—and "outer nature"—or the natural world and all its infinitely varied sentient and insentient constituents.

Adorno and Horkheimer in particular located the originary negation or repression of inner and outer nature in the shift from animism to mytho-enlightenment (i.e., Greco-Roman and Judeo-Christian thought). On their usage, enlightenment, or *instrumental reason* (the reduction of the world of experience to categories of manipulation, control, and domination), is coterminous with the disenchantment of nature, that is, with the repudiation of the animist belief that not just humans but *all* beings—mineral, vegetable, and animal—are animated by souls, and are therefore driven by intent and will.[4] With the new Enlightenment ethos of mastery over nature, "matter was to be fully controlled without the illusion of immanent powers or hidden properties."[5]

Once co-subjects, more-than-human beings had by the onset of the scientific revolution became the *objects* of scientific investigation, instruments of calculation, and eventually, raw material for capitalist exploitation.[6] This process did not, as the myth of progress would have us believe, improve humans' lot, but worsened it. In particular, they argue that enlightenment's artificial binary between the *disembodied mind* and the *sensuous body* results in shameful violence against other beings and prevents us from developing our own being to its fullest potentiality—a capacity which can only be properly grounded *in* sensuousness.[7] In their words:

> The standardization of the intellectual function through which the mastery of the senses is accomplished, the acquiescence of thought to the production of unanimity, implies an impoverishment of thought no less than that of experience; the separation of the two realms [sensual and rational] leaves both damaged.[8]

To sever thinking from sensuousness, in other words, is both to degrade our experience as natural beings and to diminish our capacity for critical thinking.

While Adorno and Horkheimer generally include both sentient and non-sentient beings under the heading "nature," they occasionally highlight the oppression of animals and its particular role in the psychic mutilation of the human subject. For example, they point to vivisectionists as the epitome of the distorted human being produced by enlightenment and its repressive mechanism. By ravaging the bodies of helpless animals in the name of putative rationality, animal experimenters play out a brutal *irrational* logic that reduces all beings—human and more-than-human alike—to mere objects of calculation. "By mistreating animals," they write, "they announce that they, and only they in the whole of creation, function voluntarily in the same mechanical, blind, automatic way as the twitching movements of the bound victims made use of by the expert."[9] Though we have conquered internal and external nature in general and other animals in particular, our "success" has only come at the expense of our own further alienation and neurosis. Ironically, in proclaiming its mastery over other beings, it was the human being who proved itself irrational and bereft. As Herbert Marcuse observes, the human subject in advanced industrial civilization has become a distorted version of what it *could* and *ought* to be.[10] Propping itself up as the great rational being on the corpses of other beings to whom it has denied subjectivity and rationality, the human subject transforms *itself* into a kind of object—an unthinking automaton, a one-dimensional shell.[11]

Our quest for mastery over inner and outer nature in general and animality and other animals in particular has also fostered brutality. Though enlightenment was supposed to free us from "barbarism" it has in fact exacerbated our proclivity for violence against both other beings and each other.[12] As Adorno and Horkheimer write, "[h]uman beings are so radically estranged from themselves and from nature that they know only how to use and harm each other."[13] According to Marcuse, the invention of the scientific method and the instrumentalization of reason and of nature which took hold during the scientific revolution, in particular, not only enabled the domination of nature but in fact laid the groundwork for the domination of humans:

> The scientific method which led to the ever-more-effective domination of nature thus came to provide the pure concepts as well as the instrumentalities for the ever-more-effective domination of man by man *through* the domination of nature.[14]

By reducing other beings to objects of control, we reduce ourselves to the same thing.

Marcuse adds another important dimension to our discussion by pointing out how advanced industrial society has cultivated Thanatos, or aggression and the death drive for the purpose of dominating of nature in general and animals in particular, at the expense of Eros—the drive for unrestrained sexual gratification, the creative life force, and the source of our potential emotional bond with other beings. Noting the distinction, already implicit in Freud's work, between "necessary" and "unnecessary" repression, Marcuse distinguishes between "basic" and "surplus" repression. The former is, in his view, necessary for humans to live together and is not oppressive, while the latter is constitutive of domination. Of surplus repression, Marcuse tells us: "[w]ithin the total structure of the repressed personality, surplus-repression is that which is the result of specific societal conditions sustained in the specific interests of domination."[15] Whereas Freud normalizes the subordination of non-genital, non-procreative sexual activity and gratification of the procreative function in the course of a human individual's sexual maturation, Marcuse insists that this process is one of the principal forms of surplus repression in patriarchal techno-capitalist society because it reduces infinitely varied free erotic expression to instrumentality. Under the reign of "genital supremacy" the body is a servant to a state-capitalist machine that demands a constant influx of efficient workers. Marcuse also brings to light the direct correlation between the repression of Eros and the body's natural erotic impulses, on one hand, and the domination of nature in general and other animals in particular, on the other. He writes,

> the entire progress of civilization is rendered possible only by the transformation and utilization of the death instinct or its derivatives. . . . [A]ggressive impulses provide energy for the continuous alteration, mastery, and exploitation of nature to the advantage of mankind. In attacking, splitting, changing, pulverizing things and animals (and, periodically, also men), man extends his dominion over the world and advances to ever richer stages of civilization.[16]

In other words, to shackle the erotic expression of human beings is to condemn other beings to chains. By the same token, to enslave other animals is to tighten humans' bonds to the apparatus of "technological rationality," which reduces every thing, every being, every action, and every breath to a *calculation*. As a result of surplus repression in patriarchal and techno-capitalist society, the human being's capacity for love is deformed into an irrational explosion of hatred and violence against both other humans and other animals.

The early Frankfurt School theorists help to illuminate the relationship between the systematic persecution of other animals and the distortion of the human subject. However, they do not develop their critique of animal repression and oppression at length, nor do they explore the particular neuroses which have developed as a result. Because we are not merely natural beings, but *animals*, the repression of animality and the oppression of animals respectively has, in my view, been especially traumatic to our individual and collective psyches. On closer examination, we can identify a number of symptoms in the modern human being that are constitutive of speciesism and its basis in repression.

MELANCHOLIA, AMBIVALENCE, AND GUILT

While on a conscious level we persist in deluding ourselves that we have expunged our animal natures once and for all, our repressed animality remains with us. Despite the apparent immensity of the repressive mechanism, repression by its very nature is not absolute. As Freud explains, "its essence consists simply in the act of turning—and keeping—something away from the conscious."[17] The powerful psychic apparatus oriented toward maximizing pleasure can never be wholly dismantled, only damaged and hidden away in the dusty corners of the unconscious. As Christopher White observes, Freud recognized that there are not only traces of drives but also of "'animal life' lingering in the human body and psyche." White continues, "the modern human subject finds himself inhabited by his most other Other."[18] The repressed animal vehemently rebels against its internment, thrashes about in our unconscious, and claws at our flesh pleading for release. Though we seldom acknowledge our inner horror at the violence we inflict upon other animals, that violence nonetheless remains with and within us, manifesting as *melancholia*. Unlike mourning, where the object of loss is known to the subject, and who thence can work the emotion through, melancholia is the result of an unknown or unconscious loss, chiefly the alienation from (or loss of) one's own ego, coupled with an attachment to the lost object.[19]

A further manifestation of the damage done by the repression-oppression complex can be observed in the neurotic ambivalence we exhibit toward other animals. In Freud's theory, ambivalence is "the reversal of a drive's content into its opposite," as, for example, in "*the transformation of love into hate*."[20] Ambivalence, he argues, most clearly manifests itself in the Oedipal complex and in the drama of the prehistorical "band of brothers" who kill their father to rob him of his exclusive sexual rights to their mother.[21] Governed as much by Eros and their love of the father as by Thanatos (or the aggression which enabled them to commit patricide), and trapped forever in the torturous web of ambivalence, the band of brothers feel tremendous guilt at their violent betrayal. In an attempt to appease their conscience and compensate for their crime, they resurrect the dead father in a surrogate—first in the form of the totemic animal and then, with the arrival of Christianity, God the Father.[22] Driven by an admixture of blood love and blood lust, the band of brothers—here a metaphor for the human species as a whole—achieves its sense of authority and autonomy, but without fully shaking off its sense of guilt or overcoming its ambivalence.[23]

Human beings are caught in a similar tug-of-war between loving and hateful impulses toward other animals. Under the rule of repressive civilization and its insistence on defining the human as *not* animal, the fundamental empathy and friendship we might otherwise have felt vis-à-vis other animals—whose needs, wants, fears, and joys are so similar to our own—have, under the process of repression, turned into antipathy and contempt. While it would be an exaggeration to say that all human beings are naturally inclined to feel affection for all other animals, it can certainly be said that many people do exhibit natural and spontaneous affection toward many other species of animals. In fact, while humans may have naturally aggressive impulses toward each other and other beings, aggression and sadism have been expressly cultivated to serve the interests of technocapitalist progress in repressive patriarchal society, while the non-dominating, loving feelings we might also inherently feel with other beings have been deliberately quashed or downplayed.

When we become conscious of our sadistic behavior toward other animals who we might otherwise feel an affinity for, profound guilt sets in. This guilt adds another dimension to our ambivalence. We kill and maim helpless animals, but we feel bad about it, at least on an unconscious level. Indeed, our repressed animality lives on in this guilt, reverberating through the depths of our psyche. Guilt is then incorporated into the structure of love itself. As Melanie Klein observed through her psychoanalysis of children, "[t]hese feelings of guilt and distress now enter as a new element into the emotion of love."[24] However, our ambivalent feelings toward other animals are more complicated. We may entertain violent impulses toward humans, but, for the most part, stop short of carrying them out (Klein gives the example of the infant's rage against the mother). However, we go a step further with other animals and, as a society, bring our bloody fantasies to fruition by committing atrocities against them on a massive scale.

Many people, tormented by feelings of ambivalence and overcome with guilt at the violence repressive civilization compels them to participate or to be complicit in, simply become numb. But this too is a symptom of the pathology of speciesism. Freud explains that "hysterical indifference" toward or lack of affect for a previously loved object are products of repression and/or of the breakdown of the repressive mechanism. In the case of the latter, "the emotive charge can be made to disappear entirely," so that a person displays total *indifference* to a previously loved object.[25] Our tendency to become "immune" to extreme violence against other animals in laboratories, factory farms, and so on is an example of the unnatural indifference that arises from repression of a former love-object. Slaughterhouse workers, for example, who slit the throats and dismember the bodies of scores of terrified animals day after day, must engage in a Herculean—or rather, *Odyssean*—feat of self-repression, suppressing what might otherwise be their natural affection toward, or sense of affinity with, their victims.[26] As Carol Adams observes, people who "work in the disassembly line of slaughterhouses . . . must accept on a grand scale a double annihilation of self . . . must be alienated from their own bodies and animals' bodies as well."[27] Rather than regard the living animal before them as an embodied subject, they are compelled to freeze their hearts, their humanity, and regard the animal as an "absent referent," that is, as a mere *symbol* for (dead) meat, without value in itself. The self-alienation in the slaughterhouse is also the result of the fragmentation of the labor process so vividly outlined by Marx, in which the once (or potentially) *whole* human being has been severed into a series of parts, limbs, like so many components of a machine, becoming a kind of "crippled monstrosity," both in body and spirit.[28]

Here, however, it is necessary to introduce a feminist perspective to this broad Freudian view of repression, alienation, and violence. Enlightenment reason is not gender-neutral but distinctly patriarchal in character—a fact highlighted in *Dialectic of Enlightenment* by Adorno and Horkheimer, who note the overlapping oppressions of women and other animals brought about by the transition to the Enlightenment and scientific worldviews. As Carolyn Merchant writes, in consolidating a worldview that depicted nature as feminine, dead, and passive, the scientific revolution "sanctioned the domination of both nature and women."[29] Women, reduced to immanence, were relegated to a position alongside other animals "below" ostensibly transcendent men. Eventually, as Adorno and Horkheimer note, "modern puritanical woman" came to represent "nature not in its wildness but in its 'domestication.'"[30] Woman was the visible embodiment of the tamed inner and outer "beast." Josephine Donovan is therefore right to insist that "the domination of nature

[is] rooted in postmedieval, Western, *male* psychology," a male psychology, of course, that is not innate, but culturally and historically determined by the demands of patriarchy, enlightenment, and techno-capitalism.[31] We therefore need not accept Freud's essentialist view that "the desire to subjugate" is inherent in male sexuality or psychology.[32] In patriarchal societies, aggression is glorified while care, nurturing, empathy, and compassion for the vulnerable are vilified as symptoms of (feminine) "sentimentality" and weakness.[33] At the same time, women must "act like men"—that is, clamp down on their natural human capacity for empathy—when the society finds it productive for them to do so. Thus, women put to work in animal processing facilities or laboratories are expected to adopt a "masculine" disposition at the expense of any nurturing impulses they might initially harbor toward other beings. Ambivalence and guilt are the fine print of their job description.

ANIMAL UNCANNY

Our perpetual struggle at once to impede and facilitate the return of our repressed animality is evinced in our frequent experience of other animals as uncanny. Though the experience of the uncanny is not a neurosis per se, it taps into unconscious and repressed fears and desires. The very term *uncanny* (*Unheimlich*), Freud relates, contains a dual and ambiguous meaning. On the one hand, *Unheimlich* means literally "un-homely," or more generally, that which is "unfamiliar." Our experience of the uncanny arouses horror, fear, or dread.[34] Yet in order for something to be *Unheimlich* it must first have been *Heimlich*. *Heimlich* means "belonging to the house, not strange, familiar . . . dear and intimate, homely."[35] We identify the familiar with that which is contained or concealed in an intimate, private space, like the home, and the unfamiliar with that which is exposed and revealed.[36] Hence German philosopher Friedrich Schelling's remark (quoted by Freud) that the uncanny is "everything that was meant to remain secret and hidden and has come into the open."[37] This exposing of what was hitherto concealed becomes a source of terror, even though, paradoxically, it is that which is most intimately known to us.

Freud's notion of the uncanny captures the ambivalent psychic struggle that results from the joint repression of our own animality and our oppression of other animals—our combined fascination and horror, our longing for connection with other animals, on the one hand, and our dread of the animal other, on the other. The animal is that which is both familiar and feared, hidden and revealed. According to White, other animals evoke the uncanny through their voices because, though they speak without words, we can nonetheless understand what they are saying. White describes a scene in William Faulkner's *As*

I Lay Dying to illustrate this point: "[c]oming from out of the wild and voiceless darkness, the sounds of the honking geese, in their uncanny proximity to speech, mock the ineffectuality of language."[38] Language itself, White suggests, is permeated with and grounded in the "other-than-human."[39] But it is not only animals' voices that arouse in us a feeling of the uncanny—their bodies, especially when pacified for human amusement, can also arouse a sense of *das Unheimlich*. "Exotic" animals on display at zoos, for example, are both familiar and foreign, and that is part of their attraction, while the circus is a kind of orgy of the uncanny. The crowds are not only amused but also dazzled and terrified by the contorted animals they see before them. In coercing other animals into performing human actions, in pressing the more-than-human into a human mold, we force closed the gap between the strange and the familiar. But only artificially. For what is *truly* familiar about these animals is their need for independence, social interaction with their family members and peers, self-determination, and care—the same needs that shape and give meaning to our own lives. The uncanny is for this very reason also at play when other animals resist their subjugation. In 1994 a female elephant named Tyke killed her trainer, Allen Campbell, in front of a crowd of spectators at Circus International. She then made a run for it down the streets of Honolulu, trying desperately to find *home*, before she was gunned down by the local police. Tyke was "meant" to be kept hidden in some dark stall and exposed under the glare of circus lights, but burst out into the open air and outside the confines of human domination—if only momentarily. And so she had to be murdered. As Adorno and Horkheimer remind us, "[e]nlightenment is mythical fear radicalized. . . . Nothing is allowed to remain outside since the mere idea of the 'outside' is the real source of fear."[40]

When we capture fleeting glimpses of animals in the "wilderness" in photographs in *National Geographic* and other media, we can also be overcome by a sense of the uncanny. There is something vaguely familiar in the faces of these more-than-human creatures, whether mammals, amphibians, or insects, which reverberates in the recesses of our unconscious. But we are also struck by their "outsideness," by the total unfamiliarity of the particular space-time continuum(s) they inhabit, of their alien "styles of being."[41] We are reminded that the "open" is in a sense the *outside*. It is a place of being that is *open to all beings* and not, as Martin Heidegger claimed, the exclusive province of humans.[42] Indeed, it is humans who, in our routinized, operationalized, mechanized lives have *closed ourselves off* from the open. "With their whole gaze / animals behold the Open. Only our eyes / are as though reversed / and set like traps around us, keeping us inside" (Rilke).[43] Our efforts to achieve transcendence through reason lead us to a self-imposed homelessness. The "emergence" of "self-awareness, reason and imagination," according to Erich Fromm, has "made man into an anomaly, into the freak of the universe. . . . He is set apart while being a part; he is homeless, yet chained to the home he shares with all other creatures."[44] We have exiled ourselves from our proper home amongst our fellow beings-in-the-world, alienated ourselves from an embodied form of being we continually try, in vain, to transcend. In beholding these creatures, we catch a glimpse of where and what we unconsciously long to be.

According to Freud, any depiction of a double, or doppelgänger, also arouses a feeling of the uncanny. In depictions of the doppelgänger in literature, he explains,

> a person may identify himself with another and so become unsure of his true self; or he may substitute the other's self for his own. The self may thus be duplicated, divided and interchanged. . . . The double was originally an insurance against the extinction of the self . . . [but] the meaning of the "double" changes: having once been an assurance of immortality, it becomes the uncanny harbinger of death.[45]

To look into another animal's eyes is uncanny because encountering our doppelgänger destabilizes our artificial sense of self as not-animal. The subjugated animal other is the uncanny harbinger of death inasmuch as its ravaged body reminds us of the (attempted) extinction of our animality. Theodore Roethke's poem, "The Bat," captures this jarring impact of the doppelgänger: "But when he brushes up against a screen / We are afraid of what our eyes have seen / For something is amiss or out of place / When mice with wings can wear a human face."[46] In a similar vein, the phenomenologist Maurice Merleau-Ponty underscored the way in which other animals' faces are like mirrors of our own—to behold them both reveals and conceals our own animality:

> this relationship [between embodied beings] is an ambiguous one, between beings who are both embodied and limited and an enigmatic world of which we catch a glimpse (indeed which we haunt incessantly) but only ever from points of view that hide as much as they reveal, a world in which every object displays the human face it acquires in a human gaze.[47]

The animal face—and the "face" of the other which, in Emmanuel Levinas' terms, solicits our ethical responsibility not to kill it and to protect it from harm—haunts us like the memory of our own (repressed) animality.[48] In the eyes of other animals we see the challenge to their oppression, their implicit rebuke of human arrogance, and the irreversibility of what makes us and other beings *animal*: our embodied consciousness and our relationality with other sentient beings. Thus, while our animal doubles may be, in one sense, the harbingers of death, in their eyes we may also glimpse *the promise of a new life*.

MIMESIS, MANIACAL LAUGHTER, AND ANIMAL FANTASIES

Not only does repression not eradicate its object, but (Freud notes) "there is an unmistakable tendency to restore the repressed idea in its entirety."[49] One way in which we attempt to revive the lost other is through identification and imitation.[50] A process of reversal occurs whereby the internal and external animal, cast out from human experience, is *re-internalized*, but now in exaggerated, distorted, or stereotyped form. Horkheimer's theory of mimesis illustrates this process well. In his view, repressed nature or animality returns in the form of a *revolt* against the subject that has repressed it. This revolt occurs when the human subject mimics the very nature she aims to transcend. Horkheimer paints a vivid picture of this mimetic tendency at play in Nazi Germany:

> Anyone who ever attended a National-Socialist meeting in Germany knows that speakers and audience got their chief thrill in acting out socially repressed mimetic drives. . . . The high spot of such a meeting was the moment when the speaker impersonated a Jew. He imitated those he would see destroyed. His impersonation aroused raucous hilarity, because a forbidden natural urge was permitted to assert itself without fear of reprimand.[51]

Similarly, as nature revolts within us we engage in acts of brutality normally ascribed to other "vicious" animals who, in reality, would cause us no harm if we simply left them alone. We hear news stories all the time of workers in sites of mechanized violence like slaughterhouses and laboratories having engaged in deliberate acts of extreme violence against animals, such as kicking already sick and injured chickens around like footballs, or beating puppies to death, laughing all the while. Through this behavior they imitate the vilified "beast" who, they imagine, ravages her victims without recourse to moral restraint. It is they, however, who, as a result of repression, lack moral restraint.

But such brutal sadism is exhibited too in the "raucous hilarity" which swells through us whenever other animals are depicted as objects of ridicule or made to suffer the brunt of our jokes. In Freud's view, jokes can be healthy outlets for repressed unconscious desires or acts of rebellion against the unnatural strictures of "ruthless morality."[52] As products of repression they may also indicate a repressed desire that needed to be released, exposed, and thereby relieved.[53] In this regard, the frequent use of animal imagery or analogies in jokes, idioms, and figures of speech may reveal society's underlying need to give voice to the repressed animality dwelling in our own unconscious, as well as to our discomfort with the knowledge of our collusion in violence against other animals. In this connection, Adorno and Horkheimer distinguish between "wrong," "diabolical," "ringing," and sadistic laughter, on the one hand, and celebratory or "reconciled" laughter, on the other.

Reconciled laughter "resounds with the echo of escape from power."[54] It is the laughter of freedom and of resistance against domination. Wrong laughter, on the other hand, resounds with the subject's enslavement to coercive power. It spews from the mouth of the oppressor and is directed at her victims—namely, the weak, who are the objects of ridicule most ready to hand. Such laughter is "wrong" because it humiliates rather than liberates those who are oppressed. It is diabolical because "there is laughter when there is nothing to laugh about," and because it laughs in the face of ethical responsibility to the other.[55] Thus, rather than foster reconciliation, wrong laughter parodies it.[56]

The endless jokes we make about other animals parody what is in truth the urgent need for reconciliation with our animality and our animal kin. Examples of such non-reconciliatory, wrong laughter at the expense of other animals abound in contemporary culture. Circus trainers beat and torture elephants, bears, lions, and so on into "performing" for us so that we can laugh at how ridiculous they look doing things that are not natural to them, such as riding bicycles, balancing on balls, and other idiotic stunts. In a similar vein, in 2009 the host of "As it Happens," a popular Canadian Broadcasting Corporation radio program, relayed the story of a pig who had managed to escape from a transport vehicle on the way to slaughter, only to be hit by a car on the highway and killed. But rather than take this incident as an opportunity to question the ethics of animal transport and factory farming (a potentially reconciliatory gesture) the host demeaned the pig further by making a pun about "pork on the grill." Similarly, on National Public Radio in the United States, a programmer jokingly asked the scientists who had killed a 405-year-old clam—the longest-lived animal ever recorded—for research (on human-induced climate change no less) whether or not they had cooked and eaten it. Here is laughter where there is nothing to laugh about.

In keeping with the dialectic of repression-oppression, meanwhile, we often find this laughter to be perversely self-directed. Chimpanzees, so similar to us, are typically depicted as idiotic versions of ourselves, and therefore attract special ridicule. With 98 percent of their DNA shared with us, with a strikingly similar physique and mannerisms but covered in fur, the chimpanzee is the *animal* double (the doppelgänger) of the human being. A double sado-masochistic humiliation is at play when a chimpanzee is made to don human clothing (a staple of satirical cartoons, TV, and movies for decades). Both the chimpanzee and her human counterpart are mocked—one for being not-quite-human, and the other for being almost-animal.

As Adams observes, wrong laughter is often specifically directed at both women and animals. The cover of a contemporary humor book (found by the present author in a U.S. bookstore) shows a real decapitated and de-feathered hen, propped up by a brick wall in an alleyway, posed to look like a prostitute, holding a cigarette, and puffing smoke out of her hollow neck. The violated body of the dead hen is equated with the soon-to-be-violated body of an almost-dead prostitute. Both the dead hen and the dead pig function as absent referents for the rape of women—that is, both are "transmuted into a metaphor for someone else's existence or fate."[57] In *The Sexual Politics of Meat*, Adams discusses a picture of one "Ursula Hamdress" (after the Swiss actress Ursula Andress) which appeared in the satirical magazine *Playboar* in the early 1980s. In the photo, a dead pig sits spread-eagled on a chair wearing women's panties, posed as though masturbating. Adams connects the sexualization of the dead pig to Gary Heidnik's kidnapping, torture, and rape of six women a few years later. (Heidnik murdered two of his victims, dismembered them, and fed their body parts to his other captives.) Adams writes, "I hold that Ursula Hamdress and the women raped, butchered, and eaten under Heidnik's directions are linked by an overlap of cultural images of sexual violence against women and the fragmentation and dismemberment of nature and the body in Western culture."[58] As Adams has demonstrated throughout her work, images of violation and dismemberment of women and animals are often presented in a joking or mocking way. But such maniacal laughter scarcely conceals the despair and guilt beneath: despair, because we know that in brutalizing other animals we mutilate ourselves psychically, and guilt, because we secretly identify with these beings we have taught ourselves to hate.

The repressed animal can also return in a less brutal and distorted form, however. Akira Mizuta Lippit suggests that Freud saw dreams in part as a "regression" or a return to (or of) a lost animality. On the topic of wish fulfillment, Freud asked, "What do geese dream of? Of Maize."[59] Not only does Freud's question and answer confirm his view that other animals in fact dream, Lippit writes, but it also indicates his belief that in our own dreams we embrace our lost animality. "If, as Freud believes, the origins of dream wishes are revealed in regression, then the recourse to animality here suggests a point of contact between the deepest recesses of memory and the animal world."[60] In other words, in dreams we restore the animality we otherwise subdue in the artificial, repressive, all-too-human world we have constructed over the millennia. Freud reduces the particular animals that appear in the dreams of his patients to *symbols* and metaphors (in other words, absent referents) for specifically human experiences.[61] But there is much more at stake, particularly in our *waking* dreams—our fantasy lives—concerning other animals than Freud conceded or perhaps comprehended.

Just as Freud posited the function of dreams to be the fulfillment of wishes, so too our fantasy lives—as played out in cultural media such as film, literature, ads, children's stories, and so forth—express the partial fulfillment of a wish to restore our own animality to a prior—or, rather, as yet unachieved—

state. Just like the band of brothers who attempt to atone for their sin of patricide by resurrecting the murdered father in the idea of God, so we attempt to compensate for the murder of our fellow sentient beings in bucolic images in stories and animated films of happy, healthy farm animals grazing and sunbathing in lush fields, joyously bounding about, scratching, sniffing the earth, cuddling their human companions, and so on. These scenes reflect a repressed desire to reconstitute, to put back together, the bodies and lives of other animals whom we have so brutally mutilated.[62] Violent fantasies are in fact often accompanied or followed by restorative ones. Thus, as Klein suggests, "if the baby has, in his aggressive phantasies, injured his mother by biting and tearing her up, he may soon build up phantasies that he is putting the bits together again and repairing her."[63] Similarly, even as we dream up new ways to genetically engineer, hybridize, and disassemble other animals into so many parts for our consumption, we recreate them symbolically on screen and in other media, desiring to make them whole again. Such images assert the powerful claim of the erotic imagination against enlightenment rationality. As Adorno and Horkheimer observed of the "culture industry" of their own time, "[c]artoon and stunt films were once exponents of fantasy against rationalism. They allowed justice to be done to the animals and things electrified by their technology, by granting the mutilated beings a second life."[64]

Our veritable fixation on animal images is therefore an indication of our unacknowledged and ambivalent *attachment* to the repressed object.[65] We also look to animal images to be reassured that we have not irreversibly revoked our profound connection with other animals. In her analysis of the proliferation of animal images in cell phone advertisements and media culture, Jody Berland describes the promise of reconnection to other animals that is granted by such images and the products they are promoting: "[t]he pictures of animals promise a sense of attachment and security which might feel analogous to the 'natural' connection between animals and man, and which is waiting to be fulfilled the way a love-struck teenager waits for a phone call."[66] Ironically, cell phones and other digital communication technologies may in fact increase our distance from animality by, for example, turning our attention from the sounds of *real* birds chirping in the trees around us to the sounds of electronic "birds chirping" in the form of ring tones. Nonetheless, so hungry are we for a renewed connectivity with our abandoned animal kin that we eat up the telecommunications' companies false promises of "connection."

In reality, animal images have ceased to be restorative and instead, in Adorno and Horkheimer's view, "merely confirm the victory of technological rationality over truth."[67] Today, art and cultural media disguise the brutal reality of our domination of other beings with an imaginary counterpart without actually effecting any transformation. As Freud explains, art only superficially reconciles the reality principle with the pleasure principle.[68] That is, in her work, the artist (or graphic designer, etc.) brings back to life the repressed pleasure principle without threatening the established order. But there is a deception involved inasmuch as the artist "shap[es] his fantasies into a new kind of reality, which are appreciated by people as valid representations of the real world."[69] When people look at the artist's work, they are momentarily convinced that the canvas depicting the fantasy world is really just a *mirror* of reality. The artist is able to deceive others into believing that he is somehow living proof of this other world "only because other people feel the same dissatisfaction he does at the renunciations imposed by reality."[70] But especially in the case of commercial or commodified cultural expression, such collective self-deception ultimately *perpetuates* this dissatisfaction. Adorno and Horkheimer emphasize how easily art can reinforce rather than challenge the status quo: "[a]s long as art does not insist on being treated as knowledge, and thus exclude itself from praxis, it is tolerated by social praxis in the same way as pleasure."[71] In other words, so long as art remains simply a representation of an unattainable ideal, and not the stuff of actual change, it reinforces or masks what *is*, at the expense of the pursuit of what *ought* to be. Indeed, as Berland further points out, there is a glaring disconnect between the image of human–animal harmony in mass culture and the reality of the devastating impact the production and disposal of cell phones have on the health and well-being of other species.[72] Restorative images, in other words, do not necessarily amount to restorative practices, but in fact can signal a general submission to the status quo.

CONCLUSION

The repression of animality and the oppression of other animals which began in classical antiquity has caused profound psychic damage to human beings. With the rise of global capitalism and consumer culture and the intensification and normalization of brutal violence against other animals—both artifactual consequences of the denial of our animality—we are arguably more alienated, more neurotic, and more psychically troubled than ever before. As Wilhelm Reich long ago pointed out, capitalism has de-animalized the human in part by imposing "a pattern of compulsory work" on the individual, whereby labor and activity are drained of any animal or erotic *pleasure*, to such an extreme degree that we effectively become the machines we use, only more terrifying for our (learned) sadism.[73] Because our animality lingers on in our embodied unconscious, however, there are limits to how far we can sustain such hysterical indifference, fragmentation, and self-alienation. Overcoming the pathology of speciesism will therefore entail not merely social, ethical, and political action, but curative *psychic* action as well.

Other animals, it goes without saying, by far suffer the brunt of speciesism. Yet we humans damage ourselves psychically, too, in denying our fundamental identity with other animals and claiming a false superiority over them. A society which confines, mutilates, and kills billions of animals each year—the same animals whose beauty overwhelms us with awe, whose affection we universally long for, and whose pain and pleasure we feel so deeply—can be neither healthy nor sane. Nor can movements claiming to represent the oppressed be true to the spirit of universal social justice so long as their members remain willfully blind to the plight of billions of sentient creatures under capitalism. To fight for indigenous rights, for ecological protection, for women's liberation, or for the elimination of racism while writing off animal liberation as an obstacle to human liberation is to remain captive to narcissistic delusion. As Cary Wolfe observes, the repression of animality is not limited to traditional, hegemonic religio-philosophical thought, but is rampant in recent discourses of social justice as well. In his words, there is a "fundamental *repression* that underlies most ethical and political discourse: repressing the question of nonhuman subjectivity, taking it for granted that the subject is always already human."[74] Those who imagine a universal freedom only in terms of *human* freedom, justice only as *human* social justice, in this way re-inscribe species privilege.[75] Repression of animality is therefore a major stumbling block in the development of truly liberatory discourses and practices, and to the well-being of all sentient beings, human and more-than-human.

Marcuse suggests a way out of this endless cycle of destructive fantasy and guilt in his analysis of the ancient Greek myths of Narcissus and Orpheus. Both myths center on humans' reunification with nature and animals and serve as examples of a new, non-neurotic, and non-repressive order. Marcuse offers Narcissus not as a symbol of solipsistic self-interest—Freud's characterization of the first few years of infancy—but rather of our potential for harmonious *relationality* and *identity* with humans and other animals. When Narcissus gazes with love at his own image in the water, he is enraptured not only with himself, but also with the other: nature or the more-than-human. In short, he does not project himself onto nature or impose a singular meaning upon the latter (as European humans did with the transition to enlightenment) but rather sees himself as a part of, and as constituted by, nature:

> The love of Narcissus is answered by the echo of nature. . . . His silence is not that of dead rigidity; and when he is contemptuous of the hunters and nymphs he rejects one Eros for another. He lives by an Eros of his own, and he does not only love himself. He does not know that the image he admires is his own.[76]

If Narcissus can be seen as the symbol of the triumph of Eros over modern humanity's hatred of itself as a natural being, as an *animal*, Orpheus represents our potential reconciliation with both ourselves and other animals. As Marcuse writes, "the song of Orpheus pacifies the animal world, reconciles the lion with the lamb and the lion with man."[77] This image brings back to life not only the animals mutilated at our hands, but our sense of kinship with them. The Orphic myth thus inspires us to overcome the repression-oppression complex and the pathology of speciesism by demonstrating that no liberation will be universal or complete so long as it leaves the other animals behind. Of course, to overcome repression and to cure modern human beings of their pathological hatred of and ambivalence toward animals will require much more than recourse to myths. Collective remembrance of what we have lost, and of our sorrow over that loss, must be transformed into *praxis*: "Remembrance is no real weapon unless it is translated into historical action."[78] Among other things, a feminist ethics of care, which recognizes overlapping oppressions and which is "grounded in an emotional and spiritual conversation with nonhuman life-forms" and in "women's relational culture of caring and attentive love," would be central to such a praxis—a way to begin reversing the impact of a repression-oppression complex that is literally suicidal, zoocidal, and ecocidal.[79] If we wish to see and think clearly, and act justly, we must embrace a praxis which eliminates the rational human/irrational animal binary opposition and restores our repressed animality to its fullest expression. Only then might we take up our proper position amongst the other beings-in-the-world.

10

Neuroscience (a Poem)

By Susan Benston

Let's take, say, a present-day Caligula
sitting down to lunch: he's hungry,
and humanity has come to consensus
that this blood-englutted one
be fed ahead of any.

And why not? That smirking mask
is our essential self. It no more preys upon us than it prays
over us; it is that tendril of ourselves that loves no other,
that malignant heart-weed growing from the core,
unapologetic. Seek no flowers from this thing,
no fragrance for a burrowing face—
the human breast sends up a triffid: a carnivorous vine.
Movie-makers say its spores arrived on meteors that struck
  the population blind,
but I would guess that it originated here
when some creature, crazed with natural selection, reared
in nuclear madness, coiled, convulsed,
and sprang a shard of wormwood DNA

which is our feeler
into our domain,
the probe we stick
into melting tundras at the pole,
into aquifers of acid rain,

the spike with which we stick the gullet of the goose,
stick the anus of the mink,
stick the cerebral cortex of the chimpanzee
to ascertain how we would feel
if leprous distillations dripped inside our skull—
this is a subtle and voracious feeler,
sticking, sticking
like a white cane tapping
unperceived topography
of suffering. A most unfeeling feeler.

Okay,
here's the deal:

hunters take their skinning knives to living seals,
while we, the bleeding hearts, hemorrhaging, write
or hold the cameras as we weep.
We document, we document—
but who'll sit in that audience for whom our gruesome film unfurls?
Who'll sit there, blandly tolerant and half-asleep?

Christ, Christ—
I know no other name to call upon
than this, proscribed by my ancestral greats:
Name in whose honor thumbscrews were applied
and fingernails torn out in Spain—
Name that, exalted, flung the Salem goodwives into flames—
Name, high syllable, made right
of teeth-gritting consonants and bright, ethereal vowel soaring to escape:

Christ!—
Christ verboten, Christ taboo,
who owes me nothing—even so:
look down upon the worldwide wretchedness
that was redeemed by You.

Look on the primate sitting in a chair
—not I, Lord, but my cousin:

Macaques and squirrel monkeys can be trained to move voluntarily from the home cage into a restraint chair.[1]

Hear us, Lord, redeem us
from our oxymorons:

Macaques and squirrel monkeys can be
trained to move *voluntarily*
from the *home cage*
into a *restraint chair.*

Christ, consider: *Your* head lolled
in the agony. You did not wear your halo,
for it might have snagged on a splinter or a knot
in the sacred wood
and held your skull inhumanly
level
as your eyes swiveled,
straining toward your God—
you did not wear your halo—.

Head-restraint systems minimize the movement of the head during neurophysiology experiments without causing discomfort if the animal is properly conditioned. Hardware, generically called a head-holder, is implanted chronically on the animal's skull. Three different styles of head-holders are generally used: implantable, headpiece, and halo.[2]

There, Lord, see how our angel sits
in saintly immobility, *properly conditioned.*
Marvel how he never lifts his brow, crowned with obligatory thorns,
to cry, *Eli, Eli,*
nor turns his eyes upward in reproach,
wearing thorns upon these, too:

[E]ye coils typically will function reliably for a limited period of time after implantation.[3]

Martyr!
look down from the safety of your throne
onto *a place called Golgotha, that is to say, a place of a skull,*[4]
and witness how we hold that skull aloft
and puppet its gaunt, imploring sockets
to our will:

for vertebrate eyesight moves in jerks,
leaping saccadically from thing to thing
and we have learned what you learned first
when vinegar was brought to quench your withered tongue:
that the eyes' saccadic leaps
can be steered remarkably

by thirst.
In his protocol, Lisberger has acknowledged the use of "severe" water deprivation . . .[5]

And about the ninth hour Jesus cried with a loud voice, saying, Eli, Eli,
lama sabachthani? That is to say,
My God, my God, why hast thou forsaken me?[6]

The ninth hour merely . . .

In instances where long-term (greater than 12 hours) restraint is required, the nonhuman primate must be provided the opportunity daily for unrestrained activity for at least one continuous hour . . . unless continuous restraint is justified for scientific reasons and approved by the Institutional Animal Care and Use Committee.[7]

And Jesus cried with a loud voice, and gave up the ghost.[8]

Alas, poor ghost![9]
Death is less decisive in this latter day
when the *anima*—that writhing, breathing sprite—is confined
till its days of nature can be burnt and purged away.
But that this animal is forbid to tell the secrets of its prison house,
it could a tale unfold whose lightest word would harrow up thy soul.[10]

—I'll speak to it:[11]

Thou com'st in such a questionable shape,[12]
so like to mine and yet, methinks, perhaps a parody:
for though thou had seemed something other than
a mere facsimile,
I am informed by a vaunted doctor of philosophy
that I am much deceived:

[T]here is a reason to cause such pain in animals, namely, to enable us better to understand the nature and functioning of pain. If we are to understand pain, we need to be able to study it in creatures simpler than ourselves, as well as in ourselves, and that is what [a scientist] does. (And if you have ever watched someone die a slow and very painful death, I think you will agree that we do need better to understand pain.) So, the pain caused in animals is not needless. Nor, again, as far as I know, is it harmful. It is, in animals, not consensual. This is an important difference between the case of animals and our own case, but that difference cuts both ways. Mere animals are not

rational beings, not free beings, not moral agents. They should be accorded the respect that is due to them, which is not the respect due to a rational, free, and moral agent.[13]

The respect that is due them . . .

And we spake unto them, saying: ye shall dwell
amid our cinderblock and wire and steel,
in our fluorescence and compressor-driven chill,
and you shall eat and fast
according to the days wherewith we shall command you;
you shall be
as the stars of the heaven
and the sands of the earth,[14] which you will never see,
that we may know your offspring, verily each,
unto the last, all counted, all accounted for.
And we shall know you to the inmost fiber of your being
and shall make ourselves known to you
in multitudes of plagues and dread afflictions.
We shall plant
caseation in your brains
and tumors in your spines,
and open the bellies of your babes
to watch them heal in untended pain
that we may see what they can tolerate
in their maturity.[15]

And Job spake
in the voice of them that weep, saying:

I am a brother to dragons, and a companion to owls.[16]

No dragon nor no owl
can ransom these. For the Moral Agent rules—
that agent which springs forth exclusively
from this: our august company
of ghouls.
Ours is the choice to wield
or not to wield—
and were we not to wield,
how should we recognize ourselves as free?
Our categorical imperative is, then,
to stand at the center of the world
hefting a hose of pain
and spray its blight in every direction but our own,

lest we be taken for *mere animals,*
not rational beings, not free beings, not moral agents.

And my interlocutor resumes:
The very fact that you and I are having this conversation
points to a fundamental difference between us and mere animals. . . .
We wonder whether we ought to be doing what we are doing,
and we reflect critically on the question.
I'd need to see some evidence that mere animals do that.
I need to know more, in particular why we
should read the impossibility of [animal] consent as you do
rather than . . . as an exemplification of the fact that mere animals are
not free.[17]

Sage scholar,
are you free? Can *you*, then, give consent
to the halo and the eye coils,
the neuromuscular blockade, the spinal catheter,
the crush injury, the prodded nerve—
consent to the restraint table and the blade,
the frigid wire-bottomed cage,
the glacial, bottomless swimming tank—
consent to every delicate design
forged by the crafty fingers of an unknown mind
on behalf of its own health?
I'd need to see some evidence that mere humans do that.

My pen-pal's case runs thus:
by choosing freely to inflict pain on others than ourselves,
we seize the moral high ground
and may then freely set upon them—and not merely
with bared teeth and claws
but slowly, elegantly,
with adroitly fashioned needles, pincers, knives, caustics,
propane torches and electrodes—
freely set upon them.

Does the scholar sleep-walk in these circles
of tautology?
How does one shed one's fealty to the sentient world,
unseat compassion for these others who share our mortal bind
of fear, anguish, misery, and pain?

How was this done?
Let's hear from a dame
a little more than kin and less than kind:[18]

Fill me from the crown to the toe top-full
Of direst cruelty! make thick my blood;
Stop up the access and passage to remorse,
That no compunctious visitings of nature
Shake my fell purpose!
Come, thick night,
And pall thee in the dunnest smoke of hell,
That my keen knife see not the wound it makes,
Nor heaven peep through the blanket of the dark,
To cry 'Hold, hold!'[19]

And heaven's mute. But we have that within
which speaks. Even the feral queen must rue the wound:

Here's the smell of the blood still: all the perfumes
of Arabia will not sweeten this little hand[20]—
and the world's preeminent scholar comes to grief
in the twelfth hour,
having pledged himself to Lucifer and Mephistophilis:
Ah, Gentlemen! I gave them my soul for my cunning.[21]

But soft: something wicked stirs within the fog,
an equal-gendered wraith incapable of mortal qualms,
chanting its malignant ode:
Eye of newt and toe of frog,
Wool of bat and tongue of dog . . .
Cool it with a baboon's blood,
Then the charm is firm and good.[22]

Behold how quizzically this grim, weird sister leers
into the human countenance
to teach us miracles of skilled dismemberment,
and how contemptuously she perseveres
in teaching us the requisite contempt.

Once more, somewhere, someone dying bleats: *See,*
see where Christ's blood streams in the firmament![23]

11

Everyday Rituals of the Master Race

Fascism, Stratification, and the Fluidity of "Animal" Domination

By Victoria Johnson

History is littered with episodes of the brutal exploitation and murder of groups that have been portrayed as subhuman animals and therefore not deserving of the moral and legal protections of human beings. Going back as far as 300 BCE, Spartans turned the newly conquered Messenians into a slave-serf class through rituals of subordination that required the Messenians to wear "dog skins," to dance while drunk to humiliate themselves, and to be hunted in an annual war the Spartans declared on them.[1] More recent examples of the "animalization" of human beings can be found throughout the colonial period, for instance in the European characterization of Native Americans as "wild beasts," a view early Spanish explorers adopted as they massacred entire towns, including women, children, and the elderly—"not only stabbing and dismembering" (de las Casas later described) "but cutting them to pieces as if dealing with sheep in the slaughter house."[2] African human beings too were treated "like animals"—branded, muzzled, collared, bred, packed into small enclosures for transportation, and sold at slave markets modeled after cattle markets.[3] Similarly, in the East, the Japanese characterized the Chinese as subhuman and "animal"-like to justify the colonization of China and its inhabitants in the early twentieth century. Thus the Japanese soldier who, later describing how he felt pushing Chinese prisoners into a pit and setting them on fire, said that it was "identical to when he slaughtered pigs."[4]

Perhaps the best-known episode of the dehumanization—which is to say, *animalization*—of human populations was the Nazi extermination of Jews during World War Two.[5] Scholars seeking to understand how engaging in acts of dehumanization "made sense" to the perpetrators of atrocities have focused especially on the cultural narratives used by the Nazis to rationalize their violence. According to Kenneth Burke, Hitler's war rhetoric constructed Jews through a "devil" function that unified those who constituted absolute good in opposition to those who constituted absolute evil, and who hence were beyond moral redemption.[6] The more recent work of Felicity Rash has identified the ways that Hitler used metaphor, metonymy, and personification to degrade opponents.[7] Not surprisingly, these forms of linguistic violence included numerous animal representations. Both Burke and Rash reveal a dualism interwoven in Hitler's rhetoric between Aryans and "subordinate" beings—specifically, the Jews, whose very nature was seen as being so fundamentally different from the "superordinate" Aryans as to constitute a separate species. In *Mein Kampf*, Hitler depicts Jews as being biologically inferior: as unable to produce culture, as lacking souls, as being less intelligent, and as being physically and mentally weaker than the "master race." The latter term might as easily have been "the master species."[8] And in fact, Hitler occasionally used the term "species" interchangeably with "race" in *Mein Kampf*.[9]

Such examples could be multiplied. But there is another dimension to the "animalization" of human persons that is often overlooked—namely, that the power of such animal metaphors depends on a prior cultural understanding of other animals themselves, as beings who are by nature abject, degraded, and hence worthy of extermination. In fact, on examination we find that Nazi narratives justifying the domination of *human* subordinates are strikingly similar to beliefs about animals that are widely held to this day, beliefs that human beings use to justify the exploitation and killing of nonhuman beings. For example, defending the use of animals for experimentation, John Martin, a cardiovascular researcher and academic in Great Britain, has argued that the superior moral status of human beings is sufficient justification for vivisection and experimentation on primates. He argues that only human beings have the ability for abstract thought and reflection, which allows us to learn over generations and to produce music and poetry.[10] A recent article in *Christianity Today* argued that "[h]umans alone have souls which confers upon them a unique moral status. . . . Scriptures tells us that animals are soulless creatures and will perish with the rest of creation."[11]

In this chapter I want to explore the nature of the relationship between animal domination and human domination, specifically the connection between discourses and practices that legitimate the degradation of animals and fascist rituals of stratification used to justify the domination of "subordinate" groups. I wish to pose two main questions. First, what discourses and practices legitimate the domination of animals and desensitize human beings to their suffering? Second, how are these discourses and practices inextricably bound up with the "animalization" of human groups to justify the latter's domination?

I answer these questions by building upon Marx's historical materialist and Marcuse's Marxist-Freudian insights to argue that as animals were integrated into the mode of production of human societies, especially through agriculture, human beings constructed elaborate rituals of stratification to legitimate this novel mode of exploitation. These rituals, which served the cultural function of creating deeply embedded caste boundaries between human beings and the rest of the animal world, necessitated the repression of empathy for and connection to the subjectivity of other sentient beings. As I show, however, the same beliefs that legitimize desensitization toward animal exploitation and suffering also inform processes of "animalization," or the rendering of *human* others abject and deserving of exploitation or even extermination. I conclude that if we want to make headway against cultural processes that legitimate violence against humans as well as nonhumans, we must eliminate the *animal caste* itself, along with all rituals of domination that continue to desensitize us to the suffering of nonhumans on a global scale. For the first time in history, I argue, technological innovations provide us with the potential to reorganize the mode of production in such a way that we would no longer need to enslave and exploit other animals to survive and flourish. Restructuring society and economy in this way would enable us to recover our repressed emotional connection to other animals, and hence to recognize them as moral subjects, while eliminating the rituals of animal domination that are too often directed at human groups.

CASTE, THE MODE OF PRODUCTION, AND RITUALS OF DOMINATION

In *The German Ideology* Marx and Engels make the insightful claim that by "producing their means of subsistence [human beings] are indirectly producing their actual material life." They continue:

> The mode of production must not be considered simply as being the production of the physical existence of individuals. Rather it is a definite form of activity of these individuals, a definite form of expressing their life, a definite *mode of life* on their part. As individuals express their life, so they are. What they are, therefore, coincides with their production, both with what they produce and *how* they produce. The nature of individuals thus depends on the material conditions determining their production.[12]

As this passage suggests, any given mode of production, or means by which human beings reproduce their conditions of life, encompasses much more than the economy: each society generates its own distinct systems of language and cultural belief, systems which mediate social relations. In stratified systems, beliefs and cultural forms serve to legitimate existing social inequalities and hierarchical relations. This has also been true of the many systems of animal domination which have formed the basis of human economic production for centuries. Those systems too have required cultural beliefs and practices in order to be sustained and reproduced.

Marx and Engels traced different stages in the mode of production, beginning roughly 11,000 years ago when agrarian and pastoral economies emerged that were able to produce surplus value through property ownership.[13] Societies with agrarian and pastoral modes of production produced surplus value and competition that resulted over time in highly stratified societies that contrasted with the "primitive communism" of hunting and gathering societies. More recent scholarship indicates that with the emergence of pastoral and agrarian societies, human beings began to "domesticate," that is to confine or enslave, other species of animals as the basis of material culture. As Jacoby and others point out, the institution of *human* slavery became prevalent during this same period, when humans first began to domesticate animals in order to exploit their bodies for labor as well as for clothing and food.[14] Animal slavery subsequently became the paradigmatic basis for enslaving other human beings—the core of a deeply embedded caste system that stratified sentient beings, humans and animals.[15]

Of all forms of stratification that function to organize and legitimate inequality within social institutions, that of *caste* is the most rigid. Members are ascribed caste positions at birth based upon presumed differences in natural ability, with members of subordinate groups consigned on that basis to different types of labor, spatial locations to inhabit, and fewer civil, economic, and political rights than superordinates. One of the earliest philosophical justifications for caste was the ancient philosophy of the great chain of being, which placed divine beings at the top of a cosmic hierarchy, with humans placed beneath them, animals beneath humans, and lower still plants, parasites, and fungi at the very bottom.[16] Beings on top were ascribed superior characteristics to lower ones, and within each caste category there was said to be a gradation of superior to inferior beings, so that the inferior beings at the bottom of a given caste were seen as coming close to the superior beings of the caste immediately beneath it. In unrecognized ways, the great chain of being continues to inform Western thought and culture. Variations of the chain of life can still be found today among any number of ethical, religious, and scientific systems of thought that put human beings in a separate and superior caste vis-à-vis other animals.

Patterns and practices of using animal bodies for meat and clothing have varied widely from society to society over time. However, despite the diversity in the cultural narratives used to justify these embedded practices, we nonetheless find a cluster of common beliefs used to justify animal caste in most pastoral and agrarian societies—in contrast to hunting and gathering societies, which often participated in rituals to expiate the transgression against animals when killing them, indicating a different type of relationship. Typically, the exploitation of animal bodies, hence too the bodies of subordinated *human* groups, has been justified on the basis of a common set of stereotypes: the "other" is said to be biologically different, less intelligent, and lacking a soul. The natural inferiority of others, their very vulnerability, is in turn said to justify the natural right of the dominant group to exercise power over them.

Caste is in turn legitimated and enacted through *ritual*—the symbolic expressive dimension of social action that communicates collective values and moral codes through everyday practices.[17] The capture, imprisonment, and murder of beings who are sentient, and who exhibit autonomous interests and signs of suffering, necessitate daily rituals of desensitization for those who engage in these practices, from slaughterhouse employees to those who hunt for sport. While we tend to think of ritual as a function only of technologically "primitive" or pre-modern cultures, ritual in fact has attended every aspect of the modern system of animal slaughter and vivisection. With urbanization and industrialization in Europe, rituals for killing other animals did not disappear; they were simply reinvented to keep them from offending modern sensibilities, chiefly through a system of avoidances and spatial dislocations.[18] These spatial rituals desensitized urban populations to animal subjectivity and suffering and hence eliminated even the possibility that consumers might experience a sense of connection to farm or wild animals, as conscious subject to conscious subject. Today, we may be intellectually aware that the "hamburger" or "bacon" we are eating once was the flesh of a conscious being. But that knowledge must be repressed or mystified. One way to make the animal's suffering and death appear inconsequential is to devalue or degrade them through humor. Similar rituals of desensitization also attend scientific experimentation on animals, even the unabashed use of religious rituals and metaphors of sacrifice to legitimate the killing of animals in the laboratory, where animals are magically transformed from subjects—living beings understood to have their own interests—to cultural objects in the form of abstracted scientific data.[19]

Notwithstanding such desensitization rituals, however, the presumption that people who hunt or otherwise harm animals to entertain themselves recognize them only as objects is not quite accurate either. In such instances animals are *subject-objects* who are attacked precisely because they are conscious beings. In other words, the culture of conquest that informs hunting for sport and animal torture today makes visible the desire to act upon beings who have their own interests—to experience a sense of power over them (otherwise, why not attack and destroy inanimate objects?). In this way, other animals' suffering at our hands becomes not merely morally inconsequential, but psychologically gratifying as well. There are therefore also rituals of conquest, demonstrations of pleasure in the domination of the weak or vulnerable.

NAZISM AND THE LANGUAGE OF ANIMALIZATION

No subordination ritual is complete without a *discourse* to justify the subordination of the vulnerable or abject group. In this regard, we find a close family resemblance between discourses of speciesism and racist discourses of caste. As Berreman observes, "[s]ocieties embracing caste systems are often described as 'racist.' Indeed racist behavior is identical to caste behavior and the ideology of racism is included within casteism."[20] Members of caste systems perceive other castes as physically different even when they share the same biological "race."[21] Castes are mediated by elaborate cultural belief systems involving philosophy, religion, science, folklore, and so forth, organized around everyday rituals that communicate the "inherent" superiority or inferiority of caste members. These beliefs and practices serve to justify access to resources, power, and prestige. The lowest castes of human beings are typically placed only slightly above the animal caste, although these lines are fluid.

The intersection of racial and animal caste can be seen most vividly in fascist ideology; no other discourse so completely authorizes absolute violence against the weak. The term *fascism* was coined by Benito Mussolini to describe his extreme right-wing movement in Italy from the 1920s to the 1940s; the term was also applied to another variant of fascism, Hitler's National Socialist Party, which governed Germany from 1933 to 1945. Today, fascism is an umbrella term used to describe patriarchal, authoritarian dictatorships exhibiting certain characteristics, among them the belief in a rigid hierarchy that entitles the "superior" to rule others, corporatism or an alliance between the state and capitalist elites exercised through single-party rule, celebration of irrationalism (such as rejection of Enlightenment reason and the egalitarian features of modernity), the glorification of nationalism, and an exaggerated militarism. While other right-wing movements and governments probably qualify as being fascist, the Italian and German cases remain paradigmatic for the sociological depiction of the most extreme and virulent forms that violence and stratification can take in human societies. For this reason, it is worth sifting through some of the discourses of fascism for clues to how the "animalization" of humans was accomplished.

Of the many German programs and publications communicating Nazi ideology during the 1920s and 1930s, the one most studied since the fall of the Third Reich has probably been Hitler's *Mein Kampf*. Central to Nazi ideology was of course Hitler's view of nature as an immutable hierarchy in which the strong dominate the weak. It was in the context of this naturalism that fascist ideologists depicted violence against the weak, or conquest of the inferior by the superior group, as purifying the species as a whole.[22] In fact, however, Hitler did not invent this discourse. In the nineteenth century, narratives of Germanic supermen and "alien" and "inferior" groups were woven into the fabric of European culture, from the social theory of Friedrich Nietzsche to the anti-Semitism of the composer Richard Wagner. Colonialism provided much of the model for the segmentation of the world into superior and inferior races: Europeans had for centuries viewed themselves as naturally superior to African, Indian, and Asian races. Hitler drew upon these cultural currents and widely accepted colonial practices to construct a worldview where separate species and "inferior" races became interchangeable in his rhetoric. For example, ideologists such as Count Arthur de Gobineau chastised egalitarians for not recognizing "inferior stock" in his "study" of the inherent inequality among races.[23] These beliefs in natural hierarchy were then used to justify the right of "superior" human beings to dominate "inferior" ones.

Meanwhile, at the core of fascist and right-wing ideology lay an analogy between the *natural* struggle between animal species and the (equally natural) *social* struggle between "superior" and "inferior" groups in human society. Fascist ideologists often depicted human groups either literally or figuratively as separate species, ascribing the characteristics commonly associated with *animality*, including biological difference, lack of intelligence, an inability to create culture, and so forth, to abject human groups. Through appropriating the cultural beliefs and practices that devalued the nature of animals, Hitler in this way de-personified Jews, representing them as "non-human entities such as animals, reptiles and bacteria" in order to justify their subordination and loss of human rights.[24] In *Mein Kampf*, for example, Hitler explained Jewish solidarity through an analogy to nonhuman animals:

> Their apparently great sense of solidarity is based on the very primitive herd instinct that is seen in many other living creatures in this world. It is a noteworthy fact that the herd instinct leads to mutual support only as long as a common danger makes this seem useful or inevitable. The same pack of wolves which has just fallen on its prey together disintegrates when hunger abates into its individual beasts. . . . The Jew is only united when a common danger forces him to be or a common booty entices him; if these two grounds are lacking, the qualities of the crassest egoism come into their own, and in the twinkling of an eye the united people turns into a horde of rats, fighting bloodily among themselves.[25]

Similarly, Hitler argued that the natures of human groups were so radically unlike as to be akin to different species. The targeted human groups were identified as being biologically different and weak, which necessitated separation and differences in treatment. He wrote:

> The stronger must dominate and not blend with the weaker, thus sacrificing his own nature. . . . The consequence of racial purity, universally valid in Nature, is not only the sharp outward delimitation of the various races, but their uniform character in themselves. The fox is always a fox, a goose a goose . . . but you will never find a fox, who in his inner attitude, might, for example, show humanitarian attitudes toward geese. . . . No more than Nature desires the mating of weaker with stronger individuals, ever less does she desire the blending of a higher with a lower race, since, if she did, her whole work of higher breeding, over perhaps hundreds of thousands of years, might be ruined with one blow.[26]

As humans have a right to dominate different species presumed to be biologically different and inferior, so Aryans have a right to dominate inferior races. The same principle of nature applies. Hitler went on to compare the exploitation of animals with "inferior races" to argue that the latter were first used for labor and later were replaced by animals, providing a useful illustration of the intermeshing of the lowest categories of the human caste with the animal caste:

> Only after the enslavement of subjugated races did the same fate strike beasts, and not the other way around, as some people would like to think. For first the conquered warrior drew the plow—and only after him the horse. . . . Hence it is no accident that the first cultures arose in places where the Aryan, in his encounters with lower peoples, subjugated them and bent them to his will. They then became the first technical instrument in the service of a developing culture.[27]

As noted above, the Nazi argument that Jews were akin to animals also turned on the common belief that other animals lacked intelligence and the capacity to create culture. Only the race/species of Aryans could create culture; the animal-like Jewish people were incapable of doing so. Aryans would therefore fall into a cultureless and artless abyss—in short, an uncivilized, animal-like existence—if they bred with lower "species."[28] Not only did fascists characterize the Hebrew scripture as lacking the spirituality of the higher-order Aryans and being inherently materialistic (hence animal-like), but Jews were at times said to lack souls. Nazi party leader Dietrich Eckart, for example, argued that Jews had no souls; as an "adversary of all humanity" they had been driven from the "temple of the Lord"—just as animals, lacking souls in Christian belief, have never been allowed to enter it.[29] But these are only a few examples of many from Nazi discourses that attest to the fluidity of the animal caste and its interchangeability with targeted human groups to justify their domination, exploitation, and termination.[30]

Before moving on to discuss how we can challenge the animalization of human groups, however, we must first respond to a question that some readers have likely already asked. Didn't the Nazis pass laws to protect animals? Don't these laws contradict the argument that Nazis animalized human groups to justify their domination? In 1933 the Nazis did pass a law for the protection of animals, and another in 1934 to limit hunting and the use of certain types of traps. In 1935 a law was passed to protect "Nature."[31]

To understand how such laws could be passed while animals were still being killed and exploited as a subordinate caste in Germany, we must first understand the Nazi conception of nature in relation to German mythology and national identity, as well as the actual practices of the German people. Building upon German mythology, the Nazis believed that human "races" were representative of different *völker* that formed through differing landscapes and were linked to the group's physical characteristics and history.[32] The characteristics of the *volk* of Germanic origins were intrinsically tied to the landscape of the forests, terrain and wildlife, which reflected the "nature" and the soul of the German people. The Nazis championed the need for pristine nature uncontaminated by human beings to maintain national heritage. It was in this context that the Nazis passed laws that placed limits on hunting—to better preserve nature so that Germans could continue to hunt within the natural terrain, with the animals native to it. Animals were to be free to struggle among themselves, so that the fittest could survive in a nature devoid of human interference. It is important for the argument in this chapter to recognize that these laws did not bestow the same legal rights to animals that humans had. Animal experimentation continued in Germany, as did the traditions of hunting and the exploitation and death of animals for labor, food, and clothing.[33]

THE WAY FORWARD: FROM REPRESSION TO CONNECTION

To summarize, speciesist beliefs emerged after human beings first took to organizing their material culture around animal agriculture, some 11,000 years ago. I have argued that this shift in the mode of production resulted in the construction of a caste system that justified the placement of animals and subordinate human groups (classified as slaves) in service to superordinate human groups. Today, however, now that technological innovation provides the potential for alternatives to the use of animal bodies for survival, our emotional connection to animal subjectivity can come to the fore of society's consciousness in ways that were not formerly possible. Reorganizing the mode of production from one of animal exploitation to the use of non-sentient alternatives provides the ontological potential for a radically new human subjectivity and relationship to the world. For the first time in history, we have the opportunity through technological innovation to eliminate the human/animal caste system, together with its rituals of "natural" superiority and inferiority that continue to underpin sexist, racist, classist, and other forms of stratification in the present.

In Marx's thought, human freedom can only be realized once society is able to overcome the realm of physical necessity. To flourish ontologically—to think, to create, to live in harmony with others, and so forth—one must first be able to eat. That is, communism could only emerge historically when the mode of production of society was sufficiently technologically developed to provide an equitable distribution of resources for all members of society. Ironically, the historical pathway to this level of technological production, hence to liberation, led through capitalism itself. After centuries of brutality and exploitation, capitalism would eventually lay the groundwork for radical societal transformation and universal emancipation.

Adapting Marx, we might similarly argue that whereas the historical exploitation of animals by humans—once a *necessity* due to resource scarcity in different geographical environments—became the eventual pathway for human physiological, intellectual, and technological development, today we no longer need to dominate and kill other animals: we have the technological potential to reorganize our mode of production in such a way that we can eliminate our violence against other sentient creatures. If this is indeed the case, however, it can also be argued that by founding our societies on systemic violence against other animals, we distorted our own "species being" in the process—in particular, by deforming our "human" capacity for empathy for the suffering of others who have been "animalized."

Here it is helpful to turn to the work of critical theorist Herbert Marcuse, who provides insights into the processes through which human beings repress emotions and become desensitized to the subjectivity and suffering of others. In *Eros and Civilization* Marcuse draws upon both Marx and Freud to explain the dynamics of societal domination. Marcuse, following Freud, argues that the human organism must forego innate "id" drives for pleasure and autonomy, or the experience of the "pleasure principle," and replace it with the "reality principle" constituted through the social repression necessary for the individual to survive within society. "Basic repression" or "modification" of natural instinct is therefore needed for the "perpetuation of the human race in civilization."[34] Revising Freud's belief that the repression of the innate drives of the id was an inevitable price of civilization,[35] however, Marcuse also argued that there are different *historical* types of social repression, each corresponding to a particular mode of production. Breaking with Freud, Marcuse thus denied that the "reality principle" was historically invariant. He wrote:

> The reality principle sustains the organism in the external world. In the case of the human organism, this is an *historical* world. The external world faced by the growing ego is at any stage a specific socio-historical organization of reality, affecting the mental structure through specific society agencies or agents. It has been argued that Freud's concept of the *reality principle* obliterates this fact by making historical contingencies into biological necessities.[36]

In contrast to Freud, thus, Marcuse identified a modern form of repression he termed "surplus repression," or a condition in which libidinal repression, rather than serving a necessary social function, serves only to maintain the dominance of elites.[37] In short, the "performance principle" (the logic of domination) becomes the "prevailing historical form of the reality principle" in repressed societies.[38]

Marcuse's analysis of "surplus repression"—the need of a socially regressive order to frustrate and repress the individual's basic life needs in order to ensure *reproduction of the system*—has important implications for the repression of our natural (if latent) predispositions to empathize with other conscious subjects, the other animals. The caste system, as we have seen, required the creation of new rituals to consolidate and rationalize the domination of subordinates. Such rituals have served two functions historically: first, to legitimate domination; and second, to *desensitize* members of dominant groups to the suffering and oppression of those they exploit and kill. Overcoming this latter function, the use of ritual and discourse to *distance* oppressors from the suffering of the oppressed, may hold the key to transforming our relations with other animals. Meanwhile, by sensitizing ourselves to the suffering and autonomy of other animals, we also erode the ability of superordinate groups to animalize other *human* groups, and hence to justify their domination.

In current industrial and post-industrial societies animal suffering is no longer materially "required," if it ever was: there are readily available alternatives to animal flesh and to the use of animal fur or skin as clothing or shoes. Yet animal domination continues, largely because corporate interests benefit directly from massive animal exploitation.[39] In other words, whereas rituals of animal killing were originally enacted by technologically "primitive" cultures due to (perceived) necessity, the surplus repression of our contemporary order constructs rituals of animal killing solely in order to shore up profit and maintain related social inequalities. The "reality principle" that "requires" the exploitation and dismemberment of billions of nonhuman animals capable of experiencing fear and suffering is the principle therefore not of survival, but of domination—*surplus* repression.

Overcoming this reality principle rooted in surplus repression—making conscious our feelings of compassion—will mean, among other things, restoring subjectivity and even a form of personhood to other animals.[40] Given the technological changes that now make it not only feasible, but advisable, for societies to change to vegetarian and/or vegan diets, we ought to move beyond our traditionally exclusionary conception of personhood to redefine it to include all who are sentient or conscious and capable of suffering, thereby making animals into full moral subjects. Thinking about how to move beyond the status quo, therefore, is as much or more a question of political strategy as it is about moral awakening and radical cultural change. In the medium term, as utopian as these ideas may now seem, we need to begin thinking about how to transition human culture toward a vegan or, at a preliminary stage, vegetarian diet. Animal agriculture, especially factory farms, is not only cruel beyond telling, it is also a notoriously inefficient and ecologically damaging form of agriculture. The wealthy nations, where meat consumption is highest, must therefore not only begin to phase out meat production, but to provide resources for poorer nations in the Third World to change practices toward animals. (If human beings can only survive through feeding animals to their children, they will do so.) And this can only happen with a more egalitarian distribution of resources among the world's population. Hence, we might say, *veganism* poses an implicit challenge to present concentrations of wealth and power, since its universal realization would require a just redistribution of global resources. Needless to say, however, added to the difficulty of overcoming literally centuries of practices and deeply embedded cultural beliefs about the inferior moral and legal status of animals, there are extremely powerful economic and political interests worldwide that violently oppose such a transition.

CONCLUSION

Through enacting rituals that justify the domination and exploitation of sentient beings constructed as less intelligent, biologically different, lacking souls, and weak, human beings continue to act like Nazis toward animals. The danger is that, to the extent that rituals of a "master race" continue to inform contemporary daily practices toward animals in most if not all human cultures, we carry around the germ of Nazi schemas through these daily practices, schemas which are drawn upon by the powerful to justify not only nonhuman domination, but also the economic, political, and cultural subordination of vulnerable human beings. Can we imagine how different society would be if there were no such readily available cultural arsenal of beliefs and practices to justify the domination, exploitation, and deaths of other sentient beings, and how the character of humanity might change once institutions, communities, and families no longer engaged in daily rituals of the master race?

While those who wish to construct their opponents as absolute evil will always find a way to do so, eliminating rituals of animal domination would dramatically limit the symbolic and discursive weapons available to the powerful when they set out to justify the violence and exploitation of targeted human groups. So long as these schemas and practices continue, then, even the most progressive human societies will be culturally ripe for the kind of animalization of human groups that we saw in Nazi Germany, given the right confluence of economic, political, and cultural crises.[41] Eliminating these schemas would also free the other animals of our own fascist practices toward them.

IV

PROBLEMS IN PRAXIS

12

Constructing Extremists, Rejecting Compassion

Ideological Attacks on Animal Advocacy from Right and Left

By John Sorenson

Questions about our relationships with nonhuman animals and how we should treat them are among the oldest of philosophical debates but lately have re-emerged to become some of the most critical ethical questions of the twenty-first century.[1] Not only is there now a greater scientific appreciation for the behavioral, cognitive, and emotional capacities of our fellow beings, but issues such as the mass production and slaughter of billions of animals for food and clothing; vivisection and the use of animals to develop pharmaceuticals, household products, and weapons; killing for sport; imprisonment and abuse of other creatures for entertainment, along with destruction of habitat and imminent extinctions on a scale not seen since the age of the dinosaurs, have all drawn the attention of a growing movement for the protection of animals. The unparalleled enormity of the suffering endured by these nonhuman animals must surely draw the attention of any serious person, but the ethical issues are not limited only to concerns about the agony of these other beings. All of these activities have implications for human beings as well, ranging from the devastating impact of a globalized meat industry upon the world's poor, contributions to global warming and environmental destruction with serious implications for human survival, and the negative health consequences of an animal-based diet for those affluent enough to consume it, to the links between the abuse of nonhuman animals and violent behavior towards other human beings. Given the gravity of these issues, along with the fact that at the heart of the animal protectionist movement exist the kindest and most compassionate of motives, one might expect that they might be met with serious consideration. Instead, across the political spectrum, the animal protectionist movement is vilified. From both the

Right and the Left, the crudest arguments are used to demonize or dismiss animal advocates and to push aside these vital matters.

WARNINGS FROM THE RIGHT

According to various right-wing journals and websites, Western civilization faces a terrible new menace, one even more dangerous than Islamist terror or gay marriage. The nature of this threat? People who want to protect animals.

Apparently alarmed by the idea of better treatment for animals, these writers depict animal advocates as the ultimate danger, a movement so powerful and violent that it is poised to destroy the very foundations of Western culture and depose "Man" from the center of the universe. The discourse they construct is part of a countermovement to animal protection, designed to protect the financial interests of those who profit from exploitation of animals. This countermovement is a well-organized, multi-million–dollar propaganda campaign by agribusiness, biomedical industries, and "sportsmen" who enjoy killing for recreation, organized to control moral capital and present their vested interests as representative of "normal people" threatened by "animal rights extremists."[2] However, as noted below, the anthropocentric prejudices underlying this discourse are not exclusively limited to corporate interests and right-wing groups: these prejudices are mirrored on the Left.

One particularly striking example of how this prejudice is mobilized against animal advocates is found in the right-wing Christian journal *U Turn* (whose editor, Ken Ewert, feels himself so directly tuned in to the supernatural that he is able to claim that a "free market economy is . . . God's economic design"[3] while other contributors explain poverty as the result of sin and complain that welfare contradicts Biblical commands).[4] Contributor Dave Matheson depicts the animal rights movement as "Man's rebellion against God" and warns:

> The animal "rights" movement is part of what Michael Novak believes is "a turning away from the biblical emphasis on the distinction between man and nature," which causes man to be "attracted by Eastern mysticism, which views man as a part of nature." Herbert Schlossberg elaborates on this theme, saying "this error plunges man into complete irrationality. . . . Everything that distinguishes man from nature disappears in this outlook, and that can only mean that man himself disappears. That is why C. S. Lewis was right to call the triumph of such a conception 'the abolition of man.'" I think Paul summed it up best; the animal rights movement is the "the doctrine of demons"![5]

Matheson's assertion that human beings are distinctly separated from the rest of nature conforms to the anthropocentric prejudices of the journal's religious ideology but it is in complete contradiction to any scientific understanding of the world. His argument is anachronistic (it is unlikely that early Christians had "the animal rights movement" in mind when discussing any "doctrine of demons"), chauvinistic (other beliefs are dismissed as mere mysticism) and selective (while embracing conservative elements of C. S. Lewis's thought, Matheson[6] overlooks Lewis's affection for animals and efforts to consider their interests within the context of his religious beliefs). The assertion that "man himself disappears" if human beings are recognized as part of the natural world is an effort to maintain an identity that seems based on equal parts grandiose self-congratulation and existential terror.

One finds the same attempt to control the social construction of moral meaning by mobilizing religious ideology to discredit animal advocacy in Australia's *Sydney Morning Herald*, where right-wing Catholic journalist Miranda Devine warns that the "obsession with animal rights is not a sign of a more compassionate society but of one which has lost respect for humanity. It has lost its belief in the soul and free will, which used to distinguish people from animals and gave existence meaning."[7] Understanding that animal advocates have gained public support for their campaigns by appealing to the compassion that many people naturally do feel for animals, Devine works to deny those compassionate feelings and transform them into something sinister, an "obsession" which somehow has decreased "respect for humanity." Indeed, this rejection of compassion for others is the very core of those discourses that oppose animal rights. Having conjured this transformation of compassion into misanthropy, Devine then links her creation in a vague way with a decline in religious beliefs, arguing that, without these superstitions, existence must be meaningless. Despite its absence of logic, her essay creates the impression that concern for animals will have immense and disastrous consequences for human beings.

Similar warnings come from another neoconservative-Christian journal, *First Things*, which promotes the views of right-wing Catholic priest Richard J. Neuhaus. For example, Thomas Derr,[8] professor of religion at Smith College, detects "a persistent strain of anti-humanism in their movement," while David R. Carlin, professor of philosophy and sociology at the Community College of Rhode Island and chairman of the Democratic Party in Newport, Rhode Island, writes that "the animal rights movement seems to be aiming at the elevation of animals. In fact, however, it is but the latest episode in a long history of attempts to degrade humans."[9] Carlin's argument is even weaker than those cited above but is equally alarmist:

> At present I cannot *prove* that the idea of animal rights is extraordinarily dangerous and inhumane; to get proof of this, we'll have to wait until the disastrous conse-

> quences of the idea reveal themselves over the next century or so. But I strongly suspect that it's a dangerous idea, and accordingly I suspect that the promoters of this idea, whatever their intentions, are enemies of the human race.[10]

Carlin acknowledges that he is unable to offer any evidence for the strange linkages he creates (i.e., that concern for animals degrades humans) and the suspicions he draws from them. Nevertheless, he is quite content to assert strong conclusions and warn that concern for animals is being promoted by "enemies of the human race."

If these hysterical fears surfaced only in obscure publications of religious fringe groups they might be dismissed as insignificant. However, these same arguments are repeated across a much wider range of right-wing publications. For example, although Alex Epstein, from the pro-capitalist Ayn Rand Institute, does not appear to believe animal advocates are actually agents of Satan, he does perceive a threat of similar magnitude. Writing about an animal advocacy conference, he detects "the true goal of their doctrine: human extermination" and states, "[a]nimal rights advocates place the lives of animals over the lives of human beings. This is a formula for human suffering and death."[11] The claim that animal advocates "place the lives of animals over the lives of human beings" refers to vivisection and medical experiments, all of which, in Epstein's world, apparently are conducted for the highest ethical objectives of saving humans from fatal diseases. The fact that not all animal advocates share a single point of view on such questions does not even enter the discussion, nor does the fact that not all these experiments—and perhaps very few—are undertaken for such noble purposes.

On his personal website, devoted to "defense of business and America," Epstein expands on these themes, condemning actions taken against Huntingdon Life Sciences (HLS), Europe's largest contract research agency, notorious for its vivisection activities. In 1989 HLS was infiltrated by the British Union for the Abolition of Vivisection, which reported on terrified dogs being force-fed chemicals, cleaning products, insecticides, and fungicides and harnessed for painful subcutaneous and skin toxicity tests; another exposé in 1996 revealed inadequate care and deliberate abuse in addition to that which was commercially motivated. In 2000 the *Daily Express* exposed cruelty in xenotransplantation procedures at HLS for Novartis, which obtained a court injunction against further publicity on the experiments. In 2003, after fighting the injunction, *The Observer* published secret documents exposing horrendous cruelty in pig-to-primate heart transplant experiments done for Novartis. In 2004 the group Stop Huntingdon Animal Cruelty exposed tests done on beagles at HLS for Daikin Industries of Osaka and the Japan Refrigeration and Air Conditioning Association of Tokyo using banned gases. While animal advocacy groups have supplied extensive evidence of hideous abuse of animals at HLS, Epstein simply ignores this in order to make unsubstantiated claims intended to vilify and arouse hatred for those groups: "[t]he goal of the animal-rights movement is not to stop sadistic animal torturers; it is *to sacrifice and subjugate man to animals*. This goal is inherent in the very notion of 'animal rights'"[12]

Andrew Bernstein, senior writer for the Ayn Rand Institute, identifies the same "man-hating psychology" among animal advocates. He suggests that they argue, "[s]ince rattlesnakes and rats are held to possess an inviolate inherent worth, it is deemed not only morally wrong to harm them, but also obligatory to sacrifice man for their sake."[13] That such an "obligatory . . . sacrifice" is mandated nowhere in the writings of animal advocates is irrelevant to Bernstein's main aim of presenting them as fanatics. Like others who oppose the animal protection movement, Bernstein simply invents material for criticism. Another luminary of the Ayn Rand Institute, Edwin Locke, writing for the Institute's online *Capitalism* magazine, engages in similar distortions and warns of similar dangers:

> The animal "rights" terrorists are like the Unabomber and Oklahoma City bombers. They are not idealists seeking justice, but nihilists seeking destruction for the sake of destruction. They do not want to uplift mankind, to help him progress from the swamp to the stars. They want mankind's destruction; they want him not just to stay in the swamp but to disappear into its muck.[14]

Locke provides no evidence beyond his own assertion for his claim that animal advocates are like the Unabomber or the Oklahoma City bombers, all of whom deliberately intended to kill people and whose ideological affiliations have absolutely no connections with animal protectionism.

Not surprisingly, such defenders of capitalism are eager to claim that this army of demonic anti-humanists they have invented is linked with the political Left. For example, Matheson claims animal advocacy has become the last refuge of the "Evil Empire":

> Did you ever wonder what became of the left wing "intelligentsia" following the humiliating collapse of the Soviet Union and its Communist puppet states? Well, they are alive and well, and they are continuing to promote the Communist ideals of state control over resources. The only things that have changed are the terminology they use, and the names of the organizations they belong to. Roll over Marx and Lenin! Today's trendy and leftist causes are animal rights and radical environmentalism.[15]

Other observers also detect left-wing conspiracies behind animal advocacy. For example, reporting to the South African Gunowners' Association on an animal rights conference in Washington, D.C., Jim Beers (federal programs coordinator for the National Trappers Association and contributor to free-market websites such as Alliance for America and the Heartland Institute) identifies the same "communist" menace, likening the event to

> a communist training program back in the 50's or 60's for a cadre of insurgents to be sent into a country to be subverted. Some are trained to control the media, others to influence politicians and control bureaucracies, still others to control religion and schools. Demonstrators were to disrupt things, and others to do the "other things" that ultimately underpin all the rest. Frightening is too weak a word to describe what it is like to watch this take place in a luxury hotel in a free country.[16]

Others also spot a nefarious left-wing plot to impose an animal rights agenda. For example, joining the strident chorus that shouts from David Horowitz's online *FrontPage* magazine about the dangers of liberalism, J. P. Zmirak links animal protection both with the political Left and with violence in his claim that "every known philosophy of the far-Left contains the seeds of murder including the animal rights movement."[17] Terror, murder, demonic doctrines, and the end of "Man"—all these are depicted as the tactics and goals of a surging tide of self-loathing animal rights fanatics engaged in a cosmic scheme of ontological mutiny. Absolutely no evidence is presented for any of these claims, and their authors readily overlook the long historical association between movements for better treatment of animals and other movements for social justice and improvements in what we now generally regard as basic human rights, such as anti-slavery campaigns, emancipation of women, and abolition of child labor. In attempting to portray a concern for animals as a perverted hatred for human beings, the authors also ignore various studies which demonstrate that those people who show compassion and empathy for animals are more likely to have similar attitudes for other human beings. Furthermore, they overlook the large body of research that demonstrates that violence toward animals frequently is linked with violence toward human beings. Both in its compassionate approach to other living beings and in its long association with other movements for social justice among human beings, the animal protectionist movement has demonstrated that it is not anti-human as these writers claim but, rather, is an expression of the most noble and progressive of human impulses.

DISMISSALS FROM THE LEFT

While right-wing commentators fret that Satan and his socialist hordes are using subversion and murder to promote their animal rights agenda, in reality, many of those considered to be on the Left seem to have very little interest in animal protection and to share many of the same instrumentalist attitudes toward animals. Some leftist groups adopt positions that are virtually identical to those of right-wing supporters of animal exploitation industries. For example, the World Socialist Website of the International Committee of the Fourth International (ICFI), a miniscule Trotskyist faction, denounces animal rights as an "extremist" movement which rejects the benefits of modern science and places the interests of other animals above those of human beings. The ICFI dismisses the issue of animal rights as a reformist one and claims to have no position on the subject, while clearly supporting the exploitation of animals and even going so far as to condemn efforts to help animals as "attacks on the personal property of scientists."[18] In a statement that could have originated from the desk of a pharmaceutical corporation or its hired public relations consultants, the ICFI's Julie Hyland expresses firm confidence in the state's regulation of vivisection and the benign intent and good corporate citizenship of the pharmaceutical industry:

> Research involving animals is closely regulated in Britain, with the Home Office reporting that 2.73 million animal experiments were conducted in the UK in 2002, of which 84 percent were on rodents. Of such procedures—most of which were for research and drug development purposes—non-toxic testing accounted for 82 percent of all experiments. Animal testing for cosmetics is banned, and despite often highly emotive campaigns by animal rights activists, dogs, cats, horses and primates account for less than 1 percent of animal experiments.[19]

The faith of these Trotskyist revolutionaries in the humanitarian intentions of the pharmaceutical corporations and the diligence of the British state in overseeing these industries for the good of the masses is rather surprising. So is their easy acceptance of animals as the "personal property of scientists" and their contemptuous dismissal of "emotive campaigns" by animal advocates because most of the living beings used in vivisection are rodents, as if these animals were of no concern. In contrast to the kindly motives of these benevolent institutions, Hyland claims to detect a "misanthropic outlook at the heart of animal rights extremism, with its denunciations of humans as no better, and in many instances much worse, than animals." As in right-wing discourses, compassion for other beings is depicted as hatred of human beings and a threat to human supremacy. As do her right-wing counterparts, Hyland neglects to provide any actual evidence of this "misanthropic outlook" but merely asserts its existence as the only possible motivating force for animal advocates. Many Marxists share with their capitalist foes an anthropocentric, instrumentalist view of nature in which the interests of animals always must be subordinated to those of human beings.

Like right-wing critics, leftist opponents of animal advocacy typically focus on violence, selecting the actions undertaken by a tiny number of activists and presenting them as typical and expressive of the "anti-human" essence of the animal protection movement. Violence committed against sentient but nonhuman beings in factory farms, slaughterhouses, vivisection laboratories, breeding mills, zoos, rodeos, circuses, and other institutions based on the exploitation of animals is simply taken for granted as acceptable practice and seldom enters the discussion. Actions taken to stop such suffering are presented as proof of the misanthropy that allegedly underlies the entire animal protection movement, although it is never explained how efforts to prevent the cruelty and suffering of other living beings actually constitute such misanthropy. Most of the "violence" committed by animal activists has consisted of illegally entering buildings in which animals are confined, subjected to extremely painful experiments, or killed, for the purpose of rescuing those animals and documenting the conditions in which they have been kept. A smaller number of actions have involved the destruction of such institutions; many of the assertions concerning such actions are vague and lack details that might confirm that they actually took place. Even those organizations that do condone illegal actions to rescue animals, such as the Animal Liberation Front, have strict guidelines about not harming people. Only a very few incidents of violence directed towards human beings have been recorded: assaults on the managing director and the marketing director of Huntingdon Life Sciences and a series of letter bombs attributed to a group identified as the Justice Department. In several cases, violence attributed to animal rights activists was found to have been staged for purposes of insurance fraud or to discredit activists, and it is conceivable that police or privately hired provocateurs have been involved in other incidents. Although it may be too much to argue that "animal rights violence" was actually invented by animal-exploitation industries and their highly paid professional propaganda organizations in order to discredit their critics, it is clear that the latter have seized upon a few actions by a very small number of people and exaggerated them out of all proportion to make it seem as if they are representative of the entire animal protection movement. Along with the total eclipsing of the actual violence that is routinely committed against nonhuman animals, in the vilest forms and on a scale that is scarcely imaginable, these distorted images of animal advocates serve to turn the animal-exploitation industries into beleaguered victims who can then call upon the state's security forces and legal system to crack down even harder on those who would oppose their operations. Far more extensive than violence committed by animal advocates is the violence committed against them. While no human fatality has ever resulted from animal rights actions, several advocates have been killed in demonstrations and others are alleged to have committed suicide in prison. Beatings by privately contracted thugs and by police are routine.[20]

That corporate media ignore the facts and promote such stereotypes of animal advocates as violent is to be expected. But it is more surprising to find them repeated by those on the Left. For example, responding to a reader's criticisms of Hyland's claims, ICFI representative Chris Talbot defends her statements, denounces animal advocates as "extremists," and expresses the organization's support for vivisection:

> Our view, and we believe it is one that most of our readers share, is that experiments on animals are of importance to medical researchers. We have no reason to believe that cruelty or neglect of laboratory animals is widespread, and we do not accept the argument of animal rights protesters that the cases of malpractice they focus on justify stopping all animal experiments.[21]

Astonishingly, Hyland and Talbot simply accept the vivisection industry's claims that animal testing is vital to develop new drugs to save human lives. Overlooking a veritable mountain of evidence, including industry documents, undercover video footage, and eyewitness accounts that shows terrible abuse of animals (often conducted for purposes that are trivial or redundant or, as in the case of military research, actually intended to harm human beings), these Trotskyite revolutionaries readily accept that vivisection is "of importance to medical researchers" and show no interest in or awareness of a growing number of studies that suggest that much of this research is actually misleading and dangerous. They share their position with industry lobbyists such as Richard Berman. For example, in advertisements in *The New Yorker* magazine (February 14 and 25, 2005) Berman's Center for Consumer Freedom, a public relations firm funded by tobacco, meat, alcohol, and junk-food industries, campaigned against what it called PETA's "violent opposition to medical research," claiming that it funded criminal organizations to block research into an AIDS cure because PETA values animals more than human beings.

Despite vivisectionists' claims to be focused on vital medical research, much testing is still done on frivolous products such as household cleaners or cosmetics.[22] Most testing is done in secret, defended on grounds of intellectual property or academic freedom. But according to statistics released by the industry-friendly Canadian Council on Animal Care that supposedly monitors testing in this country, government-mandated toxicity tests accounted for 82 percent of the procedures. Furthermore, the group Animal Alliance noted that the Canadian government spent none of its budget on developing alternatives and stated that most testing was curiosity-driven and less than 27 percent of testing was done for medical purposes.[23] Also, the military tortures vast numbers of animals in order to develop new methods of harming human beings with biological, chemical, microwave, or radiation weapons. In the

United States, at least 320,000 animals are hurt and killed by the Department of Defense in secret experiments at a cost of over 100 million dollars, and the actual numbers are far higher because these estimates do not include contracted-out research.[24] According to recent reports, the use of animals in military testing in the United Kingdom has doubled in recent years.[25] Even in cases where animals are used for medical research, leading medical journals note that few important new drugs have been found in recent years; most are variations of existing drugs, sold under different names. Much animal testing is cruel, redundant, and wasteful, devoted to reproducing existing studies or introducing slight variations that will allow competing corporations to market their own version of already-available drugs. Vivisectors often conduct pointless experiments in order to compete for grants and to further their careers. Findings are often irrelevant to human needs, and the validity of using one species as a model for another is itself questionable.

Even when research is directed to serious human problems, the utility of animal testing is questioned within the scientific community itself. For example, in an article entitled "Laboratory Routines Cause Animal Stress," published in *Contemporary Topics in Laboratory Animal Science*, ethologist Jonathan Balcombe of the Physicians Committee for Responsible Medicine reviewed 80 published studies and found that even relatively innocuous handling caused physiological reactions such as spiked blood pressure, hormone elevations, and impairment to immune responses significant enough to invalidate data obtained from experiments.[26] Balcombe noted: "[r]esearch on tumor development, immune function, endocrine and cardiovascular disorders, neoplasms, developmental defects, and psychological phenomena are particularly vulnerable to data being contaminated by animals' stress effects."[27] Balcombe's findings followed a paper in the *British Medical Journal*, titled "Where Is the Evidence that Animal Research Benefits Humans?" in which the authors concluded that much animal experimentation was wasteful, methodologically unsound, and poorly conducted while noting that, frequently, human trials were conducted concurrently with animal research and that clinical trials sometimes continued despite evidence of harm from animal experiments.[28]

Arguments from the Left and the Right thus converge in the dismissal of animals from moral consideration. Defending animal exploitation, the ICFI's Chris Talbot rejects arguments by philosopher Peter Singer, who emphasizes ability to feel pain as an important moral consideration. Talbot's claims mirror those of Edwin Locke in the Ayn Rand Institute's *Capitalism* magazine: only humans have rights because humans have special abilities and are moral agents. In a passage that would not be out of place in right-wing Christian journals, Talbot writes:

> Our position, on the contrary, is that human society is a unique phenomenon amongst all the animal species. Humans can labour with their hands and brains, can plan and develop productive techniques, and have amassed centuries of culture and knowledge that have enabled them to control and hold dominion over the rest of nature. Moreover, we hold that humans have the ability to change and develop not only the natural world in a conscious and planned way, but also human society itself—that, after all, is the central tenet of socialism. In our view, therefore, humans have infinitely more to them than the ability to experience pleasure and pain on a biological level. We disagree with the underlying conception of Singer, Tom Regan and others that the essential nature of humans can be found in their individual and biological characteristics. In other words, we oppose the view of human society that sees it as nothing more than a collection of individuals with their own "human nature" and interests.[29]

In fact, neither Regan nor Singer argue that human beings are "nothing more" than individuals; Talbot misrepresents their views while asserting a sharp dualism between humans and other animals. Although a belief in this dualism does constitute a dominant view of our relationship with other animals, it has been challenged consistently throughout much of human history and has been disproved by modern science, which has supported Darwin's observations that differences between humans and other animals are ones of degree, not of kind. New ethological observations have led to the discovery that other animals do have complex cognition, with abilities and emotions that are comparable in many ways to those of human beings. This said, it is extremely unlikely that even a single animal rights advocate could be found who would not acknowledge the obvious point that human beings are unique in various ways and that they have some abilities that other animals do not. However, these advocates do not maintain that ethical concerns about the interests of others should be based on the level of the abilities they possess, and it is surprising to find such a position being promoted by those on the Left, unless one holds a view of social justice that might award more rights to people who are more intelligent, insightful, skilled, and so forth, than others.

Talbot's idea that human beings "hold dominion over the rest of nature" is striking for its echo of Christian ideology and its suggestion that the relationship of human beings to the environment should be one of power rather than harmony. Even the British Liberal Party's policy statement on animal welfare makes more progressive claims, though these are often not carried out in actual practice, and promotes legislation to protect animals and the environment: "Liberals recognize that the world's creatures have rights too and that the human race should act as trustees of the natural world rather than its master,"[30] while the Green Party states, "Greens oppose factory farming and advocate banning cruel live exports. We want an end to animal experimentation and real investment in non-animal chemical testing."[31] The ICFI's position on environmental issues suggests that the only dilemma is capitalism and that once Marxists control production all problems will be solved. They promote technology and industrialization and see no problems with human population growth.[32] In view of the marginalization of the Left in various contemporary societies, it is possible to see the dismissal of concern for animals as a means by which some on the Left have sought to manipulate moral capital, making their own political organizations seem more acceptable by pandering to anthropocentric prejudices of "ordinary people."

The ICFI's views are narrowly focused on human interests and are not unusual on the Left. For example, Peter Staudenmaier, of the Institute of Social Ecology, reproduces the same arguments in his article "Ambiguities of Animal Rights," calling it a "moral mistake and a symptom of political confusion . . . anti-humanist and anti-ecological . . . at odds with the project of creating a free world."[33] Championing a human-centred view, Staudenmaier rejects analogies between animal advocacy and movements for human emancipation because animals cannot speak for themselves. Again, this echoes statements from industry lobbyists and capitalist ideologues. For example, Alan Herscovici,[34] propagandist for the Fur Council of Canada, makes similar arguments, proclaiming: "[ir]ronically, animal rights is often described by its advocates as an extension of the civil rights or feminist movements. 'Speaking for the animals,' however, offers some definite advantages over these models for the leadership: the oppressed cannot question their policies." Staudenmaier's assertion that animal advocacy is a "moral mistake" is echoed by Edward J. Feulner, president of the Heritage Foundation, who states, but nowhere proves, the standard denunciation that analogies about exploitation of humans and other animals reflect "a twisted moral universe [and] callousness toward human suffering."[35] The proposal that individuals do not have rights (or the ability to experience pain or even consciousness) because they cannot speak is an argument that some philosophers use to deny consideration for animals, but this also raises problems about the status of marginal cases among human beings. Furthermore, while other animals cannot speak in human languages, they can often articulate their wishes in ways that are immediately understandable to human beings. It is therefore clear they do not want to be killed in slaughterhouses or tortured in laboratories. Reproducing the claims made by the intellectuals of the Ayn Rand Institute and the ICFI about the uniqueness of human beings as moral agents, Staudenmaier argues that animal advocacy "degrades, rather than develops, the humanist impulse embodied in liberatory social movements." Oddly, he even denies the very existence of anthropocentric institutions, arguing that only elitist ones exist and that any concern about anthropocentrism only masks differences between human beings. This is obviously false, as exemplified by the presence of factory farms, slaughterhouses, and vivisection laboratories. The fact that people have different relationships with these institutions—profiting from them or being exploited within them—does not alter the basic relationships of domination over and victimization of animals. The existence of class distinctions between human beings in no way invalidates the fact that anthropocentric beliefs operate within all classes and have negative consequences for other animals.

Seeking to undermine the connections between animal advocacy and other forms of progressive social and political thought, Staudenmaier argues that animal advocacy is elitist, racist, and linked with extreme right-wing groups, including fascists and Nazis. As proof, Staudenmaier even includes the claim that Hitler was a vegetarian, an irrelevant argument but one which is rejected in Rynn Berry's book *Hitler: Neither Vegetarian Nor Animal Lover*.[36] But Staudenmaier's arguments are misleading. Although the Nazis may have placed some limits on vivisection and advocated organic foods for health reasons, they cannot be construed as supporters of animal rights policies. While the Nazis may have introduced some progressive legislation concerning animals, this hardly invalidates a concern for animals on the part of others, such as those who may be fundamentally opposed to Nazi ideology. Some leftist writers such as Alexander Cockburn[37] and Gary Francione[38] have noted the logical flaws in this analogy as a means of discrediting animal advocacy. Yet, clearly, a ferocious hostility towards animal advocacy inspires writers on both the Left and the Right to employ such distortions and dishonesties in order to defend the supremacy of "Man."

Like various right-wing writers mentioned above, Staudenmaier makes the curious but constantly repeated claim that caring about animals somehow degrades human beings or demonstrates a lack of concern towards human suffering. Any discussion of why this should be so, or any evidence that this is actually the case, is absent. This demonstrates that almost any claim, no matter how nonsensical, can be made about the animal protection movement. Compassion and concern for those who are at our mercy do not degrade us but rather are among our more noble impulses. Furthermore, it is unreasonable to assume that concern for other animals excludes concern for human beings. Nevertheless, others on the Left repeat these same ideas, along with assertions that the interests of human beings are not only more important than but separate from those of other animals and the natural world. For example, Michael Albert, co-founder of *Z* magazine and ZNet, stated in *Satya* magazine:

> when I talk about social movements to make the world better, animal rights does not come into my mind. I honestly don't see animal rights movements in anything like the way in which I see women's movements, Latino movements, youth

> movements, the anti-corporate globalization movement, labor movements, and so on. . . . It just honestly doesn't strike me as being remotely as urgent as preventing war in Iraq or winning a 30-hour work week, or overthrowing capitalism.[39]

Apart from the unwarranted assumption that one must be concerned about animal rights *or* war in Iraq *or* a reduced work week *or* overthrowing capitalism, Albert's anthropocentrism prevents him from seeing how capitalism thrives on the exploitation of all animals, not only humans, and he fails to acknowledge important connections between various forms of oppression. Concern for "one's own kind" is just as limited, whether this is based on ideas of race or of species. As Peter Singer points out in his book on the ethics of globalization, *One World*, such sentiments of partiality formed an essential part of the Nazi worldview.[40] Like Albert, many on the Left dismiss animal advocacy as a trivial, single-issue movement and see veganism as a personal or lifestyle choice. Albert's failure to recognize these connections is echoed in an even more vulgar fashion by filmmaker Michael Moore, who asserts that "vegetarianism is unhealthy" and that animal rights "just makes me want to kick my dog."[41] Due to the pervasive use of animals in our society, it is difficult to live as a vegan in our society, but the effort to do so is a powerful symbolic statement, and involvement with animal protectionism is not only in itself a genuine expression of compassion but also a means of opening doors to other issues and to understanding connections between various forms of oppression.

Those on the Left who dismiss veganism and concern for animals not only trivialize compassion but overlook the radical potential of these concerns for creating consciousness about other issues. The Left has been criticized in the past for its dogmatic views on issues of racism and sexism, dismissing the latter as secondary issues and thus alienating many who might have been potential allies. Repeating these mistakes today, much of the Left insists on the overwhelming importance of human issues, taking "Man" as the measure of all things and dismissing the plight of other living beings. However, any political theory is inadequate if it focuses on the human species alone, ignoring other living beings and the environment in which all of them exist or regarding them only as resources to be exploited.

Just as individual human activities must be seen within a historical, social, and political context, so too they must be considered in a broader ecological context. A meat-based diet is not simply a personal choice but a political one, with far-reaching consequences. The production of meat is linked to major forms of environmental destruction. Hundreds of thousands of square kilometers of rainforest have been destroyed to provide pasture for cattle. According to reports from the World Rainforest Movement, 40 percent of the forests of Central America have been destroyed, largely for ranching. Because ranching is totally unsuited to the environment, new areas of forest are soon needed. As a result, thousands of plant and animal species are being driven into extinction, indigenous people are driven off their land—often violently and always with the loss of their unique cultural traditions—and a major source of oxygen production for the planet is being eradicated.[42] In Africa, commercial cattle ranching for export was directly linked to the Sahel famine of 1968 to 1974 in which 100,000 people died.[43] Commercial fishing, shrimp farming, and pollution are destroying coral reefs and mangrove swamps, with a similar loss of irreplaceable biodiversity and damage to extensive and vital ecosystems. In North America, half the agricultural land is devoted to ranching or producing grain for animals, and some estimate that half the world's grain goes to feeding animals who are then killed for human consumption. This is an extremely impractical system; for example, far greater amounts of water are diverted into this inefficient system than would be required for a vegan/vegetarian diet, and it is estimated that production of approximately half a kilogram of beef requires 40 times as much fossil fuel as would be required to produce a similar quantity of soybeans. The huge numbers of animals crammed into factory farms produce vast amounts of waste that pollute adjacent land and water systems. As the global consumption of meat has grown and corporate factory farming has spread throughout the world, poverty has increased as small farmers have been driven out of business and forced into urban slums, while the environment has suffered.[44] Even if one is unmoved by the ghastly suffering of billions of animals who are raised and then killed in factory farms and slaughterhouses, it is not hard to see that, like other capitalist enterprises, the meatpacking industry exploits workers, preying on the poorest and weakest and exposing them to dangerous conditions for low wages.[45] Factory farming also has implications for human health. Animals are imprisoned in crowded, filthy, poorly ventilated structures creating an ideal breeding ground for disease. Numerous reports document the filthy conditions in slaughterhouses and the distribution, sale, and consumption of animal flesh tainted with various chemicals, diseases, and fecal matter.[46] Heavy use of antibiotics in factory farming has polluted the environment as animal waste saturates waterways, promoted drug-resistant bacteria, and further threatened human health. While millions of people in advanced capitalist societies suffer from obesity, diseases of overconsumption, and illnesses such as cancer, heart disease, and diabetes that are directly related to meat consumption, a billion poor people suffer malnutrition and starvation. The cost-effective strategy of feeding animal parts to other animals led to the outbreak of bovine spongiform encephalopathy ("Mad Cow disease"), and it is only a matter of time before more diseases spread from other animals to humans. Fear of an avian influenza pandemic led to the mass slaughter of birds in Canada in 2004 and throughout Asia in 2005. So the global meat system, a multi-billion–dollar industry, has serious consequences for the entire planet and the poor, increases real dangers to human health, and is no trifling matter to be overlooked or dismissed even by those who are concerned only with the welfare of human beings and care nothing for other animals.

Despite the myopic anthropocentrism of many prominent leftists today, this hostility to expressing concern for other animals was not always the case. While there is a much longer intellectual history of concern for other animals and the ethical duties owed to them, as a political movement animal advocacy is linked with the anti-slavery movement, feminism, and various educational and social reforms, such as alleviating child poverty. In late Victorian and Edwardian Britain, a circle of socialists, Fabians, social reformers, suffragettes, pacifists, and artists, including figures such as Bertrand Russell, George Bernard Shaw, Anna Kingsford, and Annie Besant, combined concern for humanitarian improvements with vegetarianism and opposition to vivisection and hunting. The socialist Henry Salt, founder of the Humanitarian League, influenced Mahatma Gandhi and his philosophies of nonviolent resistance through his works such as *A Plea for Vegetarianism* (1886) and *Animals' Rights* (1892). In the United States, socialist writers such as Jack London and Upton Sinclair also advocated for the better treatment of animals. Henry Spira, a prominent animal rights activist in the United States, developed his radical analysis as a member of the Socialist Workers Party in the 1950s and through his involvement with the civil right movement and support for Cuba against U.S. imperialism. As Peter Singer remarked in a reflection on Spira's life, "[h]e had read an article of mine about animal liberation, and realised that it was the logical extension of what he had been doing all his life: helping the downtrodden, the powerless, and the exploited."[47]

Other prominent activists and intellectuals on the Left have acknowledged how various forms of oppression are interwoven and have identified animal protection as a serious concern. For example, Noam Chomsky argues that most forms of hierarchy and domination serve only those at the top of the heap, are morally unjustified, and must be questioned. Chomsky extends this to human relationships with other animals, citing the torture of animals in research laboratories as one example of such illegitimate exploitation. Although he acknowledges vegetarianism and animal protection as serious issues and reasonable goals for those who seek to create a more progressive society, Chomsky admits that he is not a vegetarian himself and he has not addressed these issues in any depth in his own work.[48] David Nibert's book *Animal Rights/Human Rights* draws the connections between various forms of oppression and places animal rights within the context of a socialist approach.[49] Anna E. Charlton, Sue Coe, and Gary Francione have argued that the Left should endorse animal rights.[50] The Center for Animal Liberation Affairs explicitly places its concern for animals in the context of other social justice struggles.[51] Materialist ecofeminists (as opposed to those focused mainly on spiritual aspects) see the exploitation of animals as one consequence of patriarchal capitalism. Groups such as Food Not Bombs, founded in the 1980s by anti-nuclear activists, now provide vegetarian food for the homeless and at various protests, while working with anarchists, environmentalists, anti-racist groups, animal rights activists, and others opposed to capitalist globalization.

Certainly, not all animal advocates are on the Left and do not make connections between exploitation of animals and other forms of social injustice. Even within the field of animal protection itself, some have welfarist concerns only for particular animals and accept exploitation of other animals for food or other purposes. Even some who do recognize connections between various forms of oppression do not see those connections in leftist context. Some animal advocates, such as Marjorie Spiegel, recognize similarities between enslavement of Africans and enslavement of nonhuman animals but do not see a particular link between these forms of exploitation and capitalism, with Spiegel arguing that animals have not fared any better under socialism.[52] While Marxists have been too quick to dismiss animal advocacy, to overlook its progressive history, to ignore its capacity for radicalization of consciousness, and to sneer at the compassionate sentiments that often motivate those who work on behalf of animals, it is true that some animal activists do not always see their own actions in a broader framework. For example, animal advocates argue that world hunger could be solved by widespread adoption of a vegan diet. While this strategy would represent a far more efficient and sustainable use of resources and would be a healthier choice for those who gave up eating animal flesh, a shift to vegetarianism would not directly benefit the poor who do not have enough to eat. The problem is not simply a shortage in the amount of food but a matter of how food is distributed; since the world is organized on the basis of capitalist relations, this means food goes to those who can afford to buy it. Even some of the most prominent animal advocates do demonstrate some surprising lapses in their thinking. For example, Peter Singer includes as a chapter in his edited book *In Defense of Animals: The Second Wave* an interview done by Karen Dawn for Pacifica Radio with John Mackey, founder of the Whole Foods Market chain of grocery stores. Celebrating "The CEO as Animal Activist," the chapter applauds Mackey's decision to consider some welfare standards in relation to animals killed for sale as meat in his stores, his own vegan diet, and his role in creating the Animals Compassion Foundation to "help meat producers create environments and conditions to support every animal's natural physical needs, natural behaviors, and well-being."[53] While even the slightest diminution in the unspeakable agony endured by most "farm animals" is desirable, many animal advocates would be reluctant to join Dawn and Singer in accepting the Orwellian idea that "meat producers . . . create . . . [the] well-being" of animals they kill. Furthermore, willingness to hail Mackey as a New Age capitalist overlooks the fact that he is a Milton Friedman disciple who operates with "a simple and lucrative business strategy: high prices and low wages" and is notorious for his opposition to unions, describing them as "parasites."[54] Whole Foods Market refused to join even with other major grocery corporations in signing a pledge for better wages and work conditions for strawberry pickers in California. Even in relation to animal welfare, Whole Food Market prioritizes profits, as exemplified by its refusal to cooperate with Earth Island Institute's campaign to protect sea turtles from shrimp nets.[55] As an animal activist, the CEO is inconsistent, to say the least.

Fortunately, others who espouse animal protection are more progressive in their analyses. When leftists dismiss the concerns of these more critical animal advocates as mere sentimentalism and personal lifestyle choices, they overlook a powerful potential for radicalizing consciousness. Those who are motivated to help animals will inevitably be forced to confront the absolute ruthlessness of corporate interests, the distortions of the corporate media, and the power of the state that acts to protect these capitalist interests. Those who see their own positive efforts misrepresented by the media as extremism, who confront the venality and deception of corporations, and experience the repression of the police are more likely to begin to see the world differently and to start to think about alternative forms of social organization.[56]

Furthermore, sentiment itself should not be disparaged. Most people who support animal rights are motivated by feelings of compassion and justice. If the Left wants to mobilize people, there is a need to appeal to them on more than theoretical discussions of class and to engage those feelings. However, it is not merely a matter of leftist groups adopting a more sympathetic outlook in order to win new recruits. Rather, a re-examination of anthropocentrism and a willingness to address environmental and ecological issues presents opportunities for a richer politics of liberation.

That these issues are serious ones cannot be denied. Human activities are destroying other species as a massive wave of extinctions now sweeps the planet. These extinctions are occurring in a context of unprecedented ecological disaster. In 2005, the Millennium Ecosystem Assessment, based on the work of approximately 1,400 experts from 95 countries, surveying ecological effects of human activities, found 60 percent of the global ecosystem degraded by human activities, including animal exploitation industries. Atmospheric pollution from greenhouse gases, deforestation, loss of freshwater aquifers, overfishing, polluting the oceans, and introducing alien species to new regions have destroyed 20 percent of the world's coral reefs, damaged 40 percent of the river systems, and seriously disrupted global climate. Effects have been especially harsh for the poor, many of whom rely directly on these ecosystems for survival. To avert disaster, resource consumption must be reduced to levels the planet can sustain.

A society that commodifies animals and permits massive abuse and cruelty to persist is unlikely to develop compassionate policies regarding human beings. Under capitalism, these abuses are justified in terms of profit and property relationships. The fact that animal protectionists have mounted compassionate appeals that threaten these relationships has created a right-wing countermovement discourse of vilification intended to arouse hatred for these advocates. Many on the Left have overlooked the long-standing connection between concern for better treatment of animals and better treatment of human beings and, unfortunately, seem willing to allow the same exploitation of animals to continue, justifying this on the basis of an anthropocentrism which is not only callous, limited, and ugly, but completely unrealistic in the face of urgent global problems and, ultimately, suicidal. Rather than accepting the anthropocentric and instrumentalist views of the animal exploitation industries, progressive thought on the Left should embrace a more compassionate view toward animals and strive for a more inclusive version of social justice that includes nonhuman animals as well as humans.

13

"Green" Eggs and Ham?

The Myth of Sustainable Meat and the Danger of the Local

By Vasile Stănescu

The first thing I ask Salatin when we sit down in his living room is whether he's ever considered becoming a vegetarian. It's not what I had planned to say, but we've been in the hoop houses with the nicely treated hens, all happily pecking and glossy-feathered, and I've held one in my arms. Suddenly it makes little sense that this animal, whose welfare has been of such great concern, will be killed in a matter of days. Naive, I know, and Salatin seems surprised. "Never crossed my mind," he says. . . . Salatin is hitting his stride now. "We tried heritage chickens for three years and we couldn't sell 'em. I mean, we could sell a couple. But at the end of the day, altruism doesn't pay our taxes."[1]

—Interview by Gaby Woods, *The Guardian*, January 31, 2010

I think there is an enormous amount of political power lying around on the food issue, and I am just waiting for the right politician to realize that this is a great family issue. If that politician is on the Right, all the better. I think that would be terrific, and I will support him or her.

—Michael Pollan, Interview with Rod Dreher,
The American Conservative, June 20, 2008

INTRODUCTION

In 2007 Oxford University Press chose "locavore" as the word of the year.[2] Such a move, while purely symbolic, at the same time speaks to the movement's growing popularity and emerging significance in any discussion on food policy, environmentalism, or animal ethics. The essence of the locavore argument is that because it is harmful to the environment to transport food over long distances (referred to as "food miles"), people should instead, for primarily environmental reasons, choose to consume only food that is grown or slaughtered locally. This idea of locavorism has been described and defended by a range of authors, such as Barbara Kingsolver in *Animal, Vegetable, Miracle* and Michael Pollan in his *New York Times* bestselling book *The Omnivore's Dilemma,* and promoted by farmers like Joel Salatin, owner of Polyface farms and a featured personality in both *The Omnivore's Dilemma* and the recent documentary *Food Inc.* However, despite this popularity, there is much I find deeply troubling in the various rationales given for locavorism.

For example, part of Pollan's main argument against "organic" meat is that it represents a false pastoral narrative, something produced by the power of well-crafted words and images yet lacking ethical consistency, reality, or ultimately an awareness of animals themselves. Reflecting on his experience walking down the aisles of a Whole Foods supermarket, Pollan writes:

> This particular dairy's label had a lot to say about the bovine lifestyle: Its Holsteins are provided with "an appropriate environment, including shelter and comfortable resting area . . . sufficient space, proper facilities and the company of its own kind." All this sounded pretty great, until I read the story of another dairy selling raw milk—*completely* unprocessed—whose "cows graze green pastures all year long."
>
> Which made me wonder whether the first dairy's idea of an appropriate environment for a cow included, as I had simply presumed, a pasture. All of a sudden the absence from their story of that word seemed weirdly conspicuous. As the literary critics would say, the writer seemed to be eliding the whole notion of cows and grass. Indeed, the longer I shopped in Whole Foods, the more I thought that this was a place where the skills of a literary critic might come in handy.[3]

However, while I agree with Pollan about the need for literary critics in Whole Foods, many locavore advocates, including Pollan, succumb to the same error of creating an unrealistic literary pastoral in their uncritical paean to the free-range organic farmer. Therefore, as a literary critic, I hope to subject the locavore movement to the same critical scrutiny which they have subjected industrialized agriculture, in order to show how they themselves create an idealized, unrealistic, and at times distressingly sexist and xenophobic literary pastoral that carefully elides the violence being enacted against the animals themselves. My intention is not to discount the possibility of a more natural, environmentally sustainable food system—a goal I deeply support—but instead to reveal the potential dangers that focusing purely on the local, at the expense of the global, can contain for both the human and nonhuman animal alike.

PART I: THE ENVIRONMENT

"The Vegan Utopia"

Tellingly, one of the most forceful rationales for the environmental benefits of a local food system is expressed by Michael Pollan in a chapter of *The Omnivore's Dilemma* titled "The Ethics of Eating Meat." Under the pejorative subheading "The Vegan Utopia" Pollan writes:

> The vegan utopia would . . . condemn people in many parts of the country to importing all their food from distant places. . . . To give up eating animals is to give up these places as human habitat, unless of course we are willing to make complete our dependence on a highly industrialized national food chain. The food chain would be in turn even more dependent than it already is on fossil fuels and chemical fertilizers, since food would need to travel even farther and fertility—in the form of manures—would be in short supply. Indeed, it is doubtful you can build a genuinely sustainable agriculture without animals to cycle nutrients and support local food production. If our concern is the health of nature—rather than, say, the internal consistency of our moral code or the condition of our souls—then eating animals may sometimes be the most ethical thing to do.[4]

Pollan thus takes one of the animal rights movement's most powerful arguments—the significant environmental degradation that the meat industry routinely produces—and inverts it.[5] It is now *because* of the environment that one is justified in eating meat—indeed required to do so—since the only alternative given by Pollan is a polluting globalization of large-scale food importation. Indeed, the argument, if true, is even more powerful than quoted here. If eating locally slaughtered animals is the only way to prevent global warming, animal ethics itself might well dictate the necessity of eating meat because habitat destruction (in part fuelled by global warming) is already causing mass species extinction at unprecedented rates. Such an argument, therefore, represents a particularly powerful and nuanced refutation of veganism and vegetarianism that I fear few animal rights activist, or animal studies scholars, have yet to adequately address.

However, before I engage in a more detailed analysis of Pollan's argument, I first want to note that it is simply factually untrue. What is most telling about the passage quoted above is that it lacks any form of citation or footnotes, forms of documentation which otherwise pepper Pollan's books in other places of possible controversy. Pollan is far from alone in this omission, for virtually every other locavore claim for environmental supremacy also lacks any form of documentation to back up repeated claims that being vegan is *more* harmful to the environment than eating locally slaughtered animals. Instead, locavores almost universally rely upon the "common-sense" logic that since transportation harms the environment, the further a commodity must be transported, the more harmful it must be to the ecosystem. However, recent studies have brought this common-sense wisdom into question. For example, a study conducted at Lincoln University in New Zealand shows that the way apples, lamb, and dairy items are produced in New Zealand makes them more energy-efficient to buy in the United Kingdom than those same products grown on British soil. The study concludes:

> Food miles are a very simplistic concept relating to the distance food travels as a measure of its impact on the environment. As a concept, food miles has gained some traction with the popular press and certain groups overseas. However, this debate which only includes the distance food travels is spurious as it does not consider total energy use especially in the production of the product.[6]

Indeed, the only study to date to focus on whether a local or vegetarian diet is more helpful in reducing greenhouse gases, conducted by Christopher L. Weber and H. Scott Matthews at Carnegie-Mellon, reached the following conclusion:

> Despite significant recent public concern and media attention to the environmental impacts of food, few studies in the United States have systematically compared the life-cycle greenhouse gas (GHG) emissions associated with food production against long-distance distribution, aka "food-miles." We find that although food is transported long distances in general (1,640 km delivery and 6,760 km life-cycle supply chain on average) the GHG emissions associated with food are dominated by the production phase, contributing 83% of the average U.S. household's 8.1 t CO2e/yr footprint for food consumption. Transportation as a whole represents only 11% of life-cycle GHG emissions, and final delivery from producer to retail contributes only 4%. Different food groups exhibit a large range in GHG-intensity; on average, red meat is around 150% more GHG intensive than chicken or fish. *Thus, we suggest that dietary shift can be a more effective means of lowering an average household's food-related climate footprint than "buying local." Shifting less than one day per week's worth of calories from red meat and dairy products to chicken, fish, eggs, or a vegetable-based diet achieves more GHG reduction than buying all locally sourced food.*[7]

In other words, shifting from beef to vegetables for even a single day a week would in fact be more helpful in reducing greenhouse gases than shifting the entirety of one's diet to exclusively locally produced sources. This conclusion becomes less surprising when we consider the United Nations Intergovernmental Panel on Climate Change finding that meat production contributes more greenhouse gas emissions than the entire transportation industry, including all automobiles, combined.[8] In fact, recent research suggests that organic free-range animals may, in specific cases, be more harmful to the environment than animals raised "conventionally." As the Audubon society recently reported:

> Ironically, data released in 2007 by Adrian Williams of Cranfield University in England show that when all factors are considered, organic, free-range chickens have a 20 percent greater impact on global warming than conventionally raised broiler birds. That's because "sustainable" chickens take longer to raise, and eat more feed. Worse, organic eggs have a 14 percent higher impact on the climate than eggs from caged chickens, according to Williams. "If we want to fight global warming through the food we buy, then one thing's clear: We have to drastically reduce the meat we consume," says Tara Garnett of London's Food Climate Research Network. So while some of us Americans fashionably fret over our food's travel budget and organic content, Garnett says the real question is, "Did it come from an animal or did it not come from an animal?"[9]

Lack of Land

While locavores imagine all factory farms eventually turning into more sustainable small-scale family farms, that ideal is simply not physically possible given the world's current rate of meat consumption. According to the United Nations Food and Agriculture Organization's recent report *Livestock's Long Shadow*, over 55 billion land animals are raised and slaughtered every year worldwide for human consumption. This rate of slaughter already consumes 30 percent of the earth's entire land surface (approximately 3,433 billion hectares) and accounts for a staggering 80 percent of the total land utilized by humans.[10] Even when the land currently used for feed crop production is subtracted, as theoretically it might be in a fully local farm system, the total area *currently* occupied by grazing alone still constitutes, in the words of the report, "26 percent of the ice-free terrestrial surface of the planet."[11] And this number is only expected to grow as both human population and human consumption of meat and dairy continue to rise.[12] Therefore, in addition to problems of sustainability, meat consumption also entails a massive loss of biodiversity which, ironically, would actually be *increased* by a shift to a locally based diet, as even more land would have to be set aside for free-range grazing. According to the UN Food and Agriculture Organization report, "306 of the 825 terrestrial ecoregions identified by the Worldwide Fund for Nature (WWF) . . . reported livestock as one of the current threats."[13]

Nor would it be possible to keep such farms small, tied to the community, or even "local" in any meaningful sense of that term. As Joel Salatin himself admits to Pollan, in explaining why he primarily uses neighbors coming over to help out to kill the animals he raises: "That's another reason we don't raise a hundred thousand chickens. It's not just the land that couldn't take it, but the community, too. We'd be processing six days a week, so we'd have to do what the industrial folks do, bring in a bunch of migrant workers because no one around here would want to gut chickens every day. *Scale makes all the difference*."[14] I will return to Salatin's comment about migrant workers later, but my point here is that locally based meat, regardless of its level of popularity, can never constitute more than either a rare and occasional novelty item, or food choices for only a few privileged customers, since there simply is not enough arable land left in the entire world to raise the large quantities of pasture-fed animals necessary to meet the world's meat consumption. And even if such a transition were physically possible, the resulting size of such farms would undo much of their supposed sustainability and community integration and hence their very purpose in existing in the first place. Unfortunately, this simple physical reality is ignored by many in the locavore movement, such as Barbara Kingsolver, who tells her children that they cannot have fresh fruit during the winter, but instead must consume meat because it is, purportedly, more sustainable.[15]

Belgian Chocolate

Reading this literature, one is left with the feeling that local food activists themselves must realize the impracticality and marginal environmental benefit of following locavore practices, since many of them fail to follow with consistency the very practices they themselves advocate. For example, in preparing his local-based meal on Polyface farms, Pollan admits, "I also need some chocolate for the dessert I had in mind. Fortunately the state of Virginia produces no chocolate to speak of, so I was free to go for the good Belgian stuff, panglessly."[16] While this line of reasoning might make sense in terms of other arguments for going local, such as preserving local economies, in terms of global warming and greenhouse gases it is clearly not intellectually consistent. Even if, for some unspecified reason, chocolate was essential for Pollan to have, it is not at all clear why that chocolate would have to come from *Belgium* instead of any of the more local sources of chocolate from within the whole of the United States (which also might be more effective in terms of preserving local economies). Indeed, most of the locavores mentioned continue to enjoy a variety of non–local based goods such as coffee, tea, olive oil, and (in my favourite example from Kingsolver) non-locally produced Budweiser.[17]

Nor do the business practices of Joel Salatin, the owner of Polyface farms whom Pollan holds up as a possible model, make consistent environmental sense. For example, Salatin refuses to FedEx any of his meat since, he says, "I don't believe it's sustainable—or organic, if you will—to FedEx meat all around the country."[18] Instead, he tells Pollan that he will have to "drive down here" to Virginia to get it—all the way from California.[19] But asking customers to *drive* to Polyface farms in individual cars is a significantly less efficient way to transport goods than using a centralized shipping and distribution network combined with multiple products carried on a single fully loaded delivery vehicle. Yet Salatin is, in fact, proud of how far individual people will drive in order to purchase his food. As he posts on his own website, as a positive review from a customer, "I drive to Polyface 150 miles one way in order to get clean meat for my family."[20] Hence, romantic notions of face-to-face contact and perhaps even the great American road trip seem to play a greater role in the Pollan–Salatin encounter than any environmental logic.

Indeed, one of the revealing ironies associated with all of the locavore proponents mentioned is the surprisingly large amount of driving, flying, and transportation they themselves regularly and apparently "panglessly" engage in. For example, Michael Pollan travels all around the country, from Kansas to California, just within the pages of *The Omnivore's Dilemma*; Kingsolver is even more extreme, leaving by car from Arizona so that that she can farm in rural Georgia, then driving all the way to Canada (from Georgia) for a family vacation, which she particularly enjoys because she is now able to consume so many food products which otherwise would have been out of season. As she writes, "[l]ike those jet-setters who fly across the country on New Year's Eve, we were going to cheat time and celebrate the moment more than once. Asparagus season, twice in one year: the dream vacation."[21] Kingsolver and her family even fly to Europe, in part to enjoy the local cuisine.[22] And Joel Salatin, who was unwilling to ship his meat to California, recently agreed to fly there himself for a talk at Stanford. Ironically, the talk was, in part, on the environmental benefits of a local economy. Perhaps a certain amount of irony and hypocrisy within the locavore movement can be justified by the argument that while still far from fully realized, it is on the path toward ever greater locavorism. What is distressing is the manner in which violation of even the basic ideas of locally based lifestyle occur "panglessly" and the manner in which the movement justifies itself via actions that are *more* harmful for the environment than the current food system, such as driving to purchase far-away local produce or enjoying out-of-season food in Canada and Europe.

T-Shirts and DVDs

The one aspect of locavorism that most clearly belies the rationales given to justify the movement—not just in terms of the environment, but also in terms of protecting local business and protesting the abuses of globalization—is that it resolutely focuses *only on the question of food.* Neither Pollan, nor Kingsolver, nor even Salatin is attempting to learn how to weave his or her own clothing, although cotton, as an agricultural commodity, raises many of the same issues as imported food. Yet as the journal *Environmental Health Perspective* has recently documented, the environmental effects of the food industry and the fashion industry are quite similar in terms of both pollution and worker exploitation. According to the authors:

> Cotton, one of the most popular and versatile fibers used in clothing manufacture, also has a significant environmental footprint. This crop accounts for a quarter of all the pesticides used in the United States, the largest exporter of cotton in the world, according to the USDA. The U.S. cotton crop benefits from subsidies that keep prices low and production high. The high production of cotton at subsidized low prices is one of the first spokes in the wheel that drives the globalization of fashion.
>
> Much of the cotton produced in the United States is exported to China and other countries with low labor costs, where the material is milled, woven into fabrics, cut, and assembled according to the fashion industry's specifications. China has emerged as the largest exporter of fast fashion, accounting for 30% of world apparel exports, according to the UN Commodity Trade Statistics database. In her 2005 book *The Travels of a T-Shirt in the Global Economy*, Pietra Rivoli, a professor of international business at the McDonough School of Business of Georgetown University, writes that each year Americans purchase approximately 1 billion garments made in China, the equivalent of four pieces of clothing for every U.S. citizen.[23]

Hence, at least in terms of miles traveled, cotton is actually a more egregious example of ecological waste than food. Nor is this the end of the "clothing miles," as the United States purchases so much clothing that domestic charity outlets simply cannot process it all.[24] So the extra clothing is then shipped *back* to the developing world (where in most cases it was originally manufactured), where for some developing countries it actually constitutes the number one import from the United States.[25] A single cotton t-shirt, then, comes from cotton grown in the United States, is sent to the developing world to be manufactured into clothing, then back to the United States to be purchased, and finally shipped to the developing country where the clothing is either donated or purchased. And what is true for cotton is equally true for almost every other product regularly consumed in the United States. Almost everything we buy today is both produced and consumed in a global marketplace and is therefore part of these exact same systems of production and distribution. In terms of shipping distance it is just as significant to discuss "clothing miles," "computer miles," or even "cell phone miles," many of which are actually transported far longer distances than food and are far more toxic in their results. And in terms of non-environmental concerns, working conditions for many non-agricultural products may well be worse than for the more traditional rural labor of farming (excluding certain products such as coffee and chocolate).[26]

My point here is not to criticize locavores unfairly for minor hypocrisy or failures of judgment, neither of which undermine the logic of their argument as such. Rather, my concern is that a narrow focus only on food and "food miles" renders many other environmentally unsound practices invisible, whether they are conscious decisions to drive around in search of the best local food, or unconscious participation in the consumption of non-food goods with an environmental and human cost. For example, in Salatin's online gift store, in less than four lines he both states that, "[w]e do not ship food items, anytime, anywhere, period" and, at the same time, advertises for non–food based collectibles like Polyface tote bags and DVDs[27] and boasts that (for the latter), "[a]ll shipping is free! Please allow 2–4 weeks for delivery." There is no discussion of how, where, or by whom any of these other products have been made.

PART II: THE DANGER OF THE LOCAL

Blood and Soil

If being local is not then really about protecting the environment, what is it about? One answer has been suggested by Ursula Heise in her recent book, *Sense of Place and Sense of Planet: The Environmental Imagination of the Global.*[28] Heise illustrates how the emphasis on the local within the broader environmental movement as a whole can exhibit a deeply disturbing strain of conservatism, provincialism, xenophobia, and anti-immigrant sentiment. Indeed, she goes so far as to excavate genealogically the Nazi rhetoric of *Blut und Boden* (blood and soil) to show how some similar strains within contemporary environmentalism resonate with the National Socialists' interweaving of environmentalism with a hyper-nationalism based on a romanticized autochthonous relationship with both the soil and the local. Neither I nor Heise are suggesting that the locavore movement, or the move toward localism in environmentalism, is equivalent to Nazism. Rather, the relevance of Heise's analysis is that it shows how an outspoken concern for the environment can also contain and support conservatism—*against* those viewed as alien to the speaker's sense of his or her local community. In this connection, it is clear that many in the locavore movement are moved by a desire for a nonexistent literary pastoral, a nostalgia for a bygone age that never was. For example, Pollan invokes precisely this image in his description of his first local dinner at Polyface farms, when he writes, "much about dining with the Salatins had, for me, the flavor of a long-ago time and faraway place in America."[29] However, the danger of this literary pastoral fairytale is not only that it is wholly misleading (the Salatins use ATVs daily to move around their cattle) but that it has the potential to mask the darker side of the nostalgic past, including narratives of exclusion and violence that an exclusive focus on the local elides.

Women in the Kitchen

For example, since locavores choose to focus only on the question of food transportation, that focus at times blends into the negative portrayal of women, particularly feminists, who are frequently faulted for having collectively abandoned the kitchen, that is, cooking meaningful and nutritious meals for the family. Such a claim naturally leads to another: a call for society to return to traditional gender roles of heterosexual men farming and ranching while heterosexual women cook and clean. For example, both Michael Pollan and the movie *Food Inc.* specifically hold up Joel Salatin and Polyface farms as a promising paradigm for a local-based economy. But what Pollan does not tell us is that Salatin believes so firmly in traditional gender roles that in the past he did not even accept women as workers or interns for the farm labor aspect of his farm, although they could work in the kitchen.[30] Salatin's attitude—that the proper place for women is in the kitchen and that their role has somehow been "lost"—surfaced in a recent interview:

> Hey, 40 years ago, every woman in the country—I'll be real sexist here—every woman in the country knew how to cut up a chicken. . . . Now 60% of our customers don't even know that a chicken has bones! I'm serious. We have moved to an incredibly ignorant culinary connection.[31]

This critique of feminism presumably elicited no comment by Pollan because he shares a similar opinion. For example, in his review of Janet A. Flammang's book *The Taste of Civilization: Food, Politics, and Civil Society*, Pollan agrees with Flammang's essential premise, writing with approval in his most recently published work that "[i]n a challenge to second-wave feminists who urged women to get out of the kitchen, Flammang suggests that by denigrating 'foodwork'—everything involved in putting meals on the family table—we have unthinkingly wrecked one of the nurseries of democracy: the family meal."[32] These comments merely replicated his earlier comment that the

> decline [of locally produced meals] has several causes: women working outside the home; food companies persuading Americans to let them do the cooking; and advances in technology that made it easier for them to do so. Cooking is no longer obligatory, and for many people, women especially, that has been a blessing. But perhaps a mixed blessing, to judge by the culture's continuing, if not deepening, fascination with the subject.[33]

—a comment which he links, in the same article, to the description of Betty Friedan's *The Feminine Mystique* as "the book that taught millions of American women to regard housework, cooking included, as drudgery, indeed as a form of oppression."

More surprisingly, Barbara Kingsolver, too, expresses explicit gender conservatism throughout *Animal, Vegetable, Miracle*, as when she describes feminism as "the great hoodwink of my generation" because it wrongly removed the woman from hearth and home.[34] Indeed, she takes great pride in transforming herself into the type of housewife who finally knows how to make her own cheese.[35] As Jennifer Jeffrey has written in a particularly insightful article, "The Feminist in My Kitchen,"

> One day during the *Pennywise Eat Local Challenge*, as I was dashing between meetings and wondering how on earth I was going to create an evening meal composed of local ingredients within budget with almost no time to shop, this thought flashed through my head: this whole eat local concept is *so not friendly* for women who work. . . .
>
> If eating local is still a challenge for me, what about women who, voluntarily or not, log 8 to 10 hours a day, five or six days a week, in an office or hospital or courtroom? What about women who, in addition to working long hours and commuting back and forth, also have children at home who need love and affection and help with homework?
>
> . . . Can we call ourselves feminists (simply defined here as people who desire the equality of all women, everywhere) and still suggest that an ideal dinner consists of handmade ravioli and slow-simmered marinara from vine-ripened, hand-picked tomatoes and a salad composed of vegetables that (let's be honest) are Not Available at Safeway?

Jeffrey specifically connects her argument to Barbara Kingsolver's book:

> Barbara Kingsolver took a year of her life to grow a garden to feed her family, and proceeded to write a beautiful book about the experience, but what if she had done the same thing twenty-five years ago, near the start of her writing career? My guess is that such a book (if it made it to publication at all, which is doubtful), might not have had such a receptive audience, but *more importantly*, all of that weeding and watering and meal-planning might have distracted her from the hard, lonely work of learning to write.[36]

"All American"

If the locavore movement seems to be a dubious ally of feminism, it also seems uncomfortably close to nativist strands in the American discourse of race and nationhood. Consider, for example, the criteria that Joel Salatin uses to determine who will receive one of his now highly competitive internships on his farm. The very first requirement reads that the candidates must be "[b]right eyed, bushy-tailed, self-starter, eager-beaver, situationally aware, go-get-'em, teachable, positive, non-complaining, grateful, rejoicing, get'erdone dependable, faithful, perseverant take-responsibility *clean-cut, all American boy-girl appearance characters. We are very, very, very discriminatory.*"[37] Such a list of course seems to reiterate gender conservatism (since it is hard to imagine that a woman who wears only male clothes would be considered to have a "clean-cut all American girl appearance"). Nor, one imagines, would a man who wears women's clothes, much less a homosexual or a transsexual, be considered an "all-American" boy. In fact it is odd that "appearance" is such an essential category of who Salatin will, or will not, allow to work on a farm. Furthermore, we must ask what an "all American" appearance even means in a nation of such vast racial and immigrant diversity as the United States. It is not reassuring that Salatin received his undergraduate degree from Bob Jones University, the extremely conservative, evangelical Christian university that prohibited African-Americans from attending until 1975 and prohibited interracial dating in the year 2000 (leading to a media uproar and declining student attendance that finally forced the university to revise its policy).[38] Throughout its entire history, Bob Jones University has in fact prohibited, as official policy, all acts of homosexuality as perversion condemned by God.[39] Presumably, then, issues of racial inclusion, gay rights, or even social justice were not particularly strong motivating forces in Salatin's earlier life. More to the point, however, Salatin has not repudiated this relationship with Bob Jones University, which in 2009 recognized him as "alumus of the year."[40]

Salatin has also described the conservative talk show host Glenn Beck, an outspoken critic of gay marriage and illegal immigration, as "agendaless" and "truth-seeking."[41] Salatin himself is prone to making remarks concerning migrant workers that seem to cast them in a negative or demeaning light. For example, in testimony in front of Congress on how to make a more transparent meat system, Salatin claimed, "[i]ndustrialized food and farming became aromatically and aesthetically repugnant, relegated to the offcasts of society—C and D students along with their foreign workers."[42] Such sentiments should not surprise us. As Kelefa Sanneh writes in the *New Yorker*, "[a]grarianism, like environmentalism, hasn't always been considered a progressive cause, and there's nothing inherently liberal about artisanal cheese or artisanal bikes. . . . Rod Dreher, a *National Review* contributor and the author of 'Crunchy Cons,' is ardently pro-organic and ardently anti-gay marriage. Victor Davis Hanson, the author of 'Fields Without Dreams: Defending the Agrarian Idea,' is also the author of 'Mexifornia,' about the dangers posed by immigration."[43] In fact, farm worker unions attempting to use the movie as an organizing tool have been repeatedly removed from the screening of *Food Inc.*[44]

It is therefore strange that Michael Pollan should on the one hand denounce the practice of harvesting organic produce using recycled biodiesel tractors as insufficiently progressive—because of the unfair treatment of Mexican farm workers in the process—while at the same time holding up Joel Salatin as a representative of the future vanguard of a progressive and egalitarian food movement.[45] As the British columnist Yasmin Alibhai-Brown recently argued:

> Should good people be party to a vociferous movement which wants to refuse entry to "alien" foods? Look at the language used and you realize it is a proxy for anti-immigration sentiments: these foods from elsewhere come and take over our diets, reduce national dishes to third-class status, compete unfairly with Scotch broth and haggis, both dying out, excite our senses beyond decorum, contaminate the identity of the country irreversibly.
>
> Turn to the clamour for the west to cut imported foods and a further bitter taste spreads in the mouth. If we decide—as many of my friends have—not to buy foods that have been flown over, it only means further devastation for the poorest. These are the incredibly hard-working farmers in the developing world, already the victims of trade protectionism imposed by the wealthy blocs. It means saying no to Fair-trade producers too, because their products have to travel to our supermarkets. Are we now to say these livelihoods don't matter because we prefer virtue of a more fashionable kind? Shameful are the environmentalists who are able to be this cavalier. They could only believe what they do if those peasant lives do not matter at all.[46]

In fact, the "locavore" movement may possess within it the same potential for anti-immigrant sentiment that the earlier "Buy American" movement displayed in the 1970s–1990s period. For example, many of the same reasons now provided to support locavorism, including fears of globalization, support for union labor, critiques of exploitive labor practices in other countries, and a desire to protect traditional American ways of life were earlier interwoven into a similar movement which, over time, degenerated into regional nationalism, anti-immigrant sentiment, and xenophobia. As Dana Frank documents in *Buy American: The Untold Story of Economic Nationalism*:

> Popular "Buy American" advocates promised, nonetheless, to protect and to serve the American people; but the inward-looking protection of "us" against the threatening "foreigners" spiraled downward into narrower and narrower clubbishness. What began innocently at the border of Orange County, Florida, or the State of Alaska ended less innocently at an economic border drawn by race or citizenship.[47]

There is therefore ample reason to worry that a contemporary movement to prevent the importation of goods from other countries will eventually rely on or mobilize nationalistic and xenophobic fears of other nations and peoples. And this worry is perhaps all the more relevant when the boycotted product is food, due to the deep connection between a culture's identity and the food it eats.[48] Hence, to stigmatize a food purely because of where it comes from runs the extreme risk of stigmatizing an associated people as well. Diversity may also suffer as a result. As James McWilliams writes:

> A final paradox: in a sense, any community with an activist base seeking to localize the food supply is also a community that's undermining diversity. Although we rarely consider the market influences that make community diversification possible, a moment's reflection reveals a strong tie between cultural diversity and market access. Critics of globalization argue (often with ample evidence) that global forces undermine the world's range of indigenous cultures—wiping out vernacular habits, wisdom, and languages. They overlook, however, how the material manifestations of diversity are brought to us by globalization.
>
> Localization, by contrast, specifies what is and is not acceptable within an arbitrary boundary. In this sense, it delimits diversity. Anyone who doubts this claim should imagine what the culinary map of New York City would look like without open access to globally far-flung producers. It's only because globally sourced distributors are able to provide specialized ingredients that Harlem, Chinatown, and Little Italy are such vibrant emblems of urban, culinary, and cultural diversity.[49]

Saving Souls

So far, however, I have ignored what is in fact the most chilling and disturbing aspect of the locavore movement—its naturalization and explicit justification of arbitrary and unnecessary violence against other animals. Here we return to Michael Pollan's earlier claim, made in the context of putting locavore against veganism, that what solely motivates veganism is a desire for absolute moral purity, even to the point of destroying nature, in order to save the vegans' "souls." Pollan continues this theme throughout his text, referring to vegetarians as self-righteous and even claiming that they are "Puritans": "[a] deep current of Puritanism runs through the writing of the animal philosophers, an abiding discomfort not just with our animality, but with the animals' animality too. They would like nothing better than to airlift us out from nature's intrinsic evil—and then take the animals with us. You begin to wonder if their quarrel isn't really with nature itself."[50] However, the irony of this argument is that while Pollan routinely depicts vegans as self-righteous puritans, the only examples that both he and Kingsolver provide are people who, for *religious* reasons, feel no complication about killing animals because they see the latter as utterly lacking souls. As Pollan writes, "[w]hen I was at the farm I asked Joel how he could bring himself to kill a chicken. 'That's an easy one. People have a soul, animals don't; it's a bedrock belief of mine. Animals are not created in God's image. So when they die, they just die.'"[51] In fact, since nonhuman animals have no souls and are therefore wholly unrelated to people, Joel Salatin encourages even young children to slit the throats of animals:

> Interestingly, we typically have families come—they want to come and see the chicken butchering, for example. Well, Mom and Dad (they're in their late-20s early-30s), they stay out behind in the car, and the 8-, 9-, 10-, 11-year-old children come around to see this. We have not found any child under 10 that's the least bit put off by it. They get right into it. We'll even give them a knife and let them slice some throats.[52]

Salatin's callous disregard for the bodily integrity or being of other animals is in fact all too representative of the proponents of locavorism as a whole. The intellectuals at the forefront of that movement, particularly Pollan and Kingsolver, seek to re-inscribe the very speciesism that locavorism at first seems to draw into question. Indeed, it is hard to imagine how a locavore movement ever could translate into an actual improvement of animals' lives, since many of its most famous proponents hold that animals lack souls and accept "Man's" domination and consumption of them as the very definition of our humanity. For example, both Pollan and Kingsolver claim, with no citations, a laundry list of increasingly esoteric human characteristics which, supposedly, only eating meat has produced in humans, including large brains,[53] all forms of social interaction (including the undefined "pleasures of the table,"[54] human free will,[55] and even "civilization" itself.[56] In the most amusing example of this attribution of human traits, Pollan suggests that the reason marijuana works on humans is because it mimics the effects of hunting within human brains. He writes:

> Later it occurred to me that this mental state [while hunting], which I quite liked, in many ways resembled the one induced by smoking marijuana: the way one's senses feel especially acute and the mind seems to forget everything outside the scope of its present focus, including physical discomfort and the passing of time. . . . Could it be that the cannabinoid network is precisely the sort of adaption that natural selection would favor in the evolution of a creature who survives by hunting? A brain chemical that sharpens the senses, narrows your mental focus, allows you to forget everything extraneous to the task at hand (including physical discomfort and the passage of time), and makes you hungry would seem to be the perfect pharmacological tool for man the hunter.[57]

One of the oddest parts of the locavore literature is that even as its proponents graphically and indeed poetically describe the abuses of the factory farms, at the same time they remove any reason why anyone should be concerned at all. Since animals lack souls, we cannot understand what, or even if, they think or feel. Moreover, our domination of them represents the very essence of what defines us as humans. Joel Salatin has in fact repeatedly spoken out against so called "Prop 2" ballot initiatives around the country sponsored by the American Humane Society to outlaw the worst abuses of factory farming such as battery cages and gestation crates.[58] While Prop 2 initiatives are themselves controversial within the animal rights community (since they result in larger cages rather than no cages at all), Salatin's position is that people should be legally able to do whatever they want with farm animals. Hence, he actually argues for *less* oversight and control of how farmers raise their livestock. While less government oversight may or may not, as Salatin claims, help small farms who "process" animals to expand their operations, it would exonerate existing practices that cause the horrific suffering of farm animals who otherwise now enjoy at least some protection under the law, however minimal. As importantly, the locavore position effectively undercuts future efforts to protect animals, since it naturalizes the primary relation of domination upon which all forms of violence against other animals hinge.

I Am a Locavore (and a Vegan)

None of this is to deny that locavorism does not have a point to make. For example, urban community gardening, farmers' markets, Community Support Agriculture (CSAs), and organic farms that eschew the use of monoculture crops and pesticides, and treat their workers well, are all important goals which locavorism helps to forward. The trouble with the locavore movement, however, is that it continues to articulate itself on the basis of a false dichotomy between vegans and vegetarians on the one hand, and conscious food consumers on the other, as though it were impossible to be concerned about the welfare of animals, the environment, and the broader questions of food policy and food justice all at the same time. Perfectly reasonable arguments against monoculture crops thus morph into unreasonable attacks on vegetarians. However, the reality is that many vegetarian and vegans, having already taken the step to self-consciously control and direct their diet, are frequently more aware of the dangers industrial farming practices pose and are therefore more likely to seek out ethically grown fruits and vegetables—wherever in the world these may exist. As Pollan and others have pointed out, concentrated animal feeding operations (CAFOs), or "factory farms," are economically feasible only because of the massive subsidies that the government routinely provides to large-scale industrial farmers who grow vast acres of soy, wheat, and corn, which in turn are sold to the factory farms who are the largest consumer of such products in the United States. The question, therefore, is not whether we should end the movement for conscious consumption of all food products. Large-scale industrial agriculture really is deeply harmful to the environment, workers, and animals. Rather, the question is whether we can arrive at a new understanding and new articulation of the manner in which the locavore movement's goals are expressed and understood. What matters more than the overly simplistic notion of "food miles" is the total carbon footprint of our foodstuffs, as well as the total environmental impact of any food purchase. Coming at the problem from such a broader perspective can only mean significantly decreasing the amount of meat human beings consume, in addition to cutting back on the whole array of services, including clothing and electronics, now marketed in the global marketplace.

Finally, it deeply matters how and why these calls for locavorism are framed. In this connection, as I have shown, the tendency of many in the movement to unfairly and inaccurately criticize feminists and immigrants as corrupting to an idealized, romantic state of a local community is both deeply troubling and potentially quite dangerous. As the "Buy American" movement, originally started by anti–sweat shop unions, demonstrates, initially "progressive" causes that nonetheless fail to consider the intersections of gender, race, class, and citizenship can devolve into nationalism or xenophobic localism. In sum, the false dichotomy between the vegan and the local can be ended, so that both animal rights activists and food policy activists can unite into a shared and, therefore, more effective movement. We must build on the growing consensus on the need for a more just diet, but do so in a way that addresses the full panoply of social justice issues that a truly just and "green" diet must entail.

14

After MacKinnon

Sexual Inequality in the Animal Movement

By Carol J. Adams

"You become what you do not resist."

—Catharine MacKinnon

For the past thirty years, animal activists have challenged the interdependent nature of dominance and subordination vis-à-vis our relations with other species.[1] At the same time, they have largely avoided the question of how the system of *human* dominance and *animal* subordination tracks, intersects with, and diverges from *men's* dominance and *women's* subordination. Despite the work of radical feminists to identify the linkages between the oppressions of women and animals, establishing the common patriarchal roots of both groups' subjugation, a feminist perspective has yet to be incorporated into the theory and practice of the mainstream animal movement. This is unfortunate, because sexual inequality is one of the defining elements of the animal movement, defining both the status of animals whose liberation is sought, and the status of the women within the movement who seek the liberation of animals.[2]

As my title indicates, this chapter was prompted by my reading and reflecting upon Catharine MacKinnon's essay, "Of Mice and Men: A Feminist Fragment on Animal Rights" and as a result by my sense that, because of the way the animal movement is structured, it could fail to hear MacKinnon's radical feminist insights in any substantive way that would induce it to change its tactics and approaches.[3] Metaphorically, then, this chapter might be considered a musical counterpoint, an exercise in contrapuntal themes, in which I focus on the interaction of MacKinnon's insights in that essay and her other writings with my own theories. My concern throughout is with both theory and activism. To understand why MacKinnon matters, or should matter, for movements to end the human oppression of other animals, we must first have an appreciation of her radical feminist critique both of male domination, and of *liberal* understandings of gender and sex.

The basic survival issues facing women arise because of sexual inequality: women experience the social reality of domination made into sex through rape, incest, pornography, sexual harassment, forced pregnancy, and captivity in the home. Patriarchy is a global system of systemic economic inequality; of sexual violence, intimidation, and killing by men;[4] and of the racializing of that sexual violence.[5] As such, sexual inequality affects *every* woman's life. As MacKinnon sums up the predicament of women in the United States and elsewhere, "women's situation is made up of unequal pay combined with allocation to disrespected work, sexual targeting for rape, domestic battering, sexual abuse as children, and systematic sexual harassment together with depersonalization, demeaned physical characteristics, use in denigrating entertainment, deprivation of reproductive control, and forced prostitution."[6]

For MacKinnon, sexual inequality therefore means that we can't take the "sex" out of sexism, because *gender reflects a systematic inequality of power, and sexuality is a form of its practice.* Sexuality is "a social construct of male power: defined by men, forced on women, and constitutive of the meaning of gender."[7] Thus, sexuality is predicated on the domination of women by men, and "this domination is sexual."

The liberal feminist critique, by contrast, holds that gender oppression can be decoupled from sex: that the hierarchy of inequality has nothing to do with sexuality per se. This, however, only mystifies the material basis of inequality, which derives from men's sex right and the constitution of heterosexuality as such. MacKinnon writes: "[t]o notice that these practices are done by men to women is to see these abuses as forming a system, a hierarchy of inequality."[8] In other words, the liberal conception of gender neutrality ignores what is distinctively *done to* women, as well as *who is doing it* to them.[9]

In mainstream discourses about animal rights, we find a similar (and similarly unexamined) assumption operating among activists and theorists: namely, that gender and sexuality have no bearing on the problem of speciesism as such. While taking radical positions against human domination of other species, many animal activists and theorists adopt an oddly *liberal* view when it comes to questions of gender. The domination of women by men, and the domination of animals by human beings, are not only kept in separate accounts—they are seen as having nothing to do with one another. This lack of insight into the interconnections between speciesism and sexism, I want to suggest, seriously compromises the animal movement. So long as the movement fails to address the problem sex inequality poses, it remains in thrall to the dominant patriarchal culture, colluding in a regime of sexual hierarchy and domination that both hurts women and damages its own radically transformative potential. The animal movement—like other social movements and institutions in patriarchal society—both mirrors the inequalities of the larger culture, and constitutes itself through those same inequalities.

In what follows, I want to do two things. First, I want to examine some of the ways that ideologies of masculinity, male-centered definitions of reason and "the human," and female sexual subordination play themselves out in speciesist ideology and practice, in order to show why patriarchy and sexual inequality *matter* for the domination of animals by human beings.[10] Second, I want to show how the animal movement itself, by ignoring or remaining insufficiently attentive to the connections between patriarchy and speciesism, ends up reproducing women's inequality in its structure, its focus, its arguments, its use of women's labor, and in the accessibility it provides to sexual exploiters.

SEXUAL INEQUALITY ELEVATES "RATIONAL MAN" TO REPRESENT THE DEFINITION OF "THE HUMAN"

Sexual inequality elevates men to represent the definition of "human;" women represent the not-man, and thus, the not-human. As MacKinnon puts it, women are "the animals of the human kingdom, the mice of men's world."[11] This definition of human as not woman, not animals can be traced back to Aristotle. As Wendy Brown details in her study of *Manhood and Politics*,

> It was precisely the sharpness of the Athenian conception of manhood that bore with it a necessary degradation of women, a denial of the status of "human" to women. To the extent that women were viewed as part of the human species, they would recall to men the species' animal or "natural" aspect. Alternatively, women could be denied fully human status and remain the somewhat less threatening repository of the "lower elements" of existence.[12]

In other words, manhood = humanhood: those who wish to be seen as worthy must try to show how they fit into this equation. As MacKinnon writes in "Of Mice and Men":

> Men's debates among themselves over what makes them distinctively human have long-revolved around distinctions from women and animals. Can they think? Are they individuals? Are they capable of autonomous action? Are they inviolable? Do they have dignity? Are they made in the image of God? Men know they are men, meaning human, it would seem, to the degree their answer to these questions is yes for them and no for animals and women.[13]

The question MacKinnon poses in her essay is why animals must first be shown to be similar to us (fit into our definition of the *human*) before they can be deemed worthy of our attention and our respect. Why do animals have to be like us (the common tack taken by analytical moral philosophers defending animal rights) to be free of human mistreatment of them? Just as women should not need to be "like" men to be accepted as fully human, so animals should not have to be seen as similar to humans to have their lives matter to us. In fact, the whole theoretical discussion of similarity is not really a discussion about animals at all, as MacKinnon points out, but about human power *over* animals.

The Western definition of the "man of reason" coincides with gendered notions about male behavior and masculinity. The idea of a rational person draws upon "men's gender-specific criteria"[14] and more highly valued activities identified as male or "masculine." To be a person is to be *rational* and to esteem autonomy over relationship—in other words, to be the antithesis of what is thought to be female. "[T]he feminine has been associated with what rational knowledge transcends, dominates or simply leaves behind."[15] Men's experience has been mistaken as representing human experience, while rationality has been mistaken as representing the highest attribute of humans. The central categories and habits of Western political thought—concern about rights, interests, the status of the individual over and against others, what constitutes being human, and so on—have all arisen on the basis of these two errors. Has not men's experience structured and delimited the threshold issues regarding the social contract and inclusion within the moral order, by fostering the presumption that we must prove how animals are like us? Why must we prove that animals suffer (and suffer in ways like humans) in order to have them recognized as beings worthy of better treatment? Men never had to prove they suffered to "have their existence validated and harm to them seen as real."[16] "Why is just existing alive not enough? Why do you have to hurt?"

As MacKinnon notes, the term *male* "has nothing whatever to do with inherency, preexistence, nature, inevitability, or body as such. Because it is in the interest of men to be male in the system we live under (male being powerful as well as human), they seldom question its rewards or even see it as a status at all."[17] Being a powerful male is culturally constructed. It is demonstrated in part by one's use of animals—specifically, by severing one's connection to one's feelings and by "being a man" who hunts, kills, and in other ways violates the other animals (as with scientific experimentation). Emotions are denigrated as untrustworthy and unreliable, as invalid sources of knowledge. Crucially, the emphasis on rationality precludes appealing to the one aspect of ourselves as human beings that might enable us to recognize the situation of animals and hence to respond to it: our capacity to care.[18] We experience this capacity through our bodies. The devaluation of the body and its emotions, and how both have been treated in philosophy, in history, in science, and in everyday life, thus has everything to do with its equation with women, nature, and animals; and the treatment of women, nature, the body, and animals has everything do with the elevation of men.

The elevation of "rational man" in Western thought, and its corresponding devaluation of the (female/animal) body has two immediate consequences for the animal movement. First, as feminist critics have pointed out, animal rights theorists themselves often appeal to humans to stop harming animals in a way that bifurcates the human into "rational thinker" or "emotional reactor." In addressing the "rational thinker," rights theorists tacitly accept the prior ontological divisions and categories created by a world of sexual inequality. In positing its two primary texts as Peter Singer's *Animal Liberation* and Tom Regan's *The Case for Animal Rights*—texts that insist on their reasonableness—the animal movement reiterates a patriarchal disavowal of emotions as having a legitimate role in theory making. Paradoxically, theorists articulate positions against animal suffering, while at the same time they maintain that our emotional responses to this suffering can never be appropriate sources of moral knowledge. The working assumption appears to be that emotional responses to suffering are not trustworthy as the foundation of theory.

Second, the fetish of a disembodied and abstract reason in our society effectively obscures real structures of inequality and violence, by keeping the actual experiences of women and animals at arm's length. Just as women experience the social reality of domination made into sex through rape, incest, pornography, sexual harassment, forced pregnancy, and captivity in the home, animals experience the *material reality* of human oppression through a patriarchal matrix that renders them into objects of manipulation, scientific torture, mass annihilation, and consumption. What MacKinnon calls a neo-Cartesian mind game reduces the experiences of women, and of animals, to abstractions, rendering them *immaterial*. This mind game treats everything as ideas. To take one example: the common argument that corpse-eaters offer to vegetarians and vegans that "plants have life too and so we can eat animals," is implicitly patriarchal. To draw lines where lines should not exist (i.e., by claiming that eating an animal is essentially different from eating a human being) does not mean that we cannot draw lines at all (i.e., distinguishing between eating a cow and eating a carrot). Questioning the appropriateness of drawing such lines is ironically an example of Cartesian doubt, which denies the validity of ideas rooted in lived reality. As MacKinnon points out, Cartesian doubt is a function of human male privilege. This privilege enables a standpoint that views everything as made out of ideas. One might pose the "theoretical" question of whether carrots are being exploited. But once we situate ourselves within the lived, embodied reality we know as this world, we surely know that the eating of a cow, pig, or chicken is different from the eating of a carrot.

MacKinnon also sees this neo-Cartesian mind game functioning in the argument that pornography is an idea, a speech, rather than an act, a documentation of torture. Human male privilege can view everything as being made out of abstractions. But women lack such luxury when someone else's privilege is hitting them in the face, calling them "cunt" as they walk in the street, sexually abusing them as children, sexually coercing them as adults, and sexually coming on to them as they volunteer as animal activists. MacKinnon writes:

> When something happens to women, it happens in social reality. . . . In other words, the harm of second-class human status does not pose an abstract reality question. In social life, there is little that is subtle about most rapes; there is nothing complex about a fist in your face; there is nothing nuanced about genocide—although many nuanced questions no doubt can be raised about them. . . . It is the *denial* of their social reality that is complicated and raises difficult philosophical questions. Understand that the denial of the reality of such events has been a philosophical position about reality itself. Unless and until it is effectively challenged, only what power wants to see as real is granted reality status.[19]

Power, a function of human male privilege, enables a standpoint that controls what is designated "real" and considers everything as being made out of ideas, out of abstractions. For instance, when Linda Marchiano (Linda Lovelace) testified that she was forced into the making of the pornographic film *Deep Throat*, her statements about her experience of brutal sexual slavery while making that film (in *Ordeal*, her autobiography) became the subject of a libel suit. In other words, the film was seen as an "idea," hence as protected speech, rather than as a document of actual, physical torture and degradation. Her reality disappeared. Similarly, when corpse-eaters invoke the baseless image of screaming, suffering carrots, lettuce, and tomatoes in order to justify eating animals, the animals' reality disappears. Because of the perspective arising from male privilege, the reality of *suffering* gets reduced to a debate about ideas, and whatever is an idea is protected as speech.

As MacKinnon points out, through pornography, women *become* men's speech. Thus does the mind triumph over the body, men over women, ideas over reality. And privilege remains undisturbed because abstractions ignore the context of power. When the working definition of "human" is what *manhood* is, and rationality is valued as one of the qualities of manhood, then women represent what is not valued—femaleness and what femaleness is associated with: the body, emotions, and animals.

SEX INEQUALITY INSCRIBES THE USE OF ANIMALS AS PART OF ITS DEFINITION OF MANHOOD

A popular Burger King advertisement in 2006 satirically appropriated and subverted Helen Reddy's feminist song, "I Am Woman, Hear Me Roar," turning it into a paean to masculinity and meat-eating. In the ad, a man declares his right to eat meat because he is a man: "I am man hear me roar. . . . I'm way too hungry to settle for chick food. Yes I'm a guy. . . . I will eat this meat. . . . I am man." Then the voice-over proclaims, "The Texas Double Whooper. Eat like a man, man."[20] The life-and-death power over animals that men have traditionally had in the West establishes a part of the meaning of manhood. Species inequality is inscribed within the definition of manhood, a definition that grants men the right to act violently toward animals and women with impunity. Meat eating continues to be associated with male privilege, establishing meat eating as a virile, manly thing to do. Just as philosophers elevated the "man of reason" for whom mind conquers matter, and historians elevated a male idea of the professional historian who rejected the trivial, the domestic, the feminine, so too the everyday corpse-eater recapitulates these gendered rejections of the body by consuming the bloody bodies of feminized animals.

The sexual politics of the hunt in contemporary hunting culture meanwhile celebrates man as hunter and life-taker. Both associations (virility in meat-eating, virility in hunting/killing) drip with power as well as blood.[21] Many of the recent school shootings in the United States involved gunmen targeting girls and women; and even when women and girls weren't the target, the shootings have all been done by men and boys. As Daniel Moshenberg observes, "Men and boys with guns are stalking and hunting women and girls in schools repeatedly. Until we see 'the gun problem' as equally a problem of violence against women, nothing will change."[22] Men and boys thus stalk female human animals as well as nonhuman male and female ones. Gender identity as a system leads directly to male violence and domination directed against both sets of subjects.

The question of "manhood," then, clearly enters into the politics of the animal movement at all sorts of levels. One more that bears mentioning is the increasing vogue among men in the direct action wing of the movement to portray the struggle for animal liberation as a *war*. Learning about animal oppression provokes a variety of feelings—sadness, distress, anger, powerlessness, indignation, outrage, and horror among them. Men, however, are traditionally taught to perceive all negative emotions as anger. Those who feel only anger in response to animal suffering, rather than the complex of emotions that accompany anger, may experience animal activism as a battle rather than as a process. Naturally, if animal activism is seen as a war, men's feelings about the other animals can in this way be rendered comprehensible and even honorable. To be at war avoids being "unmanned" by caring about animals. But the referent is no longer the animals, it is the battle. This maintains a disengagement from feelings such as tenderness, empathy, and sympathy. And it provides a heroic, male-identified metaphorical framework for one's work to "save the animals."

Bonnie G. Smith, a feminist historian (describing Hayden White's critique of traditional tropes of history) writes that since "the past serves up accounts of violent events that are over . . . readers (including scholars) can let their violent fantasies roam freely when doing history."[23] This raises a disturbing question: Does learning about animal oppression provide a similar function in terms of allowing the roaming of violent (male) fantasies? Sometimes the focus on describing violence against the animals becomes a justification for violent actions, and frequently for the use of violent metaphors. We are told that we are engaged in a "new civil war," that violence against animal oppressors is acceptable, that our activism should be "by any means necessary." Women and men are encouraged to join this new civil war. The problem is that to be at war upholds gender dominance within the movement while it protects male activists' "manhood." It links the animal movement with extreme Right and terrorist male groups who also use the discourse of the "warrior." Further, women are already experiencing a war, a war against them. Why should we join another? And why is it necessarily a war?

Bellicose language that celebrates armies fighting, warriors redeeming, soldiers marching (under orders) for the greater good ignore one of the basic feminist insights into animal oppression, which is that the ability to care and respond to animals exists within each of us. Though our empathic imagination is actively repressed through socialization, it can also be actively accessed. Moments of interaction between a human being and an animal being often open up the ability to respond to the situation of animals. But with warrior talk, not only is the warrior talk of other (right-wing) movements legitimated, not only are the emotions of sympathy and empathy (for both animals and for one's own opponents) denied, but the traditional male response to threats against one's possessions and one's identity are reinforced: making war.

As this analysis suggests, one of the challenges for the animal movement is getting men to give up male-identified power over other beings. To be in the animal movement, the individual man must "refuse to be a man"—to use John Stoltenberg's term for the process of disowning the privilege that comes through sexual inequality. This undoubtedly goes some way toward explaining why there aren't more men in the animal movement. Logically, if the animal movement leaves the definition of "manhood" undisturbed it cannot accomplish its goals of liberating animals since, by definition, manhood involves use of and killing of animals, as well as the promotion of a "warrior" ethos that reproduces the values of aggression and masculine heroism of a patriarchal order.

SEXUAL INEQUALITY INSCRIBES A PORNOGRAPHIC "FEMININITY" ON DOMESTICATED AND DEFEATED ANIMALS

MacKinnon's understanding of how "gender is a substantive process of inequality," "a material division of power,"[24] is helpful in understanding how femaleness becomes symbolically associated with defeated animals:

> [T]o be victimized in certain ways may mean to be feminized, to partake of the low social status of the female, to be made into the girl regardless of biological sex. This does not mean that men experience or share the meaning of being a woman, because part of that meaning is that inferiority is indelible and total until it is changed for all women. It does mean that gender is an outcome of the social process of subordination that is only ascriptively tied to body and doesn't lose its particularity of meaning when it shifts embodied form. Femininity is a lowering that is imposed; it can be done to anybody and still be what feminine means. It is just women to whom it is considered natural.[25]

Sexual inequality makes the dominated animal "female" in reality or metaphorically. Cast as female, the animal becomes either immaterial or symbolic of the defeat (thus the mounting of dead animals' heads as trophies). Thus, species inequality is gendered.

Sexual inequality creates a hierarchy about animals: domesticated animals are seen as female, wild animals are seen as male—until, that is, the hunter kills the animal, at which point, as defeated prey, he or she is treated linguistically as female.[26] The victim of the hunt is a dominated power within a sexual system that is structured along lines of dominance and subordination; ergo, the dominated animal becomes symbolically female. Karen Davis argues that the reason farmed animals have been neglected by the environmental movement is because they are "creatures whose lives appear too slavishly, too boringly, too stupidly female, too 'cowlike.'" Davis shows how both wild and domestic turkeys are subject to human sexual violence.[27] Similarly, Susan Davis and Margo Demello challenge the social/sexual construction of rabbits:

> Words about women and rabbits—like "dumb bunny" and "cunt"—belittle and degrade women and rabbits simultaneously. And the very success of the Playboy Bunny—a creature that is half rabbit and half woman, after all—reveals a male penchant for a very chilling notion of female sexuality: one that is bound in notions of prey, childishness and submissiveness, on the one hand, and unbridled lust, fertility and even witchery on the other.[28]

Animal oppressive activities, including almost all forms of corpse-eating, "work" ideologically and materially by equating the individual animal with femaleness. Industrialized farming depends on domesticated female animals' reproductive labor. Consumption of domesticated animals cannot exist without the enslavement of female animals to reproductive labor. To control fertility one must have absolute access to the female of the species. Cows, sows, chickens, and female sheep are exploited in ways that merge their reproductive and productive labor. Their bodies must be reproduced so that there will be "meat" for humans, so that there will be cow's milk for humans, so that there will be eggs for humans. Female animals are not worthy of respect. Their importance is *what* they do—*reproduce*—rather than *who* they are—individual animals. They become a *what*. There is no *who*.

The status of the female of the species meanwhile establishes the status of the male domesticated animals. The slang use of species names such as *cow, sow,* and *chick* demonstrates the unworthiness of that species and anyone to whom the name is appended. All domesticated animals carry the taint of this exploitation of female reproductivity; it is one reason that animals are seen as always already replaceable (there will always be more animals because of the slavery of female animals). Farmed animals' unworthiness becomes associated with their species as such, which in turn is associated with or defined through the demeaned status of its females. Deprived of any recognizably "human" (read male) characteristic, like reason, which might redeem them as subjects and lift them out of their lowly status, male domesticated animals become merged with femaleness.

HOW THE MOVEMENT TRADES IN SEXUAL OBJECTIFICATION OF WOMEN—AND THEREFORE OF ANIMALS

How do animal oppressors change? How does someone become awakened to consciousness of his or her individual responsibility for the death of animals? How does a culture learn to care about domesticated animals? As we have seen, one powerful structural barrier to caring about animals is the ideology by which domesticated species have been "lowered" through their equation with femaleness. So effective and total is this ideology that campaigns on behalf of animals believe that they cannot win over animal oppressors simply by showing the actual lives of domesticated animals. Farmed animals are inevitably seen as a nothingness, associated as they are with femaleness. To get around this problem, some campaigns on behalf of animals have ironically chosen to substitute a different subject for their campaigns, one who has *also* been desubjectified: the woman who lives in a state of perpetual undress. In doing so, however, they are only reinforcing the very system of sexual objectification that consigns *both* women and animals to perpetual domination.

While several organizations have promoted their causes using sexual images of women, People for the Ethical Treatment of Animals (PETA) is most notable for its choices to use women models, naked women, and to associate itself with pornographers like Hugh Hefner and *Playboy*. In a world in which sex is what women have to sell, PETA provides a way to "sell" their sex for a *cause*. A January 2007 example was PETA's "State of the Union Undress" (available at YouTube for anyone who verifies they are 18 or older), a video in which a young woman is depicted (through the magic of video intercutting) addressing the U.S. Congress on the subject of animal exploitation—as she slowly strips off all her clothing. One of the implicit, if not explicit, messages of such advertisements is, *Yes, we're asking you to give up animals as objects, but you can still have women as objects! You can become aware of animals' lives, but you don't have to give up your pornography*. Thus, rather than challenge the inherent inequality of a culture structured around dominance and subordination, the ad instead tries to leverage sexual inequality on behalf of the other animals. In fact, every time PETA uses a naked or nearly-naked woman to advertise animals' concerns it not only benefits from sexual inequality, it also unwittingly demonstrates the intransigence of species inequality.

In its defense, PETA asserts that there is nothing wrong with nakedness; that feminists who object are puritanical and denying the beauty of the body; that these campaigns bring people to their website or prompt them to make phone calls to PETA where they do learn about issues relating to animals' lives. This of course is the liberal position on women's sexuality—that it can be freed from carrying the meaning of inequality. PETA's spokespeople further defend the choice of campaigns featuring women's naked or near-naked bodies by arguing that the women in their campaigns have consented to their participation. Such arguments are inherently problematic. In a world in which sex is what women have to sell, isn't the concept of consent emptied of much of its meaning? What does women's "no" to being used as a sex object actually look like in our culture? As MacKinnon has pointed out, of the debate about consent in rape cases: "when force is a normalized part of sex, when no is taken to mean yes, when fear and despair produce acquiescence and acquiescence is taken to mean consent, consent is not a meaningful concept."[29] The problem of consent surfaces at other levels of animal movement organization as well. PETA, for instance, narrows its employment pool when it asks young women applying to certain positions at the organization if they would pose in a cage, for instance, or in other ways display themselves. If their employment at PETA is predicated on their willingness to perform certain acts of selling the message through their bodies, then de facto, those women unwilling to do so are not going to be hired (some remove themselves from consideration after being asked this question). If only those who say, "Yes I will participate," are being hired, it is again hard to know what a "no" really looks like.

In *The Sexual Politics of Meat*, I proposed that animals are "absent referents" in an animal-oppressive world. They are made absent through interventions such as corpse-eating, in which the animal disappears as animal to become food, through vivisection, in which the animal becomes the "object" of study, and is reduced to his or her body, and then reduced further to the symptoms that that body exhibits. In this context, while some argue that PETA's ads using naked or nearly-naked women are liberating, not only for animals but, in transgressive ways, for women too, such practices in fact only substitute *one absent referent* for another. The challenge for the animal movement is how to restore the absent referent to a dominant culture that refuses to acknowledge it. What must be borne in mind, however, is that the absent referent is a crucial point of intersection *both* for sexual inequality and species inequality. Logically, there can be no politically liberatory *substitution* of woman for animal, because what is being replaced carries its own marker of inequality. What appears superficially as substitution is actually the layering of one oppressive system on top of another. (In another recent PETA campaign, a woman was posed as though cut up like a piece of meat, demonstrating both sexual and species inequality—the dead animal's fate was effectively layered upon the woman's fate as an object.)

Ironically, one common way that sexual inequality is imposed on farmed animals is through advertisements that sexualize meat. Conventions include fragmentation ("are you a breast man or a leg man"?), consumable females (barbecued pigs as sexy females with thrusting hips and pendulous breasts), and strip teases (animals in various stages of disrobing), rendering all domesticated animals being consumed as female. Replacing animals with women is therefore not *substitution* or potentially liberating, because the original victim's fate is still there, present through reference. A turkey posed as a prostitute, a turkey "hooker," refers not only to the turkey's fate but uncritically invokes, and thus reinforces, the debased status of the prostitute. The word *substitution* implies that the object is changed, and that substituting women for animals is somehow transgressive (e.g., as when women are substituted for cows in "Milk Gone Wild," a pornographic parody of the well-known dairy industry slogan). But it isn't a parody of a dairy industry slogan. It is a parody of the spring break beach parties (girls gone wild). What we in fact see is merely one debased subject being substituted for the other: the lowered status of the first (animal) is applied to the other (woman), who however already carries her own low status—marked as "female" in a world of sexual inequality. If animals are burdened by gender, by gendered associations, by the oppression that is gender, then clearly they can't be liberated through representations that demean women. It isn't helping animals, and it certainly isn't helping men—to continue to believe that privilege is something to hold on to, to masturbate to. We live in the world pornography has made, and so do other animals.

Contemporary capitalist agriculture has developed into a multi-billion dollar industry that, like the porn industry, makes money off of the bodies of others, that controls female sexuality, is obsessed with nipples and pregnancy and uses vibrators (yes, these are all aspects of industrialized farmings' treatment of female animals) in ways that blur the line between the pornographer's world and the world of industrialized farming. This is one meaning of the term "the pornography of meat." Another meaning to the term is found in the imposition of common conventions in pornography (rear-entry shots; sexualized poses; and language about sex) on animals, so that the message becomes that animals, too, *want* to be desired. Through such references, meat advertisements presume they are talking to users of pornography. In *The Pornography of Meat*, I showed that animals in bondage, particularly farmed animals, are shown "free" in the way that women are seen to be "free"—posed as sexually available as though their only desire is for the viewer to want their bodies. It makes animals' degradation and suffering fun by making animals' degradation sexy. Simultaneously, it makes women's degradation fun because to be effective the advertisement requires the implicit reference to women's sexualized status as subordinate. For women, through pornography, their degradation is always already sexy. The *sexualization* of animals and *the sexual objectification of women* thus overlap and reinforce one another. The body parts of females, at times dead females, are subjects pornography has already sexualized. In a fluid move, these conventions are used to sell dead bodies.

As MacKinnon and other radical feminists have argued, pornography is a central factor in women's subordination. "Pornography makes sex into a violation and makes rape and torture and intrusion into sex."[30] Pornography is a multi-billion dollar industry—larger than all regular media combined.

> Because the profit from these mass violations counts and women do not, because these materials are valued and women are not, because the pornographers have credibility and rights and powerful friends to front for their interests and women do not, the products of these acts are protected and women are not. So these things are done so that pornography can be made of them. Everyone who has been looking high and low for a "direct casual link" between pornography and harm might consider this one: it takes harming women to make it.[31]

Meat advertisements show us how pornographers do this: take a defeated being, in this case a dead animal, and pose him or her according to a pornographic convention, say, a restaurant that sells dead lobsters claiming "Nice tail;" barbecued pigs posed as young women (all pink, signifying whiteness), hanging on the arms of men; anorexic cows; chickens in high heels. In each case: she is dead and yet she wants it.[32] Wants what? Wants sex; wants to be sexually used; wants to be consumed. And so violence has been made into sex. Meat advertisements do this to animals because pornographers do it to women. Pornographers do it to women because it works for them sexually. It works for them, because *sexual inequality* is sexy. As MacKinnon explains, "[t]o be a means to the end of the sexual pleasure of one more powerful is, empirically, a degraded status and the female position."[33] Which not only explains what pornography is doing and why, but why meat advertisements would gravitate to pornographic conventions to sell their dead products. They mix death with degradation. That equation has one answer: the dead animal equals the female position. "Pornography creates an accessible sexual object, the possession and consumption of which is male sexuality, to be possessed and consumed as which is female sexuality. This is not because pornography depicts objectified sex, but because it creates the experience of a sexuality which is itself objectified."[34]

Meat adverstisements that sexualize and feminize animals have been around for more than 30 years, and during this time, they have become more widespread and more explicit. Pornographic conventions bleed into the bloodied animals that are shown wanting to be consumed, that is, wanting their own death. Similarly, pornography makes of actual women's experience an absent referent. As MacKinnon explains, "abused women become a pornographer's 'thought' or 'emotion'. . . . Once the women abused in it and through it are elided this way . . . pornography is . . . conceived in terms of what it says . . . rather than in terms of what it does."[35] Not only is species gendered through the feminizing of animals, as gender subordination, but gender is in turn animalized. This animalization is one aspect of sexual inequality. The animalizing of women and the sexualizing of animals is the point at which the structure of the absent referent overlaps, interlocks, intersects. The creation of the woman as absent referent through the sexualizing of her body and then the use of it in pornography, prostitution, rape, and battering melds with the creation of animals as absent referents by negating their individuality as living beings and by using/abusing their bodies through slaughtering, milking, experimenting upon, and hunting. There is one road, not two: a road of objectification, fragmentation, and consumption that requires and enacts the structure of the absent referent in relationship to nondominant others, whom it posits not just as objects but similar, metaphorically overlapping objects providing sexual pleasure. I have called this the *sex-species system*.

The *sex-species system* ensures that men have access to feminized animal bodies and animalized women's bodies. Another Burger King ad demonstrates this.

The "Whopperettes" shows women dancers, who suddenly, upon command from the "Burger King"—"Ladies, build your whopper!"—begin to throw themselves down upon each other in a pattern that creates a huge hamburger. While "have it your way" sounds in the background, one can also hear the "oofs" as women supposedly land on top of one another.[36] That *Hustler's* "Last All-Meat Issue" featured a woman on a hamburger bun back in 1978 shows how completely even hard-core pornographic conventions have now bled into popular culture (the Burger King ad was shown during Super Bowl 2006).

It may be that the more vegetarians make meat eaters uneasy, the more meat is sexualized. People don't know what to do with uneasiness. But they do know what to do with sexualized messages: ignore what has actually happened to the being who has been reduced into a consumable object of representation, *her* experiences, and just get it on. Sexualizing domesticated animals through advertisements for cultural consumption restabilizes assumptions about their literal consumability. When the animal movement engages in the same representational strategy, it merely recycles the terms of an order that oppresses both animals and women.

SEXUAL INEQUALITY CREATES AN ATMOSPHERE FOR STRUCTURAL INEQUALITY IN THE ANIMAL MOVEMENT

In making veganism a political decision, animal activists rightly draw attention to the relationship between the personal and the political. However, the movement has remained extraordinarily indifferent to the ways in which the seemingly impersonal structures of patriarchy introduce patterns of sexual dominance and submission within the movement itself, patterns which inevitably play out in workplace conditions and interpersonal relations. The aforementioned PETA campaign depicting women as meat, for example, could be cited as an example of the creation of a hostile work environment for women working at PETA. A judge in one recent court case (unrelated to PETA) ruled that an image displayed at a plaintiff's workplace depicting women as meat helped create a hostile work environment, forming a context in which acts of sexual harassment occurred. But sexual politics plays out in more subtle ways within the movement as well.

In the animal movement, men still predominate as leaders and speakers, women as the grassroots workers doing the day-to-day work. Just as the Gross National Product does not measure housework, it does not measure volunteer hours. Unpaid labor is more likely to be provided by women than men, whether in the animal movement or at home. Without it, the movement could not survive. In addition, the glass ceiling for employees exists in animal organizations just as it does anywhere else in our society. Meanwhile, because of sexual inequality, women are doing work for animals instead of feminist work, or feminist-animal work. While some women come to the work for animals from the feminist movement, and see animal oppression as a part of women's oppression,[37] many women may become activists for animals in order to protect themselves from recognizing their own oppression. In other words, it may be easier to work on behalf of others who are suffering rather than to confront one's own situation.[38]

Why do women make this choice? MacKinnon suggests a reason: "[p]eople feel more dignity in being part of any group that includes men than in being part of a group that includes that ultimate reduction of the notion of oppression."[39] Though it has more women than men, the animal movement has more men than the feminist movement. Meanwhile, if women want to challenge women's oppression, we hear, let them join the feminist movement. If the animal movement challenged women's oppression, the fact that women outnumber men so greatly in the movement would be more apparent and the animal movement would more explicitly experience the lowering that comes from being associated with women. The animal movement cannot afford to do this, or so it seems to believe. Among other reasons, this may be why there is such an emphasis on the fact that no one else is doing *this* work—the work for animals—whereas someone else is doing the work for women (i.e., feminists). The claim that *we must do this work because no one else is!* helps to keep everyone distracted from just *who it is* that is doing most of that work. And so, a dualism about those who experience inequality evolves: those who can speak for themselves and those who cannot. Thus, animal activists are told we are the "voice for animals" or the "voice for the voiceless." The decision that couches advocacy as *speaking for those who cannot speak* contributes to the difficulty of seeing sexual inequality and perhaps, as well, species inequality. This decision communicates that it is equally or more important to speak for those who can't speak than to speak for oneself. This often leads to the conclusion that if you can speak for yourself you are not as oppressed as those who can't. For instance, after the Michael Vick arrest for being a major part of a dog-fighting ring, a discussion occurred on the nationally-syndicated Diane Rehm talk show that went something like this: *Why all this attention to dog fighting when there are women being beaten? At least women being beaten can speak for themselves.*[40]

In fact, there are times when women being beaten cannot speak up for themselves, for in doing so they may risk their lives or the lives of their children or companion animals.[41] By emphasizing *speaking for another*, however, we send the message that as long as we are speaking for those who cannot we therefore do not have to attend to other issues regarding those who can speak for themselves. For example, we might come to believe that battered women, because they can speak for themselves, already have sufficient power to change their lives.

Moreover, when the ability to speak on behalf of animals is lifted up as the more important act, how then do we see that animals are already communicating with us in a variety of ways? Or that it shouldn't take speech (and our ability to "hear" it) to provide the proof that animals should not be oppressed? Animals protest their treatment in many ways—they escape, they turn away, they growl, snarl, hiss, bray, or bark, they resist, they flail, they flatten their ears or bite, they kick, they swish their tails, they paw the ground or the doors, they scratch, and in other ways documented by animal behaviorists exhibit displeasure, dislike, and rejection. If we bring attention to our interactions with animals, no human voice is needed to articulate what they need. As Josephine Donovan has said, "if we listen, we can hear them."[42] By setting itself up as "the voice of the voiceless," the animal movement vaunts human language while trying to create some grounds for equality of treatment for those who don't use it (the voiceless) and ignoring the social reality of those with human voices who cannot speak about their oppression. Thus it fosters a double mis-impression: about who is the "speaker" and who are the speechless. Women who speak on behalf of animals are identifying themselves as self-sacrificing, perhaps because of the tacit recognition that women continue to hold a position of subordination both within and without the animal movement.[43] Meanwhile, and ironically, because of sexual inequality and the gendered nature of speech in Western culture, men who speak are constituting themselves as men (the status quo) often through a male-identified logocentric, rational narrative.[44]

There is a further way, though, that the personal and the political merge in the animal movement: sexual inequality creates an atmosphere for the outright sexual exploitation of women in the movement by men. The animal movement is thought of as a movement of compassion for animals. Because of this, women activists may believe that the men they meet in the movement will be compassionate and that they won't be insensitive. Thinking they will find gentle men in the movement, women lower their defenses and—guess what? They find themselves as sexualized in the animal movement as they are out of it. Indeed, they are victimized by sexual exploitation in the movement. I have received numerous personal reports from victimized animal activist women. Sexual exploitation can take place many arenas, but one popular, and confusing one, is the conference circuit. Feminists in the animal movement have discussed the inappropriateness of calling serial sexual exploiters *predators*. However, to use the term *predator* for such male behavior also applies a negative meaning to actual predatory animals. Serial sexual exploiters (the term I prefer) are not acting as "nature" would have it but in a socially constructed way, and they could change. Basically they are refusing to act justly toward women. Child sexual abusers choose professions that give them access to children (the church, the educational system, scouting activities); perhaps some men choose the animal movement because it gives them access to so many women.

Serial sexual exploiters in the movement adhere to certain forms of "grooming behavior" to lower their target's defenses. "Grooming behavior" was first identified as the deliberate ways child molesters choose to acclimate children to their sexual advances (having them sit on their laps, talking sexually, showing them pornography, touching first in a "safe" place, then moving their hands). Child sexual abusers benefit from an age difference; serial sexual exploiters benefit from the lowered defenses of women in the animal movement who anticipate *humane* men.

Serial sexual exploiters in the animal movement may begin with being flirtatious in public. The grassroots woman activist may feel flattered; someone is actually noticing the work that is often unnoticed. The next step is for the serial sexual exploiter to find an environment that is private (*Can you give me a ride?*—perhaps because he's from out of town and doesn't have a car, or perhaps because they are going to a protest together). Within the private environment, he sexualizes the talk in a general way (say, discussing topics such PETA's "State of Undress" or other ways of directly discussing something having to do with sex to see if the language and the topic are tolerated). In this private environment, he tests out the boundaries further by sexualizing the conversation in a more personal manner. He might seize on some personal information that is revealed and up the ante: discussing how she looks, for example, or the energy he feels being near her. The grooming behavior continues by the selection of an environment that is supportive of the continual erosion of the target's boundaries. For instance, he might suggest going to a bar. Then, he talks about how there is *an attraction between them.* Unlike routine dating behavior, the time frame for these interactions is often accelerated (indeed this may all occur in one night). And unlike routine dating behavior, the sexual exploiter is not looking for an ongoing relationship; indeed, the behavior he exhibits is specifically to disarm the woman quickly so that he can use her and move on. He is persistent; he won't take no for an answer. She worries about being rude. There may be some threatening, *I won't work with you. You led me on.* And when the night is over, the sexual conquest achieved, suddenly the *attraction* was only a *flirtation.* When the victim protests, verbally threatening behavior occurs: "Who will believe you?" "I will accuse you." "You will hurt the movement." Traumatized by what has happened the victim may not be able to think clearly or linearly.

Meanwhile, once again assured of his dominance through this sexual conquest, the serial sexual exploiter benefits from her traumatized state. His life is not shattered by the experience; it is enhanced. He can continue to behave as always while the victim is putting the pieces back together and trying to maintain her work on behalf of animals. Not wanting to put the movement at risk by attempting to hold him accountable, she remains silent and he moves on to his next target. Since individual women aren't seen as "the movement" per se, this sexually abusive behavior is not perceived as putting the movement at risk. It would be her speaking up that would be seen as hurting the movement. If the serial sexual exploiter is a visitor, a well-known activist, or scholar, he benefits from moving on and choosing a new target far removed from the most recent victim so that the opportunity to exchange experiences will not occur. Some women may uphold men who are abusers or sexual harassers within the movement because they are thankful that someone is articulating animals issues so strongly on behalf of animals. They recognize that women will not be heard in the way that the men or some men are. They accept, even at an unconscious level, that women are not going to be as successful, so they side with someone, even if that person has harmed them, who they think will succeed. In these ways, women are silenced so that animals can be helped. Who is the voiceless now?

CONCLUSION

In this chapter, I have taken up the question of what it would mean for the movement on behalf of other animals to acknowledge women's inequality, and I have suggested that MacKinnon offers a necessary corrective to the limits of contemporary animal rights activism and critical theories of animal domination. What I have called the sex-species system keeps oppressions interlocking and interactive; indeed the sex-species system gains its strengths through its interlocking nature. Yet, problematically, many *radical* animal activists and theorists continue to adopt a *liberal* perspective regarding sexuality, seeing it as essentially gender neutral. In doing so, they obscure one of the most important bases of animal domination, which is the sex hierarchy system.

If taken seriously, however, the problem of sexual inequality raises a host of quite vital and relevant questions for those who would liberate other species: are the animal movement's theories of *why* animals are abused ignoring one of the primary reasons for that exploitation—patriarchy? Can nonhuman animals really be saved without also eradicating sexual inequality among human ones? Will animal activists also free the animals in pornography, or in situations where they are killed by batterers, killed by hunters, killed because they are female or equated with the female?

Does anyone really believe that the animal movement, because of its "pure" focus—on others who are unable to fight for themselves—is inoculated from problems of dominance within its ranks? Gender reflects a hierarchy, a division of power that is expressed and acted out, primarily sexually. There are therefore in fact two realities in current animal activism: men's and women's. These realities are determined by the dominant culture in which animal activism is trying to intervene. Failure to acknowledge these conflicting realities and the sexual inequality that creates them does harm to women and sets the animal movement back. The problem for animal activism is that it not only faces and must change a speciesist world, but also it faces and must change a sexist world that expresses its sexism through speciesism and expresses its speciesism through sexism. For the feminist, animal activism's failure to confront the problems of sexual inequality is sad; but for animal activism, such a failure may be fatal. The animal movement is trying to eradicate the oppression of animals without addressing how sexual inequality structures species inequality. But it can't be done.

What would it mean, then, for the movement on behalf of other animals to acknowledge women's inequality? As I have argued, the animal movement benefits from women's inequality in its structure, its focus, its arguments, its use of women's efforts, and in the accessibility it provides to sexual exploiters. So long as the movement refuses to acknowledge that it is a part of a dominant culture in which women's inequality still prevails, so long as it resists addressing the problem of this inequality, it will unconsciously undermine its own vision for a new kind of society, one based on genuinely universal equality, justice, and caring.

15

Sympathy and Interspecies Care

Toward a Unified Theory of Eco- and Animal Liberation

By Josephine Donovan

PREFACE FOR THIS VOLUME[1]

The outlines of a unified theory of liberation for animals seem to be emerging as four theoretical traditions come together which urge a similar approach to the question of how humans should ethically treat nonhuman creatures, as well as in a broader sense all living vegetation. The four traditions are feminism/ecofeminism, Marxism, phenomenology, and sympathy theory. This chapter treats primarily the latter with some emphasis on the early twentieth-century phenomenology tradition.

Feminist ethic-of-care theory, as applied to animals, is elaborated in a book I co-edited with Carol J. Adams, The Feminist Care Tradition in Animal Ethics.[2] *Ecofeminism's "embodied materialism" merges with phenomenology in its focus on interiority: on, as Elizabeth Behnke put it, "sensing from within" rather than "seeing from outside"—the latter the objective perspective of modern science.*[3] *Marxism with its critique of reification and the concept of standpoint theory developed by Georg Lukács offers the possibility of articulating the subjective position of an oppressed group, providing the basis for collective group resistance. In my recent article, "Feminism and the Treatment of Animals," I apply Lukácsian standpoint theory to animals, arguing that humans can engage in interspecies communication—dialogue—upon which they may base a determination of appropriate ethical responses. Phenomenological investigations are helping to develop a theoretical base for such communication.*[4]

Sympathy theory—the fourth leg in the proposed unified theory—which emerged in part as a counter to eighteenth-century rationalism, was amplified in the twentieth century by phenomenologists, in particular Husserl, Scheler, and Stein (as noted in this article).

These four theoretical traditions seem to be arriving at the same conclusion—that rationalist and scientific ontologies ignore an important aspect of reality: the subjective, the living spirit, which remains resistant to quantification and objectification and is therefore difficult to represent and analyze but not thereby to be rendered nonexistent. All of these traditions point to a recognition of the subjective reality of animals and argue that humans have an ethical responsibility to pay attention to their communications, to learn their language, and to incorporate their wishes into human ethical decision-making. The convergence of these traditions opens up the possibility of a new unified theory of animal (and indeed human, indeed earthly) liberation, what one might call eco-liberation, in which oppressed and exploited entities are redeemed from reifying constructs that elide their living realities and reduce them to objects and commodities to which one owes no ethical obligation.

Further theoretical work needs to be done, but this article, slightly modified from previous incarnations, develops the basis for one of these traditions—sympathy theory.

Jacques Derrida spoke of a two-century "war on pity" that has allowed such atrocities as factory farming, vivisection, genetic experimentation, etc. to proceed unchecked.[5] *It is time to counter this war with a revalidation of compassion and sympathy as legitimate sources of ethical knowledge.*

—J. D.

Many feminists, including myself, have criticized contemporary animal welfare theory for its reliance upon natural rights doctrine, on the one hand, and utilitarianism, on the other. The main exponent of the former approach has been Tom Regan, and of the latter, Peter Singer. However incompatible the two theories may be, they nevertheless unite in their rationalist rejection of emotion or sympathy as a legitimate base for ethical theory about animal treatment. Many feminists have urged just the opposite, claiming that sympathy, compassion, and caring are the ground upon which theory about human treatment of animals should be constructed. Here I would like to further deepen this assertion. To do so I will argue that the terms of what constitutes the ethical must be shifted. Like many other feminists I contend that the dominant strain in contemporary ethics reflects a male bias toward rationality, defined as the construction of abstract universals that elide not just the personal, the contextual, and the emotional, but also the political components of an ethical issue. Like other feminists, particularly those in the "caring" tradition, I believe that an alternative epistemology and ontology may be derived from women's historical social, economic, and political practice. I will develop this point further below.

In addition to recent feminist theorizing, however, there is a long and important strain in Western (male) philosophy that does not express the rationalist bias of contemporary ethical theory, that in fact seeks to root ethics in emotion—in the feelings of sympathy and compassion. Why this tradition has been overshadowed by rationalist theory is a question beyond my scope; what I would like to do here is, first, to summarize the main components of this sympathy tradition; second, to extend recent feminist theorizing on the subject; and third, to conclude with the idea that we need a refocus in our moral vision—a shift in the cultural ethical episteme—so that people will begin to see and attend to the suffering of animals, which is happening all about them. Here I will rely on theorizing about "attentive love" developed principally by Iris Murdoch (under the influence of Simone Weil), but anticipated by over a century of sympathy theory expounded by such major Western philosophers as David Hume, Arthur Schopenhauer, Martin Buber, and Edmund Husserl and other phenomenologists, such as Max Scheler and Edith Stein. Murdoch indeed exhibits a thorough awareness of this tradition—especially of the contribution of Hume and Schopenhauer—in her book *Metaphysics as a Guide to Morals*.[6]

It was Immanuel Kant who formulated the rationalist rights-based ethic that has dominated the contemporary field. In his preface to the *Fundamental Principles of the Metaphysics of Morals* (1785) Kant rejects feeling or inclination as a morally worthy motive for ethical action; rather, he stipulates, for an action to be ethically significant it must be performed out of a sense of duty. Indeed, "an action done from duty must wholly exclude the influence of inclination."[7]

Kant's rejection of sentiment or sympathy as a base for moral decision making or action seems to reflect three concerns: one is that emotions are volatile (what one feels today one may not feel tomorrow)[8]; two, the capacity for sentiment is not evenly distributed (and thus those who exhibit sympathy may act more morally by inclination than those who do not)[9]; three, for these reasons a sentimental ethic is not universalizable—one cannot establish thereby universal ethical laws.[10] The second and the third point suggest that an ethic based on sentiment or sympathy or care is incompatible with the claims of justice—that everyone be treated equally and fairly. Most defenses of and attacks on a sympathy-based ethic revolve around these points.

Kant also formulated what has become the dominant Western view of animals: that they are instrumental to human interests—are means to human ends but not ends in themselves worthy of moral consideration. Since Kant's views have been extensively criticized by animal rights theorists, notably Tom Regan in his *Case for Animal Rights*, I will not further treat them here. Schopenhauer, however, sounded the keynote of this critique when he exclaimed: "genuine morality [is] outraged by the proposition . . . that beings devoid of reason (hence animals) are things and therefore should be treated merely as means."[11]

> I regard such propositions as revolting and abominable. . . . Thus, because Christian morality leaves animals out of account . . . they are at once outlawed in philosophical morals; they are mere "things. . . . " They can therefore be used for vivisection, hunting, coursing, bullfights, and horse racing, and can be whipped to death as they struggle along with heavy carts of stone. Shame on such a morality . . . that fails to realize the eternal essence that exists in every living thing, and shines forth with inscrutable significance from all eyes.[12]

Kant's objection to an ethic rooted in emotional response, or sympathy, betrays a conception of emotion which construes it as irrational, uncontrollable, and erratic. Like other rationalists, Kant seems to imagine that emotional experience necessarily obliterates rational thinking. Kantian theorist Tom Regan follows in this vein when he accuses "ethic-of-care feminism" of "abjur[ing] the use of reason."[13]

But a considered and sophisticated response to such charges has been developed by sympathy theorists. They argue that experiencing sympathy is a complex intellectual as well as emotional exercise. Philip Mercer, for example, in his very useful study *Sympathy and Ethics* claims that in fact sympathy includes "a cognitive element."[14] Like Max Scheler (see below), Mercer is careful to distinguish between empathy and sympathy. Where the former may involve "losing oneself" in another's feelings, the latter requires keeping a certain distance so as to imaginatively construct the other's situation accurately and thereby to understand it intellectually as well as emotionally.[15] H. B. Acton in "The Ethical Importance of Sympathy" similarly argues that sympathy is a "form" of rationality.[16] It is not "as partial and impulsive" as critics have claimed[17]; it is "not a primitive animal feeling but an exercise of the imagination requiring self-consciousness and comparison."[18] In his phenomenological exploration of empathy Husserl identifies it as an imaginative exercise that requires judgment and evaluation: "I try to picture to myself, standing here, how I would look, how I would feel, and how the world would appear if I were there—in the place of that body which resembles mine and acts as I might. My imaginative projection into the place of another, conjoined with the two types of data given by the senses [appearance and behavior] makes empathy possible."[19] Mercer describes a similar imaginative construction but specifies that as a basis for ethical judgment and action sympathy (again not empathy) should involve not projecting oneself into another's situation but rather figuring out how the other is feeling: "it is not enough that I should imagine how I should feel if I were in the other person's place; I have to imagine how [the other] feels."[20]

The most developed analysis of sympathy remains phenomenologist Max Schelerls's *The Nature of Sympathy*.[21] Scheler elevates sympathy into a form of knowledge (*Verstehen* or understanding) which he proposes as an epistemological alternative to the objectification of the Cartesian scientific mode. Scheler indeed was a founder of the phenomenological school in the social sciences, which relies upon a method of "psychological sympathy" where the researcher attempts to imaginatively construct the reality of the subject, rather than objectifying him or her as data to fit mathematical paradigms.[22] Scheler proposed his method not just for the social sciences, however, and not just for humans. Rather, he contends, "understanding and fellow-feeling [*Mitgefühl*] are able to range throughout the *entire* animal universe. . . . The mortal terror of a bird, its sprightly or dispirited moods, are intelligible to us and awaken our fellow-feeling."[23]

Scheler argues that humans need to develop (or re-develop) their sympathetic intellectual capacities in order to decode the symbolic language of nature. Humans need to learn to read this language in order to truly understand natural life, including animals. "[W]e can understand the experience of animals," he notes, by attending to their behavioral and expressive signs: these have as their referent the animal's emotional and psychological state. "[F]or instance when a dog expresses its joy by barking and wagging its tail . . . we have here . . . a *universal grammar* valid for all languages of expression."[24] Similarly, other forms of natural life have a "grammar of expression" that humans can learn to understand; this understanding is both intellectual and emotional. "[T]he fullness of Nature in its phenomenological aspect still presents a vast number of fields in which the life of the cosmos may find expression; fields wherein all appearances have an intelligible coherence which is other and more than mechanical, and which, once disclosed by means of the universal mime, pantomime and grammar of expression is found to mirror the stirrings of universal life within."[25] Thus, Scheler is proposing that animals and other natural forms have a "language" that is accessible if humans attend to it, one that is elided by the mathematizing pretensions of modern science.

> [W]e must rid ourselves henceforward of our one-sided conception of Nature as a mere instrument of human domination. . . . [W]e must learn once more "to look upon Nature as into the heart of a friend" [*Faust* I. 3220]. . . . Hence the first task of our educational practice must be to revive the capacity for identification with the life of the universe, and awaken it anew from its condition of dormancy in the capitalist social outlook of Western man (with its characteristic picture of the world as an aggregation of movable quantities).[26]

Thus, Scheler proposes an epistemological mode of sympathetic understanding as a valid tool of knowledge, which will reveal realities that are not seen or understood by the Cartesian mathematizing mode of science. St. Francis of Assisi is presented as exemplary; in his "emotional relationship to Nature . . . natural objects and processes take on an expressive significance of their own, without any parabolic reference to . . . human relationships."[27] Humans must develop this kind of sympathetic understanding (*Verstehen*) as a cognitive mode to decipher nature's *own* language, to see organic life as it is, not as translated into manipulable objects for human use. Scheler does not, therefore, see sympathy as a whimsical, erratic, and irrational response, but rather as a systematic investigatory tool, a form of knowledge.

An interesting recent exploration of how such an approach might work in practice is to be found in Kenneth Shapiro's "Understanding Dogs through Kinesthetic Empathy, Social Construction, and History."[28] Shapiro (following Paul Ricoeur as well as Scheler) suggests that we need a new "interpretive science in which the object of study is an autonomous subject, more textlike than thinglike, and, hence, to be understood rather than explained."[29] By use of what he calls "kinesthetic empathy" Shapiro attempts to understand his dog Sabaka. He does this by imaginatively entering into the dog's bodily movements and reactions, thus deciphering the realities of the dog's "life-world" (to borrow a term from Husserl). Edith Stein, who studied with Husserl, developed a similar concept, which she called "sensual empathy" (a "sensing-in" of the body of another).[30] Such an effort yields knowledge of another's suffering. "Should I perhaps consider a dog's paw in comparison with my hand. I do not have a mere physical body . . . but a physical limb of a living body. . . . I may sense-in pain when the animal is injured."[31]

A somewhat similar approach is proposed by John A. Fisher in "Taking Sympathy Seriously: A Defense of Our Moral Psychology toward Animals." Fisher notes that "the sympathetic experience of . . . animals entails some understanding of what it is like to be them—for example, of what it is like to be huge and to walk on four legs, to have a large trunk, and so forth."[32] (Here the terms *empathy* and *sympathy* are used somewhat interchangeably, and Stein and Shapiro tend to see the experience as a kind of visceral emotion, as opposed to Fisher; but what is important is that they all maintain that a sympathetic imaginative construction of an other's reality is what is required for an appropriate moral response.)

Environmental ethicist Paul Taylor argues that such knowledge must be the basis of any environmental ethic. It is only by close study and observation of organisms that one can come to understand their reality, their telos, their needs. "As one becomes more and more familiar with the organism and its behavior, one becomes fully sensitive to the particular way it is living out its life cycle. . . . [T]he final culmination of this process is the achievement of a genuine understanding of its point of view and . . . and ability to 'take' that point of view."[33] Such a process is not anthropomorphic, nor need it deny the separate and different reality of the other organism. Rather it is a process of learning—through careful attention and observation—what the other's reality really is, respecting that different reality, and developing an ethical response that is appropriate to that creature's reality.[34]

All of these theorists are saying in answer to Kantian charges that sympathy is irrational that, on the contrary, it involves an exercise of the moral imagination, an intense attentiveness to another's reality, which requires strong powers of observation and concentration, as well as faculties of evaluation and judgment. It is a matter of trying to fairly see another's world, to understand what another's experience is. It is a cognitive as well as emotional exercise. The ability to extend the moral imagination in this way is not, they argue, necessarily a natural gift (though some, notably Scheler and Schopenhauer, assert that women are more able to exercise sympathetic understanding than men); rather, it is an intellectual and emotional practice that can be learned. As we have seen, Scheler contends that "the first task of our educational practice must be to revive the capacity for identification with the life of the universe."[35] Mercer, too, believes that people can and should be trained in emotional knowledge.[36] Feminist theorist Rosemarie Tong even suggests that a Kantian mechanistic rules-based ethic may lead to a deadening of the moral imagination.[37] Perhaps the most extensive recent plea for a reinstatement of sympathy education into the school system comes from Nel Noddings, who believes that "the maintenance and enhancement of caring [should be] the primary aim of education," and advocates instituting such practices as "caring apprenticeships," for example.[38]

Sympathy theorists argue, moreover, that one can in fact have no morality, no justice even, without first having sympathy. Acton, for example, observes that "a certain amount of sympathy is required if anyone is even to notice that someone else is in need of help."[39] And without such attention, there would be no morality, "for without [sympathy] there would be no helping, and hence no beneficence, and help and beneficence are necessary for morality."[40] In arguing therefore that sympathy is the sine qua non of ethical decision making and action, sympathy theorists contend that sympathy precedes justice. Such precedence obtains ontogenetically, some claim; logically, others claim; and metaphysically, yet others contend.

Scheler maintains that one's feelings of sympathy are rooted in earliest childhood, or in what Freudians call the preoedipal phase. One's first feelings are "the instinctive identification of mother-love."[41] Only gradually is this "replaced, in the later stages of childhood, by merely vicarious feeling," which remains as the undergirding of "fellow-feeling [*Mitgefühl*]."[42] In his introduction to Scheler's work, W. Stark amplifies this idea: "originally, the experience of self and the experience of others is in no way differentiated: the child feels the feelings and thinks the thoughts of those who form [her] social environment. It takes a long time before [perceptions are sorted out] as 'mine' and 'others.'"[43] Others, thus, "live in us,"[44] which forms the basis of sympathetic identification, preceding the emergence of egocentricity. Brian Luke in "Justice, Caring, and Animal Liberation" claims that sympathy for animals is indeed a deep, primary disposition that is only obscured and repressed by a process of intense social conditioning. Noting the extensive guilt expiation ceremonies that attend animal killing in traditional cultures, Luke suggests that the existence of such guilt (along with other social practices) is testimony to "the depth of the human-animal connection."[45] The fact that laboratory experiments and slaughterhouse practices are kept hidden from the public suggests, once again, shame or guilt over the violation of the human–animal bond. "Enormous amounts of social energy are expended to forestall, undermine, and override our sympathies for animals, so that vivisection, animal farming, and sport hunting can continue."[46]

A number of eighteenth-century theorists—including Shaftesbury, Hutcheson, Hume, and Adam Smith—claimed that humans have an innate sense of sympathy and that this is the basis for moral awareness. The Third Earl of Shaftesbury maintained that there is an innate "moral sense" that is rooted in one's sense of kinship with others.[47] Francis Hutcheson extended Shaftesbury's idea that there is an innate moral faculty, contributing further to what Keith Thomas has labeled the "new sensibilities" that developed during the century, including sensitivities to animal cruelty (many of the humane societies originated as the result of this new emphasis on the feelings as a guide to moral action).[48]

David Hume, picking up on his predecessors, insists that there is a "natural sympathy" "implanted in our nature."[49] "Would any man, who is walking along, tread as willingly on another's gouty toes, whom he has no quarrel with, as on the hard flint and pavement?"[50] From such examples, Hume maintains,

> we must, a priori, conclude it impossible for such a creature as man to be totally indifferent to the well or ill-being of his fellow-creatures, and not readily . . . to pronounce, where nothing gives him any particular bias, that what promotes their happiness is good, what tends to their misery is evil, without any further regard or consideration.[51]

"Morality," he concludes, "is determined by sentiment. It defines virtue to be *whatever mental action or quality gives to a spectator the pleasing sentiment of approbation*; and vice the contrary."[52] Moreover, "the approbation or blame . . . cannot be the work of our judgment, but of the heart; and is not a speculative proposition or affirmation, but an active feeling or sentiment."[53]

Scientific credibility has been added to eighteenth-century theorists' claims for innate, natural sympathy by Charles Darwin and, more recently, the sociobiologists. They argue that natural selection has resulted in the phenomenon of "kin altruism," which is an innate concern about the survival of one's kin (and thus one's genes) found in most animals.[54] Darwin in fact claimed in *The*

Descent of Man (1871) that in higher mammals such altruism was extended to non-kin.[55] In a recent and interesting extension of this view, "Animal Liberation and Environmental Ethics," J. Baird Callicott suggests that since domestic animals have historically been part of the immediate human community (and thus in a sense "kin"), "kin altruism" establishes a natural base for human concern and emotional attachment. There is, he claims, a kind of "evolved and unspoken social contract" between these animals and humans.[56]

Writing in direct confutation of Kant's ethical theory, Schopenhauer, like Hume, also contends that morality is rooted in sympathy: "only insofar as an action has sprung from compassion does it have moral value."[57] And compassion, he maintains, requires a kind of empathetic identification so that one can understand the other's situation. "I suffer directly with him, I feel his woe just as I ordinarily feel only my own. . . . But this requires that I am in some way *identified with* him, in other words that this *difference* between me and everyone else, which is the very basis of my egoism, is eliminated."[58] (It should be noted that later sympathy theorists, such as Scheler and Mercer, criticized Schopenhauer and Hume, respectively, for relying on empathy rather than sympathy, and thus sanctioning a loss of self in the identificatory process, which Scheler and Mercer reject).

Schopenhauer, however, emphasizes the emotional component of compassion. One understands another's pain through "the everyday phenomenon of *compassion*, of the immediate *participation* . . . in the *suffering* of another. . . . It is simply and solely this compassion that is the real basis of all *voluntary* justice and *genuine* loving-kindness."[59] And: "Boundless compassion for all living things is the firmest and surest guarantee of pure moral conduct."[60] Schopenhauer specifically includes animals in this moral community. In a compassion-based ethic "the *animals* are also taken under its protection. In the European systems of morality they are badly provided for, which is most inexcusable. They are said to have no rights . . . [and be] without moral significance. All of this is revoltingly crude, a barbarism of the West."[61]

Schopenhauer's ethical theory is rooted in his metaphysics, which entails the Indian distinction between what he called (in his magnum opus) the "Will" and the "Idea." The will is a kind of undifferentiated pool of Being to which all living creatures belong. It underlies the screen of appearances, of separate individuals, the Mâyâ or the Idea. It is through the pool of Being that we are linked to all other creatures, and it is through compassion that we know that connection; it breaks through the barriers of individuation and egoism.[62]

Like Schopenhauer and Hume, succeeding sympathy theorists claim that sympathy logically precedes justice; that is, there must first be the experience of sympathy before there can be any justice claims. Indeed, it is sympathy that determines who is to be included under the umbrella of justice. As environmentalist Fisher notes, "sympathy is fundamental to moral theory in that it determines the range of individuals to which moral principles apply."[63] And it is "our sympathetic response to animals [that] makes them a part of our moral community."[64]

Mercer also explains: if we take as the fundamental maxim of justice that one "treat everyone alike," then it becomes a question of who counts as "everyone." That decision is determined by the extent to which one can sympathize with the entity.[65] In elaborating, Mercer specifies that sympathy only occurs between creatures who can feel. "'Sympathy' has regard for 'the other' solely in respect of his [or her] capacity to feel and to suffer."[66] The sympathetic agent must be "a thinking and feeling being" and the object of sympathy must be "at least a feeling being."[67] The awareness that the other has feelings, or is a subject of feelings, means that one can no longer see that creature as an object. "If we actively sympathize with someone then we cannot treat him as an object, as an instrument for our own self-satisfaction; on the contrary we see him as a being possessing individual worth and existing in his own right."[68] In other words, sympathy engenders moral respect, and thus determines who deserves to be treated on equal terms. Justice, therefore, according to Mercer, applies only to sentient beings.[69]

Acton also maintains that sympathy establishes claims for equal treatment, or justice. This is because sympathy requires treating another's needs as *comparable* with one's own. It leads one to realize that "the other['s] distress is at least comparable with [one's own], and the road has been opened up . . . to the demand for equal treatment of equal needs. Sympathy requires that every sentient being shall count."[70] Scheler, like Schopenhauer, agrees that sympathy frees us from the "illusion" of "'egocentricity' . . . the illusion of taking one's own environment to be the world itself."[71] "The dissipation of this illusion . . . [enables] us to grasp how a [person], or living creature . . . is our *equal in worth*."[72] Thus, again, sympathy is seen as opening up and determining notions of justice. Scheler also maintains that an individual encounter with suffering should make us aware of suffering in general; thus "the pure sentiment of fellow-feeling is released as a permanent disposition, spreading far beyond the occasion which first inspired it, towards *everybody and every* good thing."[73] This brings us to the third issue Kantian theorists hold against sympathy-based ethics, that it is non-universalizable.

In *The Thee Generation* Tom Regan criticizes "ethic-of-care" feminism for its failure to provide a means of universalizing the individual experience of caring and sympathy. "What are the resources within the ethic of care that can move people to consider the ethics of their dealings with individuals who stand outside the existing circle of their valued interpersonal relationships?"[74] In fact, he argues, "most people do not care very much about what happens to [nonhuman animals] . . . their care seems to be . . . limited to 'pet' animals, or to cuddly or rare specimens of wildlife. What, then, becomes of the animals toward whom people are indifferent, given the ethic of care?"[75] In short, how does one generalize beyond the individual particular instance of caring or compassion to include all creatures within an ethic of care?

Regan argues that such extension can only come through logic. One extends one's care for one's own children to one's neighbors' children because it is illogical and inconsistent not to do so. "Whether I care or not [emotionally for the neighbors' children], I ought to and it is logic that leads me to the realization of this 'ought.'"[76] Regan's characteristic rejection of emotion or sympathy as a base for moral decision making is apparent here. Isn't it also likely that if one's neighbors' children were in harm, one would sympathize with them and care enough to help them? And isn't it unlikely that one would stop to figure out principles of logic and consistency to determine an appropriate moral action, if say, those children were crying in pain? (Of course, one can conjure up qualifying circumstances that will affect one's decision whether to help the children or not, but that is irrelevant to the question at hand—which is whether one responds on a rational or emotional basis to the suffering of non-kin). It is clear in fact that one can and often does feel sympathy for complete strangers. If I watch on TV children starving in Somalia or hear about the brutal rape of women in Bosnia, people I know little about and certainly do not know personally, I nevertheless feel sympathy; I care about their plight and am moved to try to help them. Thus, I contend—along with Hume and other sympathy theorists—that sympathy is easily universalized.

Virginia Held argues in a recent critique that rationalist ethics, in its reliance on theory based on universal, abstract "persons," neglects the experience of the "particular other," the personal emotional relationship one has with a real person. But, she contends, "particular others" need not be individual people one knows personally; rather, they can be "actual starving children in Africa with whom one feels empathy . . . not just those we are close to in any traditional context of family, neighbors, or friends. But particular others are still not 'all rational beings' or 'the greatest number'"[77]—the latter allusions to Kantian and utilitarian abstractions, respectively. It is a particular qualitative experience that is missing in contemporary rationalist theory, the emotional sympathetic understanding of another creature. It is this "personalist" dimension that sympathy theorists would restore to ethical theory.

We see now that sympathy theorists refute Kant by arguing that sympathy is in fact a form of knowledge that includes a cognitive dimension. It is not, therefore, whimsical and erratic; nor does it entail obliteration of the thinking or feeling self. It is easily universalized, although, as Luke points out, such extensions are often muted by powerful social and political institutions.

A number of feminists, including myself, have asserted that ethical theory about animal treatment should be grounded in what these earlier theorists called sympathy. In an important 1985 article Marti Kheel called for "a recognition of the importance of feeling and emotion and personal experience in moral decision making" about animals.[78] Noting that much evil is obfuscated through abstract rationalization, which serves to distance one from its actuality, Kheel suggests that personal experience of evil might bring its reality home. For example, those who "*think* . . . that there is nothing morally wrong with eating meat . . . ought, perhaps to visit a factory farm or slaughter house to see if [they] still feel the same way."[79]

Some feminists have developed Carol Gilligan's "ethic of care" as a base for animal welfare theory. See especially Deane Curtin's "Toward an Ecological Ethic of Care."[80] Though it has received much criticism and amplification, Gilligan's *In a Different Voice* remains the classic statement of the care ethic. In this framework,

> the moral problem arises from conflicting responsibilities rather than competing rights and requires for its resolution a mode of thinking that is contextual and narrative rather than formal and abstract. The conception of morality as concerned with the activity of care centers moral development around the understanding of responsibility and relationships, just as the conception of morality as fairness ties moral development to the understanding of rights and rules.[81]

Thus, Gilligan identifies an ethic that is rooted in the kind of sympathetic understanding proposed by the sympathy theorists introduced above. Such an ethic, historically, has been confined largely to the domestic sphere and to women. Leaving aside the question of whether as mothers women are biologically predisposed toward caring for their young (I leave it aside because biological determinism is simply an inadequate explanation of human [and indeed much nonhuman animal] behavior), it is apparent that women's historical social and economic practice has been of a caring nature. In addition to maternal practice,[82] women have nearly universally engaged in use-value production as their primary economic experience. Use-value production means the creation of products for immediate use or consumption by members of the household (clothes, food, etc.). It is a "caring labor," to use Hilary Rose's term.[83] A number of theorists (particularly Nancy Hartsock, Linda Nicholson, and Eli Zaretsky) have shown how in the West a division of moral labor accompanied the historical division between the public and private spheres with their divergent economic practices.[84] In an interesting exploration of the subject, "Eco-Feminism and Deep Ecology," Jim Cheney ties Gilligan's caring ethic to the gift-exchange economy characteristic of preindustrial societies. "[I]f we were to describe the ethical voices characteristic of people living within the two economies, they would be the two ethical voices described by Carol Gilligan, the (gendered) male voice associated with the market economy and the very different (gendered) female voices associated with the gift economy."[85] Cheney proceeds to argue that the Gilligan caring ethic should form the basis of environmental ethical theory.

Several theorists (in addition to Cheney, especially Virginia Held and Annette Baier) have pointed out that rights theory is rooted in the contractual relationships of a market economy. Baier in fact notes that rights theory and the Kantian rationalist ethic were developed for an elite of white property-holding males. Kant himself excluded women from the moral community of "rights-holders" (along with animals). Women, in fact, formed a kind of "moral proletariat" who carried on the necessary caring labor in the home, while men enjoyed the privileges and rights of public citizenship.[86] This is not to say that the notion of equal rights should be abolished or that ideas of justice are automatically specious; it is to say that, historically, Western women came out of a different ethical tradition than men, one that has been identified by Gilligan as the "caring ethic." It makes sense then that because there is much that is valuable in this ethic, feminists who are concerned about animal welfare would seek to locate an animal treatment ethic within this tradition.

To do so, however, feminists must insist that it be framed within a political perspective. Caring is an important ethical point of departure but to be effective it must be informed by an accurate political view. A number of theorists have made this point.[87] As a good example of how the caring perspective is enriched by a political framework, consider Marilyn Friedman's discussion of the famous Heinz hypothetical (that Gilligan among others discusses). Here the issue concerns a man, Heinz, whose dying wife can only be saved by a particular drug. The druggist's prices are unfairly high, so that Heinz cannot afford the drug. The ethical question posed in the hypothetical is what is the proper moral course for Heinz: to obey the law (and presumably let his wife die) or to steal the drug and save his wife. Friedman points out that the real answer to this question lies in a political analysis of a system that denies health care to people who cannot afford it and that "allows most health care resources to be privately owned, privately sold for profit in the market place, and privately withheld from people who cannot afford the market price."[88] While the traditional Kantian response to the Heinz dilemma is that he should not steal (Kant: "I am never to act otherwise than *so that I could also will that my maxim should become a universal law*"[89]), and the ethic-of-care response is that he should steal because in this particular context his responsibility is to his wife and because stealing is a lesser evil than death, a political ethic-of-care response would include the larger dimension of looking to the political and economic context within which people must make moral decisions. Thus, the corporate-controlled health care system becomes the primary villain in the piece, and the incident should serve to motivate action to change the system. This is the real ethical act that should emerge from the Heinz dilemma. On the other hand, a political ethic-of-care would not abandon Heinz in the abstractions of a political critique; it would also support him in obtaining the drug (by stealing, if indeed that is the only way to secure it, and if indeed the drug is as miraculous as it is supposed to be—ecofeminists are also skeptical of drug industry claims of efficacity).[90]

Carol Adams's *Sexual Politics of Meat* is a good example of a work that lays out the political (in this case, patriarchal) context of meat-eating. While a caring ethic focuses on the suffering of the animal, it is enlarged by an understanding of the symbolic cultural significances of meat-eating, which Adams explains (see also Jeremy Rifkin, *Beyond Beef*).[91] Such awareness of cultural ideologies enables the formation of appropriate ethical actions because it helps to explain who profits from certain practices, such as meat-eating, and who therefore continues to promulgate propaganda on their behalf. It is important to understand the role of the meat lobby or the National Rifle Association (in promoting hunting, for example) in furthering institutionalized sanctions of these practices. Indeed, as Luke points out, massive institutional strategies have been mobilized on a national level to obscure the reality of animal suffering. Part of any ethical response must therefore be to counter these lies, to lift the veil on animal agony.

In addition to assessing power relations, a political perspective also involves a consideration of needs. On the individual level, the caring response must include a determination of a person or animal's needs. As Rita Manning notes, caring requires "a willingness to give the lucid attention to the needs of others."[92] This attitude, which others have labeled "attentive love" (see below), goes beyond just respecting the rights of another. Within a political perspective needs assessment has a wider scope. While relatively undeveloped in liberal political theory, some Marxist theorists have focused on this issue (see Braybrooke).[93] Agnes Heller has analyzed the social construction of the artificial consumer needs that fuel a capitalist society in her *Theory of Need in Marx*.[94] She proposes the concept of "radical needs" as a revolutionary force whereby people become aware of their qualitative, spiritual needs beyond reified manufactured needs, and demand their satisfaction.

In her analysis of the Gilligan ethic Seyla Benhabib proposes (following Jürgen Habermas) a "communicative ethic of need interpretation."[95] This means an ethic where the oppressed have an opportunity to voice their needs and where ethical decision making is conducted in a dialogic process. Unlike universalistic rights-based theories, such an ethic would not elide the reality of the "concrete other," which remains "the *unthought*, the *unseen*, and the *unheard* in such theories."[96] "One consequence of this ethic . . . is that . . . moral theory is enlarged so that not only rights but needs" are addressed.[97] An assessment of animal needs must therefore be a part of any caring ethic for the treatment of animals. Indeed, further extension of needs theory into the area of animal welfare should be developed.

No ethic, therefore, exists in a political vacuum, and thus while it is important to ground ethics in the personal sympathetic response, it is also important to take a larger view, placing the individual instance within a political understanding of the cause and an assessment of the needs of the suffering. The individual response is thus generalized not in a Kantian sense but within the framework of political analysis. No ethic can therefore be apolitical; nor can any epistemology. The way we see the world—what in fact we see—is shaped by our understanding of its power relations and by our values. Much of this is taught, passed on through the mechanisms that reproduce cultural ideology, such as the schools, the churches, the media. It therefore often reflects uncritically the viewpoint and interests of the dominant powers in society.

Some feminists, notably Alison Jaggar and Nancy Hartsock, have argued that marginalized people may have an alternative perspective or standpoint that is more valid than the dominant view because it sees realities—pain and need—that are elided by controlling ideologies which distort the truth to perpetuate the status quo.[98] Women may be seen therefore as providing an alternative perspective, that codified in the "caring ethic," which is rooted, as we have seen, in women's historical social and economic practices.

In an article entitled "Moral Understandings: Alternative 'Epistemology' for a Feminist Ethics," Margaret Urban Walker calls for "a profound and original rebellion against the regnant [ethical] paradigm," which she labels the "*universalist/impersonalist tradition*"—that is, the Kantian rationalist/rights tradition noted here.[99] In its stead she proposes "an *alternative moral epistemology*, a very different way of identifying and appreciating the forms of intelligence which define moral consideration."[100] Components of this alternative epistemology include those elements of feminist ethics identified here, such as paying "attention to the particular," constructing moral issues in "contextual and narrative"[101] frames, and using a conversational or dialogical mode in moral decision making.[102] In an earlier article I argued that an ethic for the treatment of animals must be grounded "in an emotional and spiritual conversation with nonhuman life forms" (a position I amplify in "Feminism and the Treatment of Animals").[103] Such a conversation can emerge only when attentive love is directed at the other.

Attentive love is an exercise of the moral imagination, as urged by the numerous sympathy theorists cited above. The term derives, however, specifically from Simone Weil who in 1942 stated:

> The love of our neighbor in all its fullness simply means being able to say to him [or her]: "What are you going through?" It is a recognition that the sufferer exists, not only as a unit in a collection, or a specimen from the social category labeled "unfortunate," but as [an individual], exactly like us, who was one day stamped with a special mark by affliction. For this reason it is enough, but it is indispensable, to know how to look at him [or her] in a certain way.
>
> This way of looking is first of all attentive.[104]

But it is Iris Murdoch who elaborated Weil's insight into a central moral idea, one that numerous feminists have seized upon as establishing the necessary epistemology for a caring ethic.[105] Murdoch developed the idea in several articles and in her book *The Sovereignty of Good*.[106] "Attentive love" is a moral reorientation that requires developing one's powers of attention; it is a discipline similar to that exercised by great artists or scholars (Weil used the idea originally in an essay on the discipline of scholarly study). As other sympathy theorists remarked, this reorientation breaks down solipsistic barriers; it forces attention without, to others and to what they are experiencing. Murdoch notes, "[t]he direction of attention is, contrary to nature, outward, away from self which reduces all to a false unity, toward the great surprising variety of the world, and the ability to so direct attention is love."[107] In acknowledging Weil's coinage of the term, Murdoch says she meant by it "the idea of a just and loving gaze directed upon an individual reality." Such attention, Murdoch urges, is "the characteristic and proper mark of the active moral agent."[108] Like Mercer, Murdoch recognizes that actually seeing another's reality means constituting him or her as a subject with separate needs from one's own: "[t]he more . . . [it is] seen that another . . . has needs and wishes as demanding as one's own, the harder it becomes to treat a person as a thing."[109]

Recognizing the other as a subject means constituting the other as a Thou, not an It, to use Martin Buber's celebrated distinction. While Buber's moral epistemology (which is rooted in the phenomenological existentialism of some of the sympathy theorists noted above), is usually assumed to apply only to humans, promoting a kind of moral humanism, in fact Buber himself applies it to animals and other living beings. In a moving meditation on a tree Buber writes:

> I contemplate a tree.
> I can accept it as a picture. . . .
> I can feel it as a movement. . . .
> I can assign it to a species. . . .

> But it can also happen, if grace and will are joined, that as I contemplate the tree I am drawn into a relation, and the tree ceases to be an It. . . . Does the tree have consciousness, similar to our own? I have no experience of that. . . . What I encounter is neither the soul of a tree nor a dryad, but the tree itself.[110]

In his theory of environmental ethics Paul Taylor calls for a similar attentiveness to the particular reality of individual organisms as the basis for a human relationship to nonhuman life-forms.

> As one becomes more and more familiar with the organism being observed, one acquires a sharpened awareness of the particular way it is living its life. One may become fascinated by it and even get to be involved in its good and bad fortunes. The organism comes to mean something to one as a unique, irreplaceable individual. . . . This progressive development from objective, detached knowledge to the recognition of individuality . . . to a full awareness of an organism's standpoint, is a process of heightening our consciousness of what it means to be an individual living thing.[111]

Taylor further maintains that we must be "'open' to the full existence and nature of the organism . . . let the individuality of the organism come before us, undistorted by our likes and dislikes, our hopes and fears, our interests, wants, and needs. As far as it is humanly possible to do so, we comprehend the organism as it is in itself, not as we want it to be."[112]

A feminist moral epistemology calls for the just and loving attention seen in these examples. Rooting ethics in right seeing is nothing new. As Rosemarie Tong remarks, "even Aristotle said that ethical decisions rest in perception—in perceiving, in *seeing through* one's *experiences* to the moral truth beneath appearances."[113] But in the past, she argues, the great philosophers of the Western tradition "failed in their abstract moral vision because they failed in their daily moral vision. Not seeing the oppression that surrounded them, they shaped an abstract ethics that may have served to protect the interests of those in power."[114] Sympathy theory of the past, long eclipsed, is now reinforced by a powerful new wave of ethical theory proposed by "ethic-of-care" feminists, who derive their ethic from the experience of the oppressed, urging that ethics be rooted in caring practice and an epistemology of attentive love. Such a focus need not—indeed must not—lose sight of the political context in which our moral awareness develops and our moral actions take place. But it also does not lose sight of the individual case. Contrary to Kantian rationalism, it envisages *both* the personal and the political.

Like Buber, people exercising attentive love see the tree; but they also see the logging industry. They see the downed cow in the slaughterhouse pen; but they also see the farming and dairy industry. They see the Silver Spring monkey; but they also see the drug corporations and university collaboration. A political analysis is thus essential—particularly for formulating an effective and appropriate ethical response. But the motivation for that response remains the primary experience of sympathy. By redirecting the national focus to the suffering reality of individual animals, I believe we can reawaken the sympathetic response and reactivate the moral imagination, as outlined in this article. The animal welfare movement need no longer rely solely on abstract utilitarian and rights-based claims of equal justice for animals; rather it should recognize that a viable ethic for the treatment of animals can be rooted in sympathy, a passionate caring about their well-being.

Notes

INTRODUCTION

1. "Club-Swinging Ohioans," photograph by Wallace Kirkland, *Life* magazine (1944), reprinted in *The Best of Life* (New York: Time-Life Books, 1973), 100.

2. One typical account from the period: "Sam Hose was accused of killing his employer, raping his wife. . . . [He] was taken to the town square, tied to a tree and stripped naked. His ears, fingers, and penis were sliced off, and then he was burned alive. Afterward, bits of charred bone, slices of liver and even parts of the tree were sold as souvenirs." Richard Lingeman, "O Pioneer! Ida Wells-Barnett Led the Fight Against Lynching," *New York Times Book Review*, May 15, 2008, 25.

3. During the genocide, the Hutu killers reportedly lifted their voices to the songs of Simon Bikindi, the Hutu songwriter whose genocidal, anti-Tutsi lyrics won him a prison sentence of fifteen years when he was convicted by the International Criminal Court (in 2008).

4. Hugh Trevor-Roper, foreward to Ernst Klee, Willi Dressen, Volker Riess, eds., *"The Good Old Days": The Holocaust as Seen By Its Perpetrators and Bystanders* (New York: The Free Press, 1988), xii. Quoted in Dominick LaCapra, *History and Memory After Auschwitz* (Ithaca: Cornell, 1998), 31.

5. Quoted in LaCapra, 28.

6. Kirk Semple, "Scrutiny for Puerto Rico over Animal Treatment," *New York Times*, March 9, 2008, A14.

7. Unsigned Associated Press story, "China: 50,000 Dogs Killed in Rabies Scare," *New York Times*, August 2, 2006, A9.

8. U.S. news media barely took note of either event, or did so only in passing. The story about the dogs, for example, appeared in the *New York Times* on page A9, as an unsigned Associated Press story, several sentences long (there was no

follow up). As for the pogrom against cats—the *Times* ran no story at all. See Simon Perry, "Olympics Clean-Up Chinese Style: Inside Beijing's Shocking Death Camp for Cats," *Daily Mail*, August 3, 2008. At one Chinese kindergarten, teachers beat to death "six stray cats—including two pregnant females" with sticks—out of fear that the children would try to caress them, and thus expose themselves to deadly disease.

9. Jacques Semelin, *Purify and Destroy: The Political Uses of Massacre and Genocide* (New York: Columbia University Press, 2007), 302.

10. Herbert Marcuse, "Preface: A Note on Dialectic" (1968), *Reason and Revolution: Hegel and the Rise of Social Theory* (Boston: Beacon Press, 1960), ix.

11. Herbert Marcuse, *Studies in Critical Philosophy*, trans. by Joris de Bres (Boston: Beacon Press, 1973: reprint of New Left Books, 1972), 5.

12. Taking other animals seriously "requires a significant reconfiguration of conceptual analysis." Robert Garner, *The Political Theory of Animal Rights* (Manchester: University of Manchester, 2005), 158.

13. Rolf Wiggershaus, *The Frankfurt School: Its Histories, Theories, and Political Significance* (Cambridge, MA: MIT Press, 1995), 6.

14. Herbert Marcuse, *One-Dimensional Man* (Boston: Beacon Press, 1964), 237. Cited by Carl Boggs in his chapter in this volume.

15. Herbert Marcuse, *Eros and Civilization* (Boston: Beacon Press, 1966), 166.

16. Max Horkheimer and Theodor W. Adorno, *Dialectic of Enlightenment: Philosophical Fragments* (Stanford: Stanford University Press, 2002; originally published by Querido press in Amsterdam, 1947), 204. Maurice Merleau-Ponty made a similar observation about the bogus methodology of behavioral research in *La Structure Du Comportement*, though without elaborating as Horkheimer and Adorno do here on the moral horrors of such experiments. "[The] reflex-effect of a pathological disassociation characteristic not of the fundamental behavior of the living being, but of the experimental apparatus which we use in studying it . . . cannot be considered as a constituent of animal behavior except by an anthropomorphic illusion." Maurice Merleau-Ponty, *The Structure of Behavior* (Boston: Beacon Press, 1963), 45–46. See also his preceding discussion on 44.

17. Goethe, *Faust*, trans. by Philip Wayne (Baltimore: Penguin, 1956), 40.

18. Adorno and Horkheimer, *Dialectic of Enlightenment*, 6. Quoted by Bell, below.

19. Jean Chevalier and Alain Gheerbrar *Pengiun Dictionary of Symbols*, trans. John Buchanan Brown (London: Penguin Books, 1996).

20. Horkheimer and Adorno, 203–4.

21. Wilhelm Reich, *The Mass Psychology of Fascism* (New York: Farrar, Strauss, Giroux, 1971), 334–35.

22. As the late Derrida observed: "[b]eyond the edge of the *so-called* human, beyond it but by no means on a single opposing side, rather than 'the Animal' or 'Animal Life,' there is already a heterogeneous multiplicity of the living." Jacques Derrida, "The Animal That Therefore I Am," in Matthew Calarco and Peter Atterton, eds., *Animal Philosophy: Essential Readings in Continental Thought* (New York: Continuum, 2004), 124. Originally published in *L'animal autobiographique: Autour de Jacques Derrida*, ed. Marie-Louise Mallet (Paris: Galilée, 1999).

23. Reich, 338. See also Dominick LaCapra's useful discussion in *History and Its Limits: Human, Animal, Violence* (Ithaca: Cornell University Press, 2009), chapter 6, "Reopening the Question of the Human and the Animal" (149–89).

24. Walter Benjamin, another key figure at the Institut für Sozialforschung, took a serious interest in the significance of animals in Kafka's fiction, seeing the former as symbolic of humanity's desire to recuperate an ethical dimension in our encounters with the animal other. He died while fleeing the Gestapo. Beatrice Hanssen, *Walter Benjamin's Other History: Of Stones, Animals, Human Beings, and Angels* (Berkeley: University of California Press, 2000).

25. Theodor W. Adorno, *Beethoven: The Philosophy of Music*, trans. by Edmund Jephcott (Stanford: Stanford University Press, 1998), 8, fragment 202, quoted by Mendieta below. Italics added.

26. Jacques Semelin, 39.

27. Theodor Adorno, *Minima Moralia: Reflections from Damaged Life*, trans. E. F. N. Jephcott, (London: Verso, 1971), 105.

28. Charles Patterson, *Eternal Treblinka: Our Treatment of Animals and the Holocaust* (New York: Lantern Books, 2002).

29. Derrida, 122.

30. Derrida, 120. Emphasis added.

31. Adorno, 235.

32. J. M. Coetzee captures the psychological horror of the animal liberationist position through the eyes of Elizabeth Costello, the protagonist of his novels *The Lives of Animals* (Princeton, NJ: Princeton University Press, 1999) and *Elizabeth Costello* (New York: Viking, 2003).

33. Edward Maitland, "Address to the Humanitarian League," quoted in Henry Salt, *Animals' Rights: Considered in Relation to Social Progress* (New York and London: Macmillan & Co., 1894), 88.

34. The political right has made much of a controversial British study linking soy consumption to diminished sperm count, suggesting that vegetarianism is "making kids 'gay'" and "feminizing" America. See for example, Jim Rurtz, "Soy Is Making Kids 'Gay,'" *World Net Daily*, December 12, 2006, www.wnd.com/news/article.asp?ARTICLE_ID=53327.

35. "Enemies" quote by David R. Carlin, "Rights, Animal and Human," in *First Things*, No. 105, (August-September 2000), 16–7; "extermination" by Alex Epstein, "The Conference for Human Extinction" (2000), both cited by Sorenson, this volume.

36. In June 2010, thus, far-right ultranationalist activists in Japan staged rallies throughout the country to prevent movie theaters from showing *The Cove* (2009), an award-winning U.S. documentary about the slaughter of dolphins in Taiji—proof that preserving *species right* is as important to Japanese national identity as preserving convenient myths about Japan's military "heroism" during the war. Two years earlier, the same group of Japanese nationalists shut down a Chinese film about the Yasukuni World War II shrine, whose memorialized soldiers include executed Japanese war criminals.

37. Quoted in John Sorenson, this volume.

38. Joel Kovel, *The Enemy of Nature* (London: Zed Books, 2002), 210. See Boggs, this volume.

39. Email exchange on a Marxist listserv, as reported to me by the message recipient, Nancy Zeigler (late 2006).

40. Robert Garner, *The Political Theory of Animal Rights* (Manchester, UK: Manchester University Press, 2005), 165. On a personal note, in 2009 and 2010 I was involved with other international scholars and activists to help design a questionnaire that was to take the pulse of the global Left's possible interest in forming a new International. However, when I suggested to the organizer, Michael Albert (one of the editors of *Z* magazine and Znet) that one of the planks in the new organization's platform include a commitment to "ensur[ing] that the needs and interests of other animals, including their collective and individual interest in not being dominated, exploited, or killed by human beings, not be violated when organizing economic production, infrastructure . . . or devising leisure activities," Albert told me that my proposal "either makes no sense or is ludicrous." He wrote, the "fact is [that] killing many animals is essential at times." Indeed, "one might say that at times we should do it [kill] because it is a lesser evil than some other path that doesn't kill the animals in question—so, for example, we [might] eliminate some disease by wiping out a species . . . for that reason." Therefore, the animal rights position "dooms your side to a minuscule level of support, if any support at all." (personal email exchange, January 10, 2010). If Albert's point is that it is probably not possible to live and produce without injuring any other creatures *inadvertently* in the process, he has a point. But to use the fact that life is suffering, as the Buddhists teach, as a rationale for the institutionalized violence and slavery that our species inflicts on the other animals has about it the sick odor of a monumental bad faith. We are all in a great deal of trouble when leftists defend the utility of killing other animals, or even exterminating whole species—"wiping them out"—in the name of a putatively more transcendent freedom.

41. Nicholas Rupke, *Vivisection in Historical Perspective* (New York: Taylor & Francis, 1990).

42. In this regard, while Foucault and other postmodernist critics have tended to conflate liberal reforms and technologies of domination with one another, there is in fact no reason to throw the baby out with the bath by denying that universal rule of law, broad egalitarianism, and civil rights were genuine advances over what had come before. The same can be said for the new relationship of human beings with other beings in the natural world. The early vivisectionists were attacked chiefly on theological grounds (above all by the Jesuit Order, which furiously opposed the Cartesians' view of life as a machine), though not exclusively on those grounds; later philosophers and social reformers would oppose vivisection as well as other exploitative practices involving animals in the name of Enlightenment reason itself. A critique of technological domination thus arose that was at least in part immanent to that tradition, and it was this critique that eventually culminated in the work of the Frankfurt School in the early twentieth century.

43. The French Revolution seems to have helped consolidate the gains of animal welfare movements in England, Scotland, and elsewhere. See Tristram Stuart, *The Bloodless Revolution: A Cultural History of Vegetarianism from 1600 to Modern Times* (New York: W. W. Norton & Co., 2006).

44. Thomas Young, *An Essay on Humanity to Animals* (London, 1798), quoted by Salt, 119. In fact, the identification of moral concern toward animals with social justice more

broadly conceived antedates even the Age of Enlightenment by a hundred years. As Tristram Stuart demonstrates in *The Bloodless Revolution*, the antinomian sects that sprang up in the wake of the English Civil War in the seventeenth century at times united a spiritual vision of the New Jerusalem (a Christian utopia on earth) with a vegetarian ethic.

45. Stewart, 296. It should be noted, however, that Oswald's advocacy of pacifism toward nonhuman beings was also accompanied by a ferocious appetite for revolutionary violence in the name of justice—not the last time that an animal advocate would oppose violence toward nonhumans, but promote violence toward at least some humans. See Stewart's discussion, 296–300.

46. Salt, 92. Here we might note in passing that the socialist and unionist *cri de coeur* that workers ought not to be treated "like animals"—a theme made explicit in Emile Zola's novel *Germinal* (1885) about coal miners and, decades later (and more famously), in Upton Sinclair's *The Jungle* (1906), about the horrific, mechanized mass slaughter of pigs in the Chicago stockyards—were themselves indirectly indebted to the animal welfare movement, insofar as the latter had already primed public consciousness for the notion that not "even" animals deserved to be treated *like animals*. One of the most moving passages in Zola's novel concerns Bataille, a horse condemned to labor, live, and finally die underground, not having seen the sun or breathed fresh air for ten years. Although Bataille stands in metonymically for the French working class in the novel, the figuration only succeeds because the author has realistically rendered the animal's experiences, memories, and emotions, making him into a wholly sympathetic character.

47. Peter Kropotkin, *Mutual Aid: A Factor of Evolution* (Montreal: Black Rose Books, 1989), 54.

48. Charles Fourier and Julia Franklin, *Selections from the Works of Fourier* (London: Swan Sonnenschein, 1901), 203.

49. *The Marx-Engels Reader*, second edition, ed. Robert C. Tucker (New York: W. W. Norton, 1978), 496.

50. Precisely as a hunter, Engels admired the intelligence and tactical brilliance of foxes, who displayed intimate knowledge of their terrain and used a variety of consciously deceptive strategies to throw pursuing hounds off their scent. However, this fact does not appear to have left him with any qualms about participating in this murderous sport.

51. See John Sanbonmatsu, "The Subject of Freedom at the End of History: Socialism Beyond Humanism," *American Journal of Economics and Sociology*, Vol. 66, No. 1 (January 2007), 217–35. Published in Daniel Shannon and Steve Hicks, eds., *The Challenges of Globalization: Rethinking Nature, Culture, and Freedom* (Basil Blackwell, 2007).

52. The burgeoning new field of cognitive ethology, which seeks to describe the animal *mind*, is completely remapping what scientists thought they knew about animal cognition and experience. See especially, among the many works available, Lesley Rogers, *Minds of Their Own: Thinking and Awareness in Animals* (Boulder: Westview, 1998), Colin Allen and Marc Bekoff, *Species of Mind: The Philosophy and Biology of Cognitive Ethology* (Cambridge, MA: MIT Press, 1999), Marc Bekoff, *Minding Other Animals: Awareness, Emotions, and Heart* (Oxford, UK: Oxford University Press, 2002). For the reader seeking only a brief layperson's overview of some

recent experimental research in cognitive ethology, see *Inside the Animal Mind* (Nature, 2000), the three-part film series on animal cognition and experience, and *Animal Einsteins* (Scientific American Frontiers/PBS, 1998). On language use among other primates, see especially Sue Savage-Rumbaugh, Stuart G. Shanker, and Talbot J. Taylor, *Apes, Language, and the Human Mind* (Oxford, UK: Oxford University Press, 1998).

53. L. S. Sayigh, H. C. Esch, R. S. Wells, and V. M. Janik, "Facts about Signature Whistles of Bottlenose Dolpins, *Tursiops truncatus*," *Animal Behaviour*, 74(6): 1631–42.

54. Hal Whitehead, Luke Rendell, et al., "Culture and Conservation of Nonhumans with Reference to Whales and Dolphins"; Mark Peter Simmonds, "Into the Brains of Whales"; Paola Cavalieri, "Whales as Persons," in Susan J. Armstrong and Richard G. Botzler, eds., *The Animal Ethics Reader*, second edition (London and New York: Routledge, 2008), 180–92, 193–203, and 204–7, respectively.

55. Irene Pepperberg, *Alex and Me* (New York: HarperCollins, 2008).

56. As various ethologists have cautioned, however, the fact that other species "fail" the mirror test may only point to the limitations of the research apparatus, which of course privileges the visual field over other sensory qualia that may be more significant or decisive for other species.

57. David Abram, *The Spell of the Sensuous: Perception and Language in a More-Than-Human World* (New York: Vintage Books, 1997).

58. Research by Tetsuo Matsuzawa at the Primate Research Institute at the University of Kyoto. Readers can view videos of the chimpanzees beating their human peers on a memory test with stunning efficiency on YouTube.

59. "Pigeons and Baboons Are Capable of Higher-Level Cognition, Behavioral Studies Show," *Science Daily*, February 16, 2009. (www.sciencedaily.com/releases/2009/02/090212141143.htm). The quotation is from Ed Wasserman, a scientist at the University of Iowa and the director of the study cited in the article. Needless to say, in citing such studies I in no way wish to endorse the use of captive animals in scientific research.

60. Some of the most important and original work on animality and speciesism today is being done by phenomenologists, many of whom are applying Maurice Merleau-Ponty's empirical description of human embodied consciousness to other sentient beings and to our intersubjective relations with them. See especially Ralph R. Acampora, *Corporal Compassion: Animal Ethics and Philosophy of the Body* (Pittsburgh, PA: University of Pittsburgh Press, 2006), as well as Peter Steeves, ed., *Animal Others: On Ethics, Ontology, and Animal Life* (Albany: State University of New York Press, 1999), Charles S. Brown and Ted Toadvine, eds., *Eco-Phenomenology: Back to the Earth Itself* (Albany: State University of New York Press, 2003), and *Phenomenology and the Nonhuman Animal* (Corrine Painter and Christian Lotz, Springer Netherlands, 2009).

61. Nor should we discount the possibility, even the probability, that other beings "experience," if not contemplate, *metaphysical* questions. In *Lives of Animals*, novelist J. M. Coetzee speculates on the thought-process of a captive ape named Sultan who is being coerced by means of starvation to complete an absurd or

meaningless set of tasks for the obscure benefit of the human researcher: "'Sultan knows: Now one is supposed to think. That is what the bananas up there are about. The bananas are there to make one think, to spur one to the limits of one's thinking. But what must one think? One thinks: Why is he starving me. One thinks: What have I done? Why has he stopped liking me. But none of these are the right thoughts. Even a more complicated thought—for instance: What is wrong with him, what misconception does he have of me, that leads him to believe it is easier for me to reach a banana hanging from a wire than to pick up a banana from the floor. . . . At every turn Sultan is driven to think the less interesting thought. From the purity of speculation (Why do men behave like this?) he is relentlessly propelled toward lower, practical, instrumental reason (How does one use this to get that?) and thus toward acceptance of himself as primarily an organism with an appetite that needs to be satisfied. Although his entire history, from the time his mother was shot and he was captured, through his voyage in a cage to imprisonment on this island prison camp and the sadistic games . . . a carefully plotted psychological regimen conducts him *away* from ethics and metaphysics toward the humbler reaches of practical reason.'" Coetzee, 28–29. Coetzee has of course stacked his deck in favor of his audience of self-regarding primates. In point of fact, there is no reason to doubt that a cat or lobster being boiled alive knows that *this is happening to me* or that *they are doing this to me.*

Benton is therefore right to suggest that in the context of the new empirical findings, our analytical starting point as critical theorists ought to be the "recognition of a need which is common to both humans and non-human animals," rather than to set out from the presumption that the only needs that have significance, that matter, are those relating to our ostensibly "unique" capacities (language, thought, culture, and so forth). In other words, the positive need not to experience one's body being violated or dismembered, for example, like the need to feel secure in the world, is not only an objective need, but a universal one—that is, a need that transcends all species boundaries. I may not know what it is like to be a bat (to invoke Thomas Nagel's famous essay), but I can guess what it would be like to be a fully conscious bat dying of dehydration in a farmer's fruit net.

62. Bill Martin, a Marxist, has courageously defended the importance of animal liberation to socialist practice in his book *Ethical Marxism: The Categorical Imperative of Liberation* (Chicago: Open Court Books, 2008). Unfortunately, however, Martin's book is also an apologia for Mao's revolutionary excesses in China. Needless to say, in addition to the millions of *human* animals who were repressed by or suffered under Mao's policies, the nonhuman ones did not fare well either. For an account of the apocalyptic ecological consequences of Maoism, see Judith Shapiro, *Mao's War Against Nature: Politics and the Environment in Revolutionary China* (Cambridge, UK: Cambridge University Press, 2001). In keeping with anthropocentric convention, Shapiro herself does not disaggregate nonhuman animals from the category of "nature" as such, so it is not possible to get a full picture of their fate under Maoism.

63. S. Mills and Williams, "Political Animals," *Marxism Today*, April 1986: 30–33, quoted in Garner, 108.

64. As Barbara Noske shows in her book, *Beyond Boundaries: Humans and Animals* (Montreal: Black Rose Books, 1997), Marx's theory of alienation can be easily turned into a critique of the estrangement other beings experience under capitalism.

65. Salt, 93.

66. See Carolyn Merchant, *The Death of Nature: Women, Ecology, and the Scientific Revolution* (New York: Harper, 1990).

67. Karl Marx, quoted by Georg Lukács in *History and Class Consciousness*, Rodney Livingstone, trans. (Cambridge, MA: The MIT Press, 1971), 130–31.

68. Nicole Shukin, *Animal Capital: Rendering Life in Biopolitical Times* (Minneapolis: University of Minnesota Press, 2009), 87.

69. Charles Patterson, *Eternal Treblinka*.

70. Thus, by the 1940s, meat had been carefully purged of its former dark association with bloodletting and tied instead into the status needs of the rising middle class. "Sure—you're right in liking meat" read the ad copy of one ad in the period (www.starling-fitness.com/archives/2009/04/01/meat-youre-right-in-liking-it/); "Listen to the Compliments!" (Swift's Beef, 1946) read another. Adclassix.com (www.adclassix.com/ads/46swiftbeef.htm).

71. Animals also featured in the consolidation of national identity, as suggested in a 1929 advertisement that described Clark's Pork and Beans as "Canada's National Dish." The Herbert Hoover Presidential Library and Museum (http://hoover.archives.gov/info/faq.html#chicken).

72. Shukin, 16.

73. Of the 1.5 million workers employed in U.S. food manufacture today, more than one in three are employed in plants that kill and/or process animal products. Food manufacturing accounts for more than 10 percent of U.S. manufacturing activity. U.S. Bureau of Labor Statistics, 2006, www.bls.gov/oco/cg/cgs011.htm.

74. Hence propaganda outlets like the Center for Consumer Freedom, one of the shell organizations founded by right-wing corporate lobbyist Richard Berman. Stephanie Strom, "Non-Profit Advocate Carves Out a For-Profit Niche," *New York Times*, June 17, 2010, A16.

75. Frederick Kaufman, "The Food Bubble: How Wall Street Starved Millions and Got Away with It," *Harper's*, July 2010, 27–34.

76. David Nibert, "The Political Economy of Beef: Oppression of Cows and Other Devalued Groups in Latin America," paper presented to the American Sociological Association (Montreal, 2006).

77. In some cases, the crackdown on animal rights activism is merely part of a broader attempt by the state to quash dissent. In Britain, for example, the Protection from Harassment Act (1997) and Serious Organised Crime and Police Act (2005) have "effectively criminalised whole areas of peaceful political activism, or at least made its legality . . . a grey area." Gerry Nobody, "Some Observations on State Repression," *Indymedia Ireland*, April 27, 2010 (www.indymedia.ie/article/96459). In other cases, however—as in the U.S.—the state has either fashioned or retooled legislation specifically with an eye toward rolling back animal rights. Thus, "[i]n Austria, Section 278a of the Penal Code (ostensibly intended to combat organized crime) is being used to persecute the animal rights movement" (Ibid).

78. This is not to say, however, that the Continental philosophical tradition historically has historically done better than the analytic tradition in bringing animal issues to the fore of scholarly criticism. On the contrary, as Matthew Calarco and Peter Atterton acknowledge in their edited anthology, *Animal Philosophy* (New York: Continuum, 2004), "[i]t is . . . with a certain amount of incredulity and astonishment that we learn that Continental philosophy has only rarely given serious attention to the animal question" (xv). Nor is it clear that the new Continental inflection in animal studies is an unalloyed good. In particular, it is troubling that so much of that work is being written in a poststructuralist and postmodernist key. Although one can take away something valuable from such thinkers as Derrida, Agamben, and Foucault (to name a few), the poststructuralist approach is only one method among many, and it does not come without serious limitations or drawbacks for a radical politics. As Barbara Noske and Marjorie Scholtmeijer have pointed out, postmodernist and post-humanist discourses that displace the human subject have tended to displace the animal subject as well, moving critical theory from "human-centerd" discourses to "human-discourse-centered" ones (Noske, x). One consequence of this move has been to blunt the political and ethical edge of the animal liberationist critique. See, for example, Zipporah Weisberg, "The Broken Promises of Monsters: Haraway, Animals, and the Humanist Legacy," *Journal for Critical Animal Studies*, vol. 7, no. 2 (2009), 21–61. On some of the problems with poststructuralist theory as a guide to radical critique and praxis in general, see John Sanbonmatsu, *The Postmodern Prince: Critical Theory, Left Strategy, and the Making of a New Political Subject* (New York: Monthly Review, 2004). This said, the Continental tradition at its broadest and best includes radical feminism, Marxism, anarchism, phenomenology, and the Frankfurt School—approaches which potentially bring a greater complement of epistemological, political, and historical insights to bear on the nature of speciesism than we have a right to expect from the corner of a tradition that often seems preoccupied with methodistic debates about the merits of preference utilitarianism versus neo-Kantianism.

79. Carol Adams and Josephine Donovan, eds., *Beyond Animal Rights: A Feminist Caring Ethics for the Treatment of Animals* (New York: Continuum, 1996).

80. After discussing human dominion over other animals in *Dialectic of Enlightenment*, Horkheimer and Adorno then proceed to an analysis of patriarchy. "The woman is not subject. She does not produce but looks after the producers, a living monument to the long-vanished time of the self-sufficient household. She became an embodiment of biological function, an image of nature, in the suppression of which this civilization's claim to glory lay. To dominate nature boundlessly, to turn the cosmos into an endless hunting ground. It was the purpose of reason, on which man prided himself (206)." For a similar analysis, but from a contemporary feminist perspective, see Maria Mies, *Patriarchy and Accumulation on a World Scale* (London: Zed Books, 1986).

81. Catharine A. MacKinnon, "Of Mice and Men: A Feminist Fragment on Animal Rights," in Cass Sunstein and Martha Nussbaum, eds., *Animal Rights: Current Debates and New Directions* (Oxford, UK: Oxford University Press, 2004), 263–76.

82. See for instance Gary Francione, *Introduction to Animal Rights* (Philadelphia: Temple University Press, 2007), 149.

83. Chris Gale, the British Labour Party and animal rights campaigner, has drawn much-needed attention to PETA's use of misogynistic sexual imagery and even pornography in its animal rights campaigns. See Gale's website, http://chriswgale.typepad.com/.

84. For a discussion of how pornography has infiltrated and corrupted feminism and the Left more broadly, see Gale Dines, *Pornland: How Porn Has Hijacked Our Sexuality* (Boston: Beacon Press, 2010).

85. Perhaps he was merely speaking figuratively, but Peter Singer, for example, writes that it was the *idea* of animal rights that led to animal welfare and rights reforms. Peter Singer, "Ethics Beyond Species and Beyond Instincts," in Sunstein and Nussbaum, 86.

86. The analytic philosopher Tzachi Zamir, thus, suggests that animal rights can be achieved without the need to challenge any "fundamental" aspects of speciesist belief—through "pragmatic" argument alone. Tzachi Zamir, *Ethics and the Beast* (Princeton, NJ: Princeton University Press, 2007).

87. Andrew Martin, "As Recession Deepens, So Does Milk Surplus," *New York Times*, January 1, 2009, B1.

88. Jehangir S. Pocha, "Outsourcing Animal Testing: U.S. Firm Setting Up Drug-Trial Facilities in China, Where Scientists Are Plentiful but Activists Aren't," *Boston Globe*, November 25, 2006.

89. Glenn Rice, quoted by Pocha.

90. Michael H. de la Merced, "Charles River Said to Be Near a Deal for Drug Research Firm in China," *New York Times*, April 25, 2010.

91. See *Natural Relations: Ecology, Animal Rights, and Social Justice* (London: Verso, 1993), Ted Benton's important book-length defense of what a non-anthropocentric Marxism would look like.

92. I am referring here to James O'Connor's analysis of "the second contradiction" of capitalism—the tendency of the capitalist system to degrade its own conditions of production and reproduction, chiefly by destroying "natural resources." See O'Connor, *Natural Causes* (New York: Guilford, 1997).

93. See especially Bill Martin, *Ethical Marxism* (Chicago: Open Court, 2008), Part 3, and Bob Torres, *Making a Killing: The Political Economy of Animal Rights* (AK Press, 2007).

94. "This explains why the necrophile is truly enamored of force. Just as for the lover of life the fundamental polarity in man is that between male and female, for the necrophile there exists another and very different polarity: that between those who have the power to kill and those who lack this power. For him there only two 'sexes': the powerful and the powerless; the killers and the killed." Erich Fromm, *The Heart of Man: Its Genius for Good and Evil,* Religious Perspectives, vol. 12 (New York: Harper and Row, 1964), 40. Fromm's basic insight remains, but needs to be augmented with a radical feminist perspective about the implacably gendered nature of this bifurcation in human consciousness. See for example Nancy Hartsock, *Money, Sex, and Power: Toward a Feminist Historical Materialism* (New York: Longman, 1983), 155–85.

95. Adorno, 111.

CHAPTER 1

1. John Berger, "Why Look at Animals?" in *The Language of the Birds: Tales, Texts, & Poems of Interspecies Communication*, ed. David M. Guss (New York: North Point Press, 1985), 286–87.

2. Dale Jamieson, "Against Zoos," in *In Defense of Animals: The Second Wave*, ed. Peter Singer (Malden, MA: Blackwell Publishing, 2006), 139.

3. Jamieson, 140.

4. Harry R. Lewis, "America's Debt to the Hen," *National Geographic* (April 1927): 453.

5. William A. Jasper, "Marketing," in *American Poultry History 1823–1973*, ed. John L. Skinner et al., American Poultry Historical Society, Inc. (Madison, WI: American Printing and Publishing, 1974), 367.

6. Donald D. Bell and William D. Weaver, Jr., eds., *Commercial Chicken Meat and Egg Production*, 5th ed. (Norwell, MA: Kluwer Academic Publishers, 2002), 87, 805.

7. Michael Watts, "The Age of the Chicken" (paper), presented at The Chicken: Its Biological, Social, Cultural, and Industrial History: An International Conference (May 17–19, 2002), Yale University, 15–16.

8. John Webster, *Animal Welfare: A Cool Eye Towards Eden* (Oxford, UK: Blackwell Science Ltd., 1994), 156.

9. Vicki Forsberg, "Tunnel Housing" (email to Karen Davis, February 20, 2003).

10. E. Wemelsfelder, "Animal Boredom: Do Animals Miss Being Alert and Active?" *Applied Animal Behaviour: Past, Present and Future: Proceedings of the International Congress Edinburgh 1991*, ed. M. C. Appleby et al. (UK: Universities Federation for Animal Welfare, 199), 120.

11. Wemelsfelder, 122.

12. Michael W. Fox, "Animal Freedom and Well-Being: Want or Need?" *Applied Animal Ethology* 11 (1983–1984), 209.

13. David Kestenbaum, "Engineered Animals." *NPR News, Morning Edition*, December 4, 2001, 5.

14. Paul B. Thompson, "Welfare as an Ethical Issue: Are Blind Chickens the Answer?" in Richard Reynnells, ed., *Bioethics Symposium: Proactive Approaches to Controversial Welfare and Ethical Concerns in Poultry Science* (Washington, DC: U.S. Department of Agriculture, 2007), 3–5.

15. Patricia Dickenson, "Insight into Light and Reproduction: Researcher Delves into Why Naturally Blind Chickens Perform Better," *Research News*, University of Guelph, Ontario (2007). www.uoguelph.ca/research/news/articles/2007/June/light_and_reproduction.shtml

16. Barbara P. Glenn, "How Will Biotechnology Impact Agricultural Animal Welfare?" in *Future Trends in Animal Agriculture: Food Animal Agriculture in 2020*, ed. Richard Reynnells (Washington, DC: U.S. Department of Agriculture, 2007), 48.

17. Chris Sigurdson, "Purdue's 'Kinder, Gentler Chicken' Moves into Real-World Test," *Feedstuffs*, January 16, 2005, 47.

18. Wiebe Van der Sluis, "Featherless: The Future or an Un-Saleable Concept," *World Poultry*, vol. 23, no.6 (April 4, 2007). http://tinyurl.com/2c655m.

19. Aaron Priel, "The Featherless Broiler Is Ready to Go to Market," *World Poultry*, vol. 23, no. 2 (2007), 25.

20. Raphael Lemkin, *Axis Rule in Occupied Europe: Laws of Occupation, Analysis of Government, Proposals for Redress* (Washington, DC: Carnegie Endowment for International Peace, 1944).

21. Roberta Kalechofsky, *Animal Suffering and the Holocaust: The Problem with Comparisons* (Marblehead, MA: Micah Publications, 2003), 55.

22. Jean-Paul Sartre, quoted in Ward Churchill, *A Little Matter of Genocide: Holocaust and Denial in the Americas 1492 to the Present* (San Francisco: City Lights Books, 1997), 416.

23. Churchill, 421.

24. Enzo Traverso, *The Origin of Nazi Violence*, trans. Janet Lloyd (New York: The New Press, 2003), 51.

25. Traverso, 54.

26. Perrier, quoted in Traverso, 57.

27. Sartre, quoted in Churchill, 416.

28. Lewis, 457, 467.

29. GRAIN, "Fowl Play: The Poultry Industry's Central Role in the Bird Flu Crisis," February 2006, 2. www.grain.org/go/birdflu.

30. GRAIN, 13.

31. Ahmed El-Amin, "Intensive Meat Production a Danger to Food Supply, Warns FAO," *Food Production Daily.com*, September 17, 2007.

32. James V. Craig, *Domestic Animal Behavior: Causes and Implications for Animal Care and Management* (Englewood Cliffs, NJ: Prentice-Hall, 1981), 243–44.

33. David Irvin, "Control Debate, Growers Advised," *Arkansas Democrat-Gazette*, September 22, 2007. www.nwanews.com/adg/Business/202171/.

34. In *The Animal Estate: The English and Other Creatures in the Victorian Age* (Cambridge, MA: Harvard University Press, 1989), Harriet Ritvo shows how animals became surrogates for nineteenth-century agendas, in particular Britain's imperial enterprise in which "material animals" and "rhetorical animals" embodied the most powerful possible symbol of human possession and control: "As material animals were at the complete disposal of human beings, so rhetorical animals offered unusual opportunities for manipulation; their positions in the physical world and in the universe of discourse were mutually reinforcing" (Ritvo, 5).

35. NHGRI, "Chicken Genome Assembled: First Avian Genome Now Available to Scientists Worldwide," National Humane Genome Research Institute, March 1, 2004. www.nhgri.hih.gov/11510730.

36. Glenn, 46.

37. Marc Bekoff, *The Emotional Lives of Animals: A Leading Scientist Explores Animal Joy, Sorrow, and Empathy—and Why They Matter* (Novato, CA: New World Library, 2007), 33.

38. Bekoff, 55.

39. Jonathan Balcombe, *Pleasurable Kingdom: Animals and the Nature of Feeling Good* (London: Macmillan, 2006).

40. Marian Stamp Dawkins, "Feelings Do Not a Science Make," *BioScience*, vol. 57, no. 1 (2007), 84. www.biosciencemag.org.

41. Richard D. Ryder, *Animal Revolution: Changing Attitudes Towards Speciesism* (Cambridge, MA: Basil Blackwell, 1989), 163.

42. Gaby Wenig, "Humane Atonement or Animal Cruelty?" *Jewish Journal of Greater Los Angeles*, October 30, 2003, 2.

43. Glenn, 45.

44. Hannah Arendt, *Eichmann in Jerusalem: A Report on the Banality of Evil* (New York: Penguin Books, 1964), 48.

45. Arendt, 20.

46. Basant K. Lal, "Hindu Perspectives on the Use of Animals in Science," in *Animal Sacrifices: Religious Perspectives on the Use of Animals in Science*, ed. Tom Regan (Philadelphia: Temple University Press, 1986), 201.

47. Lal, 206.

48. Ibid., 200.

49. Christopher Chapple, "Noninjury to Animals: Jaina and Buddhist Perspectives," in Regan, ed., 219, 226.

50. Porphyry, *On Abstinence from Animal Food*, ed. Esme Wynne-Tyson and trans. Thomas Taylor (London & Fontwell: Centaur Press, Ltd., 1965), 36–7.

51. Richard H. Schwartz, *Judaism and Vegetarianism* (New York: Lantern Books, 2001), 125.

52. Elijah Judah Schochet, *Animal Life in Jewish Tradition: Attitudes and Relationships* (New York: Ktav Publishing House, 1984), 243.

53. Virgil Butler and Laura Alexander, "'Slaughterhouse Worker Turned Activist': UPC Talks with Virgil Butler and Laura Alexander," *Poultry Press*, vol. 14, no. 3, (Fall 2004): 1–4. www.upc-online.org/slaughter/.

54. Isaac Bashevis Singer, "The Slaughterer," *The Collected Stories* (New York: Farrar, Straus and Giroux, 1982; originally published 1935), 207.

55. Balcombe, quoted in Bekoff, 54.

56. A. W. Schorger, *The Wild Turkey: Its History and Domestication* (Norman: University of Oklahoma Press, 1966), 283–84.

57. Thompson, 3.

58. Ibid.

59. Lesley J. Rogers, *Minds of Their Own: Thinking and Awareness in Animals* (Boulder, CO: Westview Press, 1997), 185.

60. Karen Davis, *More Than a Meal: The Turkey in History, Myth, Ritual, and Reality* (New York: Lantern Books, 2001), 130–31. Karen Davis, *The Holocaust and the Henmaid's Tale: A Case for Comparing Atrocities* (New York: Lantern Books, 2005).

61. "Romania: What Happened to the Children," *Turning Point*, January 16, 1997, ABC News, Transcript #174.

62. Fox, 208.

63. Regan, 53–4.

64. Peter Singer, *Animal Liberation* (New York: Avon Books, 1990), 7.

65. Robert Burruss, "The Future of Eggs," *The Baltimore Sun*, December 29, 1993, 16A. Excerpted in Karen Davis, *Prisoned Chickens, Poisoned Eggs: An Inside Look at*

the Modern Poultry Industry, revised edition (Summertown, TN: Book Publishing Company, 2009), 142–3. See also Karen Davis, "The Experimental Use of Chickens and Other Birds in Biomedical and Agricultural Research," *United Poultry Concerns* (2003), www.upc-online.org/genetic/experimental.htm.

66. Rogers, 184–85.

67. Lesley Rogers, *The Development of Brain and Behaviour in the Chicken* (Wallingford, Oxon [UK]: CAB International, 1995), 213.

68. Andrew Purvis, "Pecking Order." *The Guardian* (UK), October 4, 2006.

69. Rogers (1997), 185.

70. Oliver Broudy, "The Practical Ethicist," *Slate*, May 8, 2006. www.salon.com/books/int/2006/05/08/singer/print.html.

71. Robert J. Etches, "Beyond Freezing Semen," Presentation, *Proceedings: First International Symposium on the Artificial Insemination of Poultry* (June 17–19, 1995), eds. M. R. Bakst and G. J. Wishart (Savoy, IL: Poultry Science Association, 1995).

72. Karen Davis, "Researching the Heart: An Interview with Eldon Kienholz," *The Animals' Agenda*, (April 1991), 13.

73. Oliver Sacks, "The Abyss," *The New Yorker*, September 24, 2007, 108.

74. Erich D. Jarvis, Onur Güntürkün, et al., "Avian Brains and a New Understanding of Vertebrate Brain Evolution," *Nature Neuroscience Reviews* vol. 6 (February 2005), 151–59. See also Avianbrain.org and Rick Weiss, "Bird Brains Get Some New Names, And New Respect," *The Washington Post*, February 1, 2005, A10. www.upc-online.org/alerts/20105post.htm.

75. Ian J. H. Duncan, "The Science of Animal Well-Being," *Animal Welfare Information Center Newsletter*, vol. 4, no. 1, (Washington, DC: National Agricultural Library, January-March 1993): 1, 4–7.

76. Marian Stamp Dawkins, *Through Our Eyes Only? The Search for Animal Consciousness* (Oxford, UK: W.H. Freeman and Company Limited, 1993), 153.

CHAPTER 2

1. Karl Marx, *Capital: A Critique of Political Economy*, vol. 3., trans. David Fernbach (London: Penguin Books, 1981).

2. Rosemary Hennessy, *Profit and Pleasure: Sexual Identities in Late Capitalism* (New York: Routledge, 2000), 95.

3. Terry Eagleton, *Ideology: An Introduction* (New York: Verso, 1991), 85.

4. James R. Simmons, *Feathers and Fur on the Turnpike* (Boston: The Christopher Publishing House, 1938).

5. Richard T. T. Forman and Lauren E. Alexander, "Roads and Their Major Ecological Effects," *Annual Review of Ecology and Systematics*, vol. 29 (1988), 212–13.

6. Roger M. Knutson, *Flattened Fauna: A Field Guide to Common Animals of Roads, Streets, and Highways* (Berkeley: Ten Speed Press, 2006), 3.

7. Ibid., 2.

8. Ingrid Newkirk, "Let Them Eat Road Kill," *The Animals' Agenda*, vol. 19, no. 3 (1999), 33.

9. PETA, "Roadkill: Meat without the Murder." http://peta.org/feat/roadkill/.

10. Barbara Noske, "Two Movements and Human-Animal Continuity: Positions, Assumptions, Contradictions," *Animal Liberation Philosophy and Policy Journal*, vol. 2, no. 1, 1–12 (2004), 3.

11. David Nibert, *Animal Rights/Human Rights: Entanglements of Oppression and Liberation* (New York: Rowman & Littlefield Publishers, 2002), 10.

12. Gary L. Francione, *Introduction to Animal Rights: Your Child or the Dog?* (Philadelphia, PA: Temple University Press, 2000), 166.

13. Craig Brestup, *Disposable Animals: Ending the Tragedy of Throwaway Pets* (Leander, TX: Camino Bay Books, 1997), 15.

14. Noske, 3.

15. Carol J. Adams, *The Sexual Politics of Meat: A Feminist-Vegetarian Critical Theory* (New York: Continuum, 1991), 47–48.

16. Bettina Heinz and Ronald Lee, "Getting Down to the Meat: The Symbolic Construction of Meat Consumption," *Communication Studies*, vol. 49, no. 1 (1998), 86.

17. Jonathan Burt, "The Illumination of the Animal Kingdom: The Role of Light and Electricity in Animal Representation," *Society and Animals*, vol. 9, no. 3 (1991), 203–28.

18. Hennessey.

19. John Berger, *About Looking* (New York: Pantheon Books, 1980).

20. Mike Michael, "Roadkill: Between Humans, Nonhuman Animals, and Technologies," *Society & Animals*, vol. 12, no. 4 (2004), 285.

21. Fredric Jameson, "Reification and Utopia in Mass Culture," *Social Text*, vol. 1, no. 1 (1979), 131.

22. Available for viewing online at www.youtube.com/watch?v=E-M5_kH5fUI.

23. Peter Freund and George Martin, "The Commodity That Is Eating the World: The Automobile, the Environment, and Capitalism," *Capitalism Nature Socialism*, vol. 7, no. 4 (1996), 3.

24. Andrew Simms, *Ecological Debt: The Health of the Planet and the Wealth of Nations* (Ann Arbor, MI: Pluto Press, 2005); Michael Renner, "Vehicle Production Continues to Expand," in *Vital Signs 2006–2007: The Trends That Are Shaping Our Future*, ed. Linda Starke (New York: W.W. Norton & Company, 2006), 64.

25. Nielsen, 150.

26. Filippo Tommaso Marinetti, *Foundation and Manifesto of Futurism* (1909). http://users.dickinson.edu/~rhyne/232/Eight/Marinetti.html.

27. Simms, 26.

28. Janet Sawin, "Making Better Energy Choices," in Linda Starke, ed. *State of the World 2004—Special Focus: The Consumer Society* (New York: W. W. Norton & Company, 2004), 29.

29. Peter Freund and George Martin, "Speaking About Accidents: The Ideology of Auto Safety," *Health*, vol. 1, no. 2, 167–82.

30. Mark Dery, "'Always Crashing the Same Car': A Head-On Collision with the Technosphere," *The Sociological Review*, vol. 54, no. s1, (2006), 228.

31. John Urry, "Inhabiting the Car," *The Sociological Review*, vol. 54, no. s1 (2006), 17–31.

32. John Bellamy Foster, *Ecology Against Capitalism* (New York: Monthly Review Press, 2002), 99.

33. Peter Freund and George Martin, *The Ecology of the Automobile* (Montreal: Black Rose Books, 1993), 86.

34. Ibid., 11.

35. Richard T. T. Forman, "Road Ecology's Promise: What's Around the Bend?" *Environment*, vol. 46, no. 3 (2004), 9.

36. Katie Alvord, *Divorce Your Car! Ending the Love Affair with the Automobile* (Gabriola Island: New Society Publishers, 2000), 117.

37. Michael, 278.

38. Noske, 6.

39. Deborah Lupton, "Monsters in Metal Cocoons: 'Road Rage' and Cyborg Bodies," *Body & Society*, vol. 5, no. 1 (1999), 57–72.

CHAPTER 3

1. Peter Singer, *Animal Liberation* (New York: Avon Books, 1975), xii.

2. Tom Regan, *The Case for Animal Rights* (Berkeley: University of California Press, 2004), xiii.

3. Jeremy Rifkin, *Beyond Beef* (New York: Penguin, 1992), 235.

4. Regan, *The Case for Animal Rights*, 332.

5. John Robbins, *The Food Revolution* (Berkeley: Conari Press, 2001), 220.

6. Gary Francione, *Introduction to Animal Rights* (Philadelphia, PA: Temple University Press, 2001), xxiv.

7. Rifkin, *Beyond Beef*, 283.

8. Jeffrey Moussaieff Masson, *When Elephants Weep* (New York: Delacorte Press, 1995), 236.

9. Jane Goodall, *Through a Window* (Boston: Houghton Mifflin, 2000), 250.

10. Singer, *Animal Liberation*, 235.

11. Ken Midkiff, *The Meat You Eat* (New York: St. Martin's, 2004), 39.

12. Upton Sinclair, *The Jungle* (Tucson, AZ: Sharp Press, 2003).

13. Robbins, *The Food Revolution*, 211.

14. Ibid., 221. See also Midkiff, 13.

15. Masson, *When Elephants Weep*, 29.

16. See Matthew Scully, *Dominion* (New York: St. Martin's, 2002).

17. For a powerful statement on stewardship values situated within a philosophical discourse, see Holmes Rolston III, "Challenges in Environmental Ethics," in Michael E. Zimmerman et al., eds., *Environmental Philosophy* (Englewood Cliffs, NJ: Prentice-Hall, 1993), 135–57.

18. Regan's views are best summarized in his *The Case for Animal Rights* (2004 edition), chapter 9. This approach, in my opinion, is superior to either the utilitarian framework adopted by Singer (in *Animal Liberation* and elsewhere) or the capabilities approach employed by Martha Nussbaum in her *Frontiers of Justice* (Cambridge, MA: Harvard University Press, 2006). Both views allow for entirely too many qualifications

and exceptions to any rule against animal cruelty and exploitation. The weaknesses of utilitarianism are well known: virtually anything can be justified if it can be said to maximize pleasure for the majority. In the case of Nussbaum, she argues forcefully for a ban on all forms of cruelty to animals but then makes room for exceptions when "there is plausible reason for the killing" (393). Elsewhere she writes that the use of animals for food and for biomedical research provide thorny, but still unresolved, moral questions (403). Regan's case for a strict abolitionism, of course, permits of no such moral ambiguity.

19. Ted Benton, *Natural Relations: Ecology, Animal Rights, and Social Justice* (London: Verso, 1998), 152.

20. "Is Meat Sustainable?" *Worldwatch* (July–August, 2004), 12.

21. The widely-acclaimed Albert Gore documentary, *An Inconvenient Truth,* provides a brilliant investigation into the problem of global warming, but contains not a single word about the impact of agriculture, meat, and dietary habits on this aspect of the ecological crisis.

22. Robbins, *The Food Revolution,* 248.

23. *Our Food, Our Future* (New York: EarthSave International, 2006), 13.

24. Lester R. Brown, *Plan B 2.0* (New York: Norton, 2006), 164.

25. David Pimentel and Marcia Pimentel, "World Population, Food, Natural Resources, and Survival," in Ervin Laszlo and Peter Seidel, eds., *Global Survival* (New York: SelectBooks, 2006), 31–33.

26. Ibid., 45.

27. See George Ritzer, *The McDonaldization of Society* (Thousand Oaks, CA: Pine Forge Press, 2000), ch. 1.

28. *Los Angeles Times,* May 12, 2006.

29. Rifkin, *Beyond Beef,* chs. 11–16.

30. Ibid., 257.

31. Eric Schlosser, *Fast Food Nation* (Boston: Houghton Mifflin, 2001), 75–77.

32. Midkiff, *The Meat You Eat,* 27.

33. Schlosser, 149–50, 154, 195.

34. Robbins, *The Food Revolution,* 60–65.

35. Masson, *When Elephants Weep,* 24.

36. Carol J. Adams, *The Sexual Politics of Meat* (New York: Continuum, 2004), 43.

37. Francione, *Introduction to Animal Rights,* 187–88.

38. Aside from journals and magazines, animal rights concerns have also been excluded from progressive radio. For example, nothing has been historically aired on the influential Pacifica stations devoted to this issue, except for a brief stint by Karen Dawn at KPFK in Los Angeles during 2004. Dawn's excellent program, however, was taken off the air after several months—the agreement was not renewed—at the insistence of the program manager.

39. Benton, *Natural Relatons,* 196.

40. William Leiss, *The Domination of Nature* (New York: George Braziller, 1972), 55.

41. See especially Ronald Aronson, *After Marxism* (New York: Guilford, 1995), 90–123.

42. See, for example, "Ecology, Capitalism, and the Socialization of Nature," an interview with *Monthly Review* editor John Bellamy Foster, *Monthly Review* (November 2004), 1–12.

43. Benton, *Natural Relations,* 23–31.

44. Probably the most comprehensive overview of the environmental crisis during the period was Barry Commoner's *The Closing Circle* (New York: Knopf, 1971).

45. John Sanbonmatsu, "Listen Ecological Marxist! (Yes, I Said *Animals!*)," *Capitalism, Nature, Socialism* (June 2005), 107.

46. Joel Kovel, *The Enemy of Nature* (London: Zed Books, 2002), 210.

47. Teresa Ebert and Mas'ud Zavarzadeh, "Our American Diet Divides Us into Classes of Workers and Bosses," *Los Angeles Times* (September 4, 2000).

48. Murray Bookchin, "What Is Social Ecology?" in Zimmerman et al., *Environmental Philosophy,* 355.

49. Bookchin, *The Philosophy of Social Ecology* (Montreal: Black Rose Books, 1990), 115–16.

50. Bookchin, *Re-enchanting Humanity* (London: Cassell, 1995), 236.

51. See George Sessions, "Ecocentrism and the Anthropocentric Detour," in Sessions, ed., *Deep Ecology for the Twenty-First Century* (Boston: Shambala, 1995), 169–77.

52. On "wild nature" see, for example, Jack Turner, "In Wildness Is the Preservation of the World," in Sessions, *Deep Ecology,* 331–38.

53. Arne Naess, "Equality, Sameness, and Rights," in Sessions, *Deep Ecology,* 222.

54. See Naess, "Deep Ecology and Lifestyle," in Sessions, *Deep Ecology,* 260.

55. Naess, "The Deep Ecological Movement," in Sessions, *Deep Ecology,* 68.

56. Timothy W. Luke, *Ecocritique* (Minneapolis: University of Minnesota Press, 1997), 23.

57. David Nibert, *Animal Rights/Human Rights* (Lanham, MD: Rowman & Littlefield, 2002), 237.

58. Herbert Marcuse, *One-Dimensional Man* (Boston: Beacon Press, 1964), 237.

59. Pimentels, in *Global Survival,* 46.

CHAPTER 4

1. K. Marx and F. Engels, *Collected Works,* vol. 3 (London: Lawrence and Wishart, 1975).

2. This essay originally appeared in slightly longer form in *Radical Philosophy,* 50 (1988), 4–18.

3. K. Marx and F. Engels, *Works,* vol. 3, 275. The secondary literature on Marx's early writings is, of course, voluminous. See especially C. J. Arthur, *Dialectics of Labor* (Oxford, UK: Blackwell, 1986); A. Cornu, *The Origins of Marxian Thought* (Springfield, IL: Thomas, 1957); G. Markus, *Marxism and Anthropology* (Assen, The Netherlands: VanGorkum, 1978); R. Noonan and S. Sayers, *Hegel, Marx and Dialectic* (Brighton, UK: Harvester Press, 1980); B. Olman, *Alienation* (Cambridge, UK: Cambridge University Press, 1971); and A. Wood, *Karl Marx* (London: Routledge, 1981). N.

Geras, *Marx and Human Nature: Refutation of a Legend* (London: Verso, 1983) is an important source on Marx's later view of human nature. Almost all commentaries mention in passing Marx's contrast between the animal and the human, but few give it sustained critical attention. J. Elster, *Making Sense of Marx* (Cambridge, UK: Cambridge University Press, 1985), ch. 2, and G. Markus (1978) are exceptions.

4. G. A. Cohen, *Karl Marx's Theory of History: A Defence* (Oxford, UK: Oxford University Press, 1979), 305.

5. Marx and Engels, Vol. 3, 297.

6. Ibid., 277.

7. Ibid., 305.

8. Ibid., 301.

9. Ibid.

10. Ibid., 296–7.

11. Ibid., 239.

12. Ibid., 276.

13. Ibid., 302.

14. See for example M. Midgley, *Beast and Man: The Roots of Human Nature* (Brighton, UK: Harvester, 1980), ch. 2.

15. Some of the most fascinating evidence of cultural transmission comes from the more than 25 years spent by Jane Goodall and her associates observing a wild chimpanzee colony at Gombe, in Tanzania. See J. Goodall, *In the Shadow of Man* (Glasgow, UK: Fontana, 1974) and *The Chimpanzees of Gombe: Patterns of Behavior* (Cambridge, MA: Harvard University Press, 1986). Chimps are frequently observed using sticks as tools to fish termites from their mounds. They first strip off leaves to make the sticks suitable for the purpose, and juveniles learn the appropriate skills by observation and imitation of their seniors. See, however, Gould's interesting discussion of Goodall's interpretations, S. J. Gould, *Ever Since Darwin* (Harmondsworth, UK: Penguin, 1981).

16. This is not, of course, to deny that there are *connections* between well-being and the fulfillment of potentials. Marx is, I think, right to argue that the opportunity to fulfill one's potential is, for humans, a need. It follows that the fulfillment of potential is a necessary constituent of well-being. But not all potentials can be actualized within the time span of an individual human life, or within the context of any particular culture. Some potentials must simply remain unactualized. Moreover, as I have suggested above, the actualization of some human potentials would be undesirable. In other cases, the simultaneous realization of two contrasting potentials may be impossible or undesirable, even though there may be nothing problematic about either taken separately.

17. Here, as elsewhere in this chapter, I might be accused of anachronistically criticizing Marx for lack of awareness of an ethological literature produced a century or more after his death. In fact, I am less interested in showing that Marx was empirically mistaken than in exposing and making constructive uses of some of the conceptual tensions and contradictions in his text. However, Marx's writings of the early and mid-1840s contrast interestingly with Darwin's notebooks (unpublished, of course, at the time) on *Man, Mind and Materialism*. These were written in 1838 and 1839 and are studded with observations and speculations on intelligence, emotional expression, and sociability in other animals and also remarks on the striking analogies between

humans and other animals in these respects. For example: "Plato says in Phaedo that our '*imaginary ideas* arise from the preexistence of the soul, are not derivable from experience'—read monkeys for preexistence. l. The young Orang in Zoological Gardens *pouts*. Partly out (of) displeasure. . . . When pouting protrudes its lips into point. Man, though he does not pout, pushes out both lips in contempt, disgust and defiance." H. E. Gruber, *Darwin on Man* (London: Wildwood House, 1974), 290. This contrasts very sharply with Marx's virtually contemporaneous position in his 1839 notebooks on *Epicurean Philosophy*: "If a philosopher does not find it outrageous to consider man as an animal, he cannot be made to understand anything." K. Marx and F. Engels, *Collected Works*, vol. 1 (London: Lawrence and Wishart, 1975), 453. It would be a worthwhile exercise to investigate the transition from this unequivocal anti-naturalism through the unstable "humanist naturalism" of the *Manuscripts* to the unequivocal pro-Darwinian stance of 1859.

18. A useful introduction to the debates surrounding biological determinism is A. L. Caplan, ed., *The Sociobiology Debate* (New York: Harper, 1978). Trenchant critiques include M. Sahlins, *The Use and Abuse of Biology* (London: Tavistock, 1977), and S. Rose, L. Kamin, and R. C. Lewontin, *Not in Our Genes* (Harmondsworth, UK: Penguin, 1984). Feminist perspectives on the issues are given in J. Sayers, *Biological Politics: Feminist and Anti-feminist Perspectives* (Londong: Tavistock, 1981) and L. Birke, *Women, Feminism and Biology* (Brighton, UK: Harvester, 1986).

19. Marx and Engels, vol. 3, 302.

20. An important figure in the development of this new understanding was the late T. McKeown—see his *The Role of Medicine* (London: Blackwell, 1979). See also the essays by L. Roger and G. Bignami in S. Rose, *Against Biological Determinism* (London: Allison and Busby, 1982) and L. Doyal with I. Pennell, *Political Economy of Health* (London: Pluto, 1979), esp. ch. 1.

21. Somewhat paradoxically, an important source for such views of need has been the work of A. H. Maslow, "A Theory of Human Motivation," *Psychological Review* (London, 1943), 370–96 and *Motivation and Personality* (New York: Harper and Row; Evanston and London, 2nd edition, 1970). Though advocating a holistic and anti-dualist view of human nature, Maslow's hierarchical classification of needs (physiological, safety, love, esteem and self-actualization) has been open to interpretations that, in effect, restore a dualism of "lower-" and "higher-" order needs. Important recent discussions of the concept of need with a direct bearing on my argument in this paper are K. Soper, *On Human Needs* (Brighton, UK: Harvester, 1981) and L. Doyal and I. Gough, "A Theory of Human Needs," *Critical Social Policy*, vol. 10 (1984), 6–38.

22. A very useful introduction to the literature on this is M. Redcliff, *Development and the Environmental Crisis* (London: Methuen, 1984), 107–10. See also W. H. Matthews, ed., *Outer Limits and Human Needs* (Uppsala, Sweden: Dag Hammarsjold Foundation, 1976).

23. Marx and Engels, *Works*, vol. 3, 336.

24. Ibid., 337.

25. Recent studies have even called into question the distinctiveness of the human capacity for language. Although earlier attempts to train captive chimpanzees and other primates to speak were not successful, R. A. and B. T. Gardner did manage to

teach the chimp "Washoe" to use sign language to some degree. E. Linden's experiments with plastic symbols have also been adduced as evidence of an intellectual capacity for language in some primates. Of course, language *can* be termed so as to exclude these as genuine eases of language learning, and all such experiments have methodological weaknesses. Nevertheless, it is hard to read this literature without being convinced of a much greater continuity between humans and other primates with respect to their reasoning and symbolizing powers than has been widely assumed. See R. A. and B. J. Gardner, "Early Signs of Language in Child and Chimpanzee," *Science*, vol. 187, (1975), 752–53; E. Linden, *Apes, Men and Language* (Harmondsworth, UK: London, 1976). A good, balanced account of the debate is given in S. Walker, *Estrangement* (London: Greenwood, 1983), chapters 9 and 10.

26. Marx and Engels, vol. 3, 304.

27. Ibid., 275.

28. Ibid., 276.

29. The use of this example might be misleading. In this case, we are, indeed, dealing with a physical need that is common to humans and animals as "natural beings." However, as I hope the above discussion has made clear, I am *not* committed to the view that all needs common to humans and (other) animals are physical needs. On the contrary, my view would also include affective, sexual, reproductive (etc.) needs as common needs in this sense. They are needs that we share with other animals, but, at the same time, they are needs that we experience, identify, and seek to satisfy in *ways* that are distinctively human (and, at a more concrete level of description, in ways that vary from one human culture, historical period, and social grouping to another).

30. For a fuller development of these arguments, see Ted Benton, *Natural Relations: Ecology, Animal Rights, and Social Justice* (London: Verso, 1993).

CHAPTER 5

1. Peter Singer, *Animal Liberation*, rev. ed. (London: Thorsons, 1990), 1. To be sure, this is less true now than when Singer originally wrote these words for the first edition of *Animal Liberation* in 1975, thanks in no small measure to the efforts of Singer himself. It is perhaps worth noting here that, unless otherwise indicated, "animal" in this text refers to nonhuman animals. "Animal liberation," as used here, refers, very roughly, to the emancipation of nonhuman animals from unnecessary forms and practices of domination, exploitation, and oppression by human beings, and should be construed as encompassing rights-based defenses of animals.

2. I shall not attempt to provide a definition of "Marxism," a term which of course covers an extraordinarily complex array of political and intellectual traditions, commitments, and positions. Let me say only that I think Donald Clark Hodges is quite right to suggest that "[t]he skeletal structure of the communist worldview dates from the [Communist] Manifesto, the rest of the edifice would be added later. Thus the Manifesto is the most succinct answer to the question, 'What is Marxism?'" (*The Literate Communist: 150 Years of the* Communist Manifesto [New York: Peter Lang, 1999], 67).

3. Ted Benton, *Natural Relations* (London and New York: Verso, 1993).

4. Angus Taylor, *Animals and Ethics* (Peterborough, Ontario: Broadview Press, 2003).

5. Taylor mentions many of these considerations in his conclusion to *Animals and Ethics*, "To Change the World." I will elaborate on this later in the chapter.

6. Taylor, *Animals and Ethics*, 177. Taylor's wording here is unfortunate, in that it may give the impression that his criticism is aimed at "industrial society" per se—a criticism that few Marxists would endorse. What he really has in mind, however, is "the basic form of industrialism [which] remains: a society organized in the interests of maximizing productivity and consumption" (Ibid.); that is to say, as he makes clear in the following sentence, *capitalism*.

7. Some aspects of the relationship between Marx and/or Marxism and animal liberation are explored in David Sztybel, "Marxism and Animal Rights," *Ethics and the Environment*, vol. 2 (1997), 169–85; Lawrence Wilde, "'The Creatures, too, Must Become Free': Marx and the Animal/Human Distinction," *Capital & Class*, vol. 72 (2000), 37–53; Katherine Perlo, "Marxism and the Underdog," *Society and Animals*, vol. 10 (2002), 303–18; Ted Benton, "Marxism and the Moral Status of Animals," *Society and Animals*, vol. 11 (2003), 73–79; and Bob Torres, *Making a Killing: The Political Economy of Animal Rights* (Edinburgh, UK and Oakland, California: AK Press, 2007), as well as in Benton's *Natural Relations*. In *Animal Rights/Human Rights* (Lanham, MD: Rowman & Littlefield Publishers, Inc., 2002), David Nibert analyzes the relationship between capitalism and animal oppression, often using arguments that Marxists would endorse. There is, however, virtually no explicit discussion of Marx and Marxism in his book.

8. This is, at any rate, what one inevitably infers from the absence of any reference to animal liberation in Marxists' references to, and analyses of, the new social movements. See, for example, the discussion of the new social movements in Ralph Miliband, *Divided Societies: Class Struggle in Contemporary Capitalism* (Oxford, UK: Clarendon Press, 1989), and Frank Cunningham, *The Real World of Democracy Revisited* (Atlantic Highlands, NJ: Humanities Press, 1994).

9. In *Deep Vegetarianism* (Philadelphia, PA: Temple University Press, 1999), Michael Allen Fox observes that in a relatively recent essay on the topic of exploitation, Allen W. Wood, a philosopher sympathetic to Marxism and the author of one of the best accounts of Marx's thought in English, "makes no mention of animals as members of the class of beings who may be exploited" (104). Likewise, neither John Bellamy Foster nor Paul Burkett addresses the moral status of animals at all in their comprehensive works on Marxism and ecology (see *Marx's Ecology: Materialism and Nature* [New York: Monthly Review Press, 2000] and *Marx and Nature: A Red and Green Perspective* [New York: Palgrave Macmillan, 1999], respectively). Animals are also ignored in Joel Kovel and Michael Löwy's "An Ecosocialist Manifesto," *Capitalism, Nature, Socialism*, vol. 13 (2002), 1–2, 155–57. For the small class of exceptions to the neglect of animal liberation on the part of Marxists, see note 7 above.

10. "He first heard of animal liberation when he came across an article about it in a Marxist magazine. The article dismissed the idea as the latest absurdity of the radical chic set associated with the *New York Review of Books*" (Peter Singer, *How Are We to Live?* [Melbourne, Australia: The Text Publishing Company, 1993], 219).

11. See the studies cited in Evelyn Pluhar, *Beyond Prejudice: The Moral Significance of Human and Nonhuman Animals* (Durham, NC, and London: Duke University Press, 1995), 127.

12. James Rachels, "Darwin, Species, and Morality," in T. Regan and P. Singer, eds., *Animal Rights and Human Obligations*, 2nd ed. (Englewood Cliffs, NJ: Prentice Hall, 1989), 95–6.

13. Singer, *Animal Liberation*, 233.

14. See Peter Singer, "Utilitarianism and Vegetarianism," *Philosophy and Public Affairs*, vol. 9 (1980), 333–4 for an argument to the effect that the adverse consequences of a society-wide conversion to vegetarianism would be short-term (while the benefits to animals would last indefinitely).

15. In this connection Singer remarks, "[W]hen nonvegetarians say that 'human problems come first' I cannot help wondering what exactly it is that they are doing for human beings that compels them to continue to support the wasteful, ruthless exploitation of farm animals" (*Animal Liberation*, 221). As it turns out, even some philosophers are given to thinking in terms of such a false dilemma; witness the opening page of Peter Carruthers' anti-liberation tract, *The Animals Issue: Moral Theory in Practice* (Cambridge, UK: University Press, 1992): "In fact, I regard the present popular concern with animal rights in our culture as a reflection of moral decadence. Just as Nero fiddled while Rome burned, many in the West agonise over the fate of seal pups and cormorants while human beings elsewhere starve or are enslaved" (xi). Quite apart from the fact that the view expressed in this passage rests on a false dilemma, it is noteworthy that Carruthers implicitly seems to appeal to a consequentialist criterion in explaining his charge of "moral decadence," even though his own framework for moral theory is hardly of a consequentialist sort. More noteworthy still are the implications of this sort of thinking, for does it not also follow that it is a sign of moral decadence that people devote their time and energy to *philosophy* "while human beings . . . starve or are enslaved"?

16. Mark Rowlands, *Animals Like Us* (London and New York: Verso, 2002), 179.

17. Here I have in mind passages in which Marx and Engels explicitly refer to animal welfare advocates, and not Marx's speculative, philosophical texts, which are the focus of Benton's analysis.

18. Karl Marx and Frederick Engels, *The Marx-Engels Reader*, 2nd ed., Robert C. Tucker, ed., (New York: W. W. Norton and Co., 1978), 496.

19. Frederick Engels, "On the History of Early Christianity," in *Marx and Engels on Religion* (New York: Schocken Books, 1964), 322. When, several decades later, Trotsky uses the phrase "vegetarian-Quaker prattle about 'sacredness of human life'" (cited in Steven Lukes, *Marxism and Morality* [Oxford and New York: Oxford University Press, 1985], 23) to criticize a certain moral position, he seems to betray the same sort of attitude.

20. Benton, *Natural Relations*, 24; cf. 23: "Few commentators on this text [the *1844 Manuscripts*] have taken seriously the fact that its central organizing concepts—species-being and estrangement—are developed by Marx in terms of a fundamental opposition between human and animal nature."

21. See Singer, *Animal Liberation*, chapter 6 for a lucid discussion, and refutation, of the most common speciesist arguments mustered against the claims of animal liberation.

22. Benton, *Natural Relations*, 59.

23. Ibid.

24. Cited in Gary Francione, series forward to *Deep Vegetarianism*, by Michael Allen Fox (Philadelphia, PA: Temple University Press, 1999), xiii.

25. Ted Benton and Simon Redfearn, "The Politics of Animal Rights—Where Is the Left?" *New Left Review*, vol. 215 (1996), 47.

26. Cited by Singer, "Utilitarianism and Vegetarianism," 330, note 9.

27. Frederic Jameson, *Postmodernism or, the Cultural Logic of Late Capitalism* (Durham, NC: Duke University Press, 1991), 314.

28. Benton and Redfearn, "The Politics of Animal Rights," 46; cf. Benton, *Natural Relations*, 72.

29. Singer, *Animal Liberation*, vii.

30. See Gary Francione, *Introduction to Animal Rights* (Philadelphia, PA: Temple University Press, 2000), 14–16, for data on the inefficiency and wastefulness of animal agriculture.

31. See, for instance, Fox, *Deep Vegetarianism*, 181, and Singer, *Animal Liberation*, 177–9.

32. Henry Salt, *Animals' Rights* (Clarks Summit, PA: Society for Animal Rights, Inc., 1980), 111; emphasis in the original. This consideration is also an important element in Fox's defense of "deep vegetarianism": "[V]egetarianism . . . is liberating as it frees us *from* the exploitation of animals, the domination of nature, and the oppression of one another, and frees us *to* discover ourselves in more positive, life-affirming ways" (*Deep Vegetarianism*, 183; emphasis in the original). Notice that this passage combines both senses in which animal liberation is said to promise human liberation.

33. Steven Sapontzis, *Morals, Reason, and Animals* (Philadelphia, PA: Temple University Press, 1987), 197.

34. In developing his (utilitarian) case against moral vegetarianism, R. G. Frey enumerates some 14 kinds of adverse socio-economic consequences that would result from a collective (i.e., society-wide) conversion to vegetarianism (*Rights, Killing, and Suffering* [Oxford, UK: Basil Blackwell, 1983], 197–203). While I believe that Frey is wrong in assuming that the harms deriving from a society-wide adoption of vegetarianism would outweigh the benefits, his list constitutes a useful corrective to simplistic and overly sanguine visions of the changes that such a shift would likely produce. For a reply to Frey's argument, see Sapontzis, *Morals, Reason, and Animals*, 101 and 103.

35. Fox, *Deep Vegetarianism*, chapter 2 contains an interesting discussion of various factors bearing on this aspect of animal liberation.

36. Benton, *Natural Relations*, 1.

37. As Fox rightly points out, "The principle of nonmaleficence (avoiding or minimizing harm) certainly seems to be about as basic a moral precept as can be imagined" (*Deep Vegetarianism*, 87), and it is for this reason that Rachels suggests that "vegetarianism might be thought of as a severely conservative moral stance," following as it does from "the rule against causing unnecessary pain," which "is the least eccentric of all moral principles" (*Created from Animals* [Oxford, UK: Oxford University Press, 1990], 212).

38. David D. DeGrazia formulates the principle as follows: "the principle that the interests of every being affected by an action are to be taken into account and given

the same weight as the like interests of any other being" ("Equal Consideration," in *Encyclopedia of Animal Rights and Animal Welfare*, M. Bekoff and C. A. Meaney, eds., [Westport, CT: Greenwood Press, 1998], 163).

39. Cf. DeGrazia: "At an abstract level, equal consideration for animals would rule out a general discounting of animals' interests, an across-the-board devaluing of their interests relative to ours. . . . At a practical level, equal consideration for animals would rule out the routine overriding of animals' interests in the name of human benefit" ("Equal Consideration," 162).

40. G. A. Cohen, *Self-Ownership, Freedom, and Equality* (Cambridge, UK: Cambridge University Press, 1995), 5. It is also true that classical Marxists were sometimes quite explicit in stating their overriding commitment to equality, even if the content of the latter remained somewhat vague. For instance, in his *Terrorism and Communism*, Trotsky defended the (communist) goal of "creat[ing] the conditions for real, economic, living equality for mankind as a member of a unified moral commonwealth" (cited in Lukes, *Marxism and Morality*, 113).

41. For a critical response to the claim that Marx was an egalitarian, see Allen Wood, "Marx and Equality," in *Analytical Marxism*, J. Roemer, ed. (Cambridge, UK: Cambridge University Press, 1986).

42. Frederick Engels, *Anti-Dühring*, Emile Burns, trans. (New York: International Publishers, 1939), 118.

43. Kai Nielsen, *Marxism and the Moral Point of View* (Boulder, CO and London: Westview Press, 1989), 219.

44. Karl Marx and Frederick Engels, *The Marx-Engels Reader*, 2nd ed., Robert C. Tucker, ed. (New York: W. W. Norton and Co., 1978), 531.

45. Wood, "Marx and Equality," 296.

46. Nielsen, *Marxism*, 221–2.

47. I borrow this construal of "needs" from Albert Weale, "Needs and Interests," in *The Concise Routledge Encyclopedia of Philosophy* (London and New York: Routledge, 2000), 620.

48. Benton, *Natural Relations*, 212.

49. Engels, *Anti-Dühring*, 309.

50. Marx and Engels, *The Marx-Engels Reader*, 5.

51. Engels, *Anti-Dühring*, 105.

52. Marx and Engels, *The Marx-Engels Reader*, 715.

53. To be sure, the notion of "moral progress" is problematic for some Marxists, namely those who insist that historical materialism does not allow for the sort of transhistorical comparisons whose validity is presupposed by the concept of "moral progress." Transhistorical comparisons, so the argument goes, require transhistorical standards, but historical materialism denies the possibility of such standards, since any values used as the basis for these standards will always be, in the last analysis, the product or result of a given mode of production. What is more, there is a kind of necessity to the values that prevail at any given time, in that these values alone correspond to the existing mode of production; and if this is the case, it is pointless to criticize these values, given that no other values were possible. This construal of historical materialism is, I believe, mistaken. I suspect that nearly all Marxists believe that

socialism would be, among other things, *morally* superior to a socio-economic arrangement based on slave labor, and in my view this belief is not inconsistent with historical materialism. However, I cannot argue for this claim here.

54. See Peter Singer, *The Expanding Circle: Ethics and Sociobiology* (New York: Farrar, Straus & Giroux, 1981).

CHAPTER 6

1. I would like to thank John Abromeit, Robert S. Eshelman, Martin Jay, Robert Kaufman, and Eric Santner for comments on earlier drafts of this article.

2. Max Horkheimer, "Materialism and Morality," *Between Philosophy and Social Science: Selected Early Writings of Max Horkheimer,* trans. G. Frederick Hunter, Matthew S. Kramer, and John Torpey (Cambridge, MA: MIT Press, 1993), 135–36.

3. Theodor W. Adorno, *Problems of Moral Philosophy*, ed. Thomas Schröder, trans. Rodney Livingstone (Stanford, CA: Stanford University Press, 2000), 145.

4. Theodor Adorno, *Minima Moralia: Reflections from Damaged Life*, trans. E. F. N. Jephcott (London: Verso, 1971; originally published 1951); *Negative Dialectics*, trans. E. B. Ashton (New York: Seabury Press, 1973); *Aesthetic Theory*, trans. Robert Hullot-Kentor (Minneapolis: University of Minnesota Press, 1997).

5. John Abromeit, "The Dialectic of Bourgeois Society: An Intellectual Biography of the Young Max Horkheimer, 1895–1937," dissertation manuscript, University of California at Berkeley, 2004, 337. Cited with permission of the author.

6. Robert Savage, "Adorno's Family and Other Animals," *Thesis Eleven*, vol. 78 (2004), 102–12. What follows in this paragraph is gleaned and loosely paraphrased from Savage's article, esp. pp. 107-8. I thank Martin Jay for bringing this article to my attention.

7. Robert Savage, 107.

8. Stefan Müller-Doohm, *Adorno: Eine Biographie* (Frankfurt/M: Suhrkamp, 2003), 525.

9. Robert Savage's article—which at times seems to be an article about the role animals played in Adorno's life—is actually a review of the recent biographies of Adorno by Stefan Müller-Doohm and Detlev Claussen.

10. Detlev Claussen, *Theodor W. Adorno. Ein letztes Genie* (Frankfurt/M: Fischer, 2003), 297. Quoted by Savage, 109.

11. Stefan Müller-Doohm, 441–3. Quoted by Savage, 108.

12. Jay Bernstein, "Mastered by Nature: Abstraction, Independence, and the Simple Concept," in *Adorno: Disenchantment and Ethics* (Cambridge, UK: Cambridge University Press, 2001), 188–99.

13. While the concepts of nature and animals obviously cannot be used interchangeably, these two concepts refer to the same problematic phenomenon that Horkheimer and Adorno seek to address in *Dialectic of Enlightenment* and that forms the point of departure in this article: the domination of nature, which they address early on in *Dialectic of Enlightenment*, and of animals, which they address in one of its later sections "Man and Animal." In this study, Horkheimer and Adorno argue that the domination of nature and of animals are intimately related.

14. Theodor W. Adorno, *Negative Dialektik, Gesammelte Schriften*, vol. 6, ed. Rolf Tiedemann (Frankfurt/M: Suhrkamp, 1997), 294. Hereafter cited as *ND*. In English, *Negative Dialectics*, trans. E. B. Ashton (New York: Seabury Press, 1973), 299. Hereafter cited as *NDe*. The first citation refers to an English translation and the second to the original German. While I refer to the English translation of this text whenever possible, in some instances slight adjustments have been made to enhance their fidelity to the original. Such modifications are identified in footnotes. "Dem Einzelnen indessen bleibt an Moralischem nicht mehr übrig als wofür die Kantische Moraltheorie, welche den Tieren Neigung, keine Achtung konzediert, nur Verachtung hat: versuchen, so zu leben, daß man glauben darf, ein gutes Tier gewesen zu sein."

15. Theodor W. Adorno and Max Horkheimer, *Dialectic of Enlightenment*, trans. John Cumming (New York: Continuum, 1972). *Dialektik der Aufklärung, Gesammelte Schriften*, vol. 3, ed. Rolf Tiedemann (Frankfurt: Suhrkamp, 1969).

16. The interest in the origins of totalitarianism was elaborated more fully in the study that was researched and written concurrent to *Dialectic of Enlightenment*, which was *The Authoritarian Personality*. This study, co-authored by Theodor W. Adorno, Else Frenkel-Brunswik, Daniel J. Levinson, and R. Nevitt Sanford, revisits earlier studies of authoritarianism, such as the Frankfurt School's 1936 *Studie über Autorität und Familie* and Max Horkheimer's 1940 essay "The Authoritarian State," written for a *Gedächtnisschrift* for Walter Benjamin that was to be published in 1942 and yet remains unpublished. On the relationship between the Frankfurt School's *Authoritarian Personality* study and Arendt's *On Totalitarianism*, see also my article "On Violence: Adorno and Arendt," in *Understanding Political Modernity: Comparative Perspectives on Adorno and Arendt*, eds. Samir Gandesha and Lars Rensmann (Cambridge, MA: MIT Press, forthcoming).

17. Adorno, "Die Aktualität der Philosophie," *Philosophische Frühschriften*, *GS* 1, 325–44. Hereafter cited as AP. In English: "The Actuality of Philosophy," *Telos*, vol. 31 (1977), 120–33. Hereafter cited as APe. The first citation refers to an English translation. The second citation refers to the German original. Here, specifically APe 130 / AP 339. "Nur eine prinzipiell undialektische, auf geschichtslose Wahrheit gerichtete Philosophie könnte wähnen, es ließen die alten Probleme sich beseitigen, indem man sie vergißt und frischweg von vorn beginnt."

18. Much of Adorno's argument here is taken up again in *Negative Dialectics*. On the undesirability and impossibility of starting with a clean slate cf. *NDe* 54-55 / *ND* 64.

19. Adorno also discusses this in the essay "Über Tradition," *Kulturkritik und Gesellschaft, Gesammelte Schriften*, ed. Rolf Tiedemann, vol. 10, no. 1 (Frankfurt: Suhrkamp, 1997): 310–20. For this particular criticism, see especially pp. 314–5.

20. Adorno, APe 129 / AP 338. "Ich sagte: Die Rätselantwort sei nicht der 'Sinn' des Rätsels in der Weise, daß beide zugleich bestehen können. . . . Vielmehr steht die Antwort in stenger Antithesis zum Rätsel; bedarf der Konstruktion aus den Rätselelementen und zerstört das Rätsel."

21. Max Horkheimer, *Kants Kritik der Urteilskraft als Bindeglied zwischen theoretischer und praktischer Philosophie* (Stuttgart, Germany: Kohlhammer, 1925).

22. Martin Jay, *Dialectical Imagination: A History of the Frankfurt School and the Institute of Social Research, 1923–1950* (London: Heinemann Books, 1973), 46.

23. Max Horkheimer, *Kants "Kritik der Urteilskraft" als Bindeglied zwischen theoretischer und praktischer Philosophie, Gesammelte Schriften*, vol. 2, eds. Alfred Schmidt and Gunzelin Schmid Noerr (Frankfurt/M: Fischer, 1987), 73–146.

24. Theodor W. Adorno and Max Horkheimer, *Dialektik der Aufklärung, Gesammelte Schriften*, vol. 3, ed. Rolf Tiedemann (Frankfurt/M: Suhrkamp, 1969), 283. Hereafter cited as *DdA*. In English, *Dialectic of Enlightenment*, trans. John Cumming (New York: Continuum, 1972), 245. Hereafter cited as *DoE*. "Die Idee des Menschen in der europäischen Geschichte drückt sich in der Unterscheidung vom Tier aus. Mit seiner Unvernunft beweisen sie die Menschenwürde."

25. For an assessment of the shortcomings of Horkheimer and Adorno's attempted revisions of the hierarchical relationship between human and animal, see Carolin Duttlinger, "Traumatic Metamorphoses: The Concept of the Animal" in Horkheimer and Adorno's *Dialektik der Aufklärung*," *Focus on German Studies*, vol. 10 (2003), 47–69.

26. Max Horkheimer, "The End of Reason," first published in *Studies in Philosophy and Social Sciences*, vol. 9 (1941). Cited here from *The Frankfurt School Reader*, eds. Andrew Arato and Eike Gebhardt (New York: Continuum, 1982), 47.

27. *DoE* 32 / *DdA* 49. "Das Wesen der Aufklärung ist die Alternative, deren Unausweichlichkeit die der Herrschaft ist. Die Menschen hatten immer zu wählen zwischen ihrer Unterwerfung unter Natur oder der Natur unter das Selbst."

28. Adorno, *Ästhetische Theorie, Gesammelte Schriften*, ed. Rolf Tiedemann, vol. 7 (Frankfurt, Germany: Suhrkamp, 1970), 537. Herafter cited as *AT*. "Naturschönes ist sistierte Geschichte, innehaltendes Werden." In English, *Aesthetic Theory*, trans. Robert Hullot-Kentor, (Minneapolis: University of Minnesota Press, 1997), 361. Hereafter cited as *AT*e, "was ich in die Waagschale zu werfen habe."

29. Theodor W. Adorno, *Probleme der Moralphilosophie*, (Frankfurt/M: Suhrkamp, 1996), 215. Hereafter cited as *PM*. In English: *Problems of Moral Philosophy*, ed. Thomas Schröder, trans. Rodney Livingstone (Stanford, CA: Stanford University Press, 2000), 144. Herafter cited as *PMP*. "den Gedanken der Vernunft als eines Endzwecks der Menschheit."

30. *PMP* 145 / *PM* 215. "Schopenhauer hat seinerzeit es als das besondere Verdienst seiner Moralphilosophie angesprochen, daß in ihr auch das Verhalten zu den Tieren inbegriffen ist, das Mitleid gegenüber den Tieren, und man hat das oft so als eine Schrulle das Privatiers behandelt. Ich glaube, daß sich an solchen exzentrischen Zügen gerade ungeheuer viel erkennen läßt."

31. As Josephine Donovan points out in her article "Attention to Suffering: Sympathy as a Basis for Ethical Treatment of Animals," using compassion as a basis for an ethical treatment of animals is by no means a universally agreed on approach for those writing about animal treatment. For example, in discussing the writings of Tom Regan and Peter Singer, she says, "however different the two theories may be, they nevertheless unite in their rationalistic rejection of emotion or sympathy as a legitimate base for ethical theory about animal treatment." Josephine Donovan, "Attention to Suffering: Sympathy as a Basis for Ethical Treatment of Animals," in *Beyond Animal Rights: A Feminist Caring Ethic for the Treatment of Animals*, eds. Josephine Donovan and Carl J. Adams (New York: Continuum, 1996), 147–69. Reprinted this volume.

32. Arthur Schopenhauer, *On the Basis of Morality,* trans. E. F. N. Payne (Providence, RI: Berghahn Books, 1995).

33. Immanuel Kant, *The Metaphysical Principles of Virtue*. vol. 2 of *The Metaphysics of Morals*, trans. James Ellington (Indianapolis, IN: Bobb-Merrill, 1964); *Critique of Practical Reason*, ed. and trans. Mary Gregor (Cambridge, UK: Cambridge University Press, 1997); *Grundlegung zur Metaphysik der Sitten*. vol. 7. *Werkausgabe*, ed. Wilhelm Weischedel. (Frankfurt, Germany: Suhrkamp, 2005).

34. Immanuel Kant, *Die Metaphysik der Sitten. Metaphysische Anfangsgründe der Tugendlehre* (Frankfurt/M: Suhrkamp, 1977), 578–9. In English: *The Metaphysical Principles of Virtue, The Metaphysics of Morals*, vol. II, trans. James Ellington (Indianapolis, IN: Bobb-Merrill, 1964), 106. "die Pflicht der Enthaltung von gewaltsamer und zugleich grausamer Behandlung der Tiere des Menschen gegen sich selbst [ist] weit inniglicher entgegengesetzt, weil dadurch das Mitgefühl an ihrem Leiden im Menschen abgestumpft und dadurch eine der Moralität, im Verhältnisse zu anderen Menschen, sehr diensame natürliche Anglage geschwächt und nach und nach ausgetilgt wird."

35. Arthur Schopenhauer, *On the Basis of Morality*, trans. E. F. N. Payne (Providence, RI: Berghahn Books, 1995), 96. For a longer study of Schopenhauer, examining not only his criticism of Kant's but also of Hegel's philosophy, particularly vis-à-vis natural history, see also Alfred Schmidt, *Idee und Weltwille: Schopenhauer als Kritiker Hegels* (Munich: Hanser, 1988), esp. 21–27.

36. *PMP* 145. "Das heißt, das Schopenhauer hatte wahrscheinlich den Verdacht, daß die Etablierung der totalen Vernunft als des obersten objektiven Prinzips der Menschheit eben damit jene blinde Herrschaft über die Natur fortsetzen könnte, die in der Tradition der Ausbeutung und der Quälerei an Tieren ihren allersinnfälligsten und faßlichsten Ausdruck hat. Er hat damit sozusagen den wunden Punkt des Übergangs der subjektiven selbsterhaltenden Vernunft in das oberste moralische Prinzip bezeichnet, welches für die Tiere und für das Verhalten zu Tieren keinen Raum läßt. Und insofern ist gerade diese Exzentrizität von Schopenhauer Zeichen einer sehr großen Einsicht."

37. Ibid., 173. "daß der Zustand geändert werden müßte in dem es Mitleid Erregendes gibt"

38. Ibid., 173-74. "in dem Mitleid, das man einem Menschen entgegenbringt, immer auch ein Stück Unrecht gegen Menschen enthalten ist, weil er nämlich an dem Mitleid immer zugleich auch die Ohnmacht und die Scheinhaftigkeit gerade der mitleidigen Handlung erfährt."

39. Quoted by Eberhard Fromm, *Schopenhauer: Vordenker des Pessimismus*, 115.

40. Max Horkheimer, "Schopenhauer Today," in *Critique of Instrumental Reason*, trans. Rodney Livingstone (New York: Seabury, 1974), 63–83.

41. Arthur Schopenhauer, *On the Basis of Morality*, 763 (German edition).

42. Arne Johan Vetlesen, "*Perception, Empathy and Judgment: An Inquiry into the Preconditions of Moral Performance* (University Park: Pennsylvania State University Press, 1994), 206.

43. Martin Jay, 44.

44. Ibid., 44.

45. John Abromeit, "The Dialectic of Bourgeois Society: An Intellectual Biography of the Young Max Horkheimer, 1895–1937," 35. Horkheimer quoted by John Abromeit.

46. Martin Jay, 44.

47. Ibid., 44.

48. Rolf Wiggershaus, *The Frankfurt School: Its History, Theories, and Political Significance*, trans. Michael Robertson (Cambridge, MA: MIT Press, 1994), 51.

49. Rolf Wiggershaus, 51.

50. Ibid., 51. Emphasis added.

CHAPTER 7

1. Steve Martin says in his acknowledgements to his wonderful book *Shopgirl* something to the effect that if writers write alone, why is it that their acknowledgments are so long? I agree with the sentiment. I certainly don't write alone: there are two dogs and two cats, running around, sitting on my writing table, warming my feet under it, nudging me when 6 o'clock (both AM and PM, depending on the deadline) rolls around. There are two children, who come over and ask when they can borrow *my computer*, and when are we going sledding, to library, or to the beach. Sometimes, they just come over and hug me. But most important, and more to the point, I did not write this chapter alone. First, I wrote an early version for a SPEP meeting, where I had some great questions. Later, I sent it Martin Woessner, who has read almost everything I have written, and always sends the best comments. But it was John Sanbonmatsu's probing questions, suggestions, and corrections that turned a conference paper into its present form.

2. Past recipients include Jürgen Habermas, Jean-Luc Godard, Pierre Boulez, Norbert Elias, Guenther Anders, Zygmut Bauman, and most recently, the composer Giorgy Ligeti.

3. Jacques Derrida, "Fichus," in Jacques Derrida, *Paper Machine*, trans. by Rachel Bowlby (Stanford, CA: Stanford University Press, 2005), 164–81.

4. Derrida, "Fichus," 177.

5. Derrida, "Fichus," 180.

6. Theodor W. Adorno, *Beethoven: The Philosophy of Music*, trans. Edmund Jephcott (Stanford, CA: Stanford University Press, 1998), 8, fragment 202. Italics added.

7. Max Horkheimer and Theodor W. Adorno, *Dialectic of Enlightenment: Philosophical Fragments*, trans. by Edmund Jephcott (Stanford, CA: Stanford University Press, 2002), 210.

8. Derrida, "Fichus," 180.

9. Giovanna Borradori, *Philosophy in a Time of Terror: Dialogues with Jürgen Habermas and Jacques Derrida* (Chicago: University of Chicago Press, 2003).

10. Jacques Derrida, "The Animal That Therefore I Am (More to Follow)," *Critical Inquiry*, vol. 28 (Winter 2002): 369–418. See also the extremely important discussion on animals and violence in Jacques Derrida and Elisabeth Roudinesco, *For What Tomorrow . . . a Dialogue*, trans. by Jeff Fort (Stanford: Stanford University Press, 2004), 62–76.

11. See Cary Wolfe, ed., *Zoontologies: The Question of the Animal* (Minneapolis: University of Minnesota Press, 2003), and David Wood, "Thinking with Cats," in Peter Atterton and Matthew Calarco, eds., *Animal Philosophy: Ethics and Identity* (London and New York: Continuum, 2004).

12. Martin Jay, *Adorno* (Cambridge, MA: Harvard University Press, 1984), 24.

13. See Theodor W. Adorno, *History and Freedom: Lectures 1964–1965*, trans. by Rodney Livingston (Cambridge, UK: Polity Press, 2006), 299–300, note 5.

14. Quoted in Stefan Müller-Doohm, *Adorno: A Biography* (Cambridge, UK: Polity, 2005), 240.

15. Detlev Claussen, *Adorno. Ein Letztes Genie* (Frankfurt am Main, Germany: S. Fischer, 2003), 301. See also the wonderful review essay by Robert Savage, "Adorno's Family and Other Animals" *Thesis Eleven*, vol. 78 (August 2004): 102–12.

16. See Herbert Marcuse, *Eros and Civilization: A Philosophical Inquiry into Freud* (Boston: Beacon Press, 1966), chapter 8, 159–171.

17. Quoted in Claussen, *Adorno*, 305.

18. Quoted in Claussen, *Adorno*, 265.

19. Horkheimer and Adorno, *Dialectics of Enlightenment*, 43.

20. Ibid., 42–43.

21. Karl Marx, "Economic and Philosophic Manuscripts of 1844," in *Karl Marx and Frederick Engels, Collected Works*, vol. 3, *Marx and Engels 1843–1844* (New York: International Publishers, 1975), 296. The passage I am paraphrasing is in the third manuscript, in the section where Marx discusses communism, and where he writes—and this merits lengthy citing—"*Communism* as the *positive* transcendence of *private property* as *human self-estrangement*, and therefore as the real *appropriation* of the *human* essence by and for man; communism therefore as the complete return of man to himself as *social* (i.e., human) being—a return accomplished consciously and embracing the entire wealth of previous development. This communism, as fully developed naturalism, equals humanism, and as fully developed humanism equals naturalism: it is the *genuine* resolution of the conflict between man and nature and between nature and man—the true resolution of the strife between existence and essence, between objectification and self-confirmation, between freedom and necessity, between the individual and the species." This passage is remarkable because it announces the rejection of a humanism that is anti-nature while affirming a humanism that is a "fully developed naturalism." This humanism is not anthropocentric, but rather post-anthropocentric. It is one of my arguments in this chapter that Adorno stands within this tradition.

22. Adorno, *Minima Moralia*, 105.

23. T. W. Adorno, *Aesthetic Theory* (Minneapolis: Minnesota University Press, 1996), 113.

24. Ibid., 119.

25. Ibid., 78.

26. Thedor W. Adorno, *Negative Dialectics* (New York: Continuum, 1983), 365.

27. Adorno, *Negative Dialectics*, 299. Translation amended.

28. Gerhard Schweppenhäuser, *Ethik nach Auschwitz: Adornos negative Moralphilosophie* (Hamburg, Germany: Argument-Verlag, 1993), 213.

29. Theodor W. Adorno, *Problems in Moral Philosophy*, trans. Rodney Livingston (Cambridge, UK: Polity Press, 2000).

30. Stefan Breuer, "Adorno's Anthropology," *Telos*, vol. 64 (Summer 1985), 15–31.

31. Adorno, *Negative Dialectics*, 124.

32. Max Pensky, "Natural History: The Life and Afterlife of a Concept in Adorno," *Critical Horizons: Journal of Social and Critical Theory*, vol. 5 (2004), 227–58.

33. Bob Hullot-Kentor, "Introduction to Adorno's 'Idea of Natural-History,'" *Telos*, vol. 60 (Summer 1984): 97.

34. T. W. Adorno, "The Idea of Natural History," *Telos*, vol. 60 (Summer 1984), 111–24.

35. Adorno, *Negative Dialectics*, 358.

36. Jacques Derrida, "The Animal That Therefore I Am (More to Follow)," *Critical Inquiry*, vol. 28 (Winter 2002), 369–418. This is a translation of one of the longest parts of the lecture series. The full translation is forthcoming with Fordham University Press in the spring of 2008.

37. Jacques Derrida and Elisabeth Rodinescou, *For What Tomorrow . . . a Dialogue*, 65.

38. Ibid., 65. Evidently, Derrida's seeming rejection of the "rights discourse" here is in keeping with his overall rejection of the norm and the order of the law. Prior to the law there is a non-normative affirmation and response to the ethical appellation of the other. Rights are posterior affirmation of our submission to a demand, the demand to respect the other in his/her/its otherness. Rights as such acknowledge a prior acknowledgement; they are responses that respond to a prior response.

39. There is now an outstanding treatment of this and related texts by Derrida. See Leonard Lawlor, *This Is Not Suffiicient: An Essay on Animality and Human Nature in Derrida* (New York: Columbia University Press, 2007). See also Kelly Oliver's *Animal Lessons: How They Teach Us To Be Human* (New York: Columbia University Press, 2009).

40. Derrida, "The Animal That Therefore I am (More to Follow)," 369.

41. Ibid., 393 ff.

42. Ibid., 397.

43. Quoted in Claussen, *Adorno*, 305.

44. Derrida, "The Animal That Therefore I Am (More to Follow)," 399.

45. Ibid., 397.

46. Adorno, *Negative Dialectics*, 15.

47. See Niles Eldredge, "The Sixth Extinction," available online at www.actionbioscience.org/newfrontiers/eldredge2.html.

48. Edward O. Wilson, *The Future of Life* (New York: Vintage Books, 2002), 102.

49. David Quammen, "Planet of Weeds," in Edward Hoagland, ed., *The Best American Essays of 1999* (Boston and New York: Houghton Mifflin Company, 1999), 212–33. This essay first appeared in *Harper's Magazine*.

50. Leo Tolstoy in *The Kreutzer Sonata*, quoted by Peter Atterton, "Ethical Cynicism," in Peter Atterton and Mathew Calarco, eds., *Animal Philosophy: Ethics and Philosophy*, 55.

CHAPTER 8

1. Theodor Adorno and Max Horkheimer, *Dialectic of Enlightenment: Philosophical Fragments* (Stanford, CA: Stanford University Press, 2007), 1.
2. Ibid., 38.
3. Ibid., 203.
4. Jacques Derrida, *The Animal That Therefore I Am* (New York: Fordham University Press, 2008), 31.
5. Adorno and Horkheimer, *Dialectic of Enlightenment*, 6.
6. Ibid., 6.
7. Agamben, *The Open*, 37.
8. Ibid., 37.
9. Ibid., 37.
10. Jacques Derrida, "'Eating Well,' or the Calculation of the Subject: An Interview with Jacques Derrida," in *Who Comes After the Subject?* ed. Eduardo Cadava, Peter Connor, and Jean-Luc Nancy (New York: Routledge, Chapman, and Hall, Inc., 1991), 112.
11. Adorno and Horkheimer, *Dialectic of Enlightenment*, 11.
12. Interestingly, late in his life Derrida claimed that the question of the animal had always been central to his work. He claimed that his arguments "since [he] began writing . . . have [been] dedicated to the question of the living and of the living animal." *The Animal That Therefore I Am*, 34.
13. Ibid., 29.
14. Ibid., 31.
15. Ibid., 31.
16. Ibid., 23.
17. "How Many Species Are There?" *The Environmental Literacy Council*, 2002, www.enviroliteracy.org/article.php/58.html, accessed June 4, 2010.
18. Derrida, *Animal I Am*, 31.
19. Adorno and Horkheimer, *Dialectic of Enlightenment*, 206.
20. Ibid., 206.
21. Matthew Calarco, *Zoographies: The Question of the Animal from Heidegger to Derrida* (New York: Columbia University Press, 2008), 131.
22. Cary Wolfe, *Animal Rites: American Culture, the Discourse of Species, and Posthumanist Theory* (Chicago: University of Chicago Press, 2003), 8.
23. Calarco, *Zoographies*, 131.
24. Christina Gerhardt, "The Ethics of Animals in Adorno and Kafka," *New German Critique*, vol. 33, no. 1 (Winter 2006), 177.
25. I maintain the use of the masculine singular pronoun in this discussion in order to preserve consistency with Hegel's original text and to make the more significant point that the subjectivity described is of an inescapably masculine character. The same can be said for the subjectivity critiqued by Adorno and Horkheimer, Derrida, and Agamben. The use of the feminine pronoun runs the risk of obscuring the patriarchal nature and origin of the subject at hand.
26. G. W. F. Hegel, *Elements of the Philosophy of Right* (New York: Cambridge University Press, 2006), 182.

27. Ibid., 182.
28. Ibid., 187.
29. Blaise Pascal, *The Provincial Letters*, as quoted in *Philosophy of Right*, 171 (italics added).
30. Hegel, *Philosophy of Right*, 433 (note by Allen Wood to page 180).
31. Ibid., 184.
32. Ibid., 182.
33. Adorno and Horkheimer, *Dialectic of Enlightenment*, 6.
34. Derrida, *Animal I Am*, 20.
35. Ibid., 25.
36. Ibid., 29.
37. Cf. Charles Patterson, *Eternal Treblinka* (New York: Lantern Books, 2002).
38. Derrida, *Animal I Am*, 26.
39. I mean "pathetic" here in the neutral, literal sense of the word, as "arousing sadness, compassion, or sympathy, esp. through vulnerability or sadness; pitiable" (Oxford English Dictionary.) It is telling that the colloquial use of the word now incites feelings of scorn or blame. Hatred of the weak and helpless is characteristic of what Adorno and Horkheimer classify as the "authoritarian personality." The modern, authoritarian subject hates all signs of weakness and vulnerability. He mocks and degrades the victim, not content with its defeat, because he is complicit in a society that has made a victim of everyone, including himself. In the end, weakness itself is enough of a provocation for violence. The numerous undercover videos of slaughterhouse workers torturing and humiliating animals, mocking the squealing of pigs and groaning of cows, demonstrates a need to lash out at those who are pathetic. What the men who slam pigs into concrete floors and tear the wings off of live chickens don't realize is that they are provoked by the distorted reflection, in the terrified faces and cowering demeanors of their victims, of their own defeated lives. Cf. "Elements of Anti-Semitism: Limits of Enlightenment" in *Dialectic of Enlightenment.*
40. Sigmund Freud, *The Standard Edition of the Complete Psychological Works of Sigmund Freud: Volume XVII* (London: Hogarth Press Ltd., 1962), 139.
41. Immanuel Kant, *Lectures on Ethics* (New York: Cambridge University Press, 2001), 212.
42. Freud, *Volume XVII*, 140.
43. Theodor Adorno, *Minima Moralia: Reflections on a Damaged Life* (New York: Verso, 2005), 247.
44. Adorno and Horkheimer, *Dialectic of Enlightenment*, 210.
45. According to Primo Levi, "there was no general rule [for survival], except entering the camp in good health and knowing German. Barring this, luck dominated. I have seen the survival of shrewd people and silly people, the brave and the cowardly, 'thinkers' and madmen." (*Survival in Auschwitz*, 180.)
46. In the United States the obvious comparison is between "farm animals" and cats and dogs, but there are far more telling cases. The rabbit is perhaps the best exemplar of our arbitrary oscillation between violence and care. She may be a loved pet, an expensive bourgeois meal, a pair of mittens, or a pair of eyes to be tortured with beauty products, depending on the context.

47. Emmanuel Levinas, *Totality and Infinity: An Essay on Exteriority* (Pittsburgh, PA: Duquesne University Press, 2007) 22 (italics added).
48. Ibid., 21.
49. Adorno and Horkheimer, *Dialectic of Enlightenment*, 140.

CHAPTER 9

1. Rainer Maria Rilke, "Sonnets to Orpheus" (n. XIII), in *In Praise of Morality: Selections from Rainer Maria Rilke's Duino Elegies and Sonnets to Orpheus*, trans. and ed. Anita Barrows and Joanna Macy (London and New York: Riverhead Books, 2005), 119.
2. Peter Singer, *Animal Liberation*, new rev. ed. (New York: Avon Books, 1990), 6.
3. I have borrowed this conception of embodied consciousness from Maurice Merleau-Ponty, who suggests that while every animal, human or otherwise, has its own "style of being," all embodied beings navigate the world and their experience "through [their] bodies." Maurice Merleau-Ponty, *The World of Perception* (London and New York: Routledge Classics, 2004), 53f.
4. Max Horkheimer and Theodor W. Adorno, *Dialectic of Enlightenment: Philosophical Fragments*, ed. Gunzelin Schmid Noerr and Edmund Jephcott (Stanford, CA: Stanford University Press, 2002), 2.
5. Ibid., 3.
6. Ibid., 2.
7. Ibid., 204.
8. Ibid., 28.
9. Ibid., 204. Freud also acknowledges the profound shifts in our relationship with other animals from animism and totemic traditions to the Greek period and points, if only in passing, to the profound psychic distress that has resulted. He points out, for example, that "in the Athenian festival of Buphonia, a formal trial was introduced after the sacrifice in which everyone taking part was interrogated," even though the deed was committed under the auspices of a fully sanctioned sacrifice. Moreover, Freud points to "a certain psychical alienation from the animal" which occurred when animistic totemic traditions submitted to the "disruption" of their practices of animal worship with the introduction of domestication. See Sigmund Freud, "Totem and Taboo: Some Correspondences between the Psychical Lives of Savages and Neurotics," in *On Murder, Mourning, and Melancholia*, trans. Shaun Whiteside (London: Penguin Classics, 2005), 137, 147.
10. Marcuse, *One-Dimensional Man*, 132f.
11. Marcuse, *Eros and Civilization*, 109.
12. Horkheimer and Adorno, xiv.
13. Ibid., 211.
14. Marcuse, *One-Dimensional Man*, 158.
15. Herbert Marcuse, *Eros and Civilization: A Philosophical Inquiry into Freud* (Boston: Beacon Press, 1966), 87.
16. Marcuse, *Eros and Civilization*, 52.

17. Freud, *The Unconscious.*, trans. Graham Frankland (London: Penguin Classics, 2005), 36.

18. Christopher T. White, "The Modern Magnetic Animal: *As I Lay Dying* and the Uncanny Zoology of Modernism," *Journal of Modern Literature*, vol. 31, no. 3 (Spring 2008), 90.

19. Freud, "Mourning and Melancholia," in *On Murder, Mourning and Melancholia*, 207.

20. Freud, *The Unconscious*, 25. (Freud's italics.)

21. Freud, "Totem and Taboo," 140–44.

22. Ibid., 151f.

23. Freud's account of the "phylogenetic" origins of repressive civilization in the patricide of the so-called "primal horde" is largely discredited, and rightly so—not least because of its racist presuppositions and its lack of historical and anthropological verifiability, and because of its reduction of diverse cultural traditions to pathology. Similarly, the anthropocentrism inherent in Freud's claim that the sacred totemic animal represents the murdered father seriously undermines the validity of this explanation. Notwithstanding these objections to Freud's theory of ambivalence in both his phylogenetic and "ontogenetic" theories of development, it appears the same neurosis is at play in our dealings with other animals. For an example of the rejection of Freud's theory of the "archaic heritage" of the primal horde, see Marcuse, *Eros and Civilization*, 59.

24. Melanie Klein, "Love, Guilt and Reparation," in *Love, Guilt and Reparation and Other Works (1921–1945)* (New York: Delacorte Press/Seymour Lawrence, 1975), 311.

25. Freud, *The Unconscious*, 43.

26. Odysseus had to have himself tied to the ship's mast in order to avoid succumbing to the lure of the Sirens' song, and to assert himself as the great man of reason and cunning, nature's mighty conqueror. See Adorno and Horkheimer, 25. It is no wonder that slaughterhouses have among the highest worker turnover rates in the United States.

27. Carol Adams, *The Sexual Politics of Meat: A Feminist-Vegetarian Critical Theory* (New York: Continuum, 2006), 53.

28. Karl Marx, *Capital: A Critique of Political Economy*, vol. 1, trans. Ben Fowkes (London: Penguin Classics, 1990), 481f.

29. Carolyn Merchant, *The Death of Nature: Women, Ecology and the Scientific Revolution* (San Francisco: Harper & Row, 1990), xvi, xxi.

30. Horkheimer and Adorno, 207.

31. Josephine Donovan, "Animal Rights and Feminist Theory," in *The Feminist Care Tradition in Animal Ethics: A Reader*, ed. Josephine Donovan and Carol J. Adams (New York: Columbia University Press, 2007), 65.

32. Sigmund Freud, *Three Essays on the Theory of Sexuality*, trans. and rev. James Strachey (New York: Basic Books, 2000), 23.

33. On how feeling is reduced to sentimentality in the context of human–animal relations, see Josephine Donovan, "Animal Rights and Feminist Theory," 59.

34. Freud, "The Uncanny," in *The Uncanny*, trans. David McLintock (London and New York: Penguin Books, 2003), 131.

35. Ibid., 132, 126.

36. Ibid., 134.

37. Ibid., 132.

38. Christopher T. White, "The Modern Magnetic Animal: *As I Lay Dying* and the Uncanny Zoology of Modernism," in *Journal of Modern Literature*, vol. 31, no. 3 (Spring 2008), 85.

39. White, 86.

40. Horkheimer and Adorno, 11.

41. See note 3.

42. According to Heidegger, "[p]lant and animal are suspended in something outside of themselves without ever being able to 'see' either the outside or the inside, i.e., to have it stand as an aspect unconcealed in the free of Being." Although Heidegger does distinguish between stones, machines, and other animals, he still denies the latter access to "the open": "[a]nd never would it be possible for a stone, no more than for an airplane, to elevate itself toward the sun in jubilation and to move like a lark, which nevertheless does not see the open." Martin Heidegger, *Parmenides*, trans. André Schuwer and Richard Rojcewicz (Bloomington: Indiana University Press, 1998), 160. In his analysis of this and other passages in *Parmenides*, Giorgio Agamben also notes contradictions in Heidegger's thought and argues that in fact for Heidegger "the animal is at once open and not open." As a way out of this metaphysical bind, Agamben posits that we "let [the animal] be *outside of being*," and abandon the question of Being altogether. Giorgio Agamben, *The Open: Man and Animal*, trans. Kevin Attell (Stanford, CA: Stanford University Press, 2004), 59, 91f.

43. Rainer Maria Rilke, "The Eighth Elegy," in *In Praise of Morality*, 49.

44. Fromm, *The Sane Society* (New York and Toronto: Rinehart & Company, 1955), 23f.

45. Freud, "The Uncanny," 141f.

46. Theodore Roethke, "The Bat," *Words for the Wind: The Collected Verse of Theodore Roethke* (Bloomington, IN, 1968), p. 25.

47. Merleau-Ponty, 54.

48. See Emmanuel Levinas, *Ethics and Infinity: Conversations with Philippe Nemo*, trans. Richard A. Cohen (Pittsburgh, PA: Duquesne University Press, 2003), 86.

49. Freud, *The Unconscious*, 44.

50. Freud, "Mourning and Melancholia," in *On Murder, Mourning, and Melancholia*, 209.

51. Horkheimer, *Eclipse of Reason* (London and New York: Continuum, 2004), 79.

52. Freud, *The Joke and Its Relation to the Unconscious*, trans. Joyce Crick (London: Penguin Classics, 2002), 107.

53. Freud, *The Unconscious*, 39.

54. Adorno and Horkheimer, 88. For further discussion of "wrong laughter" and animal oppression, see Zipporah Weisberg, "The Broken Promises of Monsters: Haraway, Animals, and the Humanist Legacy," *Journal for Critical Animal Studies*, vol. 7, no. 2 (2009), www.criticalanimalstudies.org/?page_id=396.

55. Adorno and Horkheimer, 112.

56. Ibid., 112.

57. Adams, 42.

58. Ibid., 40.

59. Akira Mizuta Lippit, "Magnetic Animal: Derrida, Wildlife, *Animetaphor*," in *MLN: Modern Language Notes*, vol. 113, no. 5, *Comparative Literature Issue* (December 1998), 1111.

60. Ibid., 1112.

61. For example, Freud tells us that dreams of lizards whose tails fall off are supposed to symbolize "the warding-off of castration" and mentions that "[m]any of the beasts which are used as genital symbols in mythology and folklore play the same part in dreams: e.g., fishes, snails, cats, mice (on account of the pubic hair), and above all those most important symbols of the male organ—snakes. Small animals and vermin represent small children." See Sigmund Freud, *The Interpretation of Dreams*, trans. and ed. James Strachey (New York: Penguin Books, 1978), 474.

62. Horkheimer and Adorno, 27.

63. Klein, 308.

64. Adorno and Horkheimer, 110.

65. Fixation is defined as "a particularly intimate attachment of a drive to an object." Freud, *The Unconscious*, 37.

66. Jody Berland, "Animal and/as Medium: Symbolic Work in Communicative Regimes," *The Global South*, vol. 3, no. 1 (Spring 2009), http://muse.jhu.edu.ezproxy.library.yorku.ca/journals/the_global_south/v003/3.1.berland.html.

67. Adorno and Horkheimer, 110.

68. Freud, *The Unconscious*, 7.

69. Ibid., 7.

70. Ibid., 7.

71. Horkheimer and Adorno, 25.

72. Berland, "Animal and/as Medium," 59.

73. Wilhelm Reich, *The Mass Psychology of Fascism*, trans. Vincent R. Carfagno (New York: Farrar, Straus & Giroux, 1971), 335f.

74. Cary Wolfe, *Animal Rites: American Culture, the Discourse of Species, and Posthumanist Theory* (Chicago: University of Chicago Press, 2003), 1. (My italics.)

75. Ibid., 7.

76. Marcuse, *Eros and Civilization,*166f.

77. Ibid., 166.

78. Ibid., 233.

79. Donovan, 76.

CHAPTER 10

1. *Guidelines for the Care and Use of Mammals in Neuroscience and Behavioral Research* (National Research Council of the National Academies, National Academies Press, 2003), 91.

2. Ibid., 77.

3. Ibid., 92.

4. Matthew 27:33.

5. Eliot Katz, DVM, letter to NIH. www.vivisectioninfo.org/ucsf/nihresponse.html.

6. Matthew 27:46.
7. Guidelines, 78.
8. Mark 15:37.
9. Hamlet I, v.
10. Ibid., v.
11. Ibid., ii.
12. Ibid., iv.
13. An academic correspondent, e-mail, March 30, 2006.
14. Genesis 22:17.
15. W. F. Sternberg, L. Scorr, L. D. Smith, C. G. Ridgway, M. Stout, "Long-Term Effects of Neonatal Surgery on Adulthood Pain Behavior," *Pain*, vol. 113 (2005), 347–53. Also W. F. Sternberg, C. Ridgway, M. Stout, H. Takahaski, J. Steinemann, "Untreated Pain on Day of Birth Permanently Alters Pain Sensitivity in Mice," *Society for Neuroscience Abstracts*, vol. 28 (2002).
16. Job 30:29.
17. Correspondent, op. cit., e-mail, April 7, 2006.
18. Hamlet I, ii.
19. Macbeth, I, v.
20. Ibid., V, i.
21. Marlowe, Doctor Faustus, XIV.
22. Macbeth IV, i.
23. Doctor Faustus, XIV.

CHAPTER 11

1. Donald D. Kyle, *Sports and Spectacle in the Ancient World* (Hoboken, NJ: Wiley Publishers, 2007).
2. De Las Casas cited in Charles Patterson, *Eternal Treblinka: Our Treatment of Animals and the Holocaust* (New York: Lantern Books, 2004), 32.
3. Marjorie Speigel, *The Dreaded Comparison: Human and Animal Slavery*, 3rd rev. ed. (New York: Mirror Books, 1997).
4. Patterson.
5. The Nazis also murdered Roma (gypsies), homosexuals, and Marxists among others groups. This paper is about the processes through which the Nazis animalized the Jews, which is not meant to minimize the atrocities committed against these other groups.
6. Kenneth Burke, "The Rhetoric of Hitler's Battle," in Joseph R. Gusfield, ed., *Kenneth Burke: On Symbols and Society* (Chicago: University of Chicago Press, 1989).
7. Felicity Rash, *The Language of Violence: Adolf Hitler's* Mein Kampf (New York: Lang Publishers, 2006).
8. Patterson.
9. Adolph Hitler, *Mein Kampf* (Boston: Mariner Book/Houghton Mifflin Company, 1996). See especially ch. 11, "Nation and Race."

10. Helen Guldberg, "Animals Are Less Valuable than Human Beings," interview with John Martin, *Spiked*, June 2, 2008. www.spikedonline.com/index.php?/site/article/355/.

11. Charles Colson and Anne Morse, "Keeping Pets in Their Place: Why We Can't Afford to Treat Animals Like They're Human Beings," *Christianity Today*, vol. 52, no. 4 (April 2008), 1-2. www.christianitytoday.com/ct/2008/april/35.80.html.

12. Karl Marx, *The German Ideology*, in David McLellan, ed., *Karl Marx: Selected Writings* (Oxford, UK: Oxford University Press, 1977), 150.

13. Friedrich Engels, *The Origin of the Family, Private Property and the State*, Eleanor Burke Leacock, ed. (New York: International Publishers, 1975).

14. Jacoby cited in Patterson.

15. The term *sentient* is used interchangeably with *conscious*. Plants are not included because they do not have nervous systems connected to brains. The reference here is to the type of subjective experience common to humans and animals capable of the experience of suffering. See Peter Singer's *Animal Liberation* (New York: Harper Collins, 1975) and Marian Stamp Dawkins, "The Scientific Basis for Assessing Suffering in Animals," in Peter Singer, ed., *In Defense of Animals: The Second Wave* (Malden, MA: Wiley-Blackwell Publishing, 2005), 26–39.

16. Arthur Lovejoy, *The Great Chain of Being* (Cambridge, MA: Harvard University Press, 1966), in Rash, *The Language of Violence* and Jim Mason, *An Unnatural Order: Why We Are Destroying the Planet and Each Other* (New York: Continuum Press, 1998).

17. Robert Wuthnow, *Meaning and Moral Order: Explorations in Cultural Analysis* (Berkeley: University of California Press, 1987).

18. Noiles Vialles, *Animal to Edible* (Cambridge, UK: Cambridge University Press, 1994).

19. Michael Lynch, "Sacrifice and the Transformation of the Animal Body into a Scientific Object: Laboratory Culture and Ritual Practice in the Neurosciences," *Social Studies of Science*, vol. 18, no. 2 (1988), 265–89.

20. Gerald D. Berreman, *Caste in the Modern World* (Morristown, NJ: General Learning Press, 1973).

21. Ibid.

22. Roger Griffin, *Fascism* (Oxford, UK: Oxford University Press, 1995); George L. Mosse, *Nazism: A Historical and Comparative Analysis of National Socialism* (New Brunswick, NJ: Transaction Books, 1978); S. J. Woolf, ed., *The Nature of Fascism* (New York: Random House, 1968); F. L. Carsten, *The Rise of Fascism* (Berkeley: University of California Press, 1967); Ernst Nolte, *The Three Faces of Fascism: Action Francaise, Italian Fascism, National Socialism* (New York: Holt, Rinehaer and Winston, 1963).

23. Arthur de Gobineau, *Inequality of Races: The Pioneering Study of the Science of Human Races* (Los Angeles: The Noontide Press, 1966; originally published 1854), 35.

24. Rash, 90.

25. Hitler, 301–2.

26. Ibid., 285–86.

27. Ibid., 295

28. In a similar vein, Hitler degraded the Jews by denying their capacity for genuine spiritualism. (It was a token of faith in Nazi writings that Jesus was actually an Aryan.)

For example: "[t]he best characterization is provided by the product of this religious education, the Jew himself. His life is only of this world, and his spirit is inwardly as alien to true Christianity as his nature two thousand years previous was to the great founder of the new doctrine. Of course, the latter made no secret of his attitude toward the Jewish people, and when necessary he even took to the whip to drive from the temple of the Lord this adversary of all humanity" (Hitler, 307).

29. See, for example, Nazi party leader Dietrich Eckart's 1919 article on "Jewishness in and around Us," in *Nazi Ideology before 1933: A Documentation*, trans. Barbara Miller Land and Leila J. Rupp (Austin: University of Texas Press, 1978; originally published 1919).

30. In the late nineteenth century, Germany was home to anti-rationalist and anti-modernist movements, as was much of Europe. Henri Bergson and Friedrich Nietzsche were theorists from the late nineteenth century whose work was drawn upon to challenge Enlightenment rationalism, modernism, and liberal democracy. Nazi official Ludwig Clauss, for example, drew upon *volk*ish mythology to argue that the "racial soul" reaches out into the world and "fashions the geographical area of this world into a landscape . . . by virtue of its species determined way of viewing its environment" (Ludwig Clauss, "Racial Soul, Landscape, and World Domination," in Mosse, 65). Against Enlightenment views of nature, which had emphasized the role of human intellect and its intervention in "taming" nature, the German anti-modernist movements understood what was natural as being unchanged by humanity, as "*outside and prior to man.*" Luc Ferry, *The New Ecological Order* (Chicago: University of Chicago Press, 1992), 97. Consequently, "nature" needed to be protected in its pristine form.

31. Ferry, 92–3.

32. Mosse, *Nazism*, 9.

33. Ferry.

34. Herbert Marcuse, *Eros and Civilization: A Philosophical Inquiry into Freud* (Boston: Beacon Press, 1955), 35.

35. Sigmund Freud, *Civilization and Its Discontents* (New York: W. W. Norton & Co., 2005).

36. Marcuse, 34

37. Ibid., 35

38. Ibid.

39. This is not to say that small businesses and family businesses do not also profit from and sustain the system of animal exploitation. However, they may do so to maintain a living or to continue family traditions, and so forth.

40. While there is considerable debate among philosophers and scientists about the extent and degree of consciousness among other sentient beings, a consensus is emerging that members of other species are aware and intelligent, experience a variety of emotions, and possess rich sensorial and psychic lives that matter greatly to them (see Dawkins and Singer's *Animal Liberation* as well as his *Practical Ethics* [Cambridge, UK: Cambridge University Press, 1993]; also David DeGrazia, "On the Question of Personhood beyond *Homo Sapiens*" in Singer, ed., *In Defense of Animals*, 40–53).

41. Human groups have been animalized by powerful political and/or economic actors in specific historical contexts. This essay does not explore the economic or

political conditions that provide a context for the animalization of subordinates. Rather, it focuses on the cultural beliefs and practices or rituals that are drawn upon in the process of animalization.

CHAPTER 12

1. Research for this chapter was carried out with the generous support of the Social Sciences and Humanities Research Council of Canada.

2. Lyle Munro, "Contesting Moral Capital in Campaigns against Animal Liberation," *Society and Animals*, vol. 7, no. 1 (1999). www.psyeta.org/sa/sa7.1/munro.html.

3. Ken Ewert, "The Bible and Private Property," *U-Turn*, vol. 6, no. 2 (1999). www.u-turn.net/6-2/property.shtml.

4. Zoltan Horvath, "A Biblical Approach to Poverty," *U-Turn*, vol. 9, no. 1 (Spring 2003). www.u-turn.net/9-1/poverty.shtml.

5. Dave Matheson, "Six Billion Chickens: The Animal Rights Movement," The King's Community Church Resources, *The Kingdom* (n.d.). www.tkc.com/resources/resources-pages/animalrights1.html. Originally published in *U-Turn* (1999). www.u-turn.net/3-3/chicken.html.

6. Dave Matheson, "Eat Your Veggies," The King's Community Church Resources, *The Kingdom* (n.d.). www.tkc.com/resources/resources-pages/animalrights2.html. Originally published in *U-Turn* (1999). www.u-turn.net/3-4/veggies.html.

7. Miranda Devine, "The Green Beast Is Out of Control," *Sydney Morning Herald*, December 2, 2004. www.maninnature.com/Management/ARights/Rights1u.html.

8. Thomas S. Derr, "Animal Rights, Human Rights," *First Things* (1992). www.firstthings.com/ftissues/ft9202/articles/derr.html.

9. David R. Carlin, "Rights, Animal and Human," *First Things*, no. 105 (August–September 2000), 16–17. www.leaderu.com/ftissues/ft0008/opinion/carlin.html.

10. Ibid.

11. Alex Epstein, "The Conference for Human Extinction" (2001). www.aynrand.org/site/News2?page=NewsArticle&id=5186&news_iv_ctrl=1084.

12. Alex Epstein, "The Terror of "Animal Rights"" (2004). www.alexepstein.com/articles/theterror.htm. (Italics in original.)

13. Andrew Bernstein, "Animal Rights vs. Human Rights" (2000). www.aynrand.org/site/News2?page=NewsArticle&id=5106&news_iv_ctrl=1084.

14. Edwin A. Locke, "Animal's [*sic*] 'Rights' Versus Man's Rights: Animal 'Rights' Activists Want to Sacrifice Man's Rights," *Capitalism Magazine* (August 1, 2000). www.capmag.com/article.asp?ID=3423.

15. Matheson, "Six Billion Chickens."

16. Jim Beers, "Conference Report: Terrorism and a Radical Agenda," South African Gunowners' Association (2001). www.saga.org.za/Animal%20Rights.htm.

17. J. P. Zmirak, "To Serve Man: A Cookbook" (2002). www.frontpagemag.com/Articles/ReadArticle.asp?ID=1578.

18. Chris Talbot, "Correspondence on Animal Rights," World Socialist Website (September 14, 2004). www.wsws.org/articles/2004/sep2004/corr-s14.shtml.

19. Julie Hyland, "Britain: Blair Government Outlines Fresh Attack on Civil Liberties," World Socialist Website. (August 10, 2004). www.wsws.org/articles/2004/aug2004/rght-a10.shtml.

20. John Sorenson, "Attacking Animal Advocacy," paper presented at the Twenty Years of Propaganda Conference, University of Windsor, May 17, 2007.

21. Chris Talbot, "Correspondence on Animal Rights," World Socialist Website. (September 14, 2004). www.wsws.org/articles/2004/sep2004/corr-s14.shtml.

22. In 1998 the British government announced it would not issue licenses for animal testing of cosmetic products or ingredients, but this took the form of a voluntary agreement with corporations, which can still test their products outside the country.

23. Animal Alliance, "The Massacre Continues . . . " (2001). www.cruelscience.ca/news-2000stats.htm.

24. People for the Ethical Treatment of Animals, "The Military's War on Animals." www.peta.org/feat/military/.

25. James Kirkup, "MoD Tests on Animals have Doubled to 21,000 a Year," *The Scotsman*, May 10, 2006. http://news.scotsman.com/uk.cfm?id=698932006; Marie Woolf, "Military Lab tests on Live Animals Double in Five Years," *The Independent*, May 14, 2006. http://news.independent.co.uk/uk/politics/article447816.ece.

26. Jonathan Balcombe, "Laboratory Routines Cause Animal Stress," Contemporary Topics in Laboratory Animal Science (Autumn 2004). www.pcrm.org/newsletter/nov04/stress.html.

27. Physicians Committee for Responsible Medicine, "Animal Experiments More Stressful than Previously Recognized," press release, December 28, 2004. www.eurekalert.org/pub_releases/2004-12/pcfr-aem122804.php.

28. Pandora Pound, Shah Ebrahim, Peter Sandercock, Michael B. Bracken, and Ian Roberts, "Where Is the Evidence that Animal Research Benefits Humans?" *British Medical Journal* (February 28, 2004). http://bmj.bmjjournals.com/cgi/content/full/328/7438/514.

29. Chris Talbot, "Correspondence on Animal Rights," World Socialist Website. (September 14, 2004). www.wsws.org/articles/2004/sep2004/corr-s14.shtml.

30. Liberal Party (UK), "Animal Welfare," policy statement (2000). www.liberal.org.uk/policy/animal.htm.

31. Green Party (UK), "Animal Rights," policy statement (2006). www.greenparty.org.uk/issues/1.

32. World Socialist Website, "An Exchange on a Socialist Approach to the Protection of the Environment" (January 10, 2001). www.wsws.org/articles/2001/jan2001/corr-j10.shtml.

33. Peter Staudenmaier, "Ambiguities of Animal Rights," Institute of Social Ecology website (June 11, 2004). www.social-ecology.org/article.php?story=2004061114081745 8&query=animal+rights.

34. Alan Herscovici, "The Rise & Fall of Animal Rights: Holding Activists Accountable," Man in Nature website (October 1998). www.maninnature.com/Management/ARights/Rights1a.html.

35. Edward J. Feulner, "Animal Rights and Wrongs," The Heritage Foundation website (November 4, 1998). www.heritage.org/Press/Commentary/ed110498.cfm.

36. Rynn Berry, *Hitler: Neither Vegetarian Nor Animal Lover* (New York: Pythagorean Publishers, 2004).

37. Alexander Cockburn,"Vegetarians, Nazis for Animal Rights, Blitzkrieg of the Ungulates: A Short Meat-Oriented History of the World, Part Three," *Counterpunch*, August 18, 2005. www.counterpunch.org/cockburn08182005.html.

38. Gary Francione, "Nazis and Animal Rights" (1996). www.animal-law.org/commentaries/fe29.htm.

39. Michael Albert, "Progressives: Outreach Is the Key: The *Satya* Interview with Michael Albert," Catherine Clyne, interviewer, *Satya* (September 2002). http://satyamag.com/sept02/albert.html.

40. Peter Singer, *One World* (New Haven, CT: Yale University Press. 2004), 153.

41. Michael Moore, *Dude Where's My Country?* (New York: Warner, 2004), 190, 192.

42. World Rainforest Movement, "Deforestation by Agriculture and Cattle-Raising," *WRM Bulletin* no. 85 (August 2004). www.wrm.org.uy/.

43. Richard W. Franke and Barbara H. Chasin, *Seeds of Famine* (Totowa, NJ: Rowman and Allanheld, 1980).

44. Jacky Turner, "Factory Farming and the Environment," Compassion in World Farming Trust (October 1999). www.ciwf.org.uk/publications/reports/factory_farming_and_the_environment_1999.pdf.

45. Human Rights Watch, "Blood, Sweat and Fear: Workers' Rights in U.S. Meat and Poultry Plants" (2005). http://hrw.org/reports/2005/usa0105/.

46. Gail A. Eisnitz, *Slaughterhouse* (Amherst, MA: Prometheus, 1997).

47. Peter Singer, "A Meaningful Life," (1999). http://home.vicnet.net.au/~abr/DecJan99/nlae.html.

48. Noam Chomsky, "Michael Albert and Noam Chomsky" (1993). www.zmag.org/chomsky/interviews/9301-albchomsky.html.

49. David Nibert, *Animal Rights/Human Rights* (Lanham, MD: Rowman & Littlefield, 2002).

50. Anna E. Charlton, Sue Coe, and Gary Francione, "The American Left Should Support Animal Rights: A Manifesto" (1993). www.animal-law.org/library/left.htm.

51. Center for Animal Liberation Affairs. www.cala-online.org/index.html.

52. Marjorie Spiegel, radio interview on *Animal Voices* by Lauren Corman (2001). www.animalvoices.ca/shows.htm#IDEA.

53. John Mackey, Karen Dawn, and Lauren Ornelas, "The CEO as Animal Activist," in *In Defense of Animals: The Second Wave*, Peter Singer, ed. (Malden, MA: Blackwell, 2006), 213.

54. Eric Bates, "Minding the Store." www.organicconsumers.org/Corp/wholefood.htm.

55. Ibid.

56. Simon Redfearn and Ted Benton, "The Politics of Animal Rights—Where Is the Left?" *New Left Review*, no. 215 (1996), 43–58.

CHAPTER 13

1. Gaby Woods, "Interview with Joel Salatin," The *Guardian*, January 31, 2010. www.guardian.co.uk/lifeandstyle/2010/jan/31/food-industry-environment. Last ac-

cessed April 2010. Salatin's answer as to why he does not use "heritage" birds (i.e., birds that have not been bred for such traits as abnormally large breasts). A print version of this article also appeared in the *Observer Food Monthly* section of the *Observer*, January 31, 2010, 44.

2. "Oxford Word of the Year: Locavore" *Oxford University Press Blog*. http://blog.oup.com/2007/11/locavore/. Last accessed April 1, 2010.

3. Pollan, M., *The Omnivore's Dilemma: A Natural History of Four Meals* (New York: Penguin Books, 2006), 135–36.

4. Ibid., 327.

5. Of course Pollan himself also indicates this same environmental degradation of factory farming and his claim is that small-scale local farms will solve the problem. My point here is simply that Pollan inverts one of the most common claims made by animal rights advocates.

6. Caroline Saunders, Andrew Barber, and Greg Taylor, "Food Miles—Comparative Energy/Emissions Performance of New Zealand's Agriculture Industry," Research Report No. 285 (New Zealand: Lincoln University, July 2006), 93.

7. Christopher L. Weber and H. Scott Matthews, "Food-Miles and the Relative Climate Impacts of Food Choices in the United States," *Environmental Science and Technology*, vol. 42, no.10 (2008), 3508. Emphasis added.

8. Richard Black, "Shun Meat, Says UN Climate Chief: Livestock Production Has a Bigger Climate Impact than Transport, the UN Believes," *BBC News* (2008). http://news.bbc.co.uk/1/hi/sci/tech/7600005.stm. See also the Food and Agricultural Organization of the United Nations (FAO) report *Livestock's Long Shadow*.

9. Mike Tidwell, "The Low-Carbon Diet," *AubobonMagizine.org*. Last Accessed April 1, 2010.

10. Steinfeld et al., *Livestock's Long Shadow: Environmental Issues and Options* (Rome, Italy: Food and Agriculture Organization of the United Nations, 2006), xxi.

11. Ibid., xxi.

12. "Growing populations and incomes, along with changing food preferences, are rapidly increasing demand for livestock products, while globalization is boosting trade in livestock inputs and products. Global production of meat is projected to more than double from 229 million tones in 1999/01 to 465 million tonnes in 2050, and that of milk to grow from 580 to 1,043 million tones." (Steinfeld et al., *Livestock's Long Shadow*, xx) To be fair, Pollan has himself, in his most recent work, started to make calls for people to decrease their meat consumption. However, these calls are both not stringent enough and not echoed in the wider movement. Given the exponential rate of projected increase for meat consumption, what is need is a significantly long-term and across-the-board decrease of the number of animals raised and killed for slaughter, not tepid calls for minor decreases in individual rates of meat consumption.

13. Steinfeld et al., *Livestock's Long Shadow*, xxiii.

14. Pollan, *The Omnivore's Dilemma*, 230. Emphasis added.

15. Barbara Kingsolver, *Animal, Vegetable, Miracle: A Year of Food Life* (New York: HarperCollins Publishers, 2007), 33.

16. Pollan, *The Omnivore's Dilemma*, 263.

17. Kingsolver, *Animal, Vegetable, Miracle*, 151.

18. Pollan, *The Omnivore's Dilemma*, 133.

19. Ibid.

20. www.polyfacefarms.com/story.aspx. Last accessed April 1, 2001.

21. Barbara Kingsolver, *Animal, Vegetable, Miracle*, 158.

22. Ibid., 243.

23. L. Claudio, "Waste Couture: Environmental Impact of the Clothing Industry," *Environmental Health Perspectives*, vol. 115, no 9. (2007), A450.

24. "Only about one-fifth of the clothing donated to charities is directly used or sold in their thrift shops. Says Rivoli, 'There are nowhere near enough people in America to absorb the mountains of castoffs, even if they were given away'" (Ibid., A450).

25. "Clothing that is not considered vintage or high-end is baled for export to developing nations. Data from the International Trade Commission indicate that between 1989 and 2003, American exports of used clothing more than tripled, to nearly 7 billion pounds per year. Used clothing is sold in more than 100 countries. For Tanzania, where used clothing is sold at the *mitumba* markets that dot the country, these items are the number one import from the United States" (Ibid., A452).

26. For example, in the case of clothing, "[a]ccording to figures from the U.S. National Labor Committee, some Chinese workers make as little as 12–18 cents per hour working in poor conditions. And with the fierce global competition that demands ever lower production costs, many emerging economies are aiming to get their share of the world's apparel markets, even if it means lower wages and poor conditions for workers" (Ibid., A450).

27. According to the Environmental Protection Agency, DVDs are a particularly egregious source of e-waste pollution since they derive from rare mined earth materials, are virtually impossible to recycle, leach into water supplies, and produce toxic results for both the environment and human health. Furthermore, as a flyer made by the EPA for school children tries to explain, "[o]nce discs are packaged, they are ready to be sent to distribution centers, retail outlets, or other locations. Transportation by plane, truck, or rail requires the use of fossil fuels for energy, which contribute to climate change."

28. U. K. Heise, *Sense of Place and Sense of Planet: The Environmental Imagination of the Global* (Oxford, UK: Oxford University Press, 2008).

29. Pollan, *The Omnivore's Dilemma*, 203.

30. "Is Back to Nature Farming Only for Men?" *Irregular Times*. www.irregulartimes.com/polyface.html, accessed May 1, 2009. Note: this may be changing due to outside pressure. However, it was certainly the case when Pollan attended the farm. Indeed Salatin's website, while stating that they will accept six men and two women, still reads at the beginning, "[a]n extremely intimate relationship, the apprenticeships offer young *men* the opportunity to live and work with the Salatins" (emphasis added). It is unclear how many, if any, women have been allowed to serve in the farm labor aspect of the apprenticeship.

31. "Interview: Joel Salatin," *Observer Food Monthly* section of the *Observer*, January 31, 2010, 44. www.guardian.co.uk/lifeandstyle/2010/jan/31/food-industry-environment. Last accessed April 2010.

32. Michael Pollan, "The Food Movement, Rising," *The New York Review of Books*, June 10, 2010. www.nybooks.com/articles/archives/2010/jun/10/food-movement-rising/?page=3.

33. Michael Pollan, "Out of the Kitchen, onto the Couch," *New York Times Magazine*, July 29, 2009. www.nytimes.com/2009/08/02/magazine/02cooking-t.html?_r=3&pagewanted=1&partner=rss&emc=rss. A version of this article also appeared in print on August 2, 2009, on page MM26 of the New York edition.

34. Kingsolver, *Animal, Vegetable, Miracle*, 127.

35. Ibid., 126–27, 156.

36. Jennifer Jeffrey, "The Feminist in My Kitchen." http://jenniferjeffrey.typepad.com/writer/2007/06/one-day-during-.html. Accessed April 1st, 2010.

37. Joel Salatin, "Polyface, Inc. Apprenticeships." www.polyfacefarms.com/apprentice.aspx. Accessed May 1, 2009. Emphasis added.

38. Bob Jones University, "Statement about Race at BJU." www.bju.edu/welcome/who-we-are/race-statement.php. Last accessed April 1, 2010.

39. *Student Handbook* (Bob Jones University, 2005), 29.

40. "Headlines: Giving Due Honor: Accolades for Students and Grades," *BJU Review*, vol. 24, no. 3 (Winter 2009), 2. http://issuu.com/bjureview/docs/bju_review_winter_2009__vol._24_no.3. Accessed April 1, 2010.

41. Lewis McCrary, "Cultivating Freedom: Joel Salatin Practices Ethical Animal Husbandry—No Thanks to the Feds," *American Conservative* (November 1, 2009). www.amconmag.com/. Accessed April 1, 2010.

42. Testimony of Joel Salatin, Polyface Farm, Swoope, Virginia, United States Congress, "After the Beef Recall: Exploring Greater Transparency in the Meat Industry," House Committee on Oversight and Government Reform, April 17, 2008. While I agree with the view the migrant workers are exploited in factory farming systems it is unclear to me how grouping them intermediately with C and D students and referring to them as social outcasts helps to improve their working conditions. Please see note 23 for additional commentary on this point.

43. Kelefa Sanneh, "Fast Bikes, Slow Food, and the Workplace Wars," *New Yorker Magazine*, June 22, 2009. www.newyorker.com/arts/critics/atlarge/2009/06/22/090622crat_atlarge_sanneh. Last accessed April 1, 2010.

44. See multiple articles on the blog by the Coalition of Immokalee Workers (CIW), www.ciw-online.org/news.html. Last Accessed April 1, 2010. Of particular interest is also the manner in which Chipotle utilizes its use of meat from Polyface farms to ward off criticism of its treatment of migrant farm workers.

45. While it could be argued that Salatin's comments about migrant labor only reflect concern about labor standards, Sanneh makes, I believe, an excellent rejoinder: "[p]roponents of homegrown food and (very) small business . . . sometimes talk about how artisanalism improves the lives of workers. But the genius of this loosely organized movement is that it's not a labor movement; it's a consumer movement." Although I have searched extensively I can find no evidence of where Joel Salatin has been directly working with farm workers unions to improve their labor conditions.

46. Yasmin Alibhai Brown, "Eat Only Local Produce? I Don't Like the Smell of That: The Language in This Debate Is a Proxy for Anti-immigration Sentiments," *The*

Independent, May 12, 2008. www.independent.co.uk/opinion/commentators/yasmin-alibhai-brown/yasmin-alibhaibrown-eat-only-local-produce-i-dont-like-the-smell-of-that-826272.html. Last accessed April 1, 2010.

47. D. Frank, *Buy American: The Untold Story of Economic Nationalism* (Boston: Beacon Press, 1999), 243.

48. For a review of some of the recent literature on this subject, see Sidney W. Mintz and Christine M. Du Bois, "The Anthropology of Food and Eating," *Annual Review of Anthropology*, no. 31 (2002), 99–119.

49. James McWilliams, "Is Locavorism for Rich People Only?" *New York Times Blog,* October 14, 2009. http://freakonomics.blogs.nytimes.com/2009/10/14/is-locavorism-for-rich-people-only/?pagemode=print. Last Accessed April 1, 2010.

50. Pollan, T*he Omnivore's Dilemma*, 322.

51. Ibid., 331.

52. "Annie Corrigan, Joel Salatin and Polyface Farm: Stewards of Creation," *EarthEats*, March 26, 2010. http://indianapublicmedia.org/eartheats/joel-salatin-complete-interview/. Accessed April 1, 2010.

53. Pollan, T*he Omnivore's Dilemma*, 291.

54. Ibid., 272.

55. Ibid., 297.

56. Kingsolver, *Animal, Vegetable, Miracle*, 222.

57. Pollan, *The Omnivore's Dilemma*, 342.

58. For one example among many, see the interview by Mandy Henderson, "Joel Salatin—The Pastor of the Pasture,"*Columbus Underground*, February 28, 2010. www.columbusunderground.com/joel-salatin-the-pastor-of-the-pasture. Last accessed April 1, 2010.

CHAPTER 14

1. Thanks to Catharine MacKinnon, John Sanbonmastu, and Josephine Donovan for all of the ways they have influenced this chapter.

2. I am uncomfortable with the term "animal liberation movement." First, there is some question whether a liberation movement can exist on behalf of another group of beings, rather than arising from the oppressed group of beings for whom liberation is being sought. I also avoid "animal rights movement" as I do not believe rights is a sufficient basis upon which to articulate the issues regarding animal oppression—see Josephine Donovan and Carol J. Adams, *The Feminist Care Tradition in Animal Ethics: A Reader* (New York: Columbia University Press, 2007). In the past I have used the term "animal defense movement"—see Carol J. Adams, *Neither Man nor Beast: Feminism and the Defense of Animals* (New York: Continuum, 1994). For this essay, I am choosing a more generic term, "animal movement," as I believe it can also incorporate "critical animal studies."

3. Catharine A. MacKinnon, "Of Mice and Men: A Feminist Fragment on Animal Rights," in Cass Sunstein and Martha Nussbaum, eds., *Animal Rights: Current Debates and New Directions* (New York: Oxford, 2004).

4. At least once in their lives, 44 percent of women are victims of rape or attempted rape (MacKinnon, *Women's Lives*, 39). Women and children are considerably less safe in the home than are adult men. Battering is the major cause of injury to adult women. The World Health Organization, in the first comprehensive documentation of global violence released in October 2002, found that 40 to 70 percent of female murder victims in Australia, the United States, Canada, Israel, and South Africa were killed by their husbands or boyfriends. Marital rape is among the most common kind of sexual assault there is. One in three American girls and one in seven boys are sexually abused. Half of all rape victims are under 18 years of age; 25 percent of rape victims are under 12 years of age. Woman battering is a major cause of homelessness for women and their children. At least 40 percent of homeless women became homeless after suffering abuse by male partners, and now face rape on the street rather than battering in the home—see Stephanie Golden, *The Women Outside: Meaning and Myths of Homelessness* (Berkeley, CA: University of California Press, 1992). Homeless women also face sexual harassment from landlords and building superintendents in seeking apartments. More than 90 percent of working women surveyed had been sexually harassed on the job.

5. Sexual inequality is racialized: "[t]he combined influence of rape (or the threat of rape), domestic violence, and economic oppression is key to understanding the hidden motivations informing major social protest and migratory movements in Afro-American history." Darlene Clark Hine, "Rape and the Inner Lives of Black Women in the Middle West: Preliminary Thoughts on the Culture of Dissemblance," *Signs: Journal of Women in Culture and Society* vol. 14, no. 4 (1989), 913. "I believe that many Black women quit the South out of a desire to achieve personal autonomy and to escape both from sexual exploitation from inside and outside of their families and from the rape and threat of rape by white as well as Black males" (Ibid., 914). Sexual harassment and rape of domestics, mainly women of color, has been well documented; Patricia Hill Collins, *Black Feminist Thought: Knowledge, Consciousness, and the Politics of Empowerment* (Boston: Unwin Hyman, 1990) refers to it as sexual extortion. Collins points out that according to statistics, black women are more likely to be victimized than white women (Ibid., 178) and Angela Davis, *Women, Race, and Class* (New York: Vintage Books, 1981) has demonstrated how sexual violence is central to the economic and political subordination of African-Americans. Byllye Avery, founder of the Black Women's Health Network, argues that we must connect the issue of black teenage pregnancy to incest. "When you talk to young people about being pregnant, you find out that most of these girls did not get pregnant by teenage boys. Most of them got pregnant by their mothers' boyfriends or their brothers or their daddies. We've been sitting on that. We can't just tell our daughters, 'Just say no.' We need to talk to our brothers. . . . We need men to stop giving consent, by their silence, to rape, to sexual abuse, to violence." Byllye Avery, "A Question of Survival/A Conspiracy of Silence: Abortion and Black Women's Health," *From Reproduction to Reproductive Freedom: Transforming a Movement,* ed. Marlene Gerber-Fried (Boston: South End Press, 1990), 79–80.

6. Catharine A. MacKinnon, *Women's Lives, Men's Laws* (Cambridge and London, UK: Cambridge University Press, 2005), 24.

7. Catharine A. MacKinnon, *Toward a Feminist Theory of State* (Cambridge, MA and London: Harvard University Press, 1989), 128.

8. Catharine A. MacKinnon, "Liberalism and the Death of Feminism," in Dorchen Leidholdt and Janice G. Raymond, eds., *The Sexual Liberals and the Attack on Feminism* (New York: Teachers College Press, 1990), 13.

9. Ibid., 6.

10. The radical feminist critique that identifies the patriarchal nature of animal oppression can be found in the following writings, among others: Carol J. Adams, *Sexual Politics of Meat: A Feminist-Vegetarian Critical Theory* (New York: Continuum, 2000) and Adams, "Bringing Peace Home: A Feminist Philosophical Perspective on the Abuse of Women, Children, and Pet Animals," *Hypatia: A Journal of Feminist Philosophy* vol. 9, no. 2; Carol J. Adams and Josephine Donovan, eds., *Animals and Women: Feminist Theoretical Explorations* (Durham, NC: Duke University Press, 1995); Norma Benney, "All of One Flesh: The Rights of Animals," in Leonie Caldecott and Stephanie, eds., *Reclaim the Earth: Women Speak out for Life on Earth* (1983), 141–50; Lynda Birke, *Feminism, Animals and Science: The Naming of the Shrew* (Buckingham and Philadephia, PA: Open University Press, 1994); Aviva Cantor, "The Club, the Yoke, and the Leash," *Ms.* (August 1983), 27–30; Andrée Collard with Joyce Contrucci, *Rape of the Wild: Man's Violence Against Animals and the Earth* (Bloomington: Indiana University Press, 1989); Genoveffa Corea, "Dominance and Control: How Our Culture Sees Women, Nature and Animals," *Animals Agenda*, 37 (1984), 20–1; Karen Davis, "Farm Animals and the Feminine Connection," *The Animals' Agenda* (January/February 1988), 38–39; Maneesha Deckha, "The Salience of Species Difference for Feminist Theory," *Hastings Women's Law Journal*, vol. 17, no. 1 (Winter 2006), 1–38; Marti Kheel, *Nature Ethics: An Ecofeminist Perspective* (Lanham, MD: Rowman & Littlefield, 2007); Lori Gruen, "Dismantling Oppression: An Analysis of the Connection between Women and Animals," in Greta Gaard, ed., *Ecofeminism: Women, Animals, Nature* (Philadelphia, PA: Temple University Press, 1993), 60–90; also Gruen, "On The Oppression of Women and Animals," *Environmental Ethics*, vol. 18, no. 4 (1996), 441–44; Roberta Kalechofsky, "Metaphors of Nature: Vivisection and Pornography—The Manichean Machine," *Between the Species*, 179–85; Suzanne Kappeler, *The Pornography of Representation* (Minneapolis: The University of Minnesota Press, 1986); also Kappeler, "Speciesism, Racism, Nationalism . . . or the Power of Scientific Subjectivity," in Carol J. Adams and Josephine Donovan, eds., *Animals and Women: Feminist Theoretical Explorations* (Durham, NC: Duke University Press, 1995), 320–52; Brian Luke, "Taming Ourselves or Going Feral? Toward a Nonpatriarchal Metaethic for Animal Liberation," in Adams and Donovan, eds., *Animals and Women*, 290–319; also Lukes, *Brutal: Manhood and the Exploitation of Animals* (Champagne-Urbana: University of Illinois Press) and "Violent Love: Hunting, Heterosexuality, and the Erotics of Men's Predation," *Feminist Studies* 24 (Fall 1998), 627–55; Jane Meyerding, "Feminist Criticism and Cultural Imperialism (Where Does One End and the Other Begin)," *Animals Agenda* (November/December 1982), 14–15, 22–23; Connie Salamone, "Feminist as Rapist in the Modern Male Hunter Culture," *Majority Report* (October 1973); and "The Prevalence of the Natural Law within Women: Women and Animal Rights," in Pam McAllister, ed., *Reweaving the Web of Life: Feminism and Nonviolence* (Philadelphia, PA: New Society Publishers, 1982).

11. MacKinnon, *Women's Lives*, 93.

12. Wendy Brown, *Manhood and Politics: A Feminist Reading in Political Thought* (Lanham, MD: Rowman & Littlefield, 2002), 56.
13. MacKinnon, "Of Mice and Men," 94–95.
14. Sandra Harding, "Is Gender a Variable in Conceptions of Rationality?" 48.
15. Genevieve Lloyd, *The Man of Reason: Male and Female in Western Philosophy* (New York: Routledge, 1986), 2.
16. Brian Luke, *Brutal: Manhood and the Exploitation of Animals* (Champagne-Urbana: University of Illinois Press, 2007), 326.
17. Catharine A. MacKinnon, *Feminism Unmodified: Discourses on Life and Law.* (Cambridge, MA and London: Harvard University Press, 1987).
18. See Donovan and Adams, *Feminist Care Tradition.*
19. Catharine A. MacKinnon, *Are Women Human? And Other International Dialogues* (Cambridge, UK and London: Cambridge University Press, 2006), 57.
20. www.youtube.com/watch?v=vGLHlvb8skQ
21. See Brian Luke, *Brutal: Manhood and the Exploitation of Animals* (Champagne-Urbana: University of Illinois Press, 2007) and Kheel, *Nature Ethics.*
22. Daniel Moshenberg, Letter, *New York Times*, October 5, 2006.
23. Bonnie G. Smith, *The Gender of History: Men, Women, and Historical Practice* (Cambridge, MA and London: Harvard University Press, 1998).
24. MacKinnon, *State*, 58.
25. Ibid., 234, n. 26.
26. Adams, *Sexual Politics*, 83.
27. Karen Davis, *More than a Meal: The Turkey in History, Myth, Ritual, and Reality* (New York: Lantern Books, 2000).
28. Susan Davis and Margo Demello, op. cit., 312.
29. MacKinnon, "Liberalism," 4.
30. MacKinnon, *Women's Lives*, 303.
31. Ibid., 302.
32. See also "Taffy Lovely," described in my *Sexual Politics of Meat* (52) or the "Turkey Hooker" found in Adams, *The Pornography of Meat* (New York: Continuum, 2003), 108.
33. MacKinnon, *Women's Lives*, 129.
34. MacKinnon, *State*, 140–41.
35. Catharine A. MacKinnon, *Only Words* (Cambridge, MA: Harvard University Press, 1993), 11.
36. www.youtube.com/watch?v=0h-A3UtguZw.
37. Emily Gaarder, "Women and Animal Rights: Why Are We the Majority?" *AV Magazine*, vol. 113, no. 1 (2005), 2–3, found that some women activists expressed empathy to animals based on shared inequities.
38. Andrea Dworkin was the first to suggest this to me.
39. MacKinnon, *Women's Lives*, 30.
40. Diane Rehm Show, August 2007 (as reported to the author by a listener).
41. Carol J. Adams, "Woman-Battering and Harm to Animals," in Carol J. Adams and Josephine Donovan, eds., *Animals and Women: Feminist Theoretical Explorations* (Durham, NC: Duke University Press, 1995).

42. Donovan in Donovan and Adams, *The Feminist Care Tradition*, 76.

43. MacKinnon identifies yet another issue: "[h]ow to avoid reducing animal rights to the rights of some people to speak for animals against the rights of other people to speak for the same animals needs further thought." *Women's Lives*, 98. Crush videos are one example, in which women in stiletto heels are shown crushing small animals to death. Crush videos also prove MacKinnon's point, made elsewhere, that "[n]owhere are the powerless as powerful as in the imagination of those with real, not imaginary, power."

44. Donovan and Adams, *Feminist Care Tradition*.

CHAPTER 15

1. This chapter originally appeared as "Attention to Suffering: A Feminist Caring Ethic for the Treatment of Animals" in the *Journal of Social Philosophy*, vol. 27, no. 1 (Spring 1996), 81–102.

2. A much shorter version of which appeared as *Beyond Animal Rights: A Feminist Caring Ethic for the Treatment of Animals* (New York: Continuum, 1996).

3. Elizabeth A. Behnke, "From Merleau-Ponty's Concept of Nature to an Interspecies Practice of Peace," in H. Peter Steeves, ed., *Animal Others: On Ethics, Ontology, and Animal Life* (Albany: State University of New York Press, 1999), 109.

4. Josephine A. Donovan, "Feminism and the Treatment of Animals: From Care to Dialogue," *Signs*, vol. 31, no. 2 (Winter 2006), 305–29.

5. Jacques Derrida,"The Animal That Therefore I Am (More to Follow)," trans. David Wills, *Critical Inquiry*, vol. 28, no. 2 (Winter 2002), 317. See also David Wood, "Thinking with Cats," in *Animal Philosophy: Essential Readings in Continental Thought*, Matthew Calarco and Peter Atterton, eds. (New York: Continuum, 2004), 141–44.

6. Iris Murdoch, *Metaphysics as a Guide to Morals* (New York: Viking Penguin, 1993).

7. Immanuel Kant, *Kant Selections*, Theodore Meyer Green, ed. (New York: Scribner's, 1957), 279.

8. Ibid., 276.

9. Ibid., 277.

10. Ibid., 281.

11. Arthur Schopenhauer, *On the Basis of Morality* (Indianapolis, IN: Bobbs-Merrill, 1965; originally published 1841), 95.

12. Ibid., 96.

13. Tom Regan, *The Thee Generation: Reflections on the Coming Revolution* (Philadelphia, PA: Temple University Press, 1991), 142.

14. Philip Mercer, *Sympathy and Ethics: A Study of the Relationship Between Sympathy and Morality with Special Reference to Hume's Treatise* (Oxford, UK: Oxford University Press, 1972), 8.

15. Mercer, 9.

16. H. B. Acton, "The Ethical Importance of Sympathy," *Philosophy*, vol. 30 (1955), 66.

17. Ibid., 65.

18. Ibid., 66.

19. Fredrick A. Elliston, "Husserl's Phenomenology of Empathy," in Elliston and Peter McCormick, eds. *Husserl: Expositions and Appraisals* (Notre Dame, IN: University of Notre Dame Press, 1977), 223.

20. Mercer, 9.

21. Max Scheler, *The Nature of Sympathy* (Hamden, CT: Archon, 1970; originally published 1913).

22. See Floyd Matson,*The Broken Image: Man, Science and Society* (Garden City, NY: Anchor, 1966), 240; Stuart H. Hughes, *Consciousness and Society: The Reconstruction of European Social Thought 1890–1930* (New York: Vintage, 1961), 187–88, 311.

23. Scheler, 48.

24. Ibid., 11.

25. Ibid., 104.

26. Ibid., 105. Scheler erroneously sees the Western dominative attitude toward nature as "a legacy of Judaism" (ibid.). While the Hebrew Bible does sanction human domination, the Christian tradition heavily reinforced this thesis, and the Cartesian epistemological basis for modern science can hardly be seen as Judaic in origin. (Scheler also, of course, strongly criticizes Christianity.) Schopenhauer also—in even more offensive terms—attributed the Western derogation of animals to Judaism (the "*foetor Judaicus*") (*On the Basis of Morality*, 175, 178, 187). Schopenhauer's anti-Semitism, as well as his sexism, is, of course, abominable.

27. Scheler, 87.

28. Ken Shapiro, "Understanding Dogs through Kinesthetic Empathy, Social Construction, and History," *Anthrozoös*, vol. 3, no. 3 (1989), 184–94.

29. Ibid., 184.

30. Edith Stein, *On the Problem of Empathy* (The Hague, The Netherlands: Martinus Nijhoff, 1966; originally published 1916), 54–55.

31. Ibid., 55.

32. John A. Fisher, "Taking Sympathy Seriously: A Defense of Our Moral Psychology toward Animals," in Eugene C. Hargrove, ed., *The Animal Rights/Environmental Ethics Debate: The Environmental Perspective* (Albany: State University of New York Press, 1992).

33. Paul Taylor, "The Ethics of Respect for Nature," in Hargrove, 109–10.

34. Ibid., 110. See also Paul Taylor, *Respect for Nature: A Theory of Environmental Ethics* (Princeton, NJ: Princeton University Press, 1986), 17, 66–67.

35. Scheler, 105.

36. Mercer, 105.

37. Rosemarie Tong, *Feminine and Feminist Ethics* (Belmont, CA: Wadsworth, 1993).

38. Nel Noddings, *Caring: A Feminine Approach to Ethics and Moral Education* (Berkeley: University of California Press, 1984), 174, 188. Noddings seems ambivalent on whether or to what extent human caring should be extended to animals. See *Caring*, chap. 7; Noddings, "Comment on Donovan's 'Animal Rights and Feminist Theory,'" *Signs*, vol. 16, no. 2 (Winter 1991), 418–22; and Donovan, "Reply to Noddings," *Signs*, vol. 16, no. 2 (Winter 1991), 423–25.

39. Acton, 62.

40. Ibid., 66. See also Kekes, "Moral Sensitivity," *Philosophy*, vol. 59, no. 227 (1984), 8–9.

41. Scheler, 98.

42. Ibid., 98.

43. W. Stark, in Scheler, xxxix.

44. Ibid., xl.

45. Brian Luke, "Justice, Caring, and Animal Liberation," *Between the Species*, vol. 8, no. 2 (Spring 1992), 106.

46. Ibid., 106.

47. See Joseph Duke Filanowicz, "Ethical Sentimentalism Revisited," *History of Philosophy Quarterly*, vol. 6, no. 2 (April 1989), 189–206, for a recent reassertion of Shaftesbury's system as "a genuine and live option for contemporary ethical theory" (189).

48. Keith Thomas, *Man and the Natural World: A History of the Modern Sensibility* (New York: Pantheon, 1983), 175–76.

49. David Hume, *An Enquiry Concerning the Principles of Morals* (La Salle, IL: Open Court, 1960; originally published 1777), 146, 67.

50. Ibid., 61.

51. Ibid., 65.

52. Ibid., 129.

53. Ibid., 131.

54. See James Rachels, *Created from Animals: The Moral Implications of Darwinism* (Oxford, UK: Oxford University Press, 1990), 77, 147–57; also Helena Cronin, *The Ant and the Peacock: Altruism and Sexual Selection from Darwin to Today* (Cambridge, UK: Cambridge University Press, 1991).

55. Rachels, 157.

56. J. Baird Callicott, "Animal Liberation and Environmental Ethics: Back Together Again," in Hargrove, 156. Callicott offers a two-communities theory here, claiming that human treatment of domestic animals should operate according to one ethic, and of wild animals, to another. Less successfully, he attempts to argue that a Humean sympathy ethic also undergirds deep ecology theory, in particular the "land ethic" of Aldo Leopold—a thesis he develops in "Conceptual Foundation" (1987)—but such an abstract use of the term *sympathy* would seem to rob it of meaning. Sympathy must be rooted in feelings for the particular, the concrete other.

57. Schopenhauer, 144.

58. Ibid., 144.

59. Ibid., 144.

60. Ibid., 172.

61. Ibid., 175.

62. Ibid., 210.

63. Ibid., 245, n.5.

64. Ibid., 228.

65. Mercer, 132.

66. Ibid., 4.

67. Ibid., 5.

68. Ibid., 124.

69. Ibid., 133.

70. Acton, 66.

71. Scheler, 58.
72. Ibid., 60.
73. Ibid., 60.
74. Regan, 95.
75. Ibid., 96.
76. Ibid., 140.
77. Virginia Held, "Feminism and Moral Theory" in Eva Feder Kittay and Diana T. Meyers, eds., *Women and Moral Theory* (Totowa, NJ: Rowman & Littlefield, 1987), 118.
78. Marti Kheel, "The Liberation of Nature: A Circular Affair," *Environmental Ethics*, vol. 7 (Summer 1985), 148.
79. Kheel, 145. See also Linda Vance, "Ecofeminism and the Politics of Reality," in Greta Gaard, ed., *Ecofeminism: Women, Animals, Nature* (Philadelphia, PA: Temple University Press, 1993), 136.
80. Deane Curtin, "Toward an Ecological Ethic of Care," *Hypatia*, vol. 6, no. 1 (Spring 1991), 60–74. Karen Warren extends the idea of care to mean intense appreciation of nature—see Warren, "The Power and the Promise of Ecological Feminism," *Environmental Ethics*, vol. 12 (Summer 1990), 125–46. In a celebrated passage she explains how in rock climbing she developed an emotional, respectful—indeed caring—attitude for the rock: "At that moment I was bathed in serenity. I began to talk to the rock in an almost inaudible, child-like way, as if the rock were my friend. . . . Gone was the determination to conquer the rock. I wanted simply to work respectfully with the rock as I climbed. . . . I felt myself caring for this rock" (Warren, 134–35). Greta Gaard points out, however, that later in the same article Warren blithely sanctions the killing of a deer, to which she does not seem to extend the same caring attitude. See Gaard, "Ecofeminism and Native American Cultures: Pushing the Limits of Cultural Imperialism," in Gaard, ed., 296–7. The reason for Warren's inconsistency, I suggest, is that she is coming out of deep ecology theory, which notoriously elides the suffering of individual animals in its rush to embrace "ecoholism." Feminists Marti Kheel and Ariel Kay Salleh have criticized deep ecology theory—see Kheel, "Ecofeminism and Deep Ecology: Reflections on Identity and Difference," in Irene Diamond and Gloria Feman Orenstein, eds., *Reweaving the World: The Emergence of Ecofeminism* (San Francisco: Sierra Club, 1990); Ariel Kay Salleh, "Deeper Than Deep Ecology: The Eco-feminist Connection," *Environmental Ethics*, vol. 6 (Winter 1984), 339–45—and I will not review these critiques here except to reaffirm that a feminist caring ethic for the treatment of animals must be rooted in appreciation, understanding, and sympathy for the animals as individuals. Following Mercer I contend that sympathy or caring obtains between feeling beings: "'Sympathy' has regard for 'the other' solely in respect of his [or her] capacity to feel and to suffer" (Mercer, 4). Thus, Warren's use of the term *caring* is inappropriate. One can appreciate or respect a rock but one cannot feel sympathetic concern for it: such compassion is appropriate only for sentient or at least living creatures.
81. Carol Gilligan, *In a Different Voice: Psychological Theory and Women's Development* (Cambridge, MA: Harvard University Press, 1982), 19.
82. See Sara Ruddick, *Maternal Thinking: Towards a Politics of Peace* (Boston: Beacon, 1989).

83. Hilary Rose, "Hand, Brain, and Heart: A Feminist Epistemology for the Natural Sciences," *Signs*, vol. 9, no. 1 (Autumn 1983), 83.

84. Linda Nicholson, "Women, Morality, and History," in Larabee, 87–101; Nancy C. M. Hartsock, *Money, Sex, and Power: Toward a Feminist Historical Materialism* (New York: Longman, 1983); Eli Zaretsky, *Capitalism, the Family and Personal Life* (New York: Harper, 1976).

85. Jim Cheney, "Eco-Feminism and Deep Ecology," *Environmental Ethics*, vol. 9 (Summer 1987), 121.

86. Annette Baier, "The Need for More than Justice," in Marsha Hanen and Kai Nielsen, eds., *Science, Morality & Feminist Theory* (Calgary, Canada: University of Calgary Press, 1987), 50.

87. See especially Ruddick and Curtain, also my own Feminist Theory: The Intellectual Traditions, 3rd ed. (New York: Continuum, 2000), 210.

88. Marilyn Friedman, "Care and Context in Moral Reasoning," in Kittay and Meyes, 202.

89. Kant, 281.

90. See Marti Kheel, "From Healing Herbs to Deadly Drugs: Western Medicine's War Against the Natural World," *Healing the Wounds: The Promise of Ecofeminism* (Philadelphia, PA: New Society, 1989), 96–111.

91. Carol J. Adams, *The Sexual Politics of Meat: A Feminist-Vegetarian Critical Theory* (New York: Continuum, 1990). Jeremy Rifkin, *Beyond Beef: The Rise and Fall of the Cattle Industry* (New York: Dutton, 1992).

92. "Rita Manning, Just Caring," in Eve Browning Cole and Susan Coultrap-McQuin, eds., *Explorations in Feminist Ethics: Theory and Practice* (Bloomington: Indiana University Press, 1992), 45.

93. David Braybrooke, *Meeting Needs* (Princeton, NJ: Princeton University Press, 1987).

94. Agnes Heller, *The Theory of Need in Marx* (London: Allison & Busby, 1978).

95. Seyla Benhabib, "The Generalized and the Concrete Other: The Kohlberg-Gilligan Controversy and Moral Theory," in Kittay and Meyers, *Women and Moral Theory*, 168.

96. Benhabib, 168.

97. Ibid., 169.

98. Allison Jaggar, *Feminist Politics and Human Nature* (Totowa, NJ: Rowman & Allenheld, 1983) and "Love and Knowledge: Emotion in Feminist Epistemology," in Jaggar and Susan R. Bordo, eds., *Gender/Body/Knowledge* (New Brunswick, NJ: Rutgers University Press, 1989); Hartsock; Donovan, *Feminist Theory*, 210–13.

99. Margaret Urban Walker, "Moral Understandings: Alternative 'Epistemology' for a Feminist Ethics," in Cole and Coultrap-McQuinn, 166, 168.

100. Walker, 166.

101. Gilligan, 19.

102. Walker, 166.

103. Donovan, "Animal Rights," 375.

104. Simone Weil, "Reflections on the Right Use of School Studies with a View to the Love of God," *The Simone Weil Reader*, George A. Panichas, ed. (New York: David McKay, 1977; originally published 1942), 51.

105. See Walker; Ellen L. Fox, "Seeing through Women's Eyes: The Role of Vision in Women's Moral Theory," in Cole and Coultrap-McQuin, 111–16; Ruddick; Robin S. Dillon, "Care and Respect," in Cole and Coultrap-McQuin, 69–81; Meredith W. Michaels, "Morality Without Distinction," *Philosophical Forum*, vol. 17, no. 3 (Spring 1986), 175–87.

106. Iris Murdoch, *The Sovereignty of Good* (New York: Schocken, 1971). I elaborated these ideas earlier in "Beyond the Net: Feminist Criticism as a Moral Criticism," *Denver Quarterly*, vol. 17, no. 4 (Winter 1983), 40–57.

107. Murdoch, *Sovereignty*, 66.

108. Ibid., 34.

109. Ibid., 66.

110. Martin Buber, *I and Thou* (New York: Scribner's, 1970; originally published 1923), 57–9. See also Buber's discussion of his exchange of glances with a cat (144–6); also his treatment of a horse as Thou in *Between Man and Man*, rev. ed. (New York: Macmillan, 1965; originally published 1947), 23. Another important work that argues for the "Thou-ness" of animals is Gary A. Kowalski, *The Souls of Animals* (Walpole, NH: Stillpoint, 1991).

111. Paul Taylor, *Respect for Nature*, 120–1. Taylor, a rationalist, would probably resist the term *loving* here, even though his description comes very close to the Murdoch/Weil notion of attentive love, applied to natural life. In his book *Respect for Nature* Taylor insists upon the Kantian distinction between acting out of rational duty and acting out of emotional inclination. He rejects the latter on familiar Kantian grounds (85, 90–1, 126–7).

112. Ibid., 120.

113. Tong, 228.

114. Ibid., 229.

Index

About the Editor and Contributors

Carol J. Adams is author of *The Pornography of Meat* (2004) and *The Sexual Politics of Meat: A Feminist-Vegetarian Critical Theory* (1989), as well as editor of several books, including, with Josephine Donovan, *The Feminist Care Tradition in Animal Ethics* (2008).

Aaron Bell is a Ph.D. candidate in the social, political, ethical, and legal (SPEL) philosophy program at SUNY Binghamton. His research interests include first-generation critical theory—especially the work of Theodor W. Adorno—psychoanalysis, and the contemporary philosophical study of animals.

Susan Benston is a poet and novelist. She is author of *Dura Mater: Poems, Deluge*, and *Munchausen: A Novel.* She teaches English at Haverford College.

Ted Benton teaches sociology at the University of Essex. His books include *Natural Relations: Ecology, Animal Rights, and Social Justice* (1993), *Philosophical Foundations of the Three Sociologies* (1977), and *The Rise and Fall of Structural Marxism* (1984).

Carl Boggs teaches political science at National University in Los Angeles. Among his many books are *The End of Politics: Corporate Power and the Decline of the Public Sphere* (2000), *Gramsci's Marxism* (1977), *Social Movements and Political Power* (1989), *Intellectuals and the Crisis of Modernity* (1993), and *Imperial Delusions: American Militarism and Endless War* (2005).

Karen Davis is a leading activist and scholar in the animal rights movement, and founder and president of United Poultry Concerns. Davis is author of *The Holocaust and the Henmaid's Tale* (2005) and *More Than a Meal: The Turkey in History, Myth, Ritual, and Reality* (2001).

Josephine Donovan is a leading feminist political philosopher, and author of *Feminist Theory* (2000) and *Sarah Orne Jewett* (2002). Her collaborative work with Carol Adams on books such as *Animals and Women* (1995) and *Beyond Animal Rights* (1996) has defined an entirely new field of theoretical and political work.

Christina Gerhardt is visiting scholar at Columbia University. She has published extensively on the Frankfurt School and especially on Theodor W. Adorno. She is editor of *Adorno and Ethics* and *New German Critique* 97 (2006), and has authored numerous articles, including on Adorno and on Kracauer, and encyclopedia entries, including on the Frankfurt School, on Adorno, and on Lukács. Her dissertation manuscript, "Language of Nature in Theodor W. Adorno's Philosophical and Aesthetic Writings," an examination of natural history, beauty, and animals in the writings of Adorno, is currently under consideration for publication.

Victoria Johnson is associate professor of sociology at the University of Missouri at Columbia, with specialization in the empirical analysis of power relations, politics, culture, and social movements. She is author of *"How Many Machine Guns Does It Take to Cook a Meal?": The Seattle and San Francisco General Strikes* (2008) and coeditor (with Jo Freeman) of *Waves of Protest: Social Movements Since the Sixties* (1999).

Renzo Llorente teaches philosophy on Saint Louis University's Madrid campus. He is the author of a variety of articles on Marx and Marxism, ethics, Latin American philosophy, and our duties to animals. He is also the author of a book of aphorisms, *Beyond the Pale: Exercises in Provocation* (2010).

Eduardo Mendieta is director of the Latin American and Caribbean Studies Center at SUNY Stony Brook, where he is associate professor of philosophy. Mendieta is the author or editor of numerous books, including *Global Fragments: Critical Theory, Latin America and Globalizations* (2007), *Adventures of Transcendental Philosophy: Karl-Otto Apel's Semiotics and Discourse Ethics* (2002), *The Frankfurt School on Religion* (2004), and *Teorías sin Disciplinas: Latinamericanismo, Postcolonialidad y Globalización en debate* (with Santiago Castro-Gómez, 1998).

John Sanbonmatsu is associate professor of philosophy at Worcester Polytechnic Institute. He is author of the book *The Postmodern Prince: Critical Theory, Left Strategy, and the Making of a New Political Subject* (2004), as well as articles in *Social Theory and Practice, The American Journal of Economics and Sociology, Socialist Register, The New York Times, Z* Magazine, and other publications.

John Sorenson is professor of sociology at Brock University (Canada). His books include *Imagining Ethiopia: Struggles for History and Identity in the Horn of Africa* (1993), *Disaster and Development in the Horn of Africa* (1995), and *Ghosts and Shadows: Construction of Identity and Community in an African Diaspora* (with Atsuko Matsuoka, 2001).

Dennis Soron is associate professor of sociology at Brock University and co-editor of *Not For Sale: Decommodifying Public Life* (2006), as well as author of numerous book chapters, articles, and interviews on consumerism, work, the environment, and the problem of depoliticization.

Vasile Stănescu is a Ph.D. candidate in the program in modern thought and literature at Stanford University. He is co-senior editor of the Critical Animal Studies Book Series published by Rodopi Press and was named Tykes Scholar of the Year by the Institute of Critical Animal Studies. His paper in this volume won the Best Graduate Student Paper at the first annual Minding Animals Conference in Australia (2009).

Zipporah Weisberg is a Ph.D. candidate in the humanities programme at York University. Her research interests include critical social and political theory and critical animal studies. Her essay "The Broken Promises of Monsters: Haraway, Animals, and the Humanist Legacy" was awarded the Critical Animal Studies Graduate Dissertation of the Year and was published in the *Journal for Critical Animal Studies* (2009).

Lightning Source UK Ltd.
Milton Keynes UK
UKHW01n0306160618
324228UK00007B/350/P